What
Doesn't Kill Us
Makes Us

What
Doesn't Kill Us
Makes Us

Who We Become After
Tragedy and Trauma

Mike Mariani

BALLANTINE BOOKS
NEW YORK

What Doesn't Kill Us Makes Us is a work of nonfiction. Some names and identifying details have been changed.

Published in the United States by Ballantine Books, an imprint of Random House, a division of Penguin Random House LLC, New York.

BALLANTINE is a registered trademark and the colophon is a trademark of Penguin Random House LLC.

Library of Congress Cataloging-in-Publication Data
Names: Mariani, Mike, author.
Title: What doesn't kill us makes us: who we become after tragedy and trauma / Mike Mariani.
Identifiers: LCCN 2021041264 (print) | LCCN 2021041265 (ebook) | ISBN 9780593236949 (hardcover) | ISBN 9780593236956 (ebook)
Subjects: LCSH: Life change events. | Psychic trauma. | Adjustment (Psychology)
Classification: LCC BF637.L53 M367 2022 (print) | LCC BF637.L53 (ebook) | DDC 155.9/3—dc23/eng/20211025
LC record available at https://lccn.loc.gov/2021041264
LC ebook record available at https://lccn.loc.gov/2021041265

PRINTED IN CANADA ON ACID-FREE PAPER

randomhousebooks.com

2 4 6 8 9 7 5 3 1

First Edition

For my parents,
whose devotion took me three decades to see

What makes Heroic? To face simultaneously one's greatest suffering and one's highest hope.

—Friedrich Nietzsche, *The Gay Science*

I'm a hero. It's easy to be a hero. If you don't have hands or feet, you're either a hero or dead.

—Rubén Gallego, *White on Black*

Contents

Invisible Kingdoms

"Out of life's school of war—what doesn't kill me,
makes me stronger."

I'VE KNOWN ABOUT FRIEDRICH NIETZSCHE'S LEAN, BRACING MAXIM
since high school, perhaps even earlier. At once a dream of invincibility and a promise to avenge oneself against misfortune, the aphorism was stitched into the cultural fabric all around me; commemorated in songs, slogans, tattoos, and social media posts; exchanged in television dialogue; and growled by our school's sports coaches. I heard it from my father, too, who recited it with his soft, measured voice and knowing glance to rouse me when my childhood discouragement pantomimed adult despair. It was the rare adage that seemed transcendent of time, culture, or ideology, gracefully leaping from one generation to the next with a cogency and force of impact that was never antiquated or diminished. Few other scrimshaws of wisdom—the Delphic adage "Know thyself," Protagoras's "Man is the measure of all things," Margaret Hungerford's "Beauty is in the eye of the beholder"—felt as immutable and immemorial. That it was true felt obvious; it was both entrenched in the annals of human wisdom and forever close at hand.

In 1888, Nietzsche set out to compose a brief primer on his iconoclastic views of subjects like ancient philosophy, morality, and free will. With his popularity growing in Germany and throughout Europe, he wanted to give his expanding readership a more accessible entry point into his oeuvre. That work, *Twilight of the Idols,* dashed off in a single week and published the following year, included the brief aphorism that would catapult far beyond the purview of nineteenth-century European thought. Though *Twilight of the Idols* turns its gimlet eye on a sprawling range of subjects, renouncing the decadence of contemporary German culture and lambasting religious moralizing, no other aspect of the book would have nearly the same boundless legacy.

When I was a teenager, Nietzsche's aphorism was grafted onto my sense of self. The philosopher's words were being poured into the bedrock of who I understood myself to be even before I could glean them with any level of care. Like an irrepressible pop song, the maxim soared over logical reasoning, thriving instead off the surge of triumph and defiance it made people feel. It allowed me to transform my family tragedies into both foundation for and evidence of the fiercer, more resilient person I believed I was. Without even fully understanding Nietzsche's words or the philosophical context out of which they arose, I had begun to construct the story of myself around them.

Then I was blindsided by a life-altering illness, and the aphorism snapped into an even more personal place for me. I used Nietzsche's line like a shield, sometimes a weapon. Yes, my pain would make me stronger—not weaker, sadder, distressed, or vulnerable—and I would move through the world a more dogged, battle-hardened person. For years I even wrote his words in the right-hand corner of nearly every page of my work notebook, so that I might glance over to them at any moment as a reminder of my intensifying strength.

The promise of Nietzsche's maxim is the idea that out of their most harrowing crucibles, human beings emerge harder and flintier, with greater reserves to draw on and a character hammered and chiseled by the trials it has endured. For 130 years his line has evoked the idea that we could become more powerful—physically, emotionally, spiritually—as long as we were able to survive whatever injury, illness, accident, or smarting twist of fate had torn our lives asunder. In Nietzsche's telling, endurance becomes synonymous with accretion: We subsume what we withstand, and our character expands in stride with the geography of our suffering. If we were up for the challenge, Nietzsche seemed to promise, adversity could transform us into superior versions of our younger, more callow, and less tested selves.

It was a challenge I'd co-opted to inform and animate my personal ethos. For a very long time, his words were the through line for the story I told myself to explain the biographical facts of my life.

ON A FRIDAY in June of 2018, I was fatigued, disoriented, and coping with an aching pain that seemed to bloom from deep within my bones. As I drove to my sister Ali's house, I pushed away the sense of an unfolding crisis that had for months become a persistent white noise in the back of my mind. Though I'd been to her brick ranch home many times before, driving north up the interstate, I struggled to recall the right exit.

After finally turning off the highway, I pulled onto her street and parked. From there we headed to the therapist's office together in her old mulberry Honda Accord. During the drive we slipped into the deep, familiar grooves of siblings who'd long had to rely on each other for advice, guidance, and emotional support. There were no masks between us—only our raw selves, as jagged and battered as lonely escarpments.

The therapy room was spacious and rectangular in a way that evoked a still, pensive courtyard. Plants sat on shelves and in corners; side tables were painted in crisp lime; and a large, framed painting of a dewy glen hung on the far wall. The effect was a kind of lushness that seemed to gesture toward self-knowledge, a fecundity that might coax out the serrated secrets and tiny, dense truths buried inside so many of us. Or at least that's what I imagined—and hoped.

The therapist, a middle-aged man with a wiry build and agile brown eyes, greeted us each with a genial handshake. He told us to take a seat on one of the red upholstered chairs, that more people should be arriving soon. As we waited, exchanging polite smiles, a sharp ache carved its way through my arms and legs. I smothered the pain with practiced composure and tried not to betray my discomfort. It was a maneuver so familiar that it had become second nature. Acknowledging the pain would only alienate me from the rest of the people in the room and crack open the door where self-pity entered. I'd learned to keep it shut.

After close to half an hour, three middle-aged women joined us. Had anybody been watching, the contrast would have been bemusing—a thirty-two-year-old man in jeans and sneakers, a half-sleeve tattoo spilling out from underneath his polo shirt, surrounded by women who could each have been his mother. I didn't feel uncomfortable, though. My sister's presence anchored me.

It was Ali's idea to attend the therapy session. She'd just become a therapist herself and had long nudged me to consider regular counseling. Lately, she'd rhapsodized about the virtues of family constellation therapy; she talked about it with something approaching reverence. She felt that even a single session could provide a potent source of catharsis and offer me a new framework for looking at my life. In a way, the therapy room we found ourselves in aptly suited both our identities: an idiosyncratic intersection point where my sister's galvanizing passions and my distinctive misfortunes met.

I'd recently moved back to the East Coast after close to two years in California, and the transition had been rocky. An acute sense of displacement now hung over my normal stable of problems, making everything harder. I'd come back to live with my girlfriend and be closer to all my friends and family, but the once-familiar northeastern setting passed through me as if one of us were a ghost. The quaint plazas, fastidious lawns, and intricately gabled colonials all looked vapid and gray, the husk of a past life I had no use for. The visceral recognition of this estrangement was setting off an alarm inside me: I didn't belong here. Even if I worked diligently to keep my slow spiraling invisible to the outside world, I was emotionally unraveling. I fixed long, vacant gazes out windows, my hands clasped around my mouth like a muzzle; I let out plangent moans of frustration in my home office when work wasn't going the way I'd hoped. Something inside me was battered and thrashed, and amid its abuse, it resorted to wild swings between fury and despair. I needed help. I held a sliver of hope that this unusual therapy might be it.

Developed in the 1990s by a German psychotherapist named Bert Hellinger, family constellation therapy draws on an assortment of inspirations, including psychodynamic theory, Zulu spiritual practices, and an obscure therapy modality known as family sculpting. The methodology works as follows. One participant sits next to the therapist—sometimes referred to as the facilitator—and the two engage in a loose form of talk therapy in front of the other participants in the room. The therapist gently teases out the participant's anxieties, resentments, hang-ups, and buried sorrows, eventually casting the others attending the session in the roles of these ideas and the people that represent them. The other participants often play parents, spouses, siblings, and children and, in some cases, embody human experiences like marriage, parenthood, recovery, and mourning. Together they form the constellation of the person's world, physically configured throughout the room. When gazed at collectively, these luminaries project the shape and story of who we are and who we might become.

Once the initial constellation is arranged, the participants silently feel out the energy in the room as they move, adjust, and adapt to each other. The therapist, meanwhile, operates as a kind of psycho-choreographer, tinkering with their configuration and working to tease out the underlying gestalt. It's his job to discern how relationships orbit one another, exact gravitational force, and develop into schemata that set the stage for a life's story. My sister had told me that the way people position themselves in the "unified field" is uncanny, reflecting an almost clairvoyant understanding of the tensions and dynamics in people's lives.

I'd always respected my sister's bent toward mysticism. While I read Jung, Huxley, and William James, and felt a strong attraction to the archetypal truths of tarot iconography and the ecstatic spiritual visions of Romantic art, Ali looked for providence in the seams of everyday life. Where I needed this or that prism to help me catch fleeting glints of numinous light, for my sister, God was what she made him, and he materialized where she saw him. It was a trait that had quietly budded in me but had effloresced in her, like the same song scoring our lives at different volumes.

Even though the implication that there's an invisible energy gently guiding people's movements sounds, at best, like a new twist on the old tropes of parapsychology and, at worst, like quantum quackery, I was past the point of expecting help from hard science—or medicine. If the session could ease the lurking alienation I felt, if it could silence the alarm whose pulsing insisted something was very wrong, then it would be worth it. I needed something to loosen the knotted rope that I'd gotten tangled up in since moving back to the East Coast. Maybe this was it.

After some stiff small talk, the therapist smiled self-consciously and shifted in his seat. His voice lost its gentle affect, becoming more forceful and direct as he turned to me and said, "So, what's your problem?" At first this jarred me. To answer felt self-indulgent, even potentially humiliating. In a dialogue this artless and transparent, I wasn't sure how my story would land. I glanced over at the expectant faces in the room. Then I fixed my eyes on some invisible anchor below them, found my footing, and calmly named the furies beating their wings inside me.

When I began, one woman's eyes were tight and hardened. As I recounted my adversities and family history, they widened and eventually fell softly to the floor. The other two women sat quietly, their expressions focused and heavy. The therapist, however, stayed keyed into my words.

Calamities have swept through my biography as a kind of retrograde circle of life, disease trailed by death trailed by grief, some parts fleeting and others as stubborn as swallowed hooks. My mother's death from breast cancer when I was in kindergarten, my sister in preschool, was for a very long time the defining event of my life.

Over the years, I would come to think of everything before it as an unreachable prehistory where our family of four was stable, balanced, and symmetrical. But that comely portrait was never our fate. Instead, we pushed on admirably, sympathetically, and fitfully as a three-legged dog.

In the years that followed, grief assumed different forms for each of us. For me it was two totaled cars in an adolescence that blazed with an appetite for danger and violence. For my sister, it was the stuffed animals she habitually held to her mouth as a little girl, a gag epitomizing the language she lacked for the emotions she could not yet speak. For my dad, it was the Carlton cigarettes, the tattered recliner, and the hand-me-down flat-screen: artifacts of a life of addictive solitude. After my mother passed, he never remarried, and he never went back to work.

But this loss—and the bitterness I felt about my father's choices after that loss—was only a prelude to a much greater crucible yet to come. In the middle of the holiday season in 2012, a catastrophe would strike in the form of chronic illness that far surpassed my earlier adversities, and it would cleave my life cleanly in two. Afterward, I would never come close to my prior existence again.

Detailing those experiences in the therapy room, I was drawing out the poison, sucking it all up to the surface of the skin. There was something clean, even dignified about that. After all, I'd never felt any shame about my hardships. Indeed, I believed my suffering had made me stronger and endowed my life with substance and meaning. I clutched this belief with the unshakable ardency of a zealot. My scripture was in my scars, my tragedies a sacred flame that lit my life from within. I would not be swayed from it.

After roughly fifteen minutes, the therapist concluded my constellation would have six characters, including someone portraying me. He used three of the women and three chairs, while my sister observed. The roles in my family constellation were my deceased mother, who passed away when I was five; my deceased grandfather, who died before I was born; my chronic illness; my grief; and my loving but melancholic father. Then, it began.

The women acting out my constellation session shifted around the room in a kind of halted, distressed dance. The large turquoise eyes of the woman who played me welled up as she described a sense of fragmentation and pain. Meanwhile, the woman playing my chronic illness and the chair assuming the role of my father locked on to me from two sides. My avatar could not move left, right, forward, or backward without one of them following like predators or parasites. Rather than showcasing a noble and powerful protagonist, my constellation revealed a person under siege, his only solace the aloof company of dead family members.

At first I felt oddly vindicated by what my constellation said about me. My experiences may have been tragic, but they also made me fierce, marked by age-old symbols about hardship and honor. The longer I pictured my avatar besieged by forces outside my control, however, the more that prideful surge of affirmation was replaced by something different, something I was much less familiar with: self-doubt.

On the car ride home with my sister, recalling the woman with wet turquoise eyes struggling to move, pinioned by wraiths of sickness and grief, I felt bare and powerless—as though my life was something that had always been acted upon, and everything else was just a response meant to disguise my own helplessness. All the selves that grew over and covered up these catastrophes—maybe I'd dreamed them up. Like ornate graffiti on the wall of a blasted building or elaborate murals painted at the site of a tragedy, my personae, I suspected, were fashioned to conceal a canvas of loss. That night, back at my father's house, I lay in my old bedroom and wondered, nervously, where the line was between self-deception and self. Had I been, all these years, a deft illusionist for an audience of one?

Long before the family constellation session, I'd known that my unique adversities made me different, that they set me apart from the people whose orbits went on undisturbed, never knocked off course. I'd kept the difference locked away, exalted but never examined. But the constellation therapy session had thrown the unadorned facts of my life into stark relief. For as long as I could remember I'd thought my trials were full of meaning, only now I couldn't identify what exactly that meaning was. I'd wholeheartedly believed my misfortunes made me stronger, in deeper contact with the molten-core truths of the world. When held under scrutiny, though, that strength and those truths seemed to wobble and fade. Combing over them too closely risked rupturing the identity I'd built around them—around Nietzsche's doubtless proclamation—and revealing a fragility underneath that, existentially, I dreaded.

At one point in Rachel Cusk's novel *Kudos,* the unnamed protagonist begins to interrogate her long-held views: "Suffering has always appeared to me as an opportunity, I said, and I wasn't sure if I would ever discover whether this was true and if so why it was, because so far I had failed to understand what it might be an opportunity for. All I knew was that it carried a kind of honor, if you survived it, and left you in a relationship to the truth that seemed closer, but that in fact might have been identical to the truthfulness of staying in one place." In the wake of that therapy session, a lifetime of idealizations about suffering, honor, and truth were ebbing away, and I was left unsure of the person looking back at me in the mirror. He appeared, now, like a beleaguered doppelgänger, stripped of his propulsive delusions and forced to reckon with his own naked vulnerability and pain.

AS I CONTEMPLATED my constellation, I began to lose confidence in Nietzsche's aphorism. If my own tribulations had given rise to these attributes, then why wasn't that relationship illustrated more clearly in the wider world? I became skeptical of how Nietzsche's claim could be reconciled with all of the world's illness, physical disability, or even adverse childhood experiences—ACEs in medical parlance—that often presage difficult adult lives. I also had trouble squaring the idea that calamities strengthen us with the growing body of evidence demonstrating how trauma negatively affects the brain.

It seemed highly possible that Nietzsche's words were, at their heart, quixotic and even irrational. I sensed that those trials that bend us to the point of breaking don't actually make us stronger—or if they do, it is an elusive, qualified strength, one that hardly exists in the vacuum that the timeless adage suggests. But if tragedy and trauma don't make us stronger, I needed to know how they *do* change us. My conviction was unraveling, and in its place was a question that seemed as pressing and vital as any I'd ever come across. When you peeled away the rhetorical romance and the rousing apothegms, how did catastrophes change people's lives and identities?

How does a person go about reconstructing their existence in the wake of calamity after much of it has been irretrievably lost? What do those whose lives have been knocked off their orbits have in common? How do we make sense of and find meaning in a life where suffering and misfortune go uncompensated? These are questions that, one way or another, affect us all.

If I was going to relinquish my certitude that the central crucibles of my life had forged me into a fiercer, more persevering person, then I needed to find another perspective to take its place. Though I could not put words to it at the time, ever since I was a child contemplating my mother—both as an emotional presence and a physical absence, a cache of memories and a void new ones would never fill—I've felt compelled to redeem tragedy and loss with meaning. I did not want to merely accept her passing and shuffle along in my newly bereft state; her loss needed to represent something beyond the rueful fact of itself. I believed that her death—and the life it cut short—needed to sculpt and shape me, to birth a way of seeing the world and living in it that I could sheath myself in for many years to come. If the tragedy of her death could transform me in some way—into a stronger or deeper person, someone more impassioned or less willing to comfortably vanish into the scenery of the status quo—then everything we lost as a mother and son would not be in vain. That urge to scrabble some existential saving grace from hardship and deprivation has stayed with me to this day.

I was fully aware of the scientific research on the subject: the statistical realities of how traumatic events and other catastrophes could erode a person's quality of life, attenuating their avenues of pleasure and envenoming their prospects for the future. But I also knew that was not my story—or, at least, it represented only a single finite layer of it. I saw how much nuance and depth studies on trauma miss when we convert them into a catchall framework for how calamities shape the rest of our lives. The only story statistics told was one of unqualified loss.

I wanted to examine the gray areas of life after catastrophe: those vast, befogged borderlands that could not be neatly mapped out by the existing instruments at our disposal. I wanted to know how a person's dreams changed after she was paralyzed, lost her sight, or was sentenced to a decade in prison. Was the transition creeping and delicate, like moseying into consciousness on a Sunday morning? Or was it as savage and abrupt as a midnight assault? I wondered how a person's relationship with joy changed following an event that irreversibly robbed him of the chief avenues through which he once drew pleasure. I envisioned, in part based on my own experience, an intricate period of adaptation, a long, private reckoning with those vacuums—conspicuous as the ghostly outlines in a room stripped of its furniture—followed by a private odyssey in search of what might replace them. I suspected that there might be some kind of pattern to the aspects of our lives that were lost forever and the means we undertook to discover what would take their place.

But if that pattern was not clearly positive or negative—if it could not be tracked with concrete measurements like health, functionality, or physical recovery—then it was liable to go undetected by our scientific research and the conventional wisdom that grew out of it. Those leading afterlives often regard the changes they've undergone and the circumstances they've been forced into with deep-seated ambivalence. Their feelings are emblazoned with contradictions, internal conflict, and a learned neutrality that bridles stronger emotions. Neither academic research nor the spirited maxims we soothe ourselves with could ever capture such layered ambiguities.

Our inner lives undergo their own progressive transformations in the months and years following a catastrophic life event. When an experience wipes out much of the architecture and skyline of our day-to-day existence, our internal landscape, deprived of what it once zealously reflected, acclimates in enigmatic ways. I wanted to map out those re-formations, describe that altered terrain, develop a cartography of these postdisaster landscapes. My intuition was that they would be desolate and dystopic for a time, but also, eventually, fertile in surprising and unforeseeable ways. It brought to mind the strange, serpentine arc of Chernobyl: Once a city glistening with futuristic promise, in 1986 it became the site of human history's worst nuclear disaster. In the decades since, though, it has gradually metamorphosed into a third phase, becoming a rubble-strewn bastion for myriad flora and fauna, its concrete ruins carpeted by lush canopies and inhabited by everything from hulking bison and lumbering bears to silvery wolves and tawny wild horses.

While an unforeseeable catastrophe meant that Chernobyl's earliest dream for itself would never be realized, in the years afterward the exclusion zone evolved into something both elemental and un-repeatable, a half-erased palimpsest that wove uncanny beauty with stirring atavism and testified to life's ardent insistence on reinventing itself so that it might find new ways to flourish. My sense—perhaps my hope—was that afterlives were similarly layered, dense vessels that contained multiple permutations from the past and the present and juxtaposed disaster with transformation and renewal.

IN THIS BOOK, I seek to investigate how much validity there is to Nietzsche's claim that people grow stronger after adverse life events. I follow the lives of six individuals who each endured a cata-strophic experience that prevented them from resuming their previous lives. My subjects include Sophie, whose traumatic brain injury permanently transformed not only her cerebellum and prefrontal cortex but also her personality; Gina, a visually impaired young woman who faced sudden, violent trauma shortly after graduating from college; Jason, whose addiction to opioids resulted in a period of life-altering incarceration; JR, a thirtysomething whose life on Guam was interrupted by a car accident that forced surgeons to amputate his legs; Valerie, a high school student in an equally devastating crash that left her paralyzed; and Sean, a seventeen-year-old involved in a fatal shooting that led to a sentence of life imprisonment.

The 150 or so people I spoke to for this book underwent a wide range of catastrophic experiences. These include limb loss; paralyzing injury; acquired blindness; war wounds and combat PTSD; rape and sexual assault; the sudden loss of a child; gun violence and mass shootings; traumatic brain injuries; strokes; long-term incarceration; and the murder of loved ones. I was looking for what I was provisionally terming before-and-after experiences: events or developments so severe and irreversible that individuals conceptualize their lives under the bifurcated terms of everything that happened prior to the event and everything that has happened since. Those people who are living in the period following these types of experiences are leading *afterlives*.

Although I cast a wide net during my reporting, I've tried to establish relatively firm parameters in terms of what I understand afterlives to be. The subjects in this book experienced a catastrophic before-and-after event in late adolescence or onward that largely defined the rest of their lives; their experience was marked by significant loss of one kind or another; and it left them permanently altered physically or psychologically. Due to the catastrophe's indelible effects on their bodies, minds, or circumstances, those leading afterlives cannot return to the lives they once led. The new terms under which they live make such resumption impossible.

To keep the book focused on afterlives as I define them, certain varieties of adversity needed to be excluded. For one, I chose not to include individuals who suffered major adversity or trauma during childhood. It would have proven precarious to separate the typical changes that come with maturing through adolescence and into adulthood from those changes engendered by a childhood catastrophe. Children's identities are incomplete paintings, and the adversities and traumas they live through—during a period in which their brains are still in the thick of development—are inextricable from the rest of the incalculable brushstrokes that contribute to their portraits.

While the subjects in this book may struggle with trauma, death, disease, and disability, most do so in a state of *relative* financial solvency. Some have, without question, endured periods of destitution, but they do not chronically struggle to feed, clothe, or house themselves. The challenges of poverty are catastrophic in their own right, and indeed can be even more oppressive and paralyzing than the experiences I examine in this book. Permanent privation is a scourge that explodes Nietzsche's aphorism to dust. But poverty is also a complex systemic issue knotted up in fundamental questions related to laws, legislative agendas, social philosophies, and inequalities that have persisted for centuries—concerns beyond my purview here. And poverty is often, though not always, an intergenerational problem ensnaring families over many decades. Because of its chronic, multigenerational nature, it would prove challenging to map onto it the specific criteria I've established for afterlives. To reach the before period for many of those immiserated in poverty, that is, one might need to reach back forty, fifty, or even one hundred years.

The stories of the six people I follow in this book reflect some of the most prevalent types of afterlives experienced in America. (Though Sophie is Canadian, the incidence rate of traumatic brain injuries is the same in both countries.) I hope their narratives provide a revealing look into how those catastrophes that are disproportionately represented in this country—including incarceration, spinal cord injuries, and the traumatic effects of gun violence—are borne by real individuals who must incorporate those experiences into complex lives and identities that had not planned for such drastic adaptations. Though I ultimately decided to include three subjects who endured devastating car accidents, their injuries were all different and their afterlives therefore completely distinct from one another. But it's also not an entirely incidental choice: Car accidents are the leading cause of death for Americans under the age of fifty-five, the leading cause of spinal cord injuries, and one of the leading causes of amputation in the United States. It is an everyday catastrophe we have in some ways chosen to accept as inextricable from and essential to modern life, an event that metes out consequences in a random, undiscriminating fashion that I'm all too familiar with as the unharmed driver in a major crash years ago. And while I also tell the stories of two individuals who experienced long-term incarceration, the circumstances surrounding their imprisonments diverge in significant ways. One offers a glimpse into both America's epidemic of gun violence and its enduring legacy of institutional racism; the other is bound up in the country's pernicious dependence on opioids. Surface similarities notwithstanding, each of the six catastrophes suffered by the subjects of this book are crucially different.

These before-and-after events do not occur in statistical vacuums. In some cases, they speak to America's underlying social, political, and economic forces and the role they play in our recurring tragedies and traumas. Ours is a Janus-faced country that enjoys substantial wealth and abundant freedoms on the one hand, and perpetuates discrimination, systemic oppression, and political inertia on the other. Parsing the specific socioeconomic contexts in which the subjects are leading their afterlives is sure to disabuse some of the hollow shibboleths about American exceptionalism. The greatest country in the world, to my mind, is one that causes the least amount of suffering while promoting the most opportunities for all of its people. We strive, in fits and starts, for the latter, but betray persistent, seemingly ineradicable flaws with respect to the former.

Individuals leading afterlives are all around us. Over a quarter of the U.S. adult population lives with a physical disability—most of which have been acquired during their lifetimes. Around three hundred thousand Americans have suffered a spinal cord injury, and over five million are living with some form of paralysis. Another two million people have lost limbs. Data from the Federal Health and Retirement Study from 1992 to 2014 showed that close to 12 percent of people over the age of fifty have lost a child. Nearly 6 percent of the U.S. population, or over twenty million Americans, will endure an event distressing enough to leave them with PTSD.

Women, people of color, and members of the trans community face an especially high probability of experiencing catastrophic events over their lifetimes. One in four American women will be raped by the time they turn forty-four, according to a recent University of Michigan study, and previous research shows that fully 33 percent of those women report contemplating suicide. For American Indian and Alaskan Native women, the figures are distressingly higher. Over half of the transgender community—which comprises two million Americans—report experiencing intimate partner violence, and nearly that many have been sexually assaulted in their lifetime.

The number of Black mothers and fathers who have lost a child, meanwhile, significantly outpaces the national average, with about one in six Black parents forced to endure such a loss. Black men are also far more likely to spend time in prison—where traumatizing violence and isolation are commonplace—with a lifetime incarceration rate of around 25 percent.

Too often, though, these are the human condition's invisible kingdoms. The stories and images in our movies, television shows, commercials, and social media feeds sweep these lives under their glamorized rugs, belying their statistical realities. Our collective imagination suffers for it. When someone we know is paralyzed in a car accident, develops a debilitating chronic illness, or loses a child, many of us begin in a place of complete ignorance. We might feel that the world has not prepared us for something so treacherous and cruel, so disorienting and difficult to accept. We may even harbor a vague sense that some kind of social contract was broken—or the fine print had concealed a great deal of suffering and woe.

We depend on popular culture and media to serve as a mirror to human experience, to show us the range of identities and realities that we may one day find ourselves inhabiting. This lexicon, alas, rarely includes life-altering calamities and the afterlives that materialize in their wakes. Because of this, when something catastrophic does happen to us, we are often left without any frame of reference for it. Our internalized inventory of cultural images—so useful when it comes to teenage angst and twentysomething romance, marriage, divorce, familial drama, and even the death of certain types of loved ones—produces a sputtering blank. As a result, we feel isolated and unseen, as though our stories and fates have been deliberately ostracized from the larger human project. The cultural mirror has misled us by offering a reflection that was a glossy deception, a specious montage that never aspired to faithfully capture the full sweep of human lives.

One wheelchair user, who suffered a major spinal cord injury during a car accident, pinpointed this vanishing act in illuminating terms. "Most movies and books that depict somebody with a disability, how often are they still disabled at the end?" she asked. "They either die because they wanted to die, or they die in some mysterious, tragic, but self-sacrificial way, or they're cured." Like Chekhov's gun in reverse, if a story introduces a character that is sick, paralyzed, or otherwise disabled, then there is an unspoken injunction that the damage be somehow undone—that they perish or be miraculously healed by tale's end. One way or another, the illness or disability must be resolved, wiped clean from a canvas that refuses to accommodate the permanent nature of such conditions.

The vast majority of the stories our culture produces feature healthy, nondisabled people, characters who are confronted with hardships and dilemmas over which they can and will ultimately triumph. Depicting the permanence of losing a limb or a child—and gaining the lifelong blight of trauma in its place—would subvert our national ethos, the narrative assumption that underlies so many of the stories we tell: faith in confronting an existential crisis and surmounting it. Whether it's an action franchise, a studio drama, or a network sitcom, protagonists are put in predicaments they will find their way out of—scathed, perhaps, but rarely altered in a severe or grievous way. Characters may face delays, accidents, or even temporary derailments, but they almost invariably find their way back to their lives' familiar tracks. Afterlives give the lie to our inculcated faith in this stability and constancy, contravening the expectation that our lives contain a continuity that cannot be permanently violated.

There is, however, an even more fundamental reason why popular culture avoids life-altering catastrophes. Banishing them from our visual language serves a highly specific purpose that's rooted in the collective psychology of our society. We might call it the preservation of our absolutes.

As children, we're taught never to imagine tragedy or trauma. When a child innocently speculates on the possibility of a catastrophe happening, their parents unfailingly respond with some version of "Don't even think about something like that." Those parents see it as their solemn responsibility to protect their children for as long as they can from bleakness and misfortune, from the swiftness with which their lives can be rent apart and then reconfigured without warning or sentimentality. But delivering these gentle admonishments has another effect, too: It shields both their children and them from the knowledge that such wrenching calamities can happen.

Scolding their children into changing conversation topics, these parents are safeguarding their *absolutes:* those false certainties we hold about the continuity and permanence of our lives, relationships, and bodies. When people hold absolutes, they subscribe to the comforting but spurious assumption that their existences will always stay within certain parameters, positioning themselves and their families inside what we might call the Always category. Conceptualizing our lives through absolutes—and instructing our children to do the same—is a convenient way of maintaining our peace of mind and protecting our cognitive bandwidth from the sprawling fertility of paranoia and dread.

For all its psychological assuagement, though, thinking in absolutes comes at a price. When people assume that their lives will always stay within certain parameters, they never bother to fathom the lived realities that exist outside those parameters. And so instead of accepting those lives as possibilities for themselves, they must create another absolute classification: the Never category. This category encompasses individuals whose lives lie outside the scope of what they're willing to conceive of for themselves. These individuals are what cultural theorists sometimes call the abject: bodies and identities that are cast off because they threaten the way people want to see human existence, human anatomy, and the range of possibilities of the self. Like the Never category, the abject exists so people in a privileged position can preserve their innocence and naïveté.

For many, such traumatic experiences as becoming paralyzed, going blind, losing a child, or being sentenced to decades in a maximum-security prison are all stowed away in this Never category. Experiences like those, many implicitly feel, are too bleak to even fleetingly glance over. And with the aid of their absolutist thinking, they rarely do. But these subconscious taxonomies become self-fulfilling prophecies: When someone declares that they "can't imagine" such a harrowing development in their life, they never make any attempt to, and that failure of imagination is perpetuated. Through this cycle, their absolute thinking is solidified. These fates are unimaginable, that is, because they've chosen to keep them that way.

Our popular culture and the representations it trades in are, perhaps unsurprisingly, complicit in this objective: Our stories and images almost exclusively reflect the Always category. As a result, certain types of people are exiled from the collective imagination, relegated to the farthest edges of visibility and awareness where they cannot challenge the delusions that whitewash our unpredictable lives and their helplessness before randomness and chance.

The consequences of this banishment of convenience are manifold. For one, we deprive ourselves of some of our most remarkable, idiosyncratic human stories, embodied by people whose experiences can imbue immeasurable texture and depth into our understanding of what it means to be a person in the world. Further, we lose the chance for such lives to serve as frames of reference for our own possible future selves, choosing instead to leave ourselves unprepared if and when we face a catastrophic event. And finally, if such an event does come to pass, it is we who become marginalized, expelled out of view.

Those leading afterlives, meanwhile, are robbed of their rightful seat at humanity's table. When we marginalize these populations in our minds—out of fear, aversion, or some misguided sense of self-preservation—their marginalization within society inevitably follows. This failure of imagination fractures the horizons of the human condition, separating us not only from each other but also from many of our possible future selves.

When our prevailing storytellers *do* delve into catastrophic change, they tend to sprinkle it with pixie dust. Protagonists who were once undistinguished and pedestrian are transformed—often through the same flavor of fate-glossed accidents that befall us in real life—into superheroes, wizards, mutants, and Jedi. These narratives slyly invoke that unmistakable before-and-after moment when a person's circumstances go from commonplace, insipid, and innocent to frightening, alien, and heavy. Instead of that moment arriving in the form of a medical diagnosis, car crash, or eruption of irreparable violence, though, it materializes through a more empowering type of metamorphosis. We cannot resist telling stories about transformation: how they shatter the neatness of our lives, tear open our blinkered viewpoints, nail us to the crosses of our higher callings. These stories, however, conceal as much as they reveal, obscuring the true face of our transformations behind a glittering mask of transcendence.

Despite their cultural invisibility, almost everyone will, at some point, lead an afterlife or know someone very close to them who is leading one. Enduring catastrophe is in some ways the least-understood, most deliberately overlooked rite of passage we have. And yet it shapes our day-to-day existences and the unfolding of our lives more than perhaps anything else. It is the fulcrum of a relationship so simultaneously urgent and timeless that we have been grappling with it, ceaselessly, since antiquity: the one between tragedy and identity.

TO UNDERSTAND HOW we change after catastrophic life events, we often focus on a difference of degree: We will be stronger, deeper, or wiser; we will be irreversibly diminished and reduced; or, perhaps, we will remain the same as we have always been. But most afterlives represent not just a difference of *degree* from previous selves, but also a difference of *kind*. When we think only in terms of degree, much is lost in translation—the lives before and the ones after the catastrophes explored in this book do not adhere to the same system of measurement. They are, in some ways, more akin to a phase change, dramatically transitioning a gas to a liquid or a solid to a gas.

The subtle deception of Nietzsche's aphorism and other popular ways of thinking about catastrophic life events is their insinuation that, following tragedy or trauma, we will emerge as an extension of who we once were. The implication is that after someone endures a disabling injury, an extreme act of violence, or a devastating loss, they can pull themselves back onto the horse they rode in on, galloping out of the wreckage. But following before-and-after experiences, we cannot get back on the horse we rode in on. That horse is gone, and we must summon the courage to search the scorched plains of our life for a new one.

I have little doubt that the vast majority of people I spoke to during this project would wish to reverse what happened to them. I know I would. Nevertheless, I would struggle immeasurably with the notion that, in enacting such a wish, I would be erasing all the insight, wherewithal, self-reliance, and inner resources my illness has forced me to call upon during these past nine years. The conundrum of catastrophe is that it strengthens and expands your character—even makes you a better person—while blighting the circumstances that character and person must live under. You are forced to call up your finest qualities, over and over, to the task of conditions that will rapaciously absorb them. Nietzsche's preface to *Twilight of the Idols* includes a Latin phrase that translates to "The spirits increase, vigor grows through a wound." That may be true, but it can never heal it.

During my reporting I found myself encountering certain ways people changed after catastrophe over and over—patterns that shaped some or even most afterlives. They became this book's chapter titles, serving as answers to the project's galvanizing question, supported and illuminated by the narratives interwoven within them. While I track the subjects' lives chronologically, the chapters are not intended to serve as distinct stages like the famous model for the five stages of grief by Elisabeth Kübler-Ross. These are not phases to be passed through; when a chapter's theme is introduced, it is there to stay, a permanent feature of the individual's world. The subjects' stories start from a place of *diminishment,* and that deprivation never leaves them. Instead, other dimensions of experience are layered over that initial loss: *Fortitude, refinement,* and *vulnerability,* for example, mark the individual's progression and maturation in an afterlife that will always have a specific diminishment as its primal loss and immutable founding myth. By using these attributes and experiences as a lens for the narratives that follow, I hope to introduce a more expansive story than the quantitative model we're so quick to use when conceptualizing our most harrowing experiences.

If we're not thinking about differences of degree, we're often considering the ways catastrophic events change us in terms of bi-naries. There are the obvious negative changes, including physical impairment, psychological trauma, and lost relationships.

And there are also, to a subtler extent, those potential positive changes: enhanced discipline, widened perspective, a noble refor-mation of our everyday priorities. But this type of thinking can be restrictive, too. When we look at our lives through the binary of positive and negative, we fail to see the ways those categories can coalesce.

When somebody becomes more vulnerable as a consequence of their trauma and is forced to confront their fragilities, they may also deepen their capacity for creative expression and raise their sensi-tivity to the private struggles of others. The state of solitude often imposed by injury and illness, meanwhile, can be a potent catalyst for *seeking*, as we undertake the urgent project of searching for meaning or developing a better understanding of ourselves and our world. Even diminishment—at face value the most categorically negative change people go through in their afterlives—can establish the conditions for a narrower but deeper life, over time laying the groundwork for a state of *devotion*, be it to a cause or a deity. These interrelated changes expose the inadequacy of trying to see our af-terlives through binary categories alone. Their relentless fluidity eschews rigid value judgments, forcing us to see how these experi-ences grow out of one another like crystals blossoming from a bed of rock.

A woman in her midthirties recalled to me the sudden, complete loss of her vision following a lifelong retinal condition. At first she was scared and despondent, as nearly anyone would be. But after a few weeks passed, she began construing her blindness differently. "Wasn't it possible for loss to also be viewed as opportunity?" she remembered asking herself. Most catastrophic life events can be un-derstood as variations on loss. That loss, however, is rarely static or one-dimensional—it cannot afford to be. The grinding despair of having our lives stripped away impels us to drive forward in search of what we can find to replace it. People who are content with their lives have no incentive to change. (As Nietzsche put it, "Joy accompanies, joy does not move.") Only loss is an adequately powerful force to trigger transformation. If necessity is the mother of invention, then our most irrevocable traumas ensure that it is also the mother of *reinvention*. We transform because inertia is no longer a bearable option.

THE CONSTELLATION THERAPY session I attended with my sister had laid bare the stark, unvarnished realities of my life. More than that, it exposed the dubious convictions I'd subscribed to about that life. I had propped up a persona that promised to turn my grief and infirmity into strength, honor, and aggrandizement, and I let that persona obscure the humbler, less glorious truths about how I'd changed. The sobering disillusionment left me rootless and rattled, my repertoire of self-assurances suddenly voided. But it also inspired a newfound willingness to understand how my adversities *had* shaped my identity. My starting point was that trauma and loss did, indeed, compel people toward radical choices and dramatic adaptations. I *had* changed in the years after my mother died and following the emergence of my illness, just not necessarily or exclusively in the ways I'd long maintained. This book represents my best attempt at answering the open question left by that constellation therapy session. Underneath all the coping mechanisms that I'd kneaded together—a "unified field" that promptly fell apart—who had I actually become?

The celebrated wildlife conservationist Alan Rabinowitz, who struggled to speak fluently throughout his childhood, said once in an interview, "Stuttering gave me my life." As a child, Rabinowitz's speech impediment was so severe that he rarely opened his mouth at school. He did find, however, that he could enunciate smoothly and without stammering to the pets at his family's Brooklyn apartment and the wildlife he lingered over at the nearby zoo. His stuttering, such a source of anguish and alienation for him during his childhood, served as the originative force for the intrepid zoologist he would later become.

Our most formidable adversities can serve as the seeds that gradually bloom into a deeper and more beloved identity. Meister Eckhart wrote how "vigilant people are alert and on the watch for their Lord for whom they wait; they look to see if he is not by chance concealed in what befalls them." To survive in afterlives, we have to look deeper to see if there is anything concealed in what befalls us. Our traumas force our hand, compelling us to adapt and make the kind of radical, courageous choices that birth more ingenious dreams. Rabinowitz allowed his adversity to reroute the trajectory of his life and sculpt the person he was to become—an audacious act that is starkly different from more simplistic empowerment narratives. A deficiency that for a child probably felt like the end of the world was also the beginning of one.

The identities people foster in their afterlives are rarely arrived at incidentally—they do not wander haphazardly into their passions, careers, perspectives, and beliefs. The individuals they become are forged in voids, sowed on fallow land, pursued against the finest of margins, and people seize on them because their survival in some sense depends on it. Catastrophes shatter the status quo we once relied on, banishing our complacency and forcing us to work against the inertia of our new circumstances to make a self we can control and be fulfilled by. That self begins as little more than a slender shadow in the dark and distant rooms of our most private thoughts: a blurry, half-discovered dream of transformation. Actualizing that dream is the long, difficult, frequently harrowing journey of afterlives.

Of the course we take through life, Saint Cyril of Jerusalem wrote, "The dragon sits by the side of the road, watching those who pass. Beware lest he devour you. We go to the Father of Souls, but it is necessary to pass by the dragon." Those people leading afterlives have passed by the dragon—faced down its scalding plumes of flame and jackknife teeth and scythe-like claws—and the confrontation could not have done anything less than change them forever.

What
Doesn't Kill Us
Makes Us

CHAPTER ONE

Diminishment

SOPHIE PAPP AND HER FAMILY HAD A RITUAL FOR THE RECENTLY departed. Whenever a relative died, she and her brother and cousins would all squeeze into a car and drive to Koksilah River, an hour north of their homes in Victoria, British Columbia. There, they would spend the day swimming in the glassy jade water, letting the current drag them along the squishy riverbed and gazing at the native arbutus trees, whose red bark peeled like crinkly snakeskin in the summer months. On September 1, 2014, shortly after her grandmother passed away, Sophie—a sweet, reserved girl with gray-blue eyes and freckles—joined her younger brother, Alex, her cousin Emily, and a close friend. They packed themselves into a navy-blue Volkswagen Golf and headed up island to the banks of the long, twisty river.

On the way, the group made a quick stop at a Tim Hortons for coffee and breakfast before pulling back onto 1 North. That's the last memory Sophie, who was nineteen years old at the time, has of that day. It would also be the last memory she would form for the entire next week of her life. Over the years, she's cobbled together the facts from those who were with her in the VW that morning to create an account of what happened next.

About forty-five minutes after the stop, Emily, who was driving, spilled her iced coffee. It started dripping onto her seat, her clothes, even trickling into her shoes, and as she scrambled to clean it she let her attention slip from the highway. The car drifted to the right, eventually veering into the gravel shoulder. The sound of the tires rumbling over the carpet of rock fragments made Emily finally look up, and when she saw how far the car had slipped off the road she panicked, yanking the steering wheel to the left. The wheels struggled to gain traction on the gravel, though, and at a speed of around seventy miles per hour, she lost control. The sedan skidded across multiple lanes in both directions before somersaulting into a ravine on the opposite side of the road.

The force of the impact knocked Sophie and Emily unconscious. Hoisting themselves from their seats, Alex and Sophie's friend were able to push the doors open and escape the mangled Golf. After around fifteen minutes, Emily regained consciousness, but Sophie remained unresponsive. When first responders arrived at the scene, they used the Jaws of Life to pull her out of the back seat. She was immediately transferred to a helicopter and medevaced to Victoria General Hospital.

Sophie was rushed into the hospital's trauma center, designated for treating the facility's most severe, life-or-death injuries. The large, high-ceilinged room was filled with beds, ventilators, and defibrillators; snakelike surgical lights swooped overhead and bathed the metallic tables and color-coded medical cabinets in bright fluorescent light. Within an hour, Sophie's parents arrived. After rushing through the automatic front doors and heading for the trauma center, they were met in the hallway by a grave-faced cluster of doctors, nurses, and paramedics attending to their daughter.

During the accident, Sophie had suffered a traumatic brain injury. At the crash site, EMTs gave her a score of six on the Glasgow Coma Scale, indicating profound trauma. She had also fallen into a coma. Standing in the trauma center, her parents, who were both doctors, canvassed their daughter frantically for any signs of encouragement. Instead, they observed how her body had assumed an unusually stiff posture—arms ramrod straight against her sides, hands tightly clenched, toes flexed upward—with minimal response to stimuli. They both knew this condition, called decerebrate posturing, was a frightening sign, one that often suggested severe and potentially fatal brain damage. Neither, however, acknowledged their observation to the other. Instead, they sat on either side of Sophie's hospital bed, stroking her curly brown hair and gently gliding their fingers over her arms. "Sophie, Mom and Dad are here," they whispered, unsure whether their reassurances were getting through. "You're going to be okay." They'd both developed the emotional poise required of physicians navigating the chaos of ER departments, and that self-possession helped during those immeasurably bleak, desolating hours. Underneath their masks of composure, though, they were scrabbling to absorb the worst day of their lives, scanning their daughter's motionless body and desperately hoping she would survive.

Sophie was eventually wheeled to the intensive care unit, where she would spend the next several days. Initially all but lifeless, she grew increasingly restless as she fluctuated between varying states of consciousness. Though still in a coma, Sophie would thrash around in her hospital bed, pull at her IVs, and mumble indecipherably to herself. At one point, while still unconscious in the neurology wing's ICU, she even attempted to stage an escape from her hospital room. Wresting off her wires, pulling out her tubes, and dragging herself out of the disheveled bed, she clambered over the rails before collapsing onto the floor.

Her mother, Jane, remained by her side nearly twenty-four hours a day. Though non-staff were technically not permitted to stay in hospital rooms overnight, Jane found crafty ways to evade the hospital's rules, and often slept a few feet from Sophie's bed, on a fauxleather chair that converted into a cot. By her fourth day in the hospital, Sophie was moved to the neurology wing and placed in an acute care unit that specialized in brain injuries. Her condition had stabilized somewhat, but her physical state remained disconcerting. Behind the glass walls of her private room, she was hooked up to a snarl of medical equipment: Wires measuring heart rate and oxygen saturation dangled from her body; an IV delivered a steady stream of fluids through a butterfly needle in her forearm; and nasogastric tubes snaked through both her nostrils, which reminded her mother of a "very disturbing" plastic bull-ring. She thrashed under the hospital bedding, and her legs were often splayed at odd angles over a rumpled tangle of papery white sheets. Because she tugged at her wires and tubes so often, staff tethered her hands to the bed railings with wrist restraints.

But Sophie survived those precarious first few days, when the extent of her brain damage was entirely unclear and her stiff, contorted posture evoked her parents' worst fears. By the end of her first week in the hospital, she was gradually emerging from her coma, her mind surfacing in short, erratic bursts. Sophie would awaken for brief, bleary snatches, offering monosyllabic responses to her parents and nurses—her first three words were "blanket," "pee," and "head"—before slipping back into a fretful, tumultuous sleep. Due to a phenomenon in the brain called neural storming, her body temperature swung dramatically, and staff cooled her down by wrapping cold compresses around her legs. When she got too hot, she fell into episodes of delirium, growing agitated and disoriented and sometimes even hallucinating conversations with people who weren't in the room. Still, she was starting to communicate regularly with the family, friends, and staff checking in on her throughout each day, something her parents found extremely heartening. Sophie, it would seem, had been spared a traumatic brain injury's grimmest scenarios.

As Sophie moved into her second week at Victoria General Hospital, though, her convalescence began to assume more perplexing qualities. Just days after regaining the most rudimentary communication skills, she was engaging in extended, in-depth conversations with everyone around her. "One day she spoke a sentence, and then not long after, she was talking endlessly, about everything," Jane recalled. She asked staff how old they were, whether they had children, what their most interesting cases had been. She peppered doctors with questions about both her condition and their personal lives. She slipped effortlessly into sincere, heartfelt exchanges with the floor's nurses' aides.

Sophie was also more direct and inquisitive than she'd been prior to the injury, demonstrating a forthright, even blunt approach that could flummox those around her. On September 14, exactly two weeks after she'd first been admitted into the hospital, she was scheduled for a morning appointment with a radiologist to discuss MRI scans she'd taken a few days earlier. (Canadian radiologists rarely review brain scans directly with their patients, but the clinician was a family friend.) Sophie was still struggling to regain the use of the left side of her body—the TBI had affected her brain's ability to send signals to nerves along her left arm and leg—and she was using one of the hospital's wheelchairs to get around. With her mother by her side, she wheeled to the wing's large elevators and traveled down several floors to the radiology department. When the radiologist began discussing the scans, Sophie interjected with one question after another. "Are any of the lesions in the cerebellum?" she asked. "Has an fMRI been done? What about the thalamus, fornix, and pons? Have they been affected?" The radiologist paused, his furrowed brow and sharp eyes training both mystification and concern on the nineteen-year-old sitting in front of him. His eyes slid over to Jane, briefly, before turning back to Sophie. "How do you know these things, Sophie?" he asked. In the days before the appointment, Sophie had convinced her father to borrow several books on neurology from the library. After he dropped off the texts on neuroscience and brain anatomy, she "read away into the night," she remembered.

All her life, Sophie, who is white, had been a soft-spoken, even taciturn girl. Though she harbored a passionate idealism about making a difference in the world and expressed fierce compassion for the least fortunate, she was never wild-eyed or strident in her tone. Her parents saw their daughter as someone whose prudence and circumspection belied her age. "She had been a fairly introverted, cautious girl," Jane remembered. As her time at Victoria General Hospital progressed, though, that girl faded more and more from view, as episodes of a newly brazen, effervescent persona piled up. When a nurse went through the neurology wing and marked each room with colored tape, Sophie snuck around and mischievously peeled them all off. One night, after most of the patients had gone to sleep, she wheeled around the floor and changed the dates on all their whiteboards to December 24. When a technician explained that he would be doing something called a "propeller rotation" while she was in the MRI machine, she told him, "It's not a helicopter, so fuck you." She found one of the neurosurgeons who made rounds on her wing handsome, and she asked him out on the spot. (He replied that he was married, and at any rate much too old for her.) With intense sincerity, she queried one of the physicians on her care team about where the source of consciousness lay in the brain. "She was really, really social, and that wasn't the Sophie that we knew from before," Jane recalled. "I didn't realize at this point that I wasn't just the same person in a different body," Sophie said. "I had different personality traits."

Because of the deep-seated, manifold ways the head trauma affected her brain, Sophie awoke from her coma a markedly different person. Of course, she would always be Sophia Papp, daughter of Jane and Jamie, born December 12, 1994, with the same singular two-decade narrative. But her personality had changed, and not just in the nuanced, incremental ways most people recognize from watching friends mature and parents soften and children blink into adolescence. Sophie's entire approach to the world and the people in it shifted in swift order, and telltale markers of the person she was before the injury evaporated without a trace. A mischievous, loquacious new temperament, meanwhile, continued materializing in its place. It was unnerving and turbulent, but also, sometimes, laced with shimmering whimsy: One minute she'd be discussing neural anatomy with a brain surgeon, and the next she'd be giving away flowers and chocolate to a favorite nurse. At times it seemed as though the Sophie Papp everyone knew had been swapped out for a charismatic, capricious changeling, a fantastical double of the person who stepped into her cousin's VW that balmy August morning.

Sophie's doctors believed that the TBI affected her executive functioning, including her inhibition control. The result was a more *disinhibited* person—one who acted freely, spoke effusively, and approached others with a directness verging on audacity that her old self wouldn't have dreamed of employing. The metamorphosis wasn't limited to the way she communicated with others, either. In her monthlong stay at VGH, Sophie grew more emotional than she'd ever been before. An even-keeled girl during most of her adolescence, that September she rose to a boil quickly, tumbled into the undertow of powerful mood swings, and broke into convulsive crying jags triggered by sudden realizations about her daunting new circumstances.

Jane and Jamie were understandably elated that Sophie's TBI hadn't rendered her more incapacitated. What was also dawning on them, however, was that their daughter was emerging from her trauma as a different person. "As soon as I started talking or trying to interact with the world, they realized that, actually, it's no longer the daughter we knew," Sophie said. For Jane, "It was like losing a child, but a physical representation of that child is still living, and we had to get to know who she was." While Jane felt positive about all the gains Sophie was making in the first weeks after the crash— she'd improved her fine motor skills and reduced the severity of her paralysis, and her mobility was increasing every day—she regarded Sophie's novel disposition with acute ambivalence. "With this extroversion, with this personality change, we were able to see that she was intensely intelligent, and that gave us great hope that she could find a way around some of her changes," she said. "At the same time, she didn't show any insight. She was completely unaware of herself or her impact on the world." Jane remembered feeling "really afraid" as she contemplated how things would play out once Sophie left the hospital. There was no telling what would happen once she was thrown back into a world whose social codes and cues, nonverbal communication, and interpersonal subtleties seemed to have been wiped clean from her brain. A single urgent question echoed through Jane's mind: *How is this going to play out in the world?*

A quiet, easygoing young woman fell into a weeklong slumber and woke up talkative, tempestuous, and inscrutable to those who clung to her old mold to try to decipher her. It was like a fairy tale that gestured toward a broader allegorical meaning, perhaps a fable about the friction between modern womanhood and traditional feminine archetypes. But Sophie wasn't an everywoman or a metaphor. She was a human being who'd been estranged from herself, a person whose very continuity of self had been ruptured forever. Her new reality forced her to reckon with an identity crisis writ large, as she began her afterlife living under the skin of somebody who'd been effectively born in the crash, a girl on the cusp of adulthood now stepping into a world in which she was an all but complete stranger.

THE TYPES OF catastrophes explored in this book all result in an abrupt loss of some or even most of the territory that individuals had once taken as a given in their lives. As a result, afterlives predominantly begin in a state of diminishment—the one clear, indisputable consequence of catastrophic life events, and an uncomplicated common ground from which to begin this investigation.

This diminishment is often unambiguous—losing a child or the use of one's legs—but it can also manifest in less explicit ways, as individuals are wrenched away from sports, socializing, recreational pursuits, and even romantic partners. The dispossessions triggered by before-and-after events take a wide variety of forms: While incarceration deprives a person of their home, their relationships, and their time on earth, blindness deprives them of what is arguably their most direct means of connecting with the world. People rarely

discuss the full multitude of losses they've suffered following catastrophes, including with loved ones. For me, such lamentations felt
futile, and I feared being accused of weakness or pessimism. Even
though I appeared, on the outside, to be largely the same person
after the onset of my chronic illness, internally I was carrying out a
desperate triage, sorting through what parts of me could be saved
and what territories would not survive the condition's scourge.
Though we may receive emotional and practical support from family, friends, and significant others, these calculations are intimate
reckonings we must confront on our own.

The past several decades have seen a steady accumulation of scientific research on how trauma and catastrophe shape and influence the lives we lead in their wake—our afterlives. While the
results can vary dramatically depending on the nature of the event—
and also, crucially, the state of an individual's circumstances entering it—the upshot in many of these studies is that people who
experience major injury, illness, or trauma move forward with a
marked reduction in certain important life outcomes.

The ways people's lives and psyches are transformed in the aftermath of catastrophic events often stand in stark counterpoint to
Nietzsche's idea of growing stronger. People who live with a chronic
illness, for example, are two to three times more likely to suffer from
anxiety, depression, and other mental health conditions. They may
also struggle to maintain even their closest relationships, and often
must significantly pare back professional aspirations. For many
with more debilitating illnesses, poverty becomes a lurking specter,
too, as sufferers are robbed of the functionality to earn as they once
did.

Physical traumas like spinal cord injuries resulting in paralysis
leave individuals even more vulnerable. The prevalence of clinical
depression among this group is as high as 30 percent, with similar
figures for generalized anxiety disorder. Because spinal cord injuries often occur during a traumatic event, those living with them are
also three times more likely to meet criteria for post-traumatic

stress disorder. Life expectancy following these types of injuries is lower, too, reduced by anywhere between several years and several decades depending on condition severity.

Meanwhile, experiences like rape and sexual assault, incarceration, and sudden bereavement put people at significantly higher risk for not only PTSD but also suicidality and other mental health disorders. Individuals who have been raped face a tremendous struggle in getting over the catastrophic event itself, and may go to extreme lengths to pacify its corrosive memory. And those who've lived through extended periods under incarceration frequently develop significant mental health challenges specific to a life of isolation, stagnancy, and violence.

Our studies and statistics tell a broad but discouraging story, one whose objectivity and rigor are undoubtedly persuasive. The veracity of such data—at least as it pertains to the first few years after profound adversities—is the inescapable starting point for an exploration into how our lives are changed following irrevocable catastrophe. As Yale psychology professor Paul Bloom unsentimentally remarked in an article in *The New Yorker* discussing whether suffering is a necessary part of being human, "Look at the data: bad things are bad." The matter still up for grabs is everything else that they are.

LIKE SOPHIE, VALERIE PIRO also saw her life permanently transformed in the aftermath of a car accident. In the winter of 2008, Valerie was a junior at Stuyvesant—an ultracompetitive specialized high school in New York City—on her way to a track meet in a van her coach was driving. Valerie was on the track team's racewalking squad (a competitive sport similar to running, but requiring participants to keep one foot on the ground at all times), competing in the 1500-meter race. A hardworking teenager who was rarely idle, Valerie rode the R and N trains every day from her family's home in Bay Ridge, Brooklyn, to her school in Lower Manhattan. Squeezed between other morning commuters, her face obscured by the open jacket of a class textbook, Valerie looked the part of the nerdy overachiever with a perfect GPA that she was.

The racewalking team was heading to Dartmouth College in New Hampshire, a five-hour drive from Manhattan along Interstate 91, cutting through swaths of Connecticut, Massachusetts, and Vermont. The coach and eight girls left from Washington Heights at ten-thirty in the morning in a Ford E-350, and after four mundane hours on flat highway roads, most of the teenagers were dozing off in the van's three rear rows. For reasons that would never come to full light, at around three P.M. the coach lost control of the van, which drifted through the passing lane and onto a cresting knoll in the center of the median. The vehicle flipped over twice, landing driver's side down in a ditch along the opposite side of the highway. Valerie blacked out. When she came to, she was hanging out of the van and the black polyester belt was pressed tightly against her neck.

"There was this very heavy metal crunching," Valerie recalled. "I felt this enormous pressure around my head, and I remember screaming as loudly as I could because I thought my head was going to implode." Within minutes, a throng of first responders inside police cars, ambulances, and an EMS helicopter converged on the van, an overturned heap of shattered windows and twisted metal. Emergency personnel removed Valerie from the van by sliding a plastic spine board underneath her and hoisting her out. Lying on the board outside the van, Valerie was startled to discover she couldn't feel most of her body. Nor could she detect the bitter sting of January cold in Vermont. When she asked a paramedic whether she would ever walk again, the uniformed woman told her she didn't know.

A medevac helicopter flew Valerie to Dartmouth-Hitchcock hospital, a few miles east of the Vermont border. There, she immediately underwent six hours of emergency surgery. Doctors determined that her seventh cervical vertebra—located at the base of the neck, just above the shoulder blades—had shattered during the accident, imploding against her spinal cord and compressing it by more than 50 percent. Surgeons removed the bone fragments and stabilized her spinal cord through a procedure known as titanium fusion, replacing part of the shattered vertebra with metal plates and screws. She'd suffered a C7 traumatic spinal cord injury, and had lost the ability to feel or move most of her body below her sternum. When she awoke from the surgery around midnight, her physical sensation was limited to her neck, shoulders, chest, and smatterings in her arms. Emerging from the narcotizing fog of anesthesia, she placed her hand on her stomach and realized that she couldn't feel her fingers running across it. "It very much felt like I was touching someone else's body," she recalled. "It felt like I was touching a body that wasn't mine."

After spending a week at Dartmouth-Hitchcock, Valerie was transported by ambulance to Rusk Rehabilitation, an NYU-affiliated medical center in New York City. She would spend the next six months there, undergoing an intensive daily regimen of stretches and exercises intended to help her regain as much functionality as possible. She'd also spend countless hours working with Rusk's occupational therapists to develop the daily skills and physical maneuvers she would need to master to adapt to her dramatically altered future. Once limber and fit, with a compact five-foot-two frame and the sculpted calves of a long-distance runner, Valerie was now paralyzed across much of her body. In addition to losing sensation in her torso and legs, nerve functioning was also damaged across parts of her hands and arms. She could feel only portions of her forearms, and while her left hand had lost some of its strength but little of its dexterity, her right hand, which she wrote with, fared worse. "I could barely type correctly, I couldn't make a fist with my right hand, I couldn't straighten out my right hand without help from my other hand," she said. When she wanted to write something with her right hand, she needed to use her left to place a pen between her fingers. And when her right hand spasmed, as it often did, she'd patiently wrench each finger out of a permanent clench, as though manually pulling out the ribs of an umbrella.

The winter and spring seasons Valerie spent at Rusk were dejecting. "It felt like one of the circles of hell," she recalled. She found the pediatric rehabilitation floor she was staying on to be overcrowded and shambolic, with inpatients there suffering from a hodgepodge of physical injuries and behavioral disorders. Every morning, a nurse and aide shuffled into her room and outfitted her in sweatpants and T-shirts her parents had brought her from home. Then they transferred her from her hospital bed to a rickety wheelchair that was much too big for her. To keep her securely fitted in the chair, they stuffed the gaps with foam padding. Staff then wrapped metal braces around her ankles to prevent drop foot, and inserted her feet into used white sneakers large enough to fit the braces. Finally, they clasped an abdominal binder around her torso to help manage her erratic blood pressure. It was a slow, leaden production, what felt to her like a ragged costume for a performance she was now, without forewarning, required to put on every day. She could only hope these grim, plodding mornings—where time moved with the methodical slowness of an octogenarian—were not also rehearsals for a character she would play for the rest of her life.

Valerie struggled to develop a strong rapport with her physical therapist, a young woman with tired brown eyes she spent at least an hour with every day. Though she appreciated the therapist's flinty approach with her patients, she was less enthusiastic about her religious dogmatism. When the therapist invoked a platitude about God never giving anyone more than they can handle, Valerie labored to conceal her irritation.

Relations were not getting along much better elsewhere in the hospital. One of the doctors at the pediatric unit was hardly the source of encouragement the Piros were searching for. When the physician observed Valerie studying for the SATs, she questioned the idea of her attending college at all. "Don't bother," she told Valerie. Instead, the doctor suggested Valerie should travel, eat what she wanted, and squeeze as much pleasure as she could out of her life while she still had it. "That did not sit well with me at all," Valerie said, "because I have been a nerd my entire life." Valerie remembered the doctor's philosophy boiling down to "Her life's over, just let her do whatever she does."

Privately, the physician delivered a pitiless prognosis to Valerie's parents. Her life span would likely be cut in half, she said; her health would continue deteriorating over that time; and she'd need to see specialists regularly for the duration of her truncated life. The brusque, unvarnished pessimism pushed her Italian American father—already anxious and overwrought—closer to full-blown panic. Valerie's mother, a stubborn and ever-skeptical woman who'd moved to the United States from Taiwan in 1980 to attend graduate school, tried to stay grounded and maintain a measured approach. Instead of taking the doctor at her word, she seriously wondered whether Rusk Rehabilitation was the best facility for her daughter.

As Valerie's time at Rusk progressed, the divergence between how she viewed her long-term recovery and what her care team felt were realistic expectations for improvement only widened. Rusk's physical therapists wanted her spending her days focused on practical skills that helped people adjust to life with paralysis, including practicing wheelchair transfers, a deceptively strenuous maneuver requiring individuals to hoist themselves into and out of their chairs. Wheelchair users need to execute these transfers multiple times a day, and learning the skill promoted independence and self-sufficiency.

But Valerie saw her prognosis very differently. In her mind, wheelchair transfers and other exercises geared toward long-term adaptation were a gross misallocation of her precious recovery time. She held an unshakable certitude that, with enough dedication and effort, she would eventually regain full use of her legs. Anything geared toward a lifetime in a wheelchair, therefore, was ultimately a waste of time. (It's worth noting that while many paralyzed individuals aspire to regain the ability to walk, plenty of others feel that adapting to and embracing life in a wheelchair is the best choice for them.) "I kept thinking, 'Yeah, I'm going to regain the use of everything and then I'm going to be up and running,'" she said. "'I'm going to run a marathon when I'm twenty-five.'"

The conflicting views between Valerie and her physical therapists were a source of ongoing tension. Most of the time Valerie bit her tongue, but during one quarrelsome session her exasperation finally bubbled over. After her physical therapist dismissed her account of regaining sensation in her abdominal muscles—and once again requested that she work on wheelchair transfers—Valerie broke down sobbing. Screaming at the therapist, she flew into a precipitate rage. Afterward, all she could recall was asking one explosive rhetorical question: "Why don't you just shoot me in the head?" The scene drew the attention of the head pediatric doctor, who would later diagnose Valerie with depression based on the incident.

Valerie had undergone a life change so abrupt and severe on that chilly January afternoon in Vermont that her psyche had simply refused to accept it. Instead, her mind defaulted to an expectation—unfounded but firmly held—that her circumstances would eventually reverse themselves to the way they were before. "When something that extreme happens so suddenly, it's like your brain can't even register what just happened," Valerie said. "I convinced myself that this is such a sudden life change that it has to be temporary. There's no way this is permanent. I just kept trying to reason with myself: How could something this swift be permanent?" Whatever the accident and surgeon's reports might have said, for Valerie the notion that the line between healthy adolescent runner and C7 tetraplegic spanned all of one second was not fathomable. The feat of acceptance was too staggering, the emotional toll of fully internalizing such a fact too immense. By refusing to believe that her paralysis was permanent, Valerie was protecting her emotional equilibrium and perhaps even her sanity.

Rationalism and self-preservation had become mutually exclusive during those harrowing winter months, and Valerie emphatically zeroed in on the latter. Her self-subscribing narrative would be one of extraordinary recovery, and she would come to latch on to a simple, straightforward conviction: If she only worked hard enough and maintained an unfailingly optimistic perspective on her circumstances, she could regain the use of her legs and reclaim the life her spinal cord injury had shattered.

In June, Valerie was discharged from Rusk. After deliberating for weeks, she and her parents eventually decided to send her to a second rehabilitation center. That summer, she spent six weeks at the Kennedy Krieger Institute in downtown Baltimore. If she remembered Rusk as an infernal ordeal where she sparred with physical therapists and navigated demoralizing prognoses, Kennedy Krieger was a place of "hope and magic and unicorns." The facility had a unit dedicated to young people with spinal cord injuries, and the wing committed all its resources to just four inpatients (there were a number of outpatients). When Valerie's dad asked the unit's head nurse whether she thought Valerie could attend college, she told him, matter-of-factly, "Yeah, she can go anywhere." The nurse's viewpoint felt like the antithesis of everything they'd heard from the doctor at Rusk, and it gave the Piros a much-needed infusion of hope—hope that Valerie could continue progressing with her rehab, resume her promising academic career, and perhaps, eventually, pursue more of the trappings of a fulfilling, uninhibited life.

At Kennedy Krieger, Valerie was able to dedicate much more of her time to regaining physical sensation than she'd been permitted to at Rusk. Therapists introduced her to advanced equipment developed to help those recovering from spinal cord injuries enhance muscle functioning and improve overall health. A nurse at Kennedy Krieger also carried out a cognitive exam on Valerie—something she couldn't recall receiving at Rusk—by reading number sequences to her and having Valerie repeat the sequences in the same order. "I did all right on it, because she ran out of number groups," Valerie said.

The following fall, Valerie returned to Stuyvesant for her senior year. Though she felt like much the same person, only now with a disability, to her peers she was transformed. Her features, along with her fondness for tucking her shoulder-length black hair into colorful hair ties, remained the same. But many of her fellow seniors seemed to register only the wheelchair, a blue-and-black model with power-assist features and two metal handles at the top over which her backpack often hung. She'd made modest improvements since her injury the previous January, and could now control most of her arms, type on a computer, and write out her homework assignments. Sensation below her chest had improved slightly, too, and she occasionally felt the upper half of her abdomen. But her control over anything in that part of her body remained minimal. Instead of her long-standing jeans-and-a-T-shirt outfits, she now needed to wear skirts down to her ankles because of catheterization, compression stockings up to her knees, and a Velcro abdominal binder that she concealed underneath baggy hoodies.

Some of the coldest receptions she received when she returned to school came from her closest friends. The other members of the racewalking team—including all of those in the van with her that morning—distanced themselves from Valerie. Some even gossiped about the accident: its fallout, whether their coach was at fault, who was getting the most attention because of their injuries. Throughout her senior year, Valerie continued to steadfastly believe that she would eventually recover from her paralysis. Her peers were more skeptical. One of her oldest friends, another runner who'd been in the van during the accident, bluntly shared her thoughts during an online conversation: "Nobody at school actually thinks you're going to get better."

As the year went on, Valerie felt increasingly ostracized from the social circles that were once the polestars of her adolescence. "I went from thinking I have friends who cared about me to becoming the reminder for the girls on the track team of what had happened," she said. "They wanted nothing to do with me." Instead of draining her resources trying to resuscitate friendships now laced with animus, Valerie began devoting almost all of her time to two priorities. There was her academic future, which she focused on through her painstaking approach to her college applications, and her health, which she addressed with an exhaustive combination of physical therapy, acupuncture, and the use of specialized medical equipment. "I became very good at channeling whatever frustration, whatever emotional pain I had, just channeling it into my work." She started avoiding the cafeteria at lunchtime, instead wheeling herself to a table in the English department offices and eating the Italian sandwiches her mom made her every day. The impression she got from her peers, she recalled, came down to a single, insurmountable distinction: "This isn't Val anymore. This is Val in a wheelchair."

A 2013 study carried out by the Christopher & Dana Reeve Foundation found that 5.4 million Americans are living with some form of paralysis—around 2 percent of the U.S. population, and far more than previously thought. A third of these people became paralyzed after a stroke, and over a quarter after a spinal cord injury, which today occur most frequently in car accidents. Among those living with a spinal cord injury, 40 percent are considered paraplegic—they can freely move their arms and hands, but have lost part or all functioning in their legs—while 60 percent are deemed tetraplegic, and have partial or total loss of nerve functioning in all four of their limbs. Valerie fell into the latter category.

Up until the 1940s, the vast majority of spinal cord injuries were fatal within the first two or three years. Sufferers developed pressure sores and urinary tract infections that went untreated, led to sepsis, and ultimately resulted in death. For centuries, those with spinal cord injuries were regarded as hopeless cases, and the medical establishment resigned itself to the notion that it could not significantly or reliably prolong the lives of these patients. While death might be staved off for a time, infections and sepsis ensured that it was unavoidable.

Once the use of antibiotics became widespread during the second half of the twentieth century, the numerous varieties of infection that arose from spinal cord injuries could be much more aggressively treated. Survival rates shot up as a result, often by decades. Today, life expectancy varies depending on a person's age and the location of the injury: Individuals who suffer a lower-level in-

jury early in life may live into their seventies, while those who become dependent on ventilators may survive for only eight or nine
years.

As with other chronic conditions, though, focusing exclusively
on the struggle to stay alive can overshadow the reality of *living* itself for those forced to adapt to such dramatically altered bodies.
Spinal cord injuries are among the most challenging of all acquired
disabilities, a condition that not only affects mobility and sensation
but also disrupts functionality across a wide spectrum of organs and
systems. SCI sufferers may struggle to control their bladders and
bowel function and maintain the health of their livers and kidneys,
complicating their daily lives in ways that even exceed the obstacles
presented by their paralysis. Those with injuries to the upper cervical region of the spine, meanwhile, risk losing part or all of their
respiratory functioning and the ability to breathe independently.
Had Valerie's head struck the inside of the van just a few inches in
either direction, impacting a different vertebra, she could have severed the connection between her brain and her respiratory muscles,
leaving her permanently hooked to a mechanical ventilator for the
rest of her life.

NIETZSCHE'S CONVICTION THAT what doesn't kill us makes us
stronger—which, in the face of modern research and statistics, feels
increasingly dubious—is today just one of several frameworks for
thinking about how tragedy and calamity change us. Perhaps the
most prevalent of those frameworks—and certainly the one most
steeped in academic research—is what we might call the science of
trauma.

When we talk about living in a state of diminishment, we are
often referring, directly or indirectly, to trauma. For most of the
twentieth century, "trauma" was used to describe the varieties of
major injury that could be incurred by our bodies: car accidents,
gunshots, stabbings, war wounds. This is the medical arena of blunt

force trauma, sharp force trauma, penetrating trauma. The medical journal *PLOS Medicine* defines the word, simply, as "physical injury to the body and its sequelae."

Toward the turn of the twenty-first century, though, trauma's usage shifted, and it started being invoked in reference to not only physical but also psychological damage. This was a strain of trauma that materialized when an experience or set of circumstances was so stressful, dire, or outright horrifying that it outstripped one's ability to cope. As Judith Herman explained in her groundbreaking work on the subject, *Trauma and Recovery,* experiences that carry a high risk for inducing psychological trauma include "physical viola-tion or injury, exposure to extreme violence, or witnessing gro-tesque death. In each instance, the salient characteristic of the traumatic event is its power to inspire helplessness and terror."

A cavalcade of metaphors has been deployed for what hap-pens next—overloaded systems, smashed apparatuses, cracked foundations—because neurologists are still mapping out the laby-rinthine ways a traumatic event can change the brain's behavior. Suffice it to say, in these situations our brain's fight-or-flight re-sponse fails to protect or deliver us, and the baffling, paradoxical consequence is that those mechanisms become trapped in the mo-ment of their failure. They are, that is, doomed to a kind of insanity in which they repeat the physiological changes the original danger triggered over and over: activating the amygdala, flooding the body with stress hormones, and rapidly escalating blood pressure and heart rate.

Research findings on this variety of trauma appear to have grown only more baleful over time. The field rapidly expanded in the 1990s, as medicine and culture came to terms with the prevalence of such experiences. Since then, clinicians and researchers have worked to ferret out psychological trauma's diffuse effects on the amygdala, hippocampus, prefrontal cortex, and other regions of the brain. Herman writes, "Traumatic events produce profound and lasting changes in physiological arousal, emotion, cognition, and memory." These changes, in turn, can negatively influence a person's lifestyle and behavior, increasing their propensity for substance abuse, psychiatric disorders, and health problems. An entire subfield is now devoted to childhood trauma, too, and the research indicates that the chronic states of dysfunction, abuse, or neglect that produce it often damage children for life, working like a slow-blooming malediction on their health, mood, and behavior.

When we think of our catastrophic life events exclusively through the lens of trauma, Nietzsche is essentially nullified. If the scientific literature on trauma tells us anything about the relationship between tragedy and identity, it's that tragedies often leave our identities in a state of vulnerability, clawing to keep hold of an existence pitted with the scars of the life-altering event. Whereas Nietzsche's maxim implied an increase—in strength, character, stamina, selfhood—trauma points to a stark reduction, constricting people's lives and forcing them to find ways to adapt to more restless, turbulent psyches.

GINA APPLEBEE GREW up on the outskirts of Charleston, in the South Carolina Lowcountry of palmettos, wraparound verandas, and sprawling salt marshes that wind like tangles of water moccasins toward the widemouthed estuaries spilling into the Atlantic. She and her twin sister, Andrea, were born in 1985 at a medical complex overlooking Charleston Harbor; during their delivery, Gina became wedged in the birth canal and started suffocating, and she barely survived. She was placed in an incubator for several weeks afterward, and as an adult she's often pointed to that incident as evidence that she's been fighting for her life since it began. Over time, her biography would come to take on a dramatic pathos that rose to the literary, with a Victorian novel's deep, textured sorrows and magical realism's spurts of intoxicating enchantment. Gina herself would come to resemble a heroine from literature, too, one whose formidable intelligence and resolve would be pitted against the implacable, age-old force of unforgiving circumstance.

When the twins were around five years old, the family moved from a single-wide metal trailer in the rural town of Walterboro to a modest brick ranch home in the Charleston suburb of Summerville. A thick, towering oak tree stood sentinel in front of the house, its sprawling crown arching across the entire width of the yard. The twins' father, Steve, used a second oak, in the back, to build the girls a tree house. Though the white family of four had moved into a more middle-class milieu, they still depended on Steve's paychecks as a UPS delivery driver as their sole source of income. Money was rarely spent frivolously, and things were often tight.

After Gina and Andrea started kindergarten, they both noticed something wasn't right: They couldn't see the words on the chalkboard, and couldn't read the alphabet pasted on the classroom wall. Concerned, their parents took them to an eye clinic in Charleston, followed by trips to several ophthalmologists in the Northeast. A Harvard retinologist eventually diagnosed both girls with enhanced S-cone syndrome, a rare genetic disorder that causes retinal cells to gradually deteriorate. While the disease's progression sometimes took decades, the condition worsened vision over time and led, invariably, to blindness. The Harvard doctor advised the family to have the girls pass as sighted for as long as they could. As demonstrably false as it was, what he said next would be impossible to unhear. "Once people realize you're blind," he told them, his tone coolly paternalistic, "your life will be over."

Steve tried to take the news in stride, maintaining a level of emotional equanimity that lent ballast to an otherwise tumultuous situation. But their mother, Natalie, was less composed. Devastated by her daughters' diagnosis, she sobbed hysterically and wandered through the house, shell-shocked, for several days afterward.

When the twins completed second grade, in 1992, Natalie pulled them out of the local public school system. She felt she could do a better job than Summerville's teachers, and also, according to Gina, thought the measure would help her maintain more control over what was being put into her daughters' heads. Beginning when they were seven, Gina and Andrea were homeschooled in a cramped

room off the attic that doubled as a storage space. Red shag carpet-
ing covered the floor, which was littered with frayed cardboard
boxes and antique bric-a-brac. The twins sat at tiny desks on opposite walls—Andrea next to a bookcase cobbled from cinder blocks
and wooden planks, Gina adjacent to a clunky old desktop
computer—working in quiet diligence as an old window-mounted
AC unit clattered out cold air from a small window near the peak of
the roof.

From a very young age, Gina and Andrea were precocious, verging on prodigious. As eight-year-olds, they tested at an eighth grad-
er's academic level, and they eventually skipped all of the sixth
grade. Their mother, a psychologically troubled woman who was
also a member of Mensa, pushed her daughters to excel but could be
cold and disapproving if their aptitude threatened her brilliance.
"My mom considered herself a genius, and tested as a genius," Andrea said. "We were always sort of both a challenge and a disap-
pointment to that." Largely sequestered from other children their
age, the twins read voraciously and could often be seen lying on
their stomachs in the tree house or on their backs on the hood of the
family's old Jeep, poring over Nancy Drew and the Hardy Boys, the
Knights of the Round Table, and the myths of ancient Greece.

Even in childhood, the twins' vision proved an unceasing obstacle. Wherever Gina went, she sought sources of light to help her
read. In the family's front and back yards, she searched for the perfect angles to capture the sun. When she was indoors and the pages
of her books weren't naturally lit, she straddled the arm of an old
living room sofa so she could position the pages directly beneath the
end table's lamplight. Gina was always chasing the light—
incandescent, fluorescent, solar, bright, dim, dappled, dying—
twisting her body like rubber to take in whatever luminescence she
could. Even then, darkness brought blindness, and she scoured her
surroundings to forestall it.

Throughout their childhood in the 1990s, Natalie shuttled her
daughters to an array of specialists in the hope of stumbling on one
who deemed their condition treatable. During appointments, they

took turns in the ophthalmologist's office, where each was put through a battery of tests involving black boxes with electrodes, flashing strobe lights, and contact lenses attached to electrical wires. Though S-cone syndrome is always degenerative, the speed of the condition's progression varies dramatically from one person to the next. By the time they were eight, Gina recognized that her retinal loss was advancing faster than her sister's. When they took eye exams at doctors' offices, she made Andrea go first so she could memorize the sequence of letters her sister shouted out in slow, halting bursts.

At the age of twelve, Gina was declared legally blind, a designation applied to anyone whose vision falls to 20/200 or less. It was around that time when she started feeling more frustrated about her condition and the limitations it imposed on her young life. "I did have a lot of grief and anger," Gina said. "At the time I thought, 'Well, I'll never be able to just pick up a newspaper and read it, or walk into a restaurant and read what's on the menu.' I knew I was never going to be able to do these little things."

None of the ophthalmologists or other specialists the family visited could tell Natalie with any certainty when the girls would lose their functional sight completely. It could happen in their twenties, thirties, or even later. Their vision was a source of instability they were forced to accept, an impermanence that kept their futures forbiddingly opaque. Gina and Andrea resolved to focus on the present, adapting to their existing circumstances as best they could. They wore large glasses with thick frames, took class notes in big, bold-tipped Sharpies. Natalie took a different tack: Rarely acknowledging her daughters' visual impairment, she appeared to completely suppress the reality of their condition. "Our mother was in total denial about it," Gina said. Save for prescription glasses, few accommodations were made for the girls in the Applebee household. "There wasn't any discussion about it, practically or emotionally," she said. "I didn't have anybody to talk to about it, so I just kind of sucked it up."

By early adolescence, the twins realized they would not be the recipients of much sympathy or support at home in relation to their vision loss. They also grew to understand that they would need to be completely reliant on themselves in adulthoods that would be inevitably colored by their disability. The family barely scraped by on Steve's salary, and their parents simply didn't have the resources to help Gina and Andrea after they graduated from high school. When that time came, they would have no choice but to survive in whatever way they knew how. After being homeschooled for seven years, in 2000 both girls won scholarships to Pinewood Prep, a prestigious private school in Summerville. They attended Pinewood from tenth through twelfth grades, earning their diplomas in 2002. Following graduation, they both set off for college at sixteen years old, an age when many teenagers are still working their way through their sophomore years of high school.

Gina enrolled at the College of Charleston, where she majored in geology, while Andrea received a full scholarship to Davidson College, in North Carolina. The hard sciences held a particularly strong appeal for Gina. Her mother had left most of those fields out of her homeschooling curriculum, preferring to espouse fundamentalist Christian views based in creationism. For Natalie, much of scientific inquiry contradicted the Bible, and was therefore heresy. But Gina's readings had left her captivated by the concrete beauty and irreducible truths of the natural world.

During Gina's time at the College of Charleston, her vision continued to decline. Though she'd become legally blind years earlier, she identified herself as severely visually impaired. (Language matters, and Gina did not yet think of herself as blind.) She struggled to decipher the words written in her textbooks and the equations scrawled over her classroom's whiteboards. Peering into the lens of a microscope—a staple for many of her science courses—was like trying to see through clouds of muddy water. Her sight was also plagued by a distracting shimmering effect that made everything tremble and shake as if a sharp wind had just rolled by. Navigating the urban campus at night was an ongoing challenge, too, and Gina used the street lamps "like sailors use constellations."

In the summer before her junior year, Gina received training to adopt a guide dog, and the following fall she returned to the lush, Spanish moss–festooned campus with an oversize yellow Lab named Mitchell by her side. Mitchell would prove himself an invaluable companion, his twitching tail and lolling tongue breaking the ice with Gina's peers and gently communicating her condition with effortlessness and even joy. By then, she'd reached a degree of inner peace regarding her visual impairment, recognizing it as an inextricable feature of her incipient identity. "By the time I had Mitchell in college, I had accepted that this is my path and this is who I was," she said.

Gina's college years were financially precarious. She'd received a need-based scholarship that paid part of her tuition, but it fell on her slight shoulders to procure the rest and cover her living expenses. She worked part-time jobs when opportunities arose, but those funds went toward the remainder of her tuition and her portion of the rent on a three-bedroom apartment on Charleston's Ashley Avenue. Most weeks, there was little left for her to feed herself. "I stole and scavenged all my food while I was in college," Gina said. "I had no money." She waited outside the city's restaurants around closing time—usually midnight or later—and cooks sometimes gave her pickup orders that were never claimed or leftovers they'd be throwing out anyway. That wasn't always enough, though, and Gina was often forced to walk into gas stations and convenience stores and slip sandwich crackers, candy bars, and other snacks up her sleeves or under her sweatshirt. With her wispy frame and bob of black hair tumbling over her face in stringy locks, she looked the part of a guileless waif barely north of adolescence. That callow appearance—scrappy but also radiating decency and innocence—likely worked to her advantage. She hardly raised alarms.

One day before class, a geology professor watched as Gina slyly pulled a sandwich out from under her sleeve. After that, the woman started keeping a stash of trail mix in her office for her. When Gina's dad came to stay with her for a few days, she decided that she wanted her refrigerator to look like it was stocked with everything "normal people had in their kitchen." She shoplifted enough to fill her fridge with foods she'd never had but thought everyone else kept in their homes, including frozen shrimp and cocktail sauce. "It was the only time I almost got caught," she said.

Gina spent her undergraduate years leading two very different lives. On one hand, there was the college student striking the proverbial balance between classwork and socializing; on the other, a girl scrabbling to feed herself and beat back the inexorable specter of hunger. It was a jarring dichotomy she rarely exposed, preferring to conceal her daily struggles behind an easygoing, even bubbly demeanor—she remembers being "very extroverted" within friend groups that included both geologists and stoners—and rely on her gritty independence to claw through. Over her four years in the college's geology department, she gained the respect and even admiration of her professors, who saw her as a fearless, enterprising student who succeeded through a combination of formidable intellect and adamantine tenacity. "Amazing is the word that comes to everybody's mind when they know her," one teacher remarked. She was "always proving she could do more than what anyone ever expected her to be able to do." On a muggy day in May 2006, Gina walked across the school's graduation stage with Mitchell trotting by her side, collecting her tightly rolled parchment diploma before a genteel throng of billowy white dresses and Southern fascinator hats.

The summer after graduation, Gina accepted a geology fellowship at the Woods Hole Oceanographic Institution on Cape Cod, Massachusetts. WHOI—affectionately pronounced *who*-eeh—is one of the foremost marine research centers in the country, and Gina hoped the fellowship would be an exhilarating foray into academia that would strengthen her candidacy for PhD programs and set her up for a long scientific career. Her eight weeks at WHOI would, in fact, have a lasting impact on her life, but it would not come in anything close to the form she anticipated.

In early June, Gina rode an old Peter Pan bus from Boston to the small seaside community on the southwestern tip of Cape Cod. She gazed out the thick glass windows as the clamor of the city relaxed into the soothing rhythms of coastal New England life. "It was just a gorgeous summertime scientific village paradise," she recalled. Long weathered piers knifed out into the careening surf; summer foliage ringed picturesque harbors peppered with cedar-shingled houseboats; and sailing skiffs with towering masts and brightly painted trims tugged at their buoys under the gentle ocean breeze. When the lapping waves that surrounded the peninsular town were pulled back out to the Atlantic, the sound of millions of tiny pebbles tumbling out to sea filled the air like ancient music. "It's deceptively beautiful, and it feels very safe," she remembered thinking.

Gina was completing her fellowship on the Sumatran mega-quakes that had recently erupted in the Indian Ocean, studying whether they were affecting deeper layers of the earth's crust and potentially even transferring stress to nearby magma chambers. Within her first few weeks of arriving at Woods Hole, she drew the eye of a white male student a number of years older than she was. When he saw her between classes and in the dormitory-style rooms where they lived, he made brusque, tasteless advances, often explicitly commenting on her body and his sexual attraction to her. Peeved but not alarmed, she quietly rebuffed him. He didn't get the message, or else he did and disregarded it. Her brush-offs only seemed to harden—and darken—his resolve.

On the night of July 20, the man slipped into Gina's apartment, a floor beneath his own in a student housing building everyone called the Barn, choked her unconscious, and raped her. When she came to, he was still on top of her, and she managed to get off a single swift punch that sent him scrambling out of the room. In a state of numbed shock, she immediately called the police, who arrived a few minutes later with an ambulance in tow. Officers interviewed her as soon as they arrived, and the ambulance then transported her to the hospital, where she underwent a complete forensic examination (also known as a rape kit). "I don't think I was even remotely aware of the level of how injured I was," Gina said. Her entire perception of her body, her identity, and the world around her had changed in a single night, the emotional valences dramatically altered without the faintest of warnings. "I was just raw, and I was just answering the questions." Never again would she be able to access that twenty-year-old girl leaning against the window in the Peter Pan bus, contemplating her future with a sense of untroubled romance and possibility.

While most of us tend to think of catastrophic life events as uncontrollable accidents or mishaps (crashes, overdoses, psychiatric breakdowns, cancerous cells), victims of sexual violence must reconcile themselves to the irreconcilable: that their bodies were violated and their lives radically altered, maliciously, by another human being. It is out of this anguishing conundrum that trauma is born, and victims of rape suffer from higher rates of it than perhaps any other group: Close to 95 percent of rape victims experience symptoms of post-traumatic stress disorder in the weeks following the assault, and for nearly a third the symptoms will persist for longer than nine months. The atrocity of such a violation is not rare, either, with as many as one in four American women enduring the trauma of rape by middle age. Judith Herman, writing in *Trauma and Recovery*, went so far as to deem the experience one of the "social rites of initiation into the coercive violence at the foundation of adult society."

Gina's assaulter was arrested the night of the attack. After he made bail, authorities moved him out of the Barn, to an apartment a mile or so away. He was charged with rape, assault and battery, and several other crimes that together carried a maximum punishment of over twenty years in prison. The police department based in Falmouth, the town that encompasses Woods Hole, opened an investigation into the incident that would last several weeks.

Prior to the assault, Gina had made arrangements to spend nine days at sea on the *Knorr*, a large research vessel owned by the Oceanographic Institution. Though she remained in a state of shock only just beginning to thaw, she decided to go through with the expedition. It was going to be her inaugural trip in the open ocean, and she didn't want the perpetrator and the atrocity he committed to spoil her first voyage out to sea.

For Gina, the ocean sojourn was a source of awe and catharsis. "I poured so much pain into the North Atlantic," she recalled. She took the graveyard shift running a research instrument that measured underwater data, including salinity, temperature, and depth, and also helped manage the ship's winch. In between tasks, she'd smoke cigarettes and gaze up at the dense clusters of pearly stars embroidering the night sky. Though she could still see in a broad sense of the term, her vision was blurry and impressionistic: Splashes of color and shimmering fragments gave her visual field the imprecise, undifferentiated quality of abstract art. But she saw the bright "shining points" coruscating across the sweeping blackness, and the spectacle of primordial light remained impossibly beautiful. Gina did her best to take in the quiet immensity that surrounded her, the stirring convergence of sea and sky inside an unbroken panorama of soothing, serene darkness. "It was just very humbling, one of those very simple but profound experiences in life that teaches you how little you are," she said.

While conducting the criminal investigation, Falmouth police interviewed other students and community members to get a sense of the defendant's background and character. Officers carried out many of these interviews while Gina was at sea, and she remembered several students speaking up on the perpetrator's behalf. "When I got back, it was like there was this collective decision that I had just made it up, or was trying to get attention, or had exaggerated what had happened," Gina said. One of the male students went so far as to walk down to her dormitory room and question her about the incident directly. "I was just horrified," she recalled. "Not only have I been through this horrible thing, but nobody believes me."

During the first week of August, Gina attended a preliminary hearing for her assailant's case in a packed courtroom that reminded her of traffic court. She had composed a written statement several days earlier and did not utter a word during the hearing. Sitting on a bench near the back right corner of the courtroom, she spent much of the proceeding with her hands clenching the edge of her wooden seat, as if she were trying to keep herself from blowing away. When she heard the perpetrator's voice, she turned her face in to her shoulder and broke into muffled sobs.

No verdict was reached that day. Instead, Gina received a letter in the mail some time later by a victim witness advocate. It stated that the defendant had agreed to plead guilty to assault and battery, one of the lesser charges on his original indictment. The rape charges were dropped in exchange for his plea. More shockingly, the perpetrator—a white man who came from considerable means— would serve no jail time. His punishment was one year of probation.

"It was a hard blow to feel that there was no justice in the legal system," Gina recalled. She was desolated by the outcome, unable to fathom how the man who violently raped her went from facing decades in prison to not serving so much as a single night behind bars. As the summer wore on, Gina fell into a bleak, rageful depression. Though still weeks shy of her twenty-first birthday, she drank heavily, and on one particular night downed an entire fifth of bourbon and needed to be hospitalized. She was put on a saline drip and stayed overnight under inpatient observation.

Toward the end of August, Gina left Cape Cod to return to South Carolina. She remained in emotional shambles. On the day of her flight, she missed her bus to Boston's Logan International Airport and had to take a two-hundred-dollar cab ride to the terminal, overdrawing on her checking account and barely reaching her departure gate. The anguish, the ostracism, the vibrations of terror inside her that signaled incipient trauma—she was lost in it all, thrashing in the dark and dumbfounded by a criminal justice system that had let her rapist go free. "It was like the ground vanished from beneath me and I fell into an abyss," she said.

THE ODDS WERE stacked against Gina long before her experience in the court system even began: Less than 3 percent of perpetrators who commit sexual assault ever serve time in prison for their actions. There are plenty of individuals in America, however, who are incarcerated for lesser crimes. Over 2 million Americans are currently locked up—including around 750,000 for victimless crimes—and our country incarcerates more people per capita than any other nation on earth. And even after years of national dialogue on addressing the systemic racism at the root of our criminal justice system and carrying out reforms, Black men remain almost six times as likely to be incarcerated in state or federal prisons compared with their white counterparts. For them, incarceration might reasonably be added to Judith Herman's "social rites of initiation" into our society's "coercive violence."

The ongoing "war on drugs" is a major driver of this prison industrial complex, as our nation remains in the virulent throes of a two-decade struggle with opioids. It seems morbid to trot out the figures that have cast a pall over us for most of this century, but it bears repeating that we continue to suffer more overdose-related deaths every year than the total number of Americans lost during the Vietnam War. The misuse of heroin, fentanyl, and the prescription painkillers that started this modern pestilence create a noxious ripple effect: The obliterating force of addiction leads not only to fatal overdoses but also injury, suicide, disability, and traumatic bereavement.

Over one-fifth of all incarcerated individuals, or close to five hundred thousand people, are in prisons or jails for drug offenses, a figure that does not include all the other crimes that were connected to or driven by substance misuse and addiction. But whatever dire straits or hijacked brain chemistry compel individuals to commit the crimes that land them in prison, those circumstances rarely match the mixture of helplessness, estrangement, and despair many experience once they find themselves marooned on a concrete island of metal fences, concertina wire, and steel doors. This loss of freedom—an abrupt confiscation of everything that once constituted their identities—is a grievous diminishment, reducing people with full, three-dimensional lives to little more than vulnerable bodies and minds.

JASON DIXON GREW up on the east coast of Central Florida, in a small town called Cocoa that his ancestors helped pioneer at the turn of the nineteenth century. They cut some of Cocoa's first roads and laid the foundations for some of its first houses, and to this day the town's central thoroughfare bears the name Dixon Boulevard. Jason, who is white, lived with his father and stepmother on the town's west side, miles from the touristy beaches and turquoise lagoon that ran along the so-called treasure coast. The Cocoa of his childhood, in the 1980s and '90s, was full of horse farms and Waffle Houses, fried alligator and NASCAR racing, flat-bottomed airboats and lifted pickups flying Confederate battle flags.

Jason's dad inherited an electrical contracting business from his father, and over the years he'd built it to a place of prominence, lighting the Daytona Speedway and several of the state's professional baseball fields. Though well-off, the Dixons lived in relative modesty among the warehouses, repair shops, and trucking outfits that filled out the working-class environs west of U.S. 1, in a two-story house with vinyl siding on a rambling property that also held their business's main offices and the stables and pastures for the barrel racing horses the family boarded.

After receiving his high school diploma in 1997, Jason joined the Marine Corps. But when a stress fracture in his leg caused an infection during training, he was discharged. Afterward, he started working at the family business for $140 a week, digging trenches and laying wiring in triple-digit temperatures and Gulf-fueled humidity. Beyond the punishing work his demanding father paid him for, Jason had no semblance of structure or direction. By his early twenties, he was committing most of his off-hours to drinking and partying, taking advantage of Cocoa's reputation as a second-tier spring break destination. It was a lifestyle that shunned the ambiguity of the future for the kinetic gratifications of the present. "I had no ambitions, wasn't going to college because I was always told college wasn't for me, and I didn't really have any skill sets other than working at my dad's company," Jason remembered.

In the late summer of 2001, when he was twenty-two years old, Jason met a young woman from Pittsburgh who'd flown down to Cocoa Beach on vacation. When she left, she invited him and his friend to come up north to visit her in Pennsylvania; within a week, the guys were driving up the coast. During the trip, Jason developed a fondness for the Keystone State: the rugged hills and mountains of the Alleghenies and the Laurel Highlands; the mixture of rural, heartland living, which he'd grown up around; and Pittsburgh's more progressive atmosphere and abundance of opportunity. Seeking out a new tack for his rudderless life, as soon as he got home Jason started planning to leave Florida. It was the end of September 2001, just weeks after the 9/11 attacks, and he prepared for the move amid a county vibrating with the steady hum of imminent war (a war he might have been readying himself for had things gone differently with the Marines). Within two weeks, he'd rented a U-Haul, scraped up his possessions, and pulled onto I-95 to make the fifteen-hour drive to Pittsburgh for good.

Days before leaving, Jason made a coldhearted decision that would reverberate across the rest of his life. An elderly relative had just moved into a nursing home, and she'd left her house filled with bottles of OxyContin and unfilled prescriptions. Knowing the drug's considerable street value, Jason pocketed the bottles and filled the prescriptions at a local pharmacy. "They'll make for good currency up there," he recalled thinking at the time. "This will be advantageous."

After arriving in Pittsburgh, Jason began dating the woman he'd met in Florida and soon moved in with her. A smooth talker with lively brown eyes and a thin strap of stubble, he quickly found a job at a mortgage refinancing company. But during his first six months in Pennsylvania, instead of selling the pain pills as he'd planned, he started using them as a hangover cure. "I was taking them to more or less recover from how much I was drinking," he said. "Then I started . . . abusing them." By the late fall, he was popping at least one nearly every day—to mollify hangovers, to bring to parties, and eventually just to attain the high. At first, he wasn't concerned. In his mind, he was taking the pills with indifference, even nonchalance, nothing like the frenzied desperation he thought characterized a stereotypical junkie. When the bulky red prescription bottles were all finally empty, though, he collapsed into agonizing sickness. Within a year of the move, and without even realizing it, Jason had become addicted to opioids. That summer, as he adjusted to a life increasingly constructed around the funding and maintenance of his addiction, he learned that his girlfriend was pregnant.

On February 18, 2003, Jason's girlfriend gave birth to a daughter named Annabella. But Jason's attention was hopelessly fractured. Lacking the income to support what he quickly discovered was a prohibitively expensive habit—a single day's high could cost him two hundred dollars if he paid OxyContin's street value—he reluctantly tried snorting heroin. Before long, he moved to injecting. "It was like a religious conversion, and that set off a very bad chain of events," he said.

One afternoon the following winter, his girlfriend walked into their living room to find him nodding off on the couch. Increasingly suspicious of his erratic behavior, she pulled up one of his sleeves. His forearm was riddled with little red puncture marks. She shook him awake. "You're fucking shooting heroin," she screamed. Jason denied it, but his lies went nowhere. That same day she moved out, taking their infant daughter with her.

With his girlfriend and daughter out of the apartment and no one to hold him accountable, Jason's spiraling gathered downhill speed. Nothing interested him except getting high. He'd nod off at home, at the office, even behind the wheel of his black SUV. Heroin ripped through his life like shrapnel sawing through flesh, and in quick succession he lost his job at the mortgage refinancing company and most of his possessions to dealers and pawnshops. "I had this really, really bad habit, and I couldn't see past the next day," he said. "I was constantly sick, constantly day-to-day hustling to figure out how to manage this drug addiction."

The year 2004 would be one of escalating recklessness and disorder for Jason. By early spring, as temperatures slowly ticked up in Pittsburgh, his life took on a helter-skelter quality, his actions acquiring an element of dangerous lunacy. With no money coming in to support his habit, he started robbing corner boys at gunpoint. After buying drugs in the area for so long, he knew all the different pickup spots in and around the city. Most of the street dealers recognized him as a regular—a clean-cut, affable guy who always paid and never hassled them to cut him a deal or front supply. When he pulled up to buy a sleeve of wax paper filled with heroin, typically bundled together with a rubber band, they ducked into his SUV without thinking twice. Moments later, Jason thrust his hand into the center console and pulled out a black stainless steel pistol. "I don't know what triggered it, other than just desperation," Jason said.

The madcap scheme didn't last long. Whenever Jason robbed a dealer in one area, he'd have to steer clear of it for some time to avoid heading into a bullet-strewn reprisal. On the one occasion when he made the mistake of returning to a neighborhood where he'd recently robbed someone, several young men pulled out handguns and started unloading their clips at his SUV. In little more than a month, he robbed around a dozen low-level pushers—luring them into his car, demanding their stash at gunpoint—and he'd exhausted every place he knew to score heroin. His addiction had devoured what appeared to be the very last, craziest means of its sustenance.

That summer, after Jason got a call about an opportunity to get back into the mortgage refinancing business, he decided to stop by a local Office Depot to pick up ink and printer paper. Dead broke and drained of his supply, he was rapidly approaching withdrawal, that vicious reckoning that now lurked like an evil eye over each day of his life. While he was standing in the checkout aisle to pay for his supplies, the clerk popped open the cash register. Struck by how full

it was, Jason's eyes lingered over the stacks of bills; there was perhaps two thousand dollars in there. By the time he'd checked out
and stepped back into his car, the murky outline of what he felt he
needed to do next started materializing in his mind. The thoughts—
sordid, violent, and bubbling up seemingly of their own malign
volition—repulsed him. Slumped down in his SUV's driver's seat in
the Office Depot parking lot, Jason allowed himself to momentarily
reflect on how awful things had gotten. "I was so tired of being sick
all the time, and having to do all this extreme shit to have drugs," he
said.

Gazing out the windshield, Jason felt an intense sense of self-
loathing, hating what he'd allowed his life to become. Five feet eight
inches tall, he was down to a gaunt, scarecrow-like 118 pounds. His
face was a sallow mask of creases and hollows, and track marks
bloomed over his arms like bruises on overripe fruit. But it would
take only a few minutes for all that remorse and repulsion to be su-
perseded by something more urgent and forceful: his unconquerable fealty to his addiction. He knew where things were headed. In
recent months, he found himself bearing witness to a phantasmagoric pattern: As he neared withdrawal, he started picturing violent
robberies, sequences that looked like scenes from some gritty crime
film. Only the scenes weren't from the movies—they were premoni-
tions of actions he would eventually take in his own life. Like Cas-
sandra standing in horror before Agamemnon's palace, he'd started
prophesying his own grisly demise.

That afternoon, with another deranged scene crystallizing before him, Jason got high in his car, strode back into the Office Depot,
and robbed the same cashier he'd just bought office supplies from.
"I just put the gun on the counter," he remembered. "I had zero intentions of hurting this girl." In the weeks that followed, he robbed
four more stores in the same area, a small town just outside Pittsburgh. "Something kind of snapped," he remembered. Jason became
a headline story on local television stations: News segments fea-
tured the brazen criminal in a baseball cap, robbing retail stores all
over town at gunpoint.

Despite the frequency of his robberies and their breathless audacity, Jason wasn't caught right away. It wasn't until several months later—after his mom convinced him to enter a rehab facility in Newport Beach, California—that a local detective put everything together. That November, he traveled back to Pennsylvania to turn himself in. When he walked into the small-town police department, officers drew their weapons, slammed him against the wall and snapped handcuffs on him, and drove him down to the county jail. He spent a week being rotated between the facility's various overcrowded holding cells, unkempt rooms with cinder block walls where men were often detoxing from heavy drug use and the only place to sleep was on the poured concrete floor. When nobody posted his bail, he was led upstairs to one of the jail's large, square-shaped blocks. He would await his trial in a narrow white-brick cell with two beds, a sink, and a toilet.

Jason still remembers the moment, a few hours later, that clearly demarcated the first twenty-six years of his life from everything that would come to pass after. When it was time for correctional officers to let the men out of their cells and into the dayroom, the automatic locks on the steel doors were released in a sequence that advanced, cell by cell, around the square block. Jason listened as the eerie *clack-clack-clack* cascaded across all 120 cell doors. "There was something about everybody coming out all at once," he recalled. The clacking noise that fanned out across the cellblock was laced with an ineffable dread, a ghastly sensation he couldn't place right away. After a few moments, a shiver of recognition ran through him: This was the reality of institutionalized life, the clockwork mechanics of living in habitual, subservient harmony to the state.

It wasn't just the palpable gloom of institutionalization that glided down his spine when the steel doors rattled open. It was also the spectacle of a brash, brutal brand of masculinity and the undercurrent of violence he sensed coursing beneath it. It could be seen, felt, and heard in the way all 240 men trampled out of their cells— shouting and slamming into one another with a physical language that was raw, swift, and coarsened. The men crashed through the prison tiers like a tornado of testosterone that would flatten anything in its path. "It was insanity, all at once," Jason said. "I had this very stark realization that I wasn't built, I wasn't ready for this." For most of his life, Jason had been confident in his ability to hold his own in threatening situations. But this was different. The speed and intensity around him, the men's loose, unbridled physicality and the visceral malice it telegraphed—it was something he'd never encountered before. "I just remember backing up and standing in the doorway of the cell, and just staring at it all. I took a step back. I needed to figure out what was happening. That person could never have survived. That person that tried to walk out on that block that day, he couldn't have made it—and he didn't."

Jason was eventually offered a plea deal by the local district attorney: seven and a half to fifteen years. Knowing that if he took his case to trial the judge could stack the charges and give him a sentence of thirty-five years or longer, he reluctantly accepted. "That was a hard, hard night," he recalled of the evening he had to make the decision. "That fucking night, man, when I saw what the future of my life looked like, was the beginning of these changes, of these big, big pieces of me being stripped away."

MOST AMERICANS DON'T perceive incarceration in the same way that they think about catastrophes like car accidents, chronic illnesses, or violent assaults. In fact, many people don't see it as a catastrophe at all. Unlike traumatic experiences that are random and undiscriminating, prison sentences imply justness. They carry the assumption that they've been triggered by the corresponding actions of a criminal offender. Those sentenced to serve time in prison are not victims, this thinking goes, but rather people who've broken the law, often by jeopardizing another person's safety or violating their rights for personal gain. The state manages these transgressions by administering retributive justice, reciprocating crime with punishment and holding individuals accountable for their criminal acts.

But this line of thinking is flawed. For one, it presumes that America's criminal justice system has the powers of discernment, impartiality, and moral clarity necessary to apply the law to every individual with unerring consistency. It takes for granted, in other words, that Lady Justice's scales are in perfect balance at all times. But an institution bound up with decades of racism and economic inequality—and propelled by a system in which powerful prosecutors are incentivized to seek maximum sentences for vulnerable populations that cannot mount a viable defense for themselves—is constitutionally at odds with such a lofty goal.

The second flaw is more abstract. When a society thinks of incarcerated people as convicts, criminals, or depraved evildoers who've transgressed some symbolic threshold and no longer deserve the same decency and humane treatment as the rest of us, we're subscribing to a dangerous brand of dehumanization. This type of dehumanization is generally a passive act: Writing off incarcerated individuals as irredeemable felons is not a direct attack or an explicit vilification. In the long run, though, it may be even worse, because that categorization permits a casual disregard for their lives that makes all the cruelty, neglect, and institutional violence that flourish behind prison walls possible. The commonplace use of solitary confinement in this country up until just a few years ago— cruel and unusual punishment by almost anyone's standards—is a testament to how thoroughly Americans had long dismissed the lived experience of incarcerated people. Widespread dehumanization of a particular group—even when that dehumanization is happening only in the collective imagination—is almost always a prerequisite for atrocities against them.

As our criminal justice system has come under increasing scrutiny, though, Americans have gradually pulled back the veil that's been thrown over prisons like a blanket over a cage. Studies and accounts from incarcerated citizens themselves attest to the soul-sapping effects of living inside these facilities. According to the Bureau of Justice Statistics, a federal agency that publishes criminal justice data, 24 percent of people in U.S. prisons and 31 percent of those in jails have some kind of major depressive disorder, compared with just 7 percent in the general population. The number of people in prisons with severe mental illnesses like schizophrenia, bipolar disorder, and substance-induced psychosis, meanwhile, is even more startling: While prevalence on the outside for these conditions hovers between 1 and 3 percent, studies have found the figure to be at least ten times higher for those incarcerated in state prisons.

Skeptics of these striking mental health disparities might reasonably claim that such figures don't distinguish between causation and correlation. Many of these men and women might have entered the criminal justice system with serious preexisting psychiatric issues. It's hard to argue, though, that the state of incarceration itself is not responsible for its own savage psychological toll. Some research indicates that nearly half of those incarcerated suffer from post-traumatic stress disorder, a devastating proportion that more than quintuples the prevalence among the U.S. general population. Life behind bars imposes a searing gauntlet of experiences that bear the capacity to inflict lasting trauma, including exposure to gruesome violence, prolonged social isolation, and the taxing hypervigilance required to survive in a perpetually hostile environment.

PTSD has emerged with such persistence among prison populations that the formerly incarcerated have coined the term "post-incarceration syndrome" to identify the unique constellation of traumatic symptoms they face. In an article published on *The Fix,* one man with the condition wrote, "Divided racial lines and the total disregard for human life were the first things that greeted me behind the grimy walls down in the swamps of Louisiana, USP Pollock. The 'slaughterhouse of the south' averaged 40 stabbings a month, while incurring 16 murders in an 18-month span." USP Pollock was just the "first of four penitentiaries in which I was beaten, stabbed, isolated, and herded throughout half my life." One man I spoke to characterized the first several months of a two-year sentence in California's prison system like this: "Your life ends, and then you realize that your life is ending, and then you have to live through hell."

Because incarceration bears the stamp of the U.S. government and the moral valence of retributive justice, many Americans will continue to perceive it differently from other catastrophes. But there is little room for questioning its status as a road that requires travelers to "pass by the dragon." In its steady onslaught of violence and deprivation, and the lacerating sorrow they produce, it forces them directly into the beast's jaws.

SEAN TAYLOR'S LIFE trajectory was also bent by the criminal justice system. The traumatic experience that changed him forever, though, took place before he ever set foot inside a prison. Sean grew up in Aurora, Colorado, a few miles outside of Denver, in a two-bedroom apartment he shared with his mother and two siblings. His mom was raising three kids on her own, in the late 1980s, when the crack epidemic reached the Denver area. She got swept up in it, along with nearly every other adult in Sean's life: two aunts, a brother-in-law whom Sean regarded as a father figure, countless other parents in his neighborhood. "Most of the adults who mattered to me, in my life, became addicted to it," Sean said. Sean's biological father, meanwhile, was serving a long prison sentence over a thousand miles away in Michigan.

As Sean's mother's presence in his life waned, he became increasingly drawn to gang life. The Bloods were the top gang in his Aurora neighborhood, and sometime after his fifteenth birthday he started working for them. Crack hollowed out a lot of opportunities in what had otherwise been a decent, relatively safe working-class Denver suburb, but it did introduce one new one: When teenagers like Sean got into gang life, they also got into the business of selling drugs. Selling made gang membership powerful, lucrative, and—to adolescents beating back poverty and assuming the responsibilities of the parental figures fading from their lives—highly attractive. A tragic irony that emerged over time, but that often escaped the grasp of those clambering to survive, was that the teenage gang members were selling the drugs that kept the adults in their neighborhoods high and hooked. "We, the kids, were selling it to them," Sean said. Some afternoons, Sean's mom asked him to buy a bag for their neighbor across the street. It was a transparent attempt at subterfuge, and Sean saw straight through it. "I would know full well that the lady across the street was there earlier, she already had her supply," he said. "This is not for her, this is for you. Yet I would still put it in her hand."

For two years, Sean, who is Black, played the role of small-time dealer, selling drugs and defending his territory against the rival Crips. One afternoon, after an associate gave him a supply of powder cocaine to move, his mom walked into the kitchen as he was bungling an attempt to cook it into crack. "You're wasting good product," she said, and showed him how to make it. Though there was a matter-of-factness to the covert presence of drugs in the apartment, his homelife wasn't unstructured chaos, either, and didn't hew to crude Hollywood stereotypes. "This wasn't *New Jack City,* where ashy-lipped crack fiends are all over the place looking like zombies," Sean said. "It's your grandmother's house, it's your mom's house. It's just people who live within that house happened to be addicted to drugs."

Some nights, Sean struggled to fall asleep. A high-level Crip lived nearby, and he'd taunt Sean and his older brother, TL, by shooting through their apartment windows and then blazing off on his motorcycle. "That's the kind of environment we were living in," Sean said.

On Saturday, September 9, 1989, Sean went for a drive with three close friends who were also members of the gang. They hopped into his friend Ernest's battered brown Ford sedan and headed for Park Hill, the Denver neighborhood that served as the unofficial headquarters for the local Bloods. After spending several hours that afternoon with gang members visiting from Los Angeles, the boys drove farther into the city to drop some friends off. As they were heading west on Thirty-sixth Avenue, they spotted a teenager walking along the street in a ski hat, an NFL Starter jacket, jeans, and sneakers. His outfit was blue from head to toe, and the sight of him immediately changed the energy in the car: All four friends knew that was the Crips' chief identifying color. Concluding that he was affiliated with their rival gang, Dejuan—a Blood who, at twenty years old, was the second oldest in the car—started harassing him from his front passenger seat. Alarmed by the sudden altercation, the teenager on the street insisted he wasn't in the Crips or any other gang. When Dejuan leaped out of the car and threatened to fight him, the boy sprinted away.

Sean and his friends laughed off the encounter. Amused by their own mischievous antics and Dejuan's display of machismo, they circled the block and started heading east to return to Park Hill. But just before crossing Colorado Boulevard, the accepted border separating the Crips' territory from the Bloods', they spotted the boy running up to a duplex house. After he banged on the door, several young men slowly filed out. Sean and the other boys in the Ford recognized them immediately: They were all Crips. Ernest slowed the car to a stop. For several moments, no one knew how to proceed. Everyone was carefully eyeing each other, the opposing gang members acutely aware of just how quickly they'd stumbled to the edge of a violent confrontation.

Having turned seventeen just three days earlier, Sean was the youngest boy in the car (the other three, Dejuan, Ernest, and Daryl, were all between eighteen and twenty). Sitting in the back seat in his maroon sweatpants and hoodie, he hastily assessed the situation. Two weeks earlier, a destitute addict had given him an old handgun in exchange for drugs. Before leaving Aurora that morning, he'd wrapped it in a T-shirt and placed it on the car floor in front of him. Now, as they silently deliberated over how to proceed, its presence felt more substantial. As the youngest member of their crew, Sean wanted to impress the older boys, to do something that would demonstrate his manhood and gain their respect. This, he felt, might be an opportunity. "I wanted to have a reputation with these guys for being a gangster," he said.

Bolting up from his seat behind the front passenger, Sean volunteered to pull out the old .45-caliber handgun—which he'd never actually used—and shoot at their crosstown rivals' house. Before firing off any shots, though, he shouted his intentions to the boys huddled on the porch outside. "Now, if I was any type of coldhearted gangster, I would have just shot them," he said. "But I made an announcement because I wanted them to, you know, take cover." Sean watched everyone scramble toward the front door and rush back into the house. Ernest, who planned on slamming the gas as soon as Sean fired, turned the key in the ignition. The car let out a long, ragged screech before stalling out. He turned it again, and the engine rattled for a second or two before finally rumbling over.

Looking toward the house, Sean saw that the front door was still cracked open a few feet. He could make out a picture frame on the wall, a coffee table with a lamp on it, part of a couch. Nobody was in sight—that much he was sure of. Confident the scene was clear, he unwrapped the black .45. It felt heavy in his hand, like a dumbbell. Reaching his arm over Daryl, who was sitting next to him in the back seat, he pointed the muzzle toward the house. As the barrel hung just outside the car window, he thought, *It will go into the screen door, it'll hit a wall, it'll be fine.* Then he squeezed the trigger, firing off a single bullet. With the sharp crack of gunfire still ringing in the boys' ears, Ernest shifted the car into drive and jammed his foot against the gas pedal. As they pulled off, Sean fired a second shot into the brick wall on the side of the house. The car sped away and headed back to the boys' homes in Aurora.

That night, Sean was watching the local ten o'clock news at Dejuan's house. A story appeared about a shooting at an apartment duplex in Denver, and the program cut to footage of the house they'd been at earlier that day. "They're showing that same apartment, that same screen door," Sean recalled. Paramedics were carrying someone out of the house on a stretcher, a white sheet drawn over his face. At first, Sean was confused. *Does that mean someone died at that house?* he thought. A reporter said that authorities already had a suspect in custody, and cameras cut to Ernest's house and the brown Ford they were riding in only hours earlier. Finally, the news program displayed a photograph of the victim: He was the teenager they'd harassed in the street that afternoon, the one who'd pleaded that he wasn't in any gang. At that point it started to dawn on Sean: "Oh my God, I caused someone's death."

It was raining that night, and a friend drove Sean home. When he got to his family's apartment, his older brother, TL, a new father, was waiting for him outside. He was standing in the driveway in the pouring rain, his face stiff and motionless as a bust. When Sean walked up to him, he saw tears streaming down his brother's cheeks. TL had heard what happened, and he knew about Sean's involvement. Before long, everyone else did, too. By eleven P.M., around a dozen friends and fellow gang members had congregated at the family's apartment, offering Sean all manner of advice. He needed to wash his hands in Comet, scrub his body with gasoline. He should start prepping to go on the run by establishing a secret bank account. His future would be that of a wanted fugitive, slipping across one set of state lines after another while on the lam for murder. "They were trying to offer me all these gangster suggestions, and the only thing I could do was stare at my brother," Sean said. Sean was closer to TL than anyone else in the world, and in their crowded living room—amid the hushed cross talk, furrowed gazes, and pregnant silences—he kept his eyes locked on to his brother's. All he could do was silently telegraph his fear and helplessness, the sense of dread rising out of the pit of his stomach and overwhelming all other thoughts. "It's starting to set in on both of us that we got ourselves involved in something that we should have never gotten ourselves involved in," Sean said.

Sean and TL didn't decide on their next move right away. They were certain, however, that Denver police officers would be arriving at their apartment very soon, banging on the front door with their weapons drawn. They resolved to call a cab and head to a family friend's house; there, they could spend the night in relative peace and plan a course of action. As the taxi headed east through Aurora, it passed a fleet of speeding police cars, their blue-and-red lights flashing and their sirens blaring long, high-pitched loops. The brothers knew exactly where the cruisers were headed. "If we'd have stayed at the house five more minutes, the police would have been there," TL recalled.

Absconding from their apartment had bought Sean and TL a bit of extra time. But a decision would still have to be made soon, one whose consequences would ripple out through the rest of both brothers' young lives. Sitting on a sofa in their friend's living room, they broke down in tears. Scrabbling for a path forward amid the paralyzing gravity of the situation, TL ran through their options. If it meant keeping his little brother safe, he was prepared to decamp with Sean that night, leaving his girlfriend and baby daughter and disappearing into another life. "We can take a bus to Massachusetts tonight," he told Sean. He suggested traveling back to the town of Springfield, where they were born. Listening to his brother sketch out far-flung, likely dangerous scenarios, Sean was less certain. Since getting a ride home several hours earlier, he'd remained almost completely silent, his eyes low and heavy and his head angled downward to whatever floor sprawled out in front of him. "It's not just you and me anymore," Sean told TL. "You just had a baby." He told his brother that he would sleep on it. They'd make a decision, he said, the next morning.

Sometime after midnight, their mother called the house where they were staying. She was hysterical—keyed up and sobbing, her frantic words fractured by heaving breaths and long, quivering sighs. When the police they'd passed on the road got to their family's apartment, she told them, they kicked down the front door. Inside, they snapped pictures of every photo of Sean they could find. There was an all-points bulletin out on her son, they warned her, and it was declaring him armed and dangerous. If they encountered him on the street, officers told her, they would likely shoot him on sight.

Though he still couldn't grasp how a single bullet fired at random had killed somebody, Sean realized that the walls were rapidly closing in on him. By the next morning, he'd made his decision. When TL woke up and walked into the living room, Sean was already sitting on the couch, his soft adolescent features transfixed on some invisible point in front of him. "I'm going to turn myself in," he told TL. "You need to take care of your daughter."

Borrowing a neighbor's car, his mom picked him up and they drove to the police station. But the decision wasn't merely guided by self-preservation. Sean was already growing consumed by guilt for what he'd done. "I didn't care about my life," Sean said. "I was just overwhelmed with the burden of having taken someone else's life." That burden would come to define the next three decades of Sean's existence.

JR VIGIL GREW up ricocheting around the islands and coasts of the Pacific Rim, and during his childhood and teen years he built up the social dexterity and emotional resilience required of a kid moving schools every few years. His dad was an aircraft load planner in the air force, and from 1980, when JR was born, through his adolescence, the family lived in the Philippines, Guam, Washington State, and New Mexico. He attended college in San Diego before returning to Guam, where he completed his degree in business and Japanese in 2008. Shortly after graduating he spent close to a year in Japan, immersing himself in a culture he'd seen tantalizing glimpses of through the Japanese expatriates he met and observed on the Micronesian island.

Before his stint in Japan, JR—whose father is white and mother is Filipino—had spent part of his twenties managing a coffee shop on Guam. Over long morning and afternoon shifts serving a clientele of locals and regulars, including small business owners and attorneys working at the courthouse across the street, JR developed a sharp sense of the local coffee industry. He knew the other café owners and where they all got their beans, and had become familiar with the island's most popular roasts. Over time, he started to grasp the business's inefficiencies and stumbling blocks. For one thing, there was no coffee roaster on Guam—everything had to be flown in from the continental United States. JR recognized this as a critical flaw in the island's supply chain and made note of it. Though he eventually moved out of the coffee business to take a position coordinating the construction of a condominium complex, he kept a thumb on his experience at the café. Such industry expertise might, he felt, open doors to future opportunities.

When he turned thirty, in 2010, JR decided that he would try to apply that expertise to an entrepreneurial venture. The fact that there were no coffee roasters on Guam practically cried out for a new business to fill the void. JR wanted to be the person to launch that business, and he started mapping out what it would take to start his own coffee-roasting facility. In between his shifts as a project coordinator, he began crafting a detailed business plan—sourcing the beans his facility would use, identifying specialized equipment it would need to operate, calculating start-up costs. From his one-bedroom apartment in the village of Chalan Pago, JR was drawing on his years of experience and fledgling business instincts to conceive of a new, more grandiose chapter of his adult life. "I saw the need," JR said. "Me being a businessperson, business-minded, and being in coffee, it made sense."

When he wasn't working at the office or conducting research for his business plan, JR could be found outside in Guam's equatorial jungle climate, running. An intensely dedicated long-distance runner—at five foot seven and 120 pounds, JR had the slender, spry physique of an endurance athlete—he carried out strenuous, exacting routines almost every day. His workouts were sophisticated regimens that resembled professional training, including not only out-and-back jogs but also interval runs, tempo runs, and hill repeats. He approached workouts with the fastidiousness of a private ritual, thrilling to every last detail. He might spend one day running past the high-rise hotels and colorful seafood restaurants lining the island's tourist district, and the next racing over the parchment-colored sands of Tumon Beach, where lissome palm trees craned overhead. On weekends, he often joined other locals for hash runs in Guam's thick, verdant rainforests, sprinting through narrow, curving paths carved into the tunnel-like understory. "I'd go through the whole day thinking about where I was going to run, plan my route out, eat depending on what kind of run I was going to do," JR said. "Running was my life."

Though JR was settling into a comfortable, proportional adulthood, balancing his day job with loftier professional ambitions and a stimulating passion, his romantic life remained a source of ambivalence. After spending his twenties dating both men and women—as well as keeping to himself for long stretches—he didn't know whether he was gay, bisexual, or straight with an experimental streak (orientations like pansexual, omnisexual, and fluid weren't on his radar). Most of his friends on Guam assumed he was bisexual, and he made little effort to refute those characterizations. For all he knew, at the time, they might have been accurate.

JR's fraught relationship with his sexuality stemmed, in large part, from the religion he was brought up in. Both his mother and father were Southern Baptists. The Southern Baptist Convention, an umbrella organization that represents Southern Baptist churches across the United States, has consistently denounced same-sex relationships for decades. A 1996 resolution from the group argued that "even a desire to engage in a homosexual relationship is always sinful, impure, degrading, shameful, unnatural, indecent, and perverted." As recently as 2017, SBC leaders issued a statement asserting that the identities of LGBTQ people are "inconsistent with God's holy purposes in creation and redemption." (The SBC does not, obviously, represent the views of all fourteen million Southern Baptists.) And while JR's parents never explicitly discussed their beliefs on the matter with him, he sensed that they disapproved of same-sex relationships. As devout Southern Baptists—his father, Anthony, and mother, Amalia, attended church at least once a week, often two or three times—they did not question the church's views. "In my mind, growing up, I thought that was never an option for me," JR said.

As an adult, JR spent years trying to compartmentalize his actions and his religious faith. Nevertheless, his family's religion continued exerting a powerful influence over how he saw his own identity. Homophobic passages like the infamous "clobber verses" from the Bible that some Southern Baptists and other antigay Christians used to condemn LGBTQ individuals loomed large in his mind—he'd heard sermons invoking them at least once a year during his childhood—and he sometimes feared for his relationship with God. Though he permitted himself a certain level of sexual fluidity, he could simply not accept the idea that he was gay. At thirty-one, the narrative he continued subscribing to was that he was just exploring the full range of his romantic curiosities until he found the right woman to settle down with and marry.

All signs were pointing to the summer of 2011 as a groundbreaking, even life-altering one for JR. Following months of researching statistics from Guam's Visitors Bureau, incorporating those figures into his business plan, and putting together his own sales projections, in late June he submitted his application for a business loan to a local bank in Guam. On July 12, the bank offered him around fifty thousand dollars to get the island's very first coffee-roasting facility up and running. "I was just elated," JR said. "I felt like my life was finally coming together after wandering for years. I thought this was the beginning of something great."

Exactly a week after receiving the offer, JR was driving his gold Nissan coupe to an evening running session in Paseo de Susana, a park in Hagatna. The vehicle was a project car JR had bought three months earlier, and in the weeks prior to July 19 he and his younger brother, Michael, had been under the hood swapping out old parts, including from the car's brake system. Though they were planning on eventually replacing the brake lines, they hadn't gotten to it yet. That night, JR was maneuvering down a sloping curve that hugged the edge of the jungle and was slick with rain. Shortly before eight P.M., he lost control of the vehicle. The Nissan slammed into a concrete telephone pole, and the car was completely severed. The accident wiped his memory from not only that day but the entire previous week, and to this day he recalls little else leading up to the collision. Photos from the accident at first appear to show two separate vehicles—the back of one and the front of the other. But it was the same car, sawed in half by the collision's devastating force of impact. After first responders arrived at the scene, JR was immediately transported by ambulance to the U.S. Naval Hospital near the center of the island.

When JR's father, Anthony, arrived at the hospital, a beige-colored facility built along cliffs overlooking the Philippine Sea, the emergency room was soaked in blood. Doctors had shut down the entire ER to focus on JR, and they told Anthony that they weren't sure his son was going to live. "They called all hands on deck," Anthony recalled, "so it was wall-to-wall people in the emergency room when they were working on him." The crash had taken a tremendous toll on JR's body. He suffered extensive damage to his legs below the knees, and doctors believed he'd also experienced a traumatic brain injury. Several of his organs, including his lungs and kidneys, were barely functioning. On his way to the operating room, on the hospital's second floor, JR's heart stopped, and staff had to resuscitate him. It was one of three times he flatlined during his first night at the facility. He was teetering on the edge of life and death, his body so battered by physical trauma that its systems seemed to be blinking out all at once. Doctors put him on a breathing machine and kidney dialysis, hoping to buy time with life support. To reduce the swelling in his brain and, quite possibly, save his life, they also induced him into a coma.

Within JR's first twenty-four hours at the Naval Hospital, surgeons were forced to amputate his left leg—which was no longer receiving blood flow—below the knee. After the surgery, they discovered a flesh-eating bacterium in the same leg and had to perform several more amputations to eradicate it. By the time doctors finally brought the bacterium under control, his left leg had been amputated four inches above the knee. Had the infection spread above the thigh and into his organs, he almost certainly would have died.

Over the next ten days, JR's body began to stabilize. His right leg, however, would never be the same. The accident had shredded much of its muscle and bone, and there was a significant likelihood that JR would never be able to walk on it again. Surgeons approached his parents, Anthony and Amalia, with an excruciating ultimatum. They could try to save their son's right leg, which might require him to use a wheelchair and would likely cause him a great deal of lifelong pain, or they could amputate it. "That was a very difficult decision," Amalia remembered. "It was really devastating for us."

After taking a day to contemplate their son's future and the dismaying options presented to them, Anthony and Amalia directed the doctors to amputate JR's right leg. Naval hospital surgeons performed the separation over six hours, removing JR's leg at the kneecap, directly below the femur. Although JR would remain in a coma for some time to come, hospital staff were already preparing his parents for the challenges that would arise once he regained consciousness. "They kept telling us that this is not a sprint, this is a marathon," Anthony said. "The psychological portion of it . . . is going to take a long time."

The Amputee Coalition estimates that there are around two million people with an amputation living in this country, or slightly more than one in two hundred Americans. The two major causes of amputation are vascular diseases, like diabetes, and major trauma, including car crashes, workplace accidents, and gun-related injuries. Limb amputation may be the single most concrete form of loss a person can experience. Part of you has been erased, and it isn't your computer hard drive or social media feed. It's a piece of the one and only corporeal body you inhabit, a body whose importance far surpasses the physical possessions and digital avatars many of us spend more time focused on. The grief that flows out of limb loss is intense and intimate, revealing dimensions of our relationship with our own flesh that we rarely contemplate unless forced to peer at them through the prism of loss. We regularly regard our bodies with some level of ambivalence or dissatisfaction; losing a limb can transform those feelings, for an instant, into a fierce, visceral love en route to a different, less familiar seat: one of permanent mourning.

JR spent forty-two days in the Naval Hospital's intensive care unit. By the end of the summer, doctors were gradually bringing him out of the medically induced coma, and he started entering the bleary, hallucinatory states that signaled a consciousness fitfully returning online. By early September he had stabilized, and there was little else Guam's military hospital could do for him. To begin the next stages of his recovery, JR was flown to St. Luke's Medical Center, a prestigious facility in Taguig in the Philippines. His parents had to purchase an entire row of seats on a commercial flight to accommodate his stretcher. Though intermittently awake during his last few weeks on Guam, he was mired in the foggy borderlands of awareness.

At St. Luke's, more of his cognitive faculties returned, including his ability to form new memories. One afternoon, JR woke up in his hospital bed and looked over to find his parents sitting next to him. His fluffy black hair had grown long, covering part of his ears and flaring out behind his neck, and his arms were as scrawny as a child's. His muscle had wasted away, and there was no fat left on his frame; his rib cage and clavicle stuck out skeletally from his body, resting, as it had for weeks, against the white sheets of a hospital mattress. "Where are we?" he asked them. "What are we doing here?" His parents handed him a copy of one of Guam's daily newspapers from nearly two months earlier—July 20, the day after the accident. Laid out on its front page was a large black-and-white photo of his car, its two halves wedged between a concrete pole and a smattering of bamboo trees.

At first, JR refused to accept he had been in that accident. "I couldn't believe that was my car," he said. "I was just in total disbelief. I was in total shock." Though his cognition and awareness were gradually improving, his brother, Michael, remembered him struggling "to acknowledge that he had lost his legs." Throughout the fall, extended family traveled from all over to visit him at St. Luke's, including relatives from other parts of the Philippines and an aunt who flew in from Alaska to spend a month with the family. His denial persisted until one of his first days in the hospital's rehabilitation center. Pushing him in his wheelchair, hospital staff positioned him in front of a full-length mirror. That's when what had happened to him, and what his physical reality was now as a result, sank in more fully. "That was the first time I saw myself without legs," he said. He hunched over in his wheelchair, his gaunt seventy-six-pound body compact and sharply angled by protruding bones, and broke down in quiet, quavering sobs.

WHETHER WE LOSE our freedom, functionality, sense of self, or underlying trust in the safety and stability of the world, catastrophes diminish aspects of our lives so omnipresent that many of us take their immutability for granted. (Such is the persuasive effect of our absolutes.) When those essential aspects of our existence are wrested away by circumstance, though, we cannot permit ourselves to be washed away in the flood of our surging grief. It is at once the human condition's deepest cruelty and its most benevolent mercy that time does not stop to honor the unimaginable, and in the period immediately following before-and-after events people find a way to resist the temptation to submit to collapse. With little alternative, they strive, morning after morning, to countenance their new voids and rise to the redoubtable trial that has come to replace their once-familiar lives.

Catalog of Losses

ON FRIDAY, DECEMBER 14, 2012, I HAD PLANS TO MEET A WOMAN I was seeing. At the time, I was working as an adjunct English professor at a local college in Westchester County, New York, commuting over the George Washington Bridge from my fourth-floor walkup in Hoboken, New Jersey, and trying to persuade distracted nineteen-year-olds to appreciate the black comedy and cryptic comeuppances of Flannery O'Connor. After walking back to my apartment from the gym, I showered and sprayed on cologne. But before I could leave, a wave of weakness and disorientation crashed over me. My balance became wobbly, and my stomach lurched forward and back. I staggered through my apartment—where I'd hosted countless parties, countless guests, countless nights where excitement and excess spilled over like the liquor that stuck to our cheap linoleum floors—as if it were the cabin of a boat heaving and pitching in a storm. This weather, I was soon to find out, would never pass.

Over the next few hours, I threw up several times, and the dizzying malaise that portends oncoming illness swept over my thoughts and rendered my movements slack and sluggish. I sank onto the comforter pulled tight around my bed in a somnolent daze, gazing up in fractured snatches at the concert poster I'd recently hung in a black plastic frame. While I still went out that night, I felt off—

languid and feeble. It was someone's birthday and she'd invited me and several dozen other twentysomethings to a downtown Hoboken bar. While everyone around me coagulated into one viscous organism, spinning to the music like a human carousel, I was stuck at half speed, wandering the sloshy floors in a different sort of stupor.

But I was twenty-six years old and used to undermining my body and its fleeting frailties. My long-standing approach to illness, whether a cold or a stomach bug, was to ignore it and continue with my normal activities in a deluded gesture of masculine contempt. (This, I felt, was toughness, tenacity, *strength*.) I assumed that, like all the previous maladies that had passed through my life—asthma attacks, walking pneumonia, chicken pox, influenza—this, too, would promptly bow out.

When a week went by and I still felt lethargic, fatigued, and mentally adrift, my nonchalance surrendered to wariness. It was December, though, and I was determined not to let this lingering illness ravage the holidays. On Christmas morning, back in the leafy Connecticut suburb where I grew up, I trudged out of my childhood bedroom cloaked in an oppressive torpor. The malaise was only thickening, a phantom millstone that grew heavier with each passing day. Kneeling barefoot with my sister, dad, and aunt around a redbrick fireplace festooned with quaint knitted socks, under the high ceilings and exposed beams of our family's den, we undid plaid ribbons and tore through sheaves of glossy wrapping paper. My sister, Ali, got me an oversize snow globe in the theme of *The Nightmare Before Christmas*—finely painted figures from the film girdled the small glass sphere encasing Christmas Town, as Jack Skellington peered over it like a scheming god. The gift aroused the saucer-eyed child in me, and for a brief moment, the holiday spirit triumphed. But I couldn't keep hold of it.

Throughout my twenties, I had been physically active to the point of extravagance. There were trips to the gym framed by the sunrise, intramural football games on cloddy high school sports fields, yoga routines in my cramped bedroom, even wind sprints along a renovated pier that jutted out into the Hudson River. Working out wasn't just a way for me to stay healthy and fit or fire off some steam from my teaching hours. It was more intimate and elevated, akin to a kind of religious ritual. Gyms, courts, and fields were the places I went to achieve spiritual sublimation and emotional catharsis, plugging myself into something soothing, dynamic, and primal.

Now, though, whenever I went for a run or played a game of pickup basketball, I felt foggy and weak for hours or even days, as if I'd been suddenly thrust into a bout with the flu. My attempts at returning to exercise and their harsh consequences piled up, and it grew unequivocally clear that almost all intensive activity was no longer an option for me. I was losing my religion, but not from apostasy. The hymnbooks where I had long found solace and joy were being torn from my barbell-calloused palms.

When classes started back up in January, I still wasn't close to full strength. Over the course of the semester, my symptoms evolved, assuming insidious new forms. While participating in a group grading session in my college's cavernous brick rotunda, I was struck by a migraine so walloping I had to excuse myself for the day, leaving a pile of ungraded final exams and a circle of quizzical colleagues around my empty chair. I rushed down several wooden staircases, across campus, and to my car, gulping fumes of embarrassment. At bookstores, I'd kneel to peruse the bottom row, and when I stood up I'd see black spots covered in stars. I was bone-weary all day. I'd toss restlessly in bed at night. My body's wiring was no longer responding to the switches that once controlled it. I was constantly short-circuiting, and no one could tell me why.

The Irish goodbyes from work became commonplace, and I vanished from my social life in a similar manner. I begged off birthdays, holiday parties, and weekend trips, spending nearly half of my waking hours resting in bed. Once accustomed to going out weekly with friends to the boisterous bars that lined Hoboken's main thoroughfare, I now spent most of my leisure time in my bedroom, reading. I simply didn't have the energy or stamina to keep hold of my old life, and so it wriggled free of my grip, fluttering away into a cloud-smeared sky from which I started to doubt it would ever return.

I racked up doctors' visits with pathological tenacity, a speed dater certain "the one" could be culled from masses of duds. I first saw a general practitioner in Connecticut who diagnosed me with bronchitis. Once it was clear that assessment was off the mark, I walked to an urgent care clinic in Hoboken, where a physician tested me for Epstein-Barr, the virus that causes mononucleosis. When it came up positive, I felt as though some degree of coherence had been restored. The symptoms of mono largely matched what I was experiencing, and the virus's enervating effects could persist for months.

For a while, I settled into the clipped, expectant rhythms of protracted convalescence. When the malaise, migraines, and muscle pain still hadn't ebbed by the summer, though, I resumed my offensive to find a physician who could treat me. My thoughts were increasingly tormented by specters insisting that something malign, perhaps permanent, was taking hold in my body. Why couldn't any professionals tell me what it was? Appointments with internists, immunologists, virologists, and other specialty clinicians yielded zero leads, and the gap between the symptoms I knew I was experiencing and the supposed expertise doctors were using to evaluate me was stretching into a vexing chasm.

Over the course of those first twelve months, I was forced to grapple with the merciless logic of life with a chronic illness—a logic that once or twice literally brought me to my knees. My condition revealed itself to be a mystifying labyrinth, a maze of M. C. Escher staircases that always led me back to where I began: no better and, if I was lucky, no worse. While I held on to my job in the college's graduate department, teaching undergraduates became too physically exhausting and mentally depleting and I eventually stopped. My workdays were acts of endurance and concealment: First I would push my pain and exhaustion down to a place where nobody, including me, could see them, and then—like an actor who's

mastered the lines and gestures for a play he silently resents—
I would assume a brittle mask of healthful calm.

If my illness had any organizing principle during that year, it was
a loose, zigzagging adherence to the stages of grief. Whether anybody else could see it or not, I had lost someone: my former, healthy
self. Early on, a procession of sanguine doctors and my friends and
family assured me I would soon get better. For a long time, many
doubted I had anything seriously wrong with me, and the steady accumulation of normal laboratory tests only bolstered that conclusion. They helped lay denial's groundwork for me. In the months
after I first fell ill, as sooty snow piled up along Hoboken's narrow
streets, I looked toward spring with an ardent, quasi-religious anticipation. It was going to be an exultant return to form, a resurrection for a life trapped in agonizing dormancy.

A truth I became increasingly aware of during that fraught season of
hope, dread, and baroque self-deceit was that the two years I lived
in Hoboken before getting sick were quite possibly the happiest of
my life. My childhood and adolescence, to be clear, were far from
unbearable; one can do a whole lot worse than an accident of birth
in the comfortable suburbs of Connecticut. But those years were
also spent grappling with the shape-shifting grief of losing my
mother to breast cancer at age five and revolting against all the desolate rooms in my father's life afterward. I staged brazen spectacles
of my own bewildered masculinity—bloody fistfights, school sus-
pensions, arrests—attempting to pry open an identity whose primary authors had, in different ways, vanished from the scene.
Because of that internal upheaval, there was a haphazard quality to
my youth and early twenties, a sense of emotional instability roiling
beneath even the more joyful times. Settling into something approximating proper adulthood in New Jersey—the inner and outer
circumstances of my life finally snapping into place—was deeply
gratifying.

I'd somehow gained a sense of fullness there. And then, like a white squall sneaking up on a summer idyll, those halcyon days were over. For months, I stared at my denial and thought I was peering into my salvation, the way someone in the grips of psychosis might glance over at a stooped, tattered panhandler on the subway and see an angel of God. But the salvation I was looking for was not holy or divine or spiritual at all; it wasn't weighed down by ponderous truths about wisdom, growth, moral character, or the arcane secrets tucked inside human suffering. I simply wanted my old life to be salvaged from whatever oblivion it had plummeted into and returned to me.

Over time, my denial—slipping the rope of the traditional "anger" stage of grief—shifted to bargaining. Just a few more months, I kept telling myself, and everything would return to normal. By the time I finished rewatching the entire series of *The X-Files*, I'd be recovered. If I can just get my hands on this one promising treatment, I thought, it would cure me. I read online articles, scanned message boards, and gleaned physician directories for anything that might nourish my flagging sense of hope. The list of my ex-doctors and their failed treatment protocols piled up. My efforts began to feel like an unconvincing charade, one in which I played the roles of both the charlatan and his mark. It slowly dawned on me that I might remain sick for years, possibly the rest of my life. It was behind this wrenching revelation where anger waited.

I watched as friends and peers went on with their lives, dating, socializing, getting promoted, getting engaged. People I thought I was close to treated the reality of my illness like a Superfund site, an awkward hazard to be avoided in favor of lighter fare.

To address my baffling predicament, it seemed, was to acknowledge the frightening messiness of the human condition. The habitual avoidance confused and upset me. It also, eventually, stirred something bitter and foul, an ugly indignation that kept itself concealed but grew larger with each passing month.

During one of our appointments, a therapist I was seeing at the time told me that anger was like drinking the poison and expecting someone else to die. I conceded her point while knowing, full well, what little it would do to dissuade me from swigging, again and again, from that black bottle. That poison coursed through my veins, replacing my flailing immune system with a sense of aggrievement that glowed like crackling red coals inside me. Anger was what I had, and I quietly put it to use—a stage as delusional as the preceding two, except draped in its own strange, addictive glamour. I'd been an angry kid, and now I was an angry adult. It was a rare through line in an otherwise ruptured narrative.

By the fall, my condition hadn't improved in the slightest, and my recovery daydreams were rapidly losing their suspension of disbelief. Finally, in September 2013—nine months after I'd first gotten sick—I visited a specialist in Manhattan who recognized the symptoms I carefully recounted in his examination room. After an hour-long appointment, he confirmed what I'd already guessed from my internet searches: I had chronic fatigue syndrome.

Combining fastidious research with the experience I now awoke to every day, I gradually learned how ruthless and perplexing chronic fatigue syndrome is for those who fall into its sinister clutches. Symptoms include lethargy, fatigue, malaise, insomnia, muscle and joint pain, and memory and concentration problems. Sufferers may struggle to hold on to their jobs, relationships, social lives, and independence. Some don't have the energy or cognitive wherewithal to leave their homes, becoming housebound. Those suffering the worst become bedbound. While I'd eluded such unlucky fates for the time being, I grew to understand that, with such an unpredictable, poorly understood condition, the trajectory could hairpin quickly. A downward spiral might lurk behind next month's—or next week's—corner. It was a stay of execution I tried not to take for granted.

After two years of coping, in 2015 I heard about a treatment, called immunoglobulin therapy, that sought to infuse my immune system with healthy antibodies from other people's blood. By that point I'd learned to navigate the medical field with icy pragmatism. I'd shuttled from one doctor to another, handling each with forceful diligence and a clinical detachment that reflected back their own. I saw through each protocol for as long as I needed to, and when the pills, injections, or supplements revealed their inefficacy, I'd move on to another. Final appointments would be tense but also mordantly comic, like an episode from a surrealist dramedy series: Physicians sat behind large, cluttered desks, bumbling through futile defenses of their treatments as I looked on with indifference and a thin, caustic smile penciled over my face. They cost me hundreds, sometimes thousands of dollars and provided none of the relief that was promised—I had no place for niceties. I was aloof but also relentless, expecting nothing but pouring absolutely everything into another doctor, another treatment, another slender wisp of hope. It was a dichotomy that kept me safe from the whiplash of foiled expectations.

Immunoglobulin was neither easy to find nor affordably priced. After scouring the tristate area for a facility that carried the unusual medication and then hounding my insurance company to cover some of its exorbitant costs, I started treatment at a sprawling medical center in suburban New Jersey. Within hours of the initial infusion, I experienced a sudden resurgence of energy. As the day progressed, my vitality continued climbing, and the symptoms that had plagued me for years dwindled.

By the first night, I was shocked to discover that I wasn't exhausted. My joints didn't hurt, and my dulled mind was as sharp as a kitchen blade. I felt, finally, normal, and it was a riveting, sublime sensation. I called my dad, euphoric. As someone who'd seen my suffering firsthand for so long, he reciprocated my enthusiasm. "That's great news!" I pictured him on the other end, beaming. "Oh, I'm so happy for you, Mike." I cautiously began exercising again. My imagination, no longer enshrouded in a thick fog, careered with ideas. The outline of a first novel grew unbidden in my mind like a lush, lascivious garden. My mischievous personality returned, and I texted friends with near-frantic glee. To feel normal was a steadily unfolding ecstasy that glowed onto every recess of my drooping, sunless being.

Then, after five intensely glorious days, my body collapsed back into illness. The regression was both staggered and abrupt, like a car running out of gasoline in the middle of the road before sputtering to a wheezy, shuddering halt. By the end of the sixth day, I was back to where I'd been prior to the infusion, my extravagant horse and carriage shriveled back into a dented pumpkin. My whole body hurt, and my newly trenchant memory slipped from my grasp. The treatment never worked for me again.

In the failed drug's aftermath, I found myself facing what two years of feverishly searching for a panacea had granted me a temporary deferment from: the fact that I would have to live, indefinitely, with this condition. Instead of chasing more doctors and treatments and quixotic narratives of a miraculous recovery, I would need to sort through the rubble CFS had left, take what could be salvaged, and go out in search of the rest. All so I could rebuild my life.

There was no point lingering in the effluvium of grief, no useful reason to draft a catalog of all the losses. My diminishments, while largely invisible, were legion: The condition had ravaged my stamina, plundered my memory, and turned me into a glitchy simulacrum of my once-effusive self. Had such a catalog been composed, though, it would have looked something like this: I could no longer play football, basketball, baseball, or any other sports; run, bike, or exercise at the gym; fall asleep naturally; wake up feeling refreshed; go out for drinks; imbibe any alcohol without inducing devastating hangovers; use recreational drugs without triggering days of physical desolation; experience the heady cascade ushered by endorphins; feel the glorious surge of an adrenaline rush; feel "sharp this morning" or be "feeling good today"; manage on less than nine hours' sleep; teach literature and composition in front of indifferent nineteen-year-olds for two hours; consistently remember movie plots, grocery store lists, the week before last, or all manner of proper nouns; stay up late into the night without sacrificing my functioning the following day; carry out math computations in my head; recall what it felt like to relate to the friends and family in my life; or participate in the world without the obfuscating screen of perpetual sickness.

These were my losses, and as I slowly, fearfully moved to a place where I understood that they would stay lost for a very long time—possibly forever—I found myself in a different sort of stage. It was not one I had seen in the capacious cottage industry of books, articles, essays, and blog posts that have proliferated out of Elisabeth Kübler-Ross's original formation on grief.

Toward the end of my twenties, I began to feel that I was suspended between the person I was before I got sick and whatever person this catastrophe was going to change me into. The tortuous path I'd long put out of my mind—the one landscaped with the heavy scenery of acceptance and adaptation, wisdom and growth—now lay before me. There was no other road to take. The question I would have to ask myself, one that would persist long after the stages of grief quieted, was whether I wanted to treat this flawed doppelgänger with the same care I treated its predecessor with. My longing for the original model haunted me. The changeling in its place was for me to salvage or squander.

CHAPTER TWO

Fortitude

THE CAMBRIDGE ENGLISH DICTIONARY DEFINES FORTITUDE AS, simply, "courage over a long period." A second dictionary definition describes it as "mental and emotional strength in facing difficulty, adversity, danger, or temptation courageously." For my part, I define fortitude as the active choice we make to draw upon our wherewithal under harrowing circumstances, marked by an intense, often thankless effort demanded day after day. Demonstrating fortitude does not imply that we are growing stronger from our adversities, though, nor that they are changing us in any sort of positive, aggrandizing way. Fortitude is a word that has not been cluttered with romance and glorification the way terms like resilience, valor, bravery, and—indeed—strength have. Its value and merit lie instead in its spareness and austerity, in the way it does not accommodate our fantasies of how hardship confers honor or insinuate a spectator's admiring gaze. Fortitude is the deglamorized act of survival, of getting through the day amid toil and strain for no other reason than to meet the next one.

When I think of fortitude, I often call to mind some of the great tortured characters from literature. Jean Valjean from *Les Misérables*—a man imprisoned for trying to feed his family, battered by the coarse abuses of the state, and emerging from two decades in one of France's most notorious prisons. Complex, malevolent Heathcliff from *Wuthering Heights,* who endures orphanhood, maltreatment from his surrogate family, and the death of his cherished Catherine, growing into a contemptuous old man as isolated near the end of life as he was at its outset. Sethe, the protagonist of *Beloved,* who lives through enslavement at the Sweet Home plantation and the horror of murdering her own child to keep her from bondage.

These characters endure abuse, immiseration, fathomless cruelty, and impossible choices. And while they face their respective plights with courage, determination, and weathered dignity, their staggering adversities impact them profoundly. Valjean returns from his two decades in prison a gruff, callous criminal, overflowing with spite for his fellow man. Heathcliff is sculpted by his abusive youth and a baneful, devouring lost love, turning him into a wicked misanthrope entranced by ghosts and death. And Sethe's narrative is centered around a literal representation of her unspeakable trauma, as the baby she was forced to kill is reincarnated in the form of a rapacious, infant-like woman who glides into her life like water and soon floods it beyond recognition.

One reason these protagonists are so unforgettable—why they've secured their permanent place in the canon and the collective consciousness of readers—is that their adversities leave them haunted, hardened, and traumatized. I see them as embodiments, even archetypes, of fortitude, as their narratives allow them to brave catastrophe without protecting or inoculating them from all the lifelong depredations of it. Instead, Sethe, Heathcliff, and Jean Valjean are transformed by violence, loss, and tragedy, for better and worse and in ways whose depths we cannot always parse but are consistently fascinated by. They demonstrate perseverance but not immunity, as they survive unforgiving circumstances but cannot keep those circumstances from shaping their character, spirit, and relationships for the remainder of their lives. In these novels, fortitude is the bedrock on top of which all other strata—trauma, reckoning, withdrawal, redemption, reinvention—layer themselves. And it is an indispensable attribute in real-life afterlives for the same reason, allowing individuals to survive and endure as they press on toward future identities that will be transformed by their catastrophes in an incalculable number of ways.

THE FIRST FEW weeks after Sophie awoke from her coma were blurry and fragmented. The traumatic injury had impacted her brain in a thicket of ways that nobody—including her doctors—had a firm handle on. She vacillated from insuppressible exuberance to deep sleep within a single hour. Her memory came and went, and she might vividly recall a single incident but form no other memories from that day. For long periods, she operated with a blissful, almost angelic detachment from her circumstances, only to be abruptly seized by visceral terror of what lay ahead.

As different regions of Sophie's brain and their corresponding functions gradually returned—the hippocampus and memory formation, the limbic system and emotional responses, the frontal lobe and speech production—she was forced to navigate their whipsaw impact, the way they simultaneously flooded her with a new layer of awareness and awakened her to her unwitting deprivation. It was like someone playing with the circuit board after a power outage, flipping switches up and down haphazardly as fluorescent light flooded one room, red digits flickered on in another, and a third still lay in eerie, uninterrupted darkness. "Translating my awareness from that time into words now is really difficult," Sophie said. "It was like I was some sort of primal animal at that point, that had no concept of what was or will be."

Sophie spent all of September at Victoria General Hospital, going from the trauma room to the intensive care unit to several different floors within the neurology department. She was finally discharged to her parents' two-floor stucco house in Victoria on October 1, 2014. Almost as soon as she returned home, she found life outside the hospital's steady, predictable rhythms to be unbearably turbulent. The part of Sophie's brain responsible for filtering stimuli had been severely affected by the TBI, and she started suffering from disarming bouts of sensory overload. She often felt under siege by the sprawling panoply of shapes, textures, and minutiae that most people's brains conveniently bypass, trapped in a world that was in a perpetual state of disorienting clamor. "It was like every single detail, every sound or sight or feeling, was just bombarding my brain," Sophie said.

When Sophie sat down to dinner at the house of close family friends, the table setting left her flustered and agitated. "I was looking at lines, and contours, and every single aspect of an object," she said. A few weeks later, she was out at a pub with friends on Halloween night when she was forced to abruptly leave the restaurant. The hectic din of voices, cross talk, and live music became too much for her to handle. Standing outside the pub, her slate-blue eyes ringed with red, she grappled with a single irrepressible fact: She would not be able to slip so easily back into her old life. Her consciousness no longer felt manageable or trustworthy, and it often left her perplexed, exasperated, even frightened. "Everything you think is normal and you understand about how your body reacts to things was no longer reliable for me," she said.

There was a lamentable irony in the way Sophie's ongoing troubles with sensory overload thwarted her ability to spend extended periods of time with other people. Because of the way her brain injury affected her executive functioning and its inhibitory control, she'd become an extremely outgoing, extroverted person. And while those personality traits had persisted, they were complicated by her sensitive threshold for sensory overload. "If all things were firing right, then I was the life of the party," she said. But her neural fragility ensured that was not often the case, and so the charismatic young woman who'd formed bonds with uncanny ease at Victoria General Hospital was largely concealed beneath her swirling, tumultuous perception of the world.

Sophie's sustained injury appeared to create new personae that were either obscured or revealed depending on her circumstances.

In this sense, one might say that the multiplex layers of her personality came to resemble Russian Matryoshka dolls. One interpretation of these quaint wooden matriarchs is as a metaphor for the
many selves one person can inhabit over a lifetime. For Sophie,
however, the dolls evoked something even more dynamic: the multiple selves that coexisted at any one time, dimensions of a human
being that surfaced, vanished, or reemerged according to the knot of
vagaries happening in real time. Her struggles with sensory input
frequently sealed off the gregarious version of herself that thrived
when "all things were firing right," which had itself been snapped
into place over the more circumspect adolescent who existed before
the accident. One of the questions she'd have to grapple with in the
years following her injury was how she wanted to understand and
define her recovery. Should she try reclaiming the smaller nesting
dolls, the ones representing who she'd been—and perhaps could
still be—or was she better off crafting larger and larger dolls, painted
in visages that might come to look less and less like the predecessors
they eclipsed?

Though an onslaught of sights and sounds had been barreling
into her fragile perception from the first hours she returned home,
Sophie's chief focus following her discharge was something simpler: relearning to walk. Because the left side of her body had been
partially paralyzed by the TBI, she continued struggling to put
weight on her left leg, maintain her balance, and walk on her own.
Beginning in the hospital, she underwent an intensive rehabilitation routine to reverse the paralysis and regain the sensation and
mobility she'd lost. Pushing a metal walker, Sophie shuffled through
the hallways of the neurology department wearing what had at the
time become her trademark beatific smile. By the beginning of October, when she was discharged, she'd transitioned to her grandfather's old cane. And after she'd regained enough strength and
sensation at home, she started ambulating with Nordic poles. Eventually, Sophie weaned herself off the physical aids and began to once
again walk on her own.

Had things turned out differently on that morning drive just a month or so earlier, she'd have been spending October as a first-year student at the University of Victoria, immersing herself in the vibrant warp and weft of coed life. As it stood, however, Sophie—who would not turn twenty years old for another two months—hobbled around her house for hours each day, muddling along with a gait belt that allowed her parents, Jane and Jamie, and brother, Alex, to grab hold of fabric straps whenever she faltered. Her injured body, mercurial brain, and drastically altered circumstances were part of a cosmic bait and switch she was forced to reconcile herself to regularly.

Sophie's mother, Jane, took time off from her family medical practice to support her daughter's recovery. The two spent the fall months driving to local parks and embarking on gentle walks through serene nature trails blanketed by the region's thick, rippling cedars and multistory Douglas firs. From her earliest days out of the hospital, Sophie possessed a stubborn drive to reverse the effects of the paralysis and recover her full physical faculties. "I remember being really, really determined to get better," she said. No matter how much progress she made, she continued shifting her focus to her next goal. At a golf course near her family's home, she slogged through laps around a paved track. At a local outdoor gym, she tested her coordination on a balance beam, putting one trembling, unsteady foot in front of the other. She hoisted herself up staircases, trudged over Victoria's log-covered beaches, and sharpened her awareness of her body in space—known as proprioception—by walking around her block at night. Her determination left no room for modest or incremental gradations of improvement; she meant to reclaim her abilities as soon as humanly possible, ideally sooner. "I was always very focused on, okay, we're doing it, right now," Sophie said. "I need to walk. Okay, let's do it." Jane recalled, "It seemed to me that her physical pain and headaches, her physical suffering, her emotional suffering, was taking a back seat to her pushing herself."

The TBI had also disrupted Sophie's sleep cycle, leaving her with bouts of insomnia that persisted for hours. She often woke up in the middle of the night, shifting and tossing on her mattress and struggling to drift back into sleep. To get through these wakeful periods, she started binge-watching television shows, including *Grey's Anatomy,* with its young, frazzled resident physicians. "I made a point of pausing the show every time they mentioned something, looking up the medical condition, and learning about it," Sophie said. Though she didn't think much of the medical soap, she got so swept up in her practice of discovering new medical terms that she eventually started a Google doc cataloging them all. Ever since high school, she'd wanted to be a doctor—as both her parents were—and she saw this as a modest measure toward deepening her knowledge base about diseases, treatments, and the intricate overlapping systems that comprise human physiology.

On the days when Sophie wasn't feeling overstimulated, she conversed with her friends, family, and acquaintances with fervent, hot-blooded exuberance. Her communication style had changed since the accident, and she spoke her mind in a blunt, unselfconscious manner that could throw people off or leave them baffled, even discomfited. In some cases, her language and tone could be hurtful to those who'd known her for her entire life. Impulsivity is a hallmark symptom of people with traumatic brain injuries, and Sophie not only spoke but also, occasionally, acted with a headlong lack of restraint—usually in the service of her drive to improve her condition, but sometimes in less constructive ways. She called people at late hours, befriended strangers throughout Victoria, and burned up what had become a very short fuse when those close to her didn't see things through the same black-and-white lens she often adopted.

Some of Sophie's closest relationships suffered under the strain of all her disconcerting changes. While her parents had prepared themselves for jarring shifts in her personality, others had a harder time adjusting to someone they now struggled to read or understand. Sophie's younger brother, Alex—with whom she had been extremely close—would leave conversations with her confused or upset. One afternoon in November, while Alex was studying for a college exam, Sophie grew so enraged at him for refusing to acquiesce to her viewpoint that she threw a glass of milk onto his class notes. "She was really volatile," Jane said. Toward the end of the fall, Alex confided in his mom, "It feels like Sophie's not Sophie anymore."

Sophie's best friend since childhood was particularly disillusioned with her sudden transformation. Though she didn't express her feelings directly to Sophie, she began pulling away and gradually drifted out of her friend's life. For a long time, Sophie didn't understand why. Years later, during a candid conversation, her friend told her, "It was just really weird to see you but not know you anymore. Before the accident, I could look at your face and know exactly what you were thinking. After the accident, I couldn't gauge you. You were just a different person." Others responded similarly. "Her character was so vastly different, that her friends didn't know how to handle that," Jane recalled. "She lost almost all of her friendships for a very long time, and she was desperately lonely."

Increasingly frustrated with the complex, insidious effects of her brain injury, Sophie started conducting her own research into the condition. While an inpatient at Victoria General Hospital, she'd had just one half-hour meeting to discuss how her TBI might affect her daily life. A neurorehabilitation specialist went over some common symptoms, followed by a cursory interpretation of how her brain could be impacted based on MRI scans. Sophie had found the appointment brief and boilerplate, conspicuously thin on details pertaining to her specific injury or guidance on setting expectations for recovery. A month had passed since she'd been discharged, and while her physical recovery was progressing—she could walk largely unaided during the day, though she still struggled with her proprioception at night—her cognitive symptoms continued roiling her daily life. Desperate to grasp what was going on, she started investigating traumatic brain injuries online. It didn't take long for her to amass much more information than she'd received at the hospital—web pages, online articles, statistics, scientific studies. The information she was uncovering filled her with a keen sense of dread. "Things didn't look good," Sophie said. "And I got really, really scared."

Sophie discovered that people with even moderate traumatic brain injuries often suffered permanent physical and mental impairments, many severe enough to leave them unable to work. A significant number of brain-injured people actually reported feeling worse five years after their injury, too, and the group was on average far more vulnerable to seizures, infections, and other illnesses than the general population. The research focused on long-term prognoses was even more discouraging. Poring over Google searches in her bedroom, her back propped against a pillow, Sophie found several academic journal articles showing how people with moderate to severe TBIs (hers was somewhere in between) had shortened life expectancies. Other literature pointed to evidence suggesting that TBI sufferers were at a significantly heightened risk for both Parkinson's and Alzheimer's disease later in life. "I want to be able to live," Sophie remembered thinking. "And I want to do all these things. What if I want to work, or get a career, or go to school?"

For weeks, Sophie perused the depth of information on the internet with escalating unease, tumbling down one dispiriting rabbit hole after another. The revelations were stoking a persistent anxiety that was becoming sharper and more acute, mutating into "pure fear" about her future and what her capabilities would be in it. The concerns for a young woman in her situation were seemingly endless, and her mind now locked on to this chilling infinitude. Anxious dread swarmed over her.

Despite the blaring alarms her prognosis was setting off in her psyche, Sophie continued researching. She'd discovered too much already, and her anxiety wouldn't let her simply step away. Digging deeper into the literature on brain injury, she uncovered research examining the relationship between TBIs and IQ. Like everything else she'd read, the papers' takeaways were demoralizing. In one work, researchers carried out a controlled study over a period of years and determined that TBIs typically lowered a person's IQ, often for the rest of their lives. Online sources corroborated many of the paper's assertions.

For Sophie, who'd always prided herself on her intelligence, it was the most agonizing discovery of them all. Afterward, she spent many of her waking hours ruminating on the notion that the injury had diminished her intellect and compromised her potential in the world. She paced feverishly outside her house, stared anxiously into the glowing abyss of her laptop, and spent days at a time with one foot thrust into the dizzying vortex of a panic attack. The notion that she was no longer capable of attending college tormented her, nudging her closer to full-blown depression. Eventually, she bottomed out. After weeks of living in the hungry quicksand of paranoia and self-doubt, she arrived at the only path forward she could think of: She refused to accept the scientific conclusions. "One of my acute fears was that I could no longer do anything," Sophie said. "I really wanted to prove to myself that I could."

Throughout the fall following the accident, doctors had strongly recommended that Sophie wait two years before starting college. Resuming her studies any sooner, they warned, could be too overwhelming, and might also wreak emotional havoc. Taking demanding university courses alongside neurotypical peers, they seemed to imply, not only would push her mental wherewithal to its breaking point but could also throw her impairments into starker relief, administering a further jolt to an already rattled psyche.

Sophie found the doctors' recommendations unacceptable. After all the fatalistic academic literature she'd read, she resolved, finally, that following the path of least resistance—the path carved by "evidence-based" guidelines, studies and statistics, and the prescriptions of people who weren't walking in her shoes—would be consigning herself to deprivation. To still have a chance at the life she wanted for herself, she would need to scorn the experts and their conventional wisdom, proceeding instead according to her own furious drive. It was a motivating force with the galvanizing power of vengeance, and she consistently drew from it. Her crowning achievement would be to prove "experts" and their lowered expectations for her flatly wrong.

In December, without telling anyone, Sophie enrolled herself in two classes at a local community college in Victoria. The courses would start in January, little more than four months after her cousin's Volkswagen skidded across three lanes and crashed down a steep embankment. "She signed herself up for chemistry and psychology, and I was in disbelief that she thought she could do this," Jane recalled. The night before classes started, Sophie asked her mom for a ride to the campus. Jane had only recently learned of her decision, and she remained deeply skeptical that her daughter was in any condition to attend courses, follow lectures, or even maintain her composure inside a college classroom. "How are you going to get to school when you can't even walk, you can't bus, you can't even sit in a room for more than fifteen minutes without losing your mind?" Jane fumed.

"I'm just going to do it," Sophie replied.

RESPONDING, IN PART, to the bleak accumulation of research on trauma, a different framework for thinking about calamity and misfortune began gathering currency in the mid-2000s. Decades earlier, in the 1960s and '70s, University of Minnesota psychologist Norman Garmezy began studying a relatively rare subset of children who were regularly exposed to adverse circumstances—poverty, neglect, alcoholism—but who nonetheless managed to avoid the stereotypical pitfalls of "troubled kids" and thrive in their academic and social environments. Garmezy eventually alighted on a term to describe the adaptive and advantageous capacity that these children possessed: resilience. In the 1980s and '90s, as the field grew and accrued greater academic credibility, other developmental psychologists picked up the thread of Garmezy's pioneering research. Garmezy had established that certain individuals could fortify themselves against hardship and affliction through resilience; his successors set out to identify exactly what characteristics generated that resilience and, crucially, whether we had any control over cultivating them.

As journalist Maria Konnikova pointed out in *The New Yorker,* "Resilience presents a challenge for psychologists. Whether you can be said to have it or not largely depends not on any particular psychological test but on the way your life unfolds." In other words, one cannot measure resilience, but rather must infer it by patiently observing whether a person successfully pursues a healthy, well-adjusted life in the face of inimical circumstances.

The famous Kauai longitudinal study, published in 1989, spent thirty-two years engaging in just that type of patient observation. Psychologist Emmy Werner recruited nurses, pediatricians, and mental health workers on the Hawaiian island of Kauai to help track 698 children from their births—all in 1955—to their early thirties. In her paper, Werner identified several characteristics demonstrated by the study's resilient children—those who grew up amid multiple ongoing adversities but still kept pace with more privileged peers. Even when the children were toddlers, pediatricians and psychologists "noted their alertness and autonomy, their tendency to seek out novel experiences, and their positive social orientation, especially among the girls," Werner wrote. When assessed upon graduating from high school, "the resilient youth had developed a positive self-concept and an internal locus of control." Children who evinced from an early age independence, self-confidence, sociability, and personal agency were the ones most likely to forge resilience. That constellation of traits, along with subtle variations that would spring up over subsequent decades, grew synonymous with the increasingly recognizable term.

It took over a decade for the concept of resilience to spread beyond academia and reach the airwaves of popular culture. When it finally did, though, it was received like a sacred dispatch. Journalists, teachers, therapists, and even business leaders seized on it with a kind of uniform, homogenizing zeal. Whether it was from the vantage of grade school children or global corporations, resilience seemed to carve a secret inviolable path through the craggy slopes and sheer-faced bluffs that were all but assured to lie ahead. For a few years, the concept appeared to be nothing less than life's glinting skeleton key: No matter your variety of adversity or the particular crucible you might one day be throttled by, embodying resilience could inoculate you from it. Why suffer when you could be resilient instead?

Parul Sehgal, writing in *The New York Times Magazine* in 2015, observed how the term resilience "is fleet, adaptive, pragmatic," and yet, also, "so conveniently vacant that it manages to be profound and profoundly hollow." Celebrities gracing the covers of lifestyle magazines were breathlessly described as personifications of resilience following divorce, infidelity, child-custody battles, and substance abuse issues. Media headlines and nonprofit campaigns spotlighting communities reeling after shooting rampages and natural disasters deployed the term to near-indistinguishable effect. By this point, the zeitgeist had all but drained resilience dry—in its most insipid invocations, it seemed to mean nothing more than staying alive and being momentarily photogenic—leaving it a pliable husk devoid of much of the substance and specificity that Garmezy and others had spent decades excavating.

What has endured—and even solidified—in the intervening years is what we might call the gospel of resilience. This is the belief in resilience as a character trait that confers a type of immunity or even invulnerability, allowing people to weather everything from competitive academic environments and the demise of a relationship to bankruptcy and life-threatening illness. Like Nietzsche's maxim, resilience has a useful one-size-fits-all quality, a malleability that has helped propel its omnipresence while also rendering it generic to the point of vacuousness.

One aspect of the concept's original DNA has managed to survive its pop culture bastardization, though, and it distinguishes resilience from Nietzsche's adage in an important way. The psychologists that originally studied and defined resilience were looking for individuals who endured adversity and trauma and emerged no differently for them. The special mark of resilience was not to be made stronger by life's slings and arrows; it was, rather, to not be impacted by them at all. That is the gospel of resilience's promise: the tenet that if we can only sculpt and burnish a sufficiently enterprising character, brew the ideal blend of independence, agency, and self-possession, the tragedies and traumas life has in store for us won't zag the trajectory of our lives in any permanent way. At its loftiest true-believer heights, the philosophy's devotees may even come to believe that they've wriggled free of an old saw: When *they* tell God their plans, he doesn't laugh but instead furrows his brow and nods respectfully.

Espousing neither Nietzsche's accretion nor trauma's reduction, this school of thought instead promises the preservation and continuation of who we have always been. Resilience, in other words, is the armor that deflects change.

While the coveted trait can be wonderfully pragmatic for thinking about how to mitigate the effects of adversity and trauma—especially in childhood—its implication is, in some sense, incompatible with the idea of afterlives. If the subjects of this book embodied Garmezy's version of resilience, then they would be, by definition, largely indistinguishable from those of us who've never endured life-altering catastrophe. But my project, of course, is to identify the ways in which such lives *are* different, to discern the characteristics and patterns that set their identities and narratives apart. While resilience is a notoriously malleable term, at its heart it implies the ability to return to a previous state, to absorb an outside force and then reclaim one's preexisting form.

But some events make such reclamation and immunity impossible. Acquired disability, for example, is a clear refutation of this understanding of resilience. In those instances, people's bodies have been permanently altered, and no amount of the traits that resilience champions—traits like a positive self-concept, an internal locus of control, or a sense of autonomy—will bring back their old lives. (Further, seeing the return to one's preexisting form as an intrinsically preferable or superior development can in itself be an ableist concept.) Many of the subjects with acquired disabilities *did* demonstrate these traits, but their narratives continued progressing in directions that bore only partial resemblances to that of the people they once were. In those cases, it is *fortitude* that more faithfully describes what people are demonstrating—a tenacious perseverance that nevertheless remains vulnerable to irrevocable change. Fortitude is a more humble, unprepossessing trait, an admission of the stark limits to what we can control that does not promise more than life can deliver.

GINA FLEW BACK to Charleston from Cape Cod at the end of August 2006. Returning to the Lowcountry where she and her twin sister, Andrea, had shown such brilliant academic promise as children and teenagers, she moved into a room she'd rented while an undergrad at the College of Charleston. It was on the top floor of a canary-yellow clapboard house, in a less affluent part of the city miles away from the Greek Revivals, Italianates, and ornately latticed Victorian homes that lined more fashionable districts. The house sat near an old corner store where the regulars, Black men in their fifties and sixties, drank beers and shot the breeze in front of an old box television set, and you could get your bread and cigarettes on credit when you needed to. The wooden floors were sinking, paint was flaking off the siding, and a colony of bats had taken up residence between the walls. Gina could hear the clattering of clawed feet at dusk, and the pumping of their wings as they fluttered out into the bruised night sky. But a long, elegant porch also wrapped around the second story, and Gina's room had two large rectangular windows and a pair of small wooden hatches underneath them that, when opened together, kept her room cool during the sweltering summer months. Even as it fell into decay the house clung to its sense of old-fashioned grandeur, and for Gina it was the closest thing she had to a safe, soothing space. After everything she'd been through at the Woods

Hole Oceanographic Institution—where she was sexually assaulted in her own living room—that counted for something. "My room was a special place for me," she said. "There was always a sense of coming home there."

As summer turned to fall in Charleston, the city's swampy heat and scorching pavement gradually surrendered to cooler air and gentle breezes wafting in from the harbor. Gina picked up shifts as a dishwasher for a local restaurant and resumed a modeling gig for drawing and painting classes at her alma mater, where she sat on a large metal platform in the center of a cluttered, high-ceilinged studio for hours at a time. It was not the circumstances one might have predicted for a young woman who read at a high school level when she was ten years old, received a full scholarship from a prestigious prep school, and graduated from college—with cum laude distinction—at the age of twenty. But if Gina's intellect showed signs of astounding promise, the obstacles she faced as a woman recovering from severe trauma were a potent countervailing force. Her fate seemed suspended somewhere between her uncommon intelligence and her hard luck, her future consigned to a space perhaps equidistant from the two.

As Gina labored to fully inhabit strenuous poses in the college art studio, she tried to suppress the stress and anxiety she felt over her expenses, her academic future, and the state of limbo she now found herself living in. "I was having a hard time just showing up for my life," she remembered. She regularly reminded herself that these were just temporary jobs in a temporary situation, a stopgap between one leg of her academic career and the next. Her focus remained sharply trained on geology, the subject that had for so long ignited her imagination and given her a stirring sense of connection to the physical world and its everyday mysteries. She badly wanted to continue her studies, and eventually conduct research at the university level. That fall, she started preparing applications for PhD programs.

For months, Gina shared the story of her rape with only two people: her boyfriend, Christopher, and a close friend named Joe. After the anguish of not being believed in Cape Cod, she was hesitant to disclose the event to anyone she wasn't completely confident would trust her account. She even struggled to open up to her family, including her twin sister, Andrea. "It was such a hard thing to say out loud—I was raped," Gina said. "I couldn't even say those words. I would say, 'Well this happened and that happened and that happened.' But I couldn't bring myself to say the word 'rape.'"

That fall, trauma began bubbling up and seeping into Gina's daily life. Whenever she heard that cold, cutting word, the one she couldn't bring herself to say, it would stir a coagulated mass of ugly, wrenching emotions in her mind that she compared to lahars—turbulent mudflows that surged from the mouths of volcanoes and ripped through everything in their molten path. She could be peacefully going about her day, washing dishes, studying for graduate school exams, or reading at a local coffee shop, when she'd overhear somebody—often a male college student—make a flippant remark about a woman being sexually assaulted. "That would be the end of my day," Gina said. "That's it. I was going home, I was going to cry in the shower, and nothing else was going to get done."

Other things could also call to mind the attack: an accent that resembled her assaulter's, a particular song she'd heard that night. In each case, the triggering experience led to a blizzard of psychic pain, a squall of anger, grief, and isolation mixed with a sense that she was a helpless passenger strapped into her own unraveling. These subtle but devastating blips in her environment could put Gina in a "kind of nonverbal, deeply upset" state, forcing her to take refuge at home, where she'd spend hours decompressing. The charming college town she'd lived in and around for so long was becoming unpredictable, even menacing terrain, a geography pitted with trapdoors that could with zero warning send her right back to that horrific night in Woods Hole.

Gina also found herself fitful and restless at night, her sleep laced with disturbing dreams that snapped her awake, panting for breath and scanning her bedroom for shadowy threats. "I couldn't subconsciously approach the event itself, so it was a lot of not being able to close the door, an intruder breaking in, somebody trying to hide," Gina remembered. Her nightmares were suffused with "the constant sort of boundary violation, pursuit theme."

As part of the Falmouth court's decision, the judge granted Gina eight sessions of psychotherapy—at no cost to her—to help her recover from the assault. Despite her strong ambivalence toward seeking professional help, one afternoon that September, Gina walked the six blocks from her house to the Medical University of South Carolina for her first session. Stepping into a small office bathed in fluorescent light, she was greeted by a female psychologist. Gina felt uncomfortable almost immediately. "I was totally out of my element," Gina said. "It felt very clinical." Sitting in a spinning office chair, clipboard in hand, the psychologist ran through a diagnostic checklist to make an initial assessment. Gina tucked herself against the far corner of a couch facing the door, nervously adjusting her weight and avoiding any direct eye contact. She responded to the clinician's queries in a clipped murmur, her gaze fixed on the floor.

Are you afraid to walk down the street at night? *No.*
Do you find yourself constantly looking over your shoulder? *No.*
Are certain sights, sounds, words, or phrases triggering? *Yes.*
Are you having trouble sleeping? *Yes.*
Are you experiencing nightmares? *Yes.*

When the psychologist finished the checklist, she offered Gina her preliminary evaluation. "I believe you have pretty severe posttraumatic stress disorder," she told her. After hearing those words, Gina sat through the session's remaining time in a state of carefully concealed autopilot. The clinician discussed plans for future appointments, and the outward-facing version of Gina nodded affirmatively. The inward one, meanwhile, had already stepped out the door. "I didn't see any reason to explain that this is not helpful to me in this moment in my life," Gina said. "I just left and it didn't even occur to me to ever go back. There was no mental debate."

For Gina, the appointment—well-intentioned though it was—

ultimately amounted to another marginalizing label. "One more pathologizing thing that was quote-unquote wrong with me," she said. "In addition to my blindness, and in addition to having gone through this shitty experience, I now had a label that is patholo-gized." Whatever support Gina might have received from the psy-chotherapy sessions needed to be weighed against the prospect of living with a mental disorder many Americans at the time associ-ated with battered, psychically scarred war veterans. PTSD, she felt, was another stigma being heaped upon a woman who was already a visually impaired victim of rape. "I wasn't willing to have a disorder put on me and have the stigma of that for the rest of my life," she said.

Though still enduring the emotional spiraling during the day and the invasive dreams at night, Gina was determined to move for-ward with graduate school. By October, she'd submitted a handful of applications to some of the nation's top geophysics programs, in-cluding the University of Washington, the University of Oregon, and several schools in California's competitive UC system. But when she started hearing back from the schools later that month, all she was getting were rejection letters. Though impossible to know for certain, Gina suspected that many of the schools she applied to were apprehensive about accepting somebody with such a signifi-cant visual impairment. "I didn't hide that in my application and recommendation letters," Gina said. The broader professional land-scape underscored the challenge she was facing: There were only a handful of geophysicists with visual impairments like hers working in the entire country. "It was unheard of," she said. Despite a strong application—she'd had a 3.6 major GPA and glowing recommenda-tion letters and boasted an impressive array of undergraduate re-search projects—she was getting "denial after denial after denial."

Toward the end of October, Gina slipped into dejection. Between her PTSD symptoms; the raw, thawing emotional pain from the at-tack; and the growing uncertainty about her academic future, she was losing faith that making a better life for herself was possible. In an act of desperation, around Halloween she sent an email detailing her hopelessness to the three people who, she felt, comprised her support network: her old academic adviser from the College of Charleston, a counselor from the local nonprofit People Against Rape, and her boyfriend, Christopher. "I don't know how to do this anymore," she wrote. "I don't know how to make my life better."

Within a few hours, all three arrived at the old yellow house on Ashley Avenue to provide whatever support they could offer. One of Gina's most prized possessions was an old-fashioned vinyl record player with a polished wooden base and a magnetic arm, and shortly after her friends stepped into her living room, on the second floor, one of them placed the needle down. "They put the record on, and it's the first song on the Beatles' *Help!* album," Gina said. The lyrics—"Help! I need somebody. Help! Not just anybody"—spoke to her circumstances with uncanny prescience, immediately boosting her spirits. The eclectic group, which ranged almost two decades in age, sat around a small wooden table in the living room, ordered pizzas, and brainstormed how to get Gina into graduate school. She found it to be a "critical moment where I went from feeling a lot of despair and just very disheartened to feeling like I was supported and I was worth something," she said. "That there was hope for building what I've always thought of as a good and decent life."

While that night provided Gina with a much-needed respite from her troubles, it was not a permanent solution for coping with her trauma. Addressing that would require her to draw on her inner resources—specifically, a strategy she'd cultivated years before during a challenging childhood and adolescence. Ever since the assault, her sensitivity to specific triggers was derailing her days, chipping away at what had once been such a stalwart will. She felt smoldering anger toward her assaulter, a rage that covered up a pummeling sadness within herself. Her rage was so powerful that she sometimes thought about killing the man who'd raped her, a fantasy of vigilante justice in which she delivered the fair punishment that the justice system was too rigged and patriarchal to do itself.

As she reached the end of the year, Gina scrabbled for a foothold amid the dizzying blur of her fury and pain. Eventually, she landed on a powerful insight: Her violent reveries and the emotions they carried weren't just deadweight; she needn't let them drag her down. Her seething desire for vengeance could be sublimated into something potent and useful, a source of motivation that could overpower the paralysis of trauma. For Gina, demonstrating fortitude was not just a matter of endurance or wherewithal—it was also a creative act, a spell invoked from deep inside herself that transformed her aggrievement into a propulsive drive. "In the depths of my deepest, darkest, loneliest, most upset moment, I had a very strong need of defiance," Gina said. "When it came to that moment of picking myself up from the bottom of the shower and sending in another graduate application, it was that kind of energy that assisted me."

Gina was rediscovering what she could do with her negative energy. It was an old trick, one she'd used as a child for dealing with a mother who could be narcissistic and even cruel to her daughters. "I had been a witness to her converting rage into power since we were kids," Andrea remembered. Once she started tapping into that old technique as an adult, Gina's sense of hopelessness started to ebb. "There's something so empowering about converting that rage and need for vengeance into doing something that's good for yourself and good for your life," Gina said. "I began to really ferociously go after making a meaningful life for myself. And that became my vengeance."

It was in some ways a logical progression for Gina, whose long-standing adaptive nature had led her to handle tribulations as a matter of inexorable course. When she was a college student with no money and a stomach groaning with hunger, she hung around restaurants in the early morning hours. And when her vision deteriorated, as it periodically did, she'd find bolder markers, brighter lights, better assistive technology. Out of stark necessity, Gina had an unsentimental instinct for adaptation. Though she'd lose a haze of hours here and there to her PTSD, over time she learned not to dwell too long in the miasma of grief and despair. Past experiences taught her that all one's internal resources needed to be marshaled to the task of overcoming. When she framed her pursuit of a future as an act of defiance—indirect retribution against the man who attempted to ruin it—she could pull herself up and keep moving forward.

Later that fall, Gina's College of Charleston adviser gave her some encouraging news: The University of Missouri was looking to fill a spot in its master's program for marine geophysics. Though she knew little about the program and even less about the state, Gina applied almost immediately. By the time the holidays came around, she was officially accepted into the school.

Gina left for Columbia the following May. "I was so eager to get away, and sort of have that fresh start," she said. "I wanted this pretend clean slate." She sold most of her things before the move, keeping only a few possessions of irreplaceable value: a guitar she'd had for years, a silver-handled teakettle her sister had given her, and a few dozen old vinyl records from Pink Floyd, Led Zeppelin, the Clash, and other staples of her youth. On a hectic, harried morning before the downtown air began thickening with Charleston's early summer heat, her dad met her and her guide dog, Mitchell, at the dilapidated yellow house she'd called home since her sophomore year of college. After packing his station wagon, they headed to the airport. She felt excited to be returning to academia after an agonizing year of turmoil and doubt, but it was also bittersweet: She was leaving a place whose every street corner, intersection, and storefront was mapped out in her mind. She'd memorized the city's bridges and beachfronts, the college's intricate web of brick paths, and the cement walkway that wrapped around the patrician, picturesque Battery, not just because they were how she navigated the city as a visually impaired person, but because they'd been the settings that landscaped the panels of her life. "I was leaving my home, I was leaving the ocean, I was leaving Christopher, I was leaving everything that was familiar," she said.

Once she began settling into her new home in Missouri, though, Gina felt a sense of "enormous relief." She was scraping away at the residue of the previous year, delivering herself from the trauma that had embedded itself in her beloved hometown. But while the University of Missouri might not have been laced with the same corrosive memories, it would present its own gauntlet of challenges. There, she would be forced to adjust to a new identity, one as precarious as it was rare: a young visually impaired woman in the academic sciences.

LIKE GINA, INDIVIDUALS who've suffered catastrophic life events are forced to call upon levels of courage, willpower, and equanimity not previously fathomable to them. They pull together whatever strength they can find, because it is the coin of their new realm. Every day demands that they quietly enlarge themselves sufficiently to meet the exigencies of newly fractured identities.

It's in this straightforward sense that Nietzsche's aphorism rings most true. Individuals leading afterlives *are* almost always stronger than they were before their catastrophes, because their altered circumstances require them to be. Waking up in the morning without legs and traversing the routines and responsibilities of your day will always represent a greater challenge, a steeper summit to scale, than navigating life as a healthy, nondisabled person. "Strength" is the vague, porous term we use to describe what individuals marshal to make up the difference in those respective climbs.

Nietzsche's famous aphorism was hardly the only thing he had to say about the virtues of suffering. That specific crackling language—"What does not kill me makes me stronger"—appears just once, in *Twilight of the Idols*. Nietzsche suffered from grave health woes for much of his adult life, and he used other opportunities to expound a more intricate philosophy regarding hardship and affliction. For him, one of humanity's loftiest, most sacrosanct tasks was to find a way to leverage our misfortune to a meaningful and productive end. "He who has a *why* to live for can bear with almost any *how*," he wrote. In Nietzsche's view, it fell on individuals to apply their intellectual and imaginative faculties to adversities and divine something meaningful in them. This was the creator aspect of a person, what Nietzsche called "the sculptor, the hardness of the hammer, the divinity of the spectator, and the seventh day." Suffering was an inkblot, an abstract painting, a sphinx's riddle, and it was up to the sufferer to endow it with lasting significance and redemptive power.

But Nietzsche was concerned with more than just mining meaning from his trials. He also felt that suffering served as one of life's chief motivating forces, inciting people toward discipline, adaptation, and advancement. Strength, will, and even self-worth, as far as he was concerned, were directly proportionate to individuals' ability to shape their hardship into something stimulating and profound. Because of the way suffering rendered the present so distressing, Nietzsche argued, it triggered humanity's instinct for adaptation and evolution, electrifying us into transforming our character.

In *Beyond Good and Evil,* Nietzsche asks, "That tension of the soul in misfortune which communicates to it its energy, its shuddering in view of rack and ruin, its inventiveness and bravery in undergoing, enduring, interpreting, and exploiting misfortune, and whatever depth, mystery, disguise, spirit, artifice, or greatness has been bestowed upon the soul—has it not been bestowed through suffering, through the discipline of great suffering?" In Nietzsche's eyes, suffering forced people into a state of being that might be best described as the antithesis of complacency: a tautness of mind and spirit, one that homed in on their resourcefulness and ingenuity to doggedly pursue the steep, harrowing paths that might lead them toward a higher plane of existence. Shuddering in view of rack and ruin, we must become our most artful, enterprising selves.

The strength Nietzsche believed sprang from adversity was in that "tension of the soul," that whetted will that spurns resignation and utilizes everything at its disposal to survive and transcend what would otherwise be unbearable circumstances. It is a more complex, dynamic attribute than either resilience or fortitude, suggesting that we can use our own suffering to transform into more determined, potent versions of ourselves. Unlike resilience, which seeks to maintain the status quo, Nietzsche conceived of strength as something we leveraged to the end of evolving our inner selves and actualizing our buried potential. And while fortitude does not suggest that we have any control over whether and how we change after sustaining adversity, Nietzsche's strength represents a "triumph of the will," a declaration that we can use suffering to tighten our grip on our lives and expand the responsive repertoire of our spirits. If you are ready to "burn yourself in your own flame," he suggests, then you can augment and elevate your being.

When we plumb deeper into the relationship between strength and catastrophe, though, we start to run into the contradictions that expose Nietzsche's aphorism and its surrounding philosophy as oversimplification. Life-altering adversities may drive us to call forth greater reserves of strength, but if those adversities become permanent features of our lives, then that newfound strength will always be applied to the task of coping with them. This is where one of the paradoxes of afterlives dwells: the strength that is demanded by illness, injury, and trauma is immediately absorbed by the crucibles themselves. It's like discovering a deceased relative has left you a lavish inheritance, only to subsequently learn you must forfeit all the money to pay off his outstanding debt. The will and wherewithal born out of catastrophe cannot be showcased, glorified, or even reliably observed, because it is subject to constant confiscation, a daily toll that must be paid so that the embattled may continue progressing through their lives. Misfortune may create a "tension of the soul" that confers "inventiveness and bravery," but some circumstances ensure that those qualities never transcend the misfortune that begot them. Catastrophe creates that which it requires, and the attributes fostered in its churning wake rarely escape it for very long.

ON SEPTEMBER 10, 1989, Sean turned himself in. The previous afternoon, he'd made the biggest mistake of his life—the biggest mistake, perhaps, a person could make—firing a gun he'd never used before in the direction of a house and accidentally killing a teenager inside. His mom dropped him off at the police department, and officers remanded him to a juvenile detention facility in Denver called the Gilliam Youth Services Center.

During his first few weeks at the multibuilding complex—which from the outside resembled a public school save for a perimeter of towering brick walls—he barely ate and spoke to no one. "I still couldn't believe what I did and how my life had come to this," Sean said. He remembered feeling "a lot of guilt and unbelief and sadness and despair and depression." During the day, he kept to himself in his dorm-like room, staring morosely at the ceiling, the wall, the floor. Concerned about the mental state of a seventeen-year-old boy who appeared to have completely shut down, Gilliam officials put him on suicide watch. A pink slip hung from his doorknob, and counselors came into his room every few hours to check on him and make attempts, however futile, at conversation. "When I was in that juvenile cell, I wanted to kill myself," he said, "because I killed someone." His guilt remained a smothering force, his thoughts a hellish realm that never let him forget why he was in there and what he had done.

A month after arriving at Gilliam, Sean attended a hearing in a small juvenile courthouse inside the facility. A representative from the Denver District Attorney's Office had set a meeting with the judge to file a motion requesting that Sean be tried as an adult—a request that was all too common for Black teenagers at the time. The judge agreed, and Sean was transferred to the Denver County Jail the very same day. He would never see the juvenile court system again.

As was becoming increasingly customary by the late 1980s, the Denver DA eventually offered Sean and his court-appointed lawyer a plea deal. If Sean pleaded guilty, he would be charged with second-degree murder and sentenced to twenty-four to forty-eight years. "At the age of seventeen, I couldn't even comprehend those kinds of numbers," Sean said. As far as he was concerned, twenty-four to forty-eight years *was* a life sentence—or hardly any different from one. What did he have to lose, then, by fighting the charges? He told his lawyer to take the case to trial. Prosecutors responded by pursuing a first-degree murder conviction.

The trial, which took place in April 1990, lasted four days. The three other boys in the old Ford sedan with Sean that afternoon, all of whom were twenty-one or younger and affiliated with the Bloods, testified against him in exchange for their immunity from prosecution. The DA's office used a Colorado statute that allowed for the pursuit of first-degree murder in instances where a homicide demonstrated "an attitude of universal malice manifesting extreme indifference to the value of human life." Instead of trying to prove premeditation or even willful intent—the bar for a first-degree murder conviction in most U.S. states—prosecutors used the statute and argued that Sean showed a violent disregard for people's lives that afternoon.

When the verdict came in, Sean was sitting at the defendant's table with his head down. The jury filed out of the deliberation room, and the foreperson announced their decision: guilty, sentenced to life in prison. At the time, a sentence of life imprisonment mandated that the offender serve forty calendar years before he even became eligible to be seen by a parole board. After officers escorted Sean to the courthouse's holding tank, he walked over to the cell wall and let his back fall against it. Dressed in the county-jail-issued orange jumpsuit, he slid slowly down the concrete wall, his eyes partly open but registering nothing, before collapsing on the cold floor in silent sobs.

During the trial, Sean learned how the seventeen-year-old boy—whose name was Dean—was killed. After Sean clumsily announced his intentions to fire his weapon, the teenager appeared to scramble inside the house along with the Crips gang members. But because he didn't actually know any of the other boys (he wasn't a member of the Crips), he wasn't comfortable running all the way in. Instead, he crouched behind the front doorjamb, hoping to shield himself there. Sean then fired a single shot. The bullet ripped through the doorjamb, pierced the boy's shoulder, passed underneath his armpit, and traveled into his chest. Finally, it entered his heart. When the round exited his heart, it exploded, killing him instantly. If the scenario was played out a hundred times—Sean firing a single bullet in no particular direction—the same result would be unlikely. But the vagaries of chance were, perhaps inevitably, lost during the criminal trial, and Sean was painted as the ruthless gang member who'd robbed a teenager of his life. From the perspective of the Denver DA's office, it was convicting a killer and putting him away for good—an unequivocal victory for retributive, eye-for-an-eye justice.

After being found guilty, Sean was eventually sent to the Denver Reception and Diagnostic Center, a classification prison for evaluating incarcerated men and women and determining the state correctional facility best suited to house them. At the DRDC, he underwent a battery of physical and psychological examinations. One morning early that summer, Sean was on his way to breakfast at the facility's chow hall when he got into an argument with a captain. (Correctional institutions adhere to rigid, militaryesque hierarchies, and captains are high in the chain of command.) After a heated exchange, he cursed her out. The facility took disciplinary action immediately, and the consequences were swift: Sean was sent to Centennial Correctional Facility in central Colorado, at the time the state's sole maximum-security prison. It would be a brutal taste of what life could be like under incarceration.

At Centennial, which sits at an elevation of around fifty-three hundred feet in the foothills of the Rocky Mountains, Sean was placed in a single-person corner cell on his unit's second floor. "They dropped me off in my cell with just a bedroll and everything in a bag," Sean remembered. "When the door closed, there was a finalization about this life that I was now living that was just shocking." The building was so dilapidated that a large fissure had formed where the wall met the ceiling, directly exposing his cell to the out-side. In the wintertime, the crack would fill with ice, and with the building's unreliable heat, Sean was often freezing. Some nights he grew so cold that he cradled an illuminated metal lamp underneath his blankets for warmth. As an administrative segregation unit, or disciplinary prison, Centennial imposed twenty-three-hour lock-downs at all times. The men housed there were, in effect, living in a state of solitary confinement every single day. (In a 2019 article for *The Colorado Independent,* the state's director of prisons admitted that some men in maximum-security facilities "go years without stepping into daylight.") "That was the start of me feeling a deep type of depression that I've never felt before, but I would become very familiar with," Sean said.

With minimal contact with other human beings, Sean observed the other men on the block and learned how to use thread from his bedding to pass and receive books and magazines between cells. Using playing cards as weights, men crouched at the bottom of their doors and executed a single powerful slide that sent yards of it in the direction of another person's thread, where they tangled like fishing line and allowed the recipient to pull everything in. The only other way men at Centennial communicated with each other was by shouting from their cells, and during the eighteen months he spent there Sean heard a lot of voices that had been shaped by years be-hind bars. He tried to soak up the constructive advice that came his way, while filtering out anything that reflected the inimical thinking that had contributed to his own crime. He paid heed to older men who urged him to pursue his GED, recommended edifying books, and frowned on a prison hierarchy that lured in men with the prize of becoming what they called "king of the dumpster."

Despite the extreme isolation he lived under, Sean still witnessed episodes of barbarity that plastered themselves to the recesses of his psyche. Men who were beefing on the block found crafty ways to fight inside each other's cells—where correctional officers couldn't see them clearly—and the assaults could be merciless. "Everything in a cell is made of concrete and steel, and everything in a cell is used in a fight," Sean said. "Sometimes it gets so ugly that I have seen people actually lose control of their bowels from being beaten so bad in a fistfight." The entrenched culture of violence extended beyond incarcerated men, too. Sean once watched, from behind his thick plexiglass window, as correctional officers carried out a "cell extraction" on an older white man who'd been disobeying orders. Half a dozen guards charged into the man's cell, rammed electrified shields against his body, slammed his face onto the concrete floor, and handcuffed him. He was then led to the disciplinary unit, where he was stripped naked and thrown into a cell emptied of everything except a concrete bench and a metal toilet.

Centennial itself could be characterized by Colorado's first-degree murder statute of "universal malice manifesting extreme indifference." Rarely seen or acknowledged by guards or other incarcerated men, Sean increasingly felt as though his existence and suffering held no consequence to the world around him. Almost as a matter of course, he fell into a woebegone state. But he didn't let hopelessness overtake him completely: Finding a way to survive each day, he never fell apart or tried to take his own life. Given the circumstances, that alone could be counted as a significant feat—an act of tenacity and mettle that easily exceeded anything he'd done in his previous eighteen years. He burrowed deep inside himself and tried not to let the bleak tableau of maximum-security-prison life pierce him too deeply, forming a raw perseverance almost entirely beyond the purview of other human beings. "I couldn't just stay in a state of depression and think that it was going to go away if I just curled up in bed and put the covers over my head," Sean said. "What I learned was, men learn how to survive."

After spending eighteen months in administrative segregation, in late 1991 Sean was transferred to Limon Correctional Facility, a Level IV prison around ninety miles east of Denver. Although he'd started to see the self-destructive futility of gang life during his time at Centennial, once he entered the general population at Limon he felt an urge to cling to something familiar. For Sean, the one familiar feature in Limon's intimidating landscape was the Bloods, and it didn't take long for him to join up with the members on his block. Underneath the facade of a hard, fearless gangster, though, the guilt for what he'd done remained the true crux of his identity. He felt, perhaps more strongly than anything else, that he deserved his oppressive punishment.

During his first year at Limon, while Sean played the role of a Blood, his feelings of remorse for his crime festered beneath his gangster artifice like an uncleaned wound. With no tools or outlets to redirect the implacable guilt, he watched helplessly as it spawned cycles of anxiety and depression. He had the persistent sense that he was receiving two separate sentences: the external circumstances of his incarceration, and the state of private anguish that stayed buried but that nevertheless colored every day of his life. Though distinct, they both seemed to effect the same end of paralyzing his will.

In the fall of 1992, after Sean had been at Limon for close to a year, another member of the Bloods was standing in line at the prison commissary when he heard someone affiliated with the Crips mutter something disrespectful. The Bloods decided to retaliate, and the next day Sean and another gang member jumped the offending Crip in the prison gym. It was an act of blind loyalty, and Sean didn't interrogate it too closely before participating in the beating. Afterward, though, he felt terrible. He ruminated in his cell for hours. "I'm like, 'Okay, I'm committing crimes again, I'm doing the same thing that I was doing before I got locked up with all this time,'" he said. "I haven't changed." The violence in the prison gym stemmed from the same impulsive, myopic mentality that he'd employed on that life-changing—and life-ending—day in September. Seeing his fatal mistake repeating itself, under new circumstances but driven by the same unreflective recklessness, was unbearable.

As he contemplated his rash decision on the thin cot in his cell in the days after, Sean started to see that he didn't have to keep deepening the furrows of his self-loathing. Gang life and everything that it required simply weren't aligned with the person he wanted to be and the character he wanted to cultivate—not anymore. Why re-enact actions and behaviors that served as reflections of his one mortal regret when there were other options? He'd been spending more time with an old acquaintance from the Denver neighborhood where he grew up, a young man who'd converted to Islam and given himself a Muslim name. Others at Limon with similar backgrounds to Sean's had embraced the religion, too, and, though he couldn't put his finger on precisely what it was, he saw something in them that he wanted for himself. He sensed that Islam might offer him the tools to rebuild himself from the inside out, and perhaps even guide him to the righteous decisions that could allay some of his asphyxiating remorse.

Later that week, Sean met with several other Bloods from his block at Limon's basketball courts. His plan was to tell them that he wanted out, to cut ties with the gang for good. Lined up against the wall, examining Sean with a hard, impenetrable silence, the gang members resembled nothing so much as a military tribunal. Bloods were rarely allowed to leave gang life without consequences, and the young men standing before Sean that afternoon would determine the nature of those consequences for him. With his broad six-foot-two frame and hulking shoulders squared up to the other gang members in the gym, he declared his intentions as clearly and directly as he could. "I'm going to become a Muslim," Sean told them. "I'm going to study it, I'm going to become a teacher of it, and I'm going to change my life."

IN ONE OF his letters to the Corinthians, Saint Paul wrote that "strength is perfected in weakness." When we are pushed into diminished states that force us to rely on our character alone—rather than the advantages that we have been afforded by birth, circumstance, or God—then our strength is being perfected. In the Hebrew Bible and the Old Testament's Book of Judges, Samson possesses a physical prowess bestowed on him by the Lord himself. He has used it to slaughter the Philistines, the Israelites' chief adversaries, on enough occasions that he's become the sole target of full-scale military offensives by them. After a number of astonishing feats—including slaying a lion with his bare hands and vanquishing one thousand Philistine soldiers with only the jawbone of a donkey—Samson falls in love with a woman, Delilah, who brings about his undoing. Bribed handsomely by the Philistines to learn the secret of Samson's indomitable physical strength, Delilah eventually coaxes him into divulging that it lies in his hair, which "no razor has touched." One day, after he falls asleep, she orders a servant to shear his long locks off. Sapped of his divine power, Samson is subsequently captured by his enemies, who gouge out his eyes and put him to work grinding grain in a prison house in Gaza.

While Samson eventually regrows his hair and carries out one final act of destruction against the Philistines, I am more interested in the period when his hair is shorn and he is forced to turn a millstone with a body that's been drained of its divinity. We might say that this is Samson's afterlife, a profound diminishment in which he is stripped of his sight and his superlative strength. And yet, it is precisely after he is blinded, weakened, and enslaved that Samson demonstrates the greatest fortitude. What once came easily—thanks to talents that were literally God-given—must now be earned through his own toil, with only the willpower and resolve that he himself is able to call on. Seen through this lens, one might say, paradoxically, that after Samson's hair is cut he actually becomes *stronger*—in at least one specific sense. The life of a blind slave demanded incomparably more from him than a fortuitous existence as the mighty vessel of an omnipotent God. He may have captured glory and won adoration with the feats he amassed over his lifetime, but it wasn't until the Philistines maimed and imprisoned him that he was forced into a position where survival depended on genuine fortitude—a position of weakness, that is, where strength is perfected.

Samson's story illustrates both the type of strength we have been glorifying ceaselessly for thousands of years and the kind we've collectively ignored. His passages in the Book of Judges begin and end with external displays of power and achievement, with slaying foes and conquering beasts and carrying out acts of triumphant vengeance. For most, these are the measures and qualities that make him legendary and beloved—a worthy successor to ancient Greek demigods and a predecessor to our modern panoply of superheroes. His period of blindness and enfeeblement, on the other hand, is seen as little more than a woeful humbling, a plot point en route to the restoration of his power and eventual death. (Recall the wheelchair user who cited the movies and books where disabled characters either die in a "tragic but self-sacrificial way, or they're cured"—Samson accomplished both nearly simultaneously.)

It is the qualities Samson demonstrates in the grain mill in Gaza—amid deprivation, vitiation, and loss—that I would argue are more worthy of our reverence. Instead of leaning on the sacred gifts that were arbitrarily bestowed on him, Samson is forced to rely completely on his own character without the cushion divinity had long provided. Swimming against the current is always a mightier feat than swimming with it. As a society, however, we've long preferred the vivid, cinematic strength that comes out of fortune and advantage to the quieter, more internal one that must be called upon to withstand its opposites.

IT WAS LATE in the afternoon on the last day of March 2009, roughly fifteen months since the van Valerie was riding in flipped over and shattered her seventh cervical vertebra, leaving her paralyzed below the chest. She was sitting in her wheelchair in her family's lime-green semi-attached home in the Bay Ridge neighborhood of Brooklyn, on a leafy residential street near clusters of takeout restaurants and beauty salons, when an email appeared in her inbox. The previous fall, the industrious teenager and onetime high school race-walker had applied to a half dozen colleges—including several Ivy League schools—and by early spring she was hearing back. The email was titled, simply, "Your Application to Harvard College."

When she opened it, she found herself so nervous that all she could do was scan the text haphazardly, her eyes flitting from one cluster of words to the next like ricocheting pinballs. When she didn't see the word "congratulations," or any of the exclamation points that normally telegraphed a letter of acceptance, she assumed Harvard had either rejected or wait-listed her. It wasn't until her mother walked over and read the letter more carefully that they discovered Harvard had, in fact, accepted Valerie. They stared at each other—Valerie's mouth open, her mother's pulled into a wide smile—before high-fiving and hugging with uncharacteristic exuberance. Valerie's father, a working-class New Yorker in a long line of Italian Americans rooted in Brooklyn, scrambled to the home phone to call as many extended family members as he had the numbers for.

That June, Valerie's senior class held its graduation ceremony at the Beacon Theatre, a historic concert hall on Manhattan's Upper West Side. For Valerie, it would be the last time she saw in person many of the people she'd grown up with, close friends and acquaintances who had, over the course of her senior year, made it clear to her they "no longer wanted me in their life," she said.

But even as her academic prospects shone brighter than ever, Valerie remained singularly focused on her recovery. She and her parents decided to defer her admission to Harvard until the following fall, so that she could spend a full year doing the rehabilitation work that was so critical to her regaining sensation and movement in her body. Ever since the accident, doctors had been telling the Piros that individuals in Valerie's situation got back all the sensation and mobility they ever would within the first two years after their injuries. Because the car crash happened in early 2008, that meant that the rest of 2009 and the first months of 2010 would have enormous implications for her lifelong health and functionality. If Valerie and her parents subscribed to the doctors' timeline, there was a rapidly narrowing window for her recovery. Either her dreams would have to be realized over the next year, or they would be shut out forever.

In July, Valerie began a rigorous rehabilitation schedule. Three days a week, her mom drove her from their Brooklyn home to Push to Walk, a rehab center in northern New Jersey. She spent several hours there carrying out a regimen of stretches and exercises to help her manage her unsteady blood pressure and regain the sensation she'd lost. Afterward, they'd head back to Brooklyn, where her mom dropped Valerie off at a local Barnes & Noble before heading to her shift at the New York City Transit Authority's HR department.

During those leisurely afternoons, Valerie learned to navigate her wheelchair through Brooklyn's tightly packed sidewalks. She developed the limber, vigorous arms required to propel her body through space while sharpening her feel for the precise movements she needed to execute to pass through the shifting gaps between passersby. Valerie began embracing the unique new mechanics that dictated how she moved through the world, gripping her chair's rubber wheels with the forceful dexterity of a rock climber wrapping her fingers around a jutting crag. After grabbing lunch at a nearby restaurant—often a favorite pizzeria—she wheeled herself into the bookstore, rode the elevator, and headed to her regular spot, a wide aisle near two fiction bookcases where few people passed. There, Valerie lost herself in some of the towering classics she'd missed during her high school years—*The Brothers Karamazov, Sense and Sensibility, Frankenstein, The Hunchback of Notre-Dame*. The slow-moving afternoons, which she had all to herself, were tranquil anodynes during a turbulent, uncertain time. They were so peaceful, in fact, that Valerie sometimes dozed off in her chair, her head slumping against the wall as the book slid down her lap.

The rest of the week, which Valerie spent largely at home by herself, took on a much different cast. She and her parents set up a functional electrical stimulation bike—a stationary cycle that issued electrical impulses to her legs to keep paralyzed muscles active and healthy—and a standing frame in the living room so Valerie could keep up her rehabilitation between trips to Push to Walk. Still, she had a great deal of unoccupied time to herself. "I really didn't see a lot of people who weren't my parents or the people who worked at Push to Walk," she said. "It just became very lonely." Almost all of her Stuyvesant peers were preparing for the mass ritual of moving away to college, but "I felt like my life was on pause," Valerie said.

Her daily forays into social media confirmed Valerie's sense of estrangement. When she logged on to Facebook—which she found herself gravitating toward too often during the empty hours she spent at home by herself—it seemed to underscore the divergence between her circumstances and those of her Stuyvesant peers. She scrolled through glittering photos chronicling summer getaways, college move-in days, and new bonds budding in the fertile soil of first-year dorms. Some days, the chasm she felt between those jubilant images and her own solitude was agonizing. Valerie sobbed, threw household objects against the wall, and at one point even called a suicide hotline, not because she was contemplating taking her own life but because she was desperate for someone to talk to—a person who might listen as she articulated her punishing loneliness. "I was feeling that I didn't have any friends," she said, "and that I would never have friends again." On the worst days, Facebook's dense tessellation of curated photos made her feel like her peers "were rubbing it in my face: like, oh, look how perfect our lives are now that Val is out of them," she said.

Valerie's extreme focus on her recovery, meanwhile, took its own distinct emotional toll. Because she put so much pressure on herself and her body to show consistent progress, instances where it stalled or regressed could be excruciating. "When you have this biologically unattainable goal, it's very easy to get frustrated with even the tiniest of setbacks," Valerie said. If she wasn't regaining sensation in one of her arms at a pace she deemed acceptable, for example, it not only caused momentary aggravation but also dealt a major blow to her internal expectations for her improvement. Every aspect of her body's functioning was connected to the larger arc of her improvement, each day's physical performance fraught with subjective implications she alone deciphered.

Individuals leading afterlives can become so engrossed and even obsessed with their recovery that every day becomes a fresh referendum on the state of their health. There's always another test measuring their improvement, a new point shifting the shape of the scatterplot. These private self-assessments can consume their inner landscapes, leaving them desolated by repetitive cycles of unfulfilled hopes. People grow so finely attuned to their bodies and how they perform from one day to the next that they start detecting the subtlest variations in their symptoms and functionality. The result is a high-stakes arena only they can see, one where each day has the power to fill them with elation or demoralize them entirely. The obsessive attention to health is a double-edged sword, helping people retain maximum vigilance over their recovery while tethering their moods to an invisible sphere even those closest to them will never know.

Valerie dreamed of fully recuperating from her paralysis. She longed to regain sensation in her legs, walk again, and maybe one day even run. One of the most powerful instruments she possessed for reaching such a rarefied goal, she believed, was a mindset of imperturbable optimism. Even her loftiest recovery hopes were firmly achievable, she'd insist to herself, but it was on her shoulders to put in the work and demonstrate the wherewithal to achieve them. But as she got deeper into her gap year, this zeal and certitude often backfired. When her progress didn't line up to her expectations, Valerie's intense investment in her improvement could lead to meltdowns. Her ambitious recovery targets were both fueling her rehabilitation and laying waste to her emotional equilibrium, leaving her tortured by the very motivation she felt was the single most important key to getting better. The conspicuous dichotomy—optimism on the one hand and volatility on the other—was becoming just another aspect of her tempestuous daily life.

Throughout her gap year, Valerie scoured the internet for accounts of people who'd made complete recoveries from spinal cord injuries. Her sense was that any evidence she turned up could be used to nourish her hopes of eventually walking and even running again. What she found, however, were narratives that only frustrated her vision of complete, unalloyed recuperation. She read about a woman who'd been paralyzed from the waist down, regained the ability to walk, but never recovered sensation in her legs. A tetraplegic man made such miraculous strides that he eventually competed in marathons, but continued struggling with bladder control and temperature regulation. "I never found a person who had the recovery I was envisioning," Valerie said.

Reading these stories, Valerie began to feel a cognitive dissonance surrounding her recovery. Though one part of her continued believing she would walk again, another grew more open to the vast, uncharted space the alternative occupied. Holding these opposing ideas in her mind was not a source of conflict, though, but rather a form of psychological adaptation: a way to hedge her bets and avoid the stark emotional perils that came with fully accepting one scenario over the other.

Valerie was also internalizing the messages propagated by a culture whose representations of female wheelchair users were largely nonexistent. "I was thinking I probably won't get married, because at that time I didn't know of any women in wheelchairs who were married," she said. "I just thought, 'Okay, I'm going to make peace with that.'" But she knew she could still be a lawyer, like her older sister, so she kept that goal anchored firmly in her mind. These internal negotiations would become an increasingly large part of how she approached her future—a process of slowly determining what she could hold on to and what she might, eventually, need to let go of. To stanch the grief, to limit the sense of loss, Valerie started considering a different sort of existence for herself.

As her gap year came to a close, Valerie looked toward Harvard with a mixture of apprehension and hope. She would be the only wheelchair user in a first-year class of over seventeen hundred students. Would she be able to live independently in the dorms? Get to all her classes on her own? Replace the lost friendships that ended with such frigid permanence? In late August 2010, she and her parents made the four-and-a-half-hour drive from Brooklyn to Cambridge, Massachusetts, where she would settle into her new life and find out.

In the first two years following her life-altering accident, Valerie exemplified a fortitude that could be extremely subtle, even invisible, so submerged was it in the unremitting task of keeping her going. Sophie, Gina, and Sean all exhibited this attribute as well, a strength that is "perfected in weakness." Their fortitude was not something they could flash, flaunt, or brandish, because fortitude is not an external, preening trait like beauty, coordination, or wit. It does not exist in abundance—as Nietzsche's strength slyly implies of itself—nor does it possess the dazzling frisson of a professional athlete or a strapping cinematic hero. It is the unsung courage and stamina stripped of the glamour we project onto those traits in a culture that likes to pretend we live in a world where they are rewarded.

In his poem "Among School Children," W. B. Yeats asks, "How can we know the dancer from the dance?" Perhaps it's impossible to separate an individual from the raw biographical material of her life, but in afterlives it is nevertheless a crucial distinction. The outward-facing realities for people living with injury, illness, and trauma illustrate only part of the story, a superficial portrait that may be characterized, in part, by grief, constriction, and diminishment. But the identity immersed within those challenging circumstances tells a dramatically different tale, a private history defined by dignity, effort, and quiet, unbending valor. It is an immeasurable strength, one that is almost always internal and opaque, a silent, unceasing exchange between the dancer and the dance.

CHAPTER THREE

Demons

WHEN OUR PERSONAL NARRATIVE AND SENSE OF SELF ARE RUP-
tured, our mind reels. We're convulsed not just by everything
that's been lost—all the buildings that have collapsed in the private
skylines we awake to each day—but by the sudden disruption in coherence. This rupture can leave us destructively betrothed to a past
that William Faulkner famously declared is "not even past." We are
left straddling who we were and who we've only started to become,
consumed with the impossible task of suturing the biographical fissure.

The word "demons" has a slew of applications and definitions in
religion, culture, and secondhand psychology. For people leading
afterlives, I see demons functioning in four primary ways. First, in
the form of a harmful and maladaptive relationship with the person
or identity that existed before catastrophe struck. In these instances,
individuals continue to cling to the lives they once led. They fanta-
size about or seek irrational means to resuscitate that life, or they
compare current and past circumstances in a way that undermines
the person they've become. The latter presents a kind of cognitive
dissonance of identity: When the before and after periods of our
lives confront each other, it can produce a sense of instability within
the self and evoke intense ambivalence. With little forewarning, this

cognitive dissonance can violently uproot a person—psychologically at least—from conditions that have taken years for them to accept and adapt to.

Second, an obsession with the before-and-after event itself. For a time, I went through the days leading up to and immediately after the viral onset of my CFS with painstaking attention to every detail. The day I came down with the triggering illness assumed a kind of fetishistic power, cycling through my mind like a faulty film reel rolling the same frame over and over. I analyzed every person, place, and activity proximate to the onset of my illness with forensic diligence, dusting for fingerprints in a feverish attempt to unveil a hidden connection or buried clue that might be brought to bear. Here we are haunted by the breakage itself, the hour, day, week, or month when beloved swaths of our lives were lost forever.

As Jordan Kisner writes in her essay "Thin Places," about people suffering psychiatric breakdowns, "When the integrity of the story is violated, people get stuck at the point of fracture. They might re-form themselves around the brokenness, or they might restlessly circle forever, trying to understand what broke and why." The compulsion could just as easily be applied to catastrophic life events more broadly. In these cases, it's as though our brains are operating according to a blurred metaphysical logic: We start confusing time with space, believing that if we can only examine the moment of fracture closely and perceptively enough, we might go back and retrieve what was wrenched away.

Third, negative or even baleful feelings toward one's prior self that may have been crystallized by the catastrophe. Individuals may see the event as a scathing indictment on the person they used to be, to the point where the event becomes a damning proxy for their entire character. Consumed with guilt, shame, or loathing for that person, their intense emotional attachment traps them in a rueful irony: The self that evokes such repulsion is also one they refuse to let go of.

Finally, a pathological attitude toward a specific aspect of themselves that was changed by the catastrophic event. In these instances, individuals nurse an obsessive fixation with either reversing a feature of their diminishment or proving to themselves that it has really not changed all that much. I've never had a particularly good memory, but the indisputable fact is that it has been made worse by my CFS. This has been a chronic source of frustration and occasional embarrassment—if only in my head—and I frequently find myself either rationalizing memory lapses as consistent with my inherent deficits or pushing myself to recall dinners, family gatherings, and movie plots as though I were buzzing in on a game show with great stakes hinging on my powers of recollection. In either case, I'm uncomfortable with the unprepossessing truth of my flawed memory, and act quickly to disguise or transfigure that bald fact. This restless shame is a comparatively minor demon, I know, and others undertake significantly larger crusades, driven by their own magical thinking, to nullify some inconsolable aspect of what has happened to them.

Running through all these cases is the shadow and memory of who we once were—a ghostly but withering force that shapes all afterlives by reminding those leading them, over and over again, of a self that's vividly fixed in their minds but they know beyond doubt does not exist anymore.

JASON SPENT OVER a year at the Allegheny County Jail in downtown Pittsburgh. Finally, in January 2006, his court date arrived. Prosecutors had offered him and his lawyer a plea deal of seven and a half to fifteen years, and he decided to accept it. During the proceedings—in which he pleaded guilty to all five counts of armed robbery—the prosecutor read a victim impact statement from a teenage employee Jason had robbed at gunpoint during her evening shift at a Pier 1 home design store. That night, she was terrified that Jason was going to shoot her at point-blank range and kill her. The experience had traumatized her, and she'd sought out serious counseling in the aftermath. Jason was shaken by the statement's raw emotion, the window it offered into a vulnerable human being he'd wounded with his actions. "It allowed me to look at myself objectively, through the eyes of someone I had hurt," he said. "I remember just feeling like, that person was my identity. That's who I'd been for a couple of years." The girl's words sent his mind spiraling toward all the other victims whose terrifying encounters with him might have left them permanently seared by trauma. It was one of the first times he'd ever let the reality of his victims' subjective experiences sink in, and the feeling never left him. He'd made people fear for their lives.

In an ironic way, the opioid addiction that drove him to commit so many acts of violence had also shielded him from the terror and destruction his actions wrought. The dependency kept his blinders up, instilling a rigid tunnel vision that shut out the possibility for empathy and the remorse it might have inspired. Now that he was sober, imprisoned, and thawing out from beneath what had been a frozen-hearted life, though, he was no longer insulated from the pain he'd unleashed. "I was extremely ashamed," he said. "To see that I was this piece of shit that traumatized kids, teenagers, to fuel a drug habit, I just felt worthless." Fully exposed for the first time in years, he felt toward himself a sense of almost unbearable disgust.

After accepting the plea deal, Jason spent several months in a classification prison in central Pennsylvania. Before dawn one spring morning, correctional officers woke him up and led him to a building where men were processed before being transported to a longer-term facility. In the early morning's tenuous half-light, the air was sharp, the surrounding environs empty and silent save for the guards in the gun towers gripping their carbon steel rifles. At processing, officers stripped Jason down, checked his body for anything that could be used to pick locks, and told him to put on a bright orange jumpsuit. Then they shackled his feet to a long chain that ran up to handcuffs snapped shut over his wrists, escorted him to a handful of other prisoners, and led the men to a large gray bus with tinted windows that were covered in rows of horizontal black bars. The bus headed west on U.S. 22, which cuts across the length of

Pennsylvania. As it rumbled along the highway, an officer positioned behind a metal cage at the front glanced back and forth between the largely empty road and the sleepy-eyed inmates in their tangerine garb, his arms wrapped around a semiautomatic 12-gauge shotgun.

Riding through the belly of the state and into the northern reaches of the Allegheny Mountains, Jason silently peered out the thick windows. Gazing over the cars flitting past the lurching bus, he contemplated all the mundane, everyday activities the men and women inside them were freely carrying out. On his side of the thick, bulletproof glass, men were trapped inside ten- and twenty-year sentences. "The normalcy around me, versus everyone on that bus," Jason said. "The contrast was all I could think about." Moments like that hammered down his guilt like an anchor stake, underscoring just how far his narrative had veered away from most people's. The jobs they were driving to, the errands they were running—it was all unrelatable to Jason, artifacts of a bygone existence that appeared chillingly remote to him now.

After several hours, the bus pulled up to a sprawling redbrick complex. The imposing edifice was festooned with steep gables, sharp spires, and a corniced facade; its stone arches, small recessed windows, and black conical roof reminded Jason of a Gothic castle. He knew he'd been assigned to SCI Somerset, and he desperately hoped the sinister fortress in front of him wasn't it. As he sat bolted to his seat, his shackled hands resting tensely on his knees, he listened to a correctional officer call out the names of the men being transferred to the glowering complex looming before them. His stomach pitched forward, and fear banged around his chest like a swooping bat. As more and more names were called, though, it gradually dawned on him that they weren't at Somerset. They were in front of SCI Huntingdon, Pennsylvania's oldest operating correctional facility and one of its level-five, maximum-security prisons. After the bus finished dropping off the men assigned to Huntingdon and prepared to head west for Somerset, Jason felt intense relief. "Then as we're leaving, I start thinking, 'What the fuck do I have to be relieved about? Where I'm going could be worse.'"

SCI Somerset turned out to be a much newer, less intimidating complex. Its beige bricks, green metal roofs, and boxy buildings gave it the bland, benign appearance of a rest stop on the Pennsylvania Turnpike. It was located in the Laurel Highlands of southwestern Pennsylvania, built in 1993 on old farmland and surrounded by long, jagged ridgelines and deep, sloping valleys blanketed with scraggly trees and dappled with lingering winter snow. Somerset was a level-three, medium-security prison, which meant that inmates were confined to their cells for around fourteen hours a day but ate at a chow hall, could go to the yard and the dayroom every day, and had access to vocational programs and continuing education courses. (Compared to the maximum-security prisons men like Sean were forced to live inside, these were significant freedoms.) A row of colossal windmills peeked over the tree lines encircling the prison grounds. Jason would mordantly recount to others on the yard how he had often driven past those same windmills as a free man, thinking how he might like to live within sight of them one day.

Jason's cell, in the prison's only nonsmoking block, was twelve by seven feet, with gray concrete walls and a concrete floor in a slightly darker hue. Bunk beds were stacked in a steel frame on the left side, opposite a single metal structure that comprised both a sink and a toilet. Past the sink and toilet were two deep, wide lockers, and beyond that a steel desk bolted to the far corner. A gray steel door with two vertical plexiglass windows slid open and closed like a barn hatch, controlled remotely by prison staff. The cell was austere and utilitarian in the extreme, the kind of sterile, spartan space you might picture in an Antarctic research facility or on a dystopian spaceship. Its utter lack of specificity, detail, or flourish gave one the sense that it was built to dehumanize the humans who inhabited it.

By the middle of spring, after Jason had started settling into his new home, the days slowed to a crawl. "Once I got on my block, where I was going to spend the next couple years, and started realizing how slow this world moved, it felt like my perception of time changed also," he said. "I became really swallowed by it." His days were exercises in vapid, inexorable routine—breakfast at six-thirty, lunch at eleven, dinner at five, lockdown at nine. He worked out in the weight room a few days a week, but besides that he spent the majority of his time in the narrow slat of space he shared with another man. There was so little differentiating one daily cycle from the next, so few markers landscaping the passage of time, that one day could feel like a week, one week could feel like a month, and one month could feel like a day. It was all the same, and the stifling monotony—a sense of utter, almost surreal futility—started chipping away at him.

By the summer of 2006, Jason was withdrawing into himself more and more, and days would go by without him speaking a word. When someone said something to him in Somerset's large, green-tiled mess hall, he'd reply in a distant pitch, as though his vocal cords had to conjure a voice that had drifted into faraway exile. The institutionalization was hollowing him out. "I was like this piece of state property that got up off the shelves and wandered around at night," he said. "I felt like I had been lost in space, set adrift into the void," Jason later wrote in an essay about that time. "My existence was only periodically verified through recurring feelings of hate, fear, loss, isolation, and a loneliness I will probably not be able to articulate in this lifetime."

One afternoon, Jason was playing cards on a long steel table in the dayroom when he noticed the men around him were no longer looking at their hands. Their eyes darted furtively around the room, and they'd shifted their bodies so they could see as much of it as possible. In a span of a few seconds, several other men closed in on the person sitting next to Jason, forming a semicircle that shrouded him from most of the room. One of them lunged forward, stabbing him with a makeshift knife tucked inside his fist. At the same time, the other cardplayers all stood up and backed away, distancing themselves from the attack with both swiftness and calm. But Jason didn't move. "By the time I knew what was happening, they must have stabbed him ten to fifteen times," Jason said. The target slumped off the bench, the holes in his prison uniform filling with crimson, and collapsed onto the ground. It would be the first of several spurts of hideous violence he witnessed during his time at Somerset.

Though the target survived and Jason wasn't hurt, at least one man would later call him out on his ineptitude. There was an unspoken code regarding how to respond to stabbings and other prison attacks, and Jason had conspicuously disregarded it. He learned two important lessons that day. The first was that you needed to act fast to physically separate yourself from the violence that periodically shattered the prison's plodding sterility. If you didn't, you could either get pulled into the carnage or brought in for questioning by correctional officers later, which was worse. Second, in order to distance yourself you had to possess a keen grasp of Somerset's highly specific rhythms. "I suddenly became aware that there was a movement to this place," Jason said. "There's a cadence to prison. And your life can very easily depend on detecting a disturbance in that cadence."

Not long after the attack at the card table, Jason was caught in the thick of another gory confrontation. As he was walking through a narrow sally port, on his way back from the gym, a man took out a sharp piece of steel and swung it at another prisoner. The victim didn't have time to shield himself, and the swipe slashed his face open. As soon as the fight broke out, guards surveilling the room locked both exits, trapping Jason inside. Grasping for the far wall, he glued himself against it and tried to stay out of the way. Jason, who was five foot eight and weighed around 165 pounds, watched as two brawny, lumbering men, each over six feet and pushing 250 pounds, fought viciously—swinging wildly, grappling with their hands and arms, spattering blood all over the port's floor and walls. By the time the blood-soaked brawl was over, dozens of officers were waiting outside. The irruption of violence and claustrophobic nature of the experience rattled Jason, forcing him to start coming to terms with just how unavoidable disturbances to the prison's cadence actually were. "It's like you're surfing and there's sharks in the water—they're out there," he said. "That violence is out there somewhere, and it's going to happen near me . . . it's going to happen to me."

Adapting to prison life felt like a continuous curve—as soon as Jason had begun adjusting to one of its coarser aspects, another would rear its head, sending a fresh jolt to his still-reeling psyche. "That same feeling I had when I went to step out of the cell that day at the county," he said, "I was still feeling that way all over again because of these stabbings." He struggled to keep up, never feeling like he had enough time to reach his equilibrium between one distressing event and the next. Despite the desolate expanse of time unraveling before him and the stultifying boredom it inspired, he was forced to remain vigilant. He could not shutter himself away in some psychic crawl space, because it would leave him unable to detect the subtle tremors that signaled an impending attack. Those demands, however, weren't enough to thwart his psychological descent. "Once I figured out how to survive in my new surroundings, what needed to happen, my brain was polite enough to just kind of check out, and I became this shell," Jason said.

What coherent thinking Jason did do in the midst of his vacant, dejected state was frequently centered on a growing distaste for the person he was leading up to his arrest. "I was deeply ashamed of what I had done," he recalled. As he contemplated the man he'd been in his twenties—the fast-talking, quick-witted braggart who abused drugs and rarely showed up for anybody—he felt increasingly repulsed by him. "I never had to pay the check," Jason said. "I was always able to get around it or get out of it. And that was kind of my whole MO. That's just how I existed, which makes for a really toxic personality."

Jason was starting to feel like the arrogance and gratuitous self-regard he'd brandished on the outside were not legitimately founded, and stemmed from either "things I never had to earn," or "stuff I made up in my head and projected out into the world." One might say he was finally contending with his privilege, the way he rested on laurels that were not earned but rather inherited by the accident of birth. At the same time, he was learning that Somerset had zero tolerance for fraudulent personas. Its hardened population disdained egos built on air, bluster masquerading as gravitas, and nobodies who deployed the slippery armor of insouciance to project the impression of importance. Men at Somerset who exaggerated their stature or biography were rooted out like traitorous moles and made to suffer the same violent repercussions. "If you're portraying yourself as somebody or something, you're going to get called on that," Jason said.

The parties, the drugs, the connections from Pennsylvania to Florida that gave Jason a sense of chintzy grandeur—piece by piece, it was all being torn down and ripped away. Friends stopped writing to him, and some went as far as changing their phone numbers. Most family members ceased replying to his letters. "I had nothing," he said. "I just had this place, and I had all this time, and I had these fucking boots that I hated, and I had all this fucking razor wire, and concrete, and cell doors slamming. I kept falling down this hole." Life in prison had erased his identity, such as it was, and left him reduced to a kind of midlife tabula rasa: scraped clean of all the material that once added up to a person, with an empty white space for whoever it was who was going to materialize in the forthcoming years. Jason didn't have the vaguest idea of who might one day fill that cavernous void. What he did know, though, was that if he wanted to survive prison's barbarous ecosystem, that person would need to be someone with more substance and character. "This shit gets cooked away, and you start becoming the actual version of yourself without all these constructs," he said.

IN *THE ORESTEIA*, Orestes avenges the death of his father, Agamemnon, by killing his mother, Clytemnestra. Following the matricide, a trio of ancient goddesses known as the Furies plunge down on Orestes and torment him mercilessly. The goddesses appear to Orestes as sneering, scowling old women in tattered black robes, their heads topped by snarls of snapping vipers. While pursuing Orestes they sing a ghoulish, incantatory song intended to achieve their all-consuming purpose: driving him into permanent madness.

The concept of demons has been around for thousands of years, predating all three Abrahamic religions and the serpents and satanic adversaries found in them. Ancient Egyptians regarded demons as malevolent spirits that wandered the earth and sowed suffering in defiance of more benevolent deities; a millennium later, Christ traveled the Judean countryside casting them out of possessed "demoniacs." But what the Furies meant to the ancient Greeks may actually come closest to what demons represent to us today—the insidious feelings that haunt us for our transgressions, the malevolent shadows of past acts that led us into dark corners from which we never fully returned. These are the demons formed from our festering guilt, shame, and remorse, the unburied knowledge of our own grave erring. They bubble up from that material within us that is repressed or expediently forsaken, embodiments of our need for internal cohesion.

But demons have come to signify even more than just the weight of unrepented sins. What was once seen as a sinister force hailing from the spiritual realm is now invoked to illuminate various afflictions we understand as either psychological or otherwise rooted in the brain, reflecting a larger cultural shift in how we explain pain and suffering. Today we conjure demons to refer to everything from addictions and psychiatric disorders to traumatic experiences and ongoing struggles to break ties with parts of our past. When an addict relapses, when malevolent voices resume whispering in a man's head, or when a woman is abruptly pulled into revisiting the horrific abuse from her past, we might colloquially remark that they are each struggling "against their demons." What connects all these distinct incarnations is the notion that there are parts of ourselves that we've lost control of—thoughts, memories, and compulsions that have splintered away from the agency and self-preservation that govern the rest of our minds, taking refuge in the distant hills and valleys of our psyche. Lurking there, the living excrescence of when our brains went haywire, our demons are always biding their time for a chance to claw their way into the present, hauling the refuse we thought we'd banished for good.

Individuals leading afterlives grapple with a related but separate phenomenon; to wit, they have their own order of demons. Life-altering catastrophes create a narrative rupture that our minds do not easily absorb and move on from. In the aftermath, we're compelled to search for the sense of continuity and coherence that was destroyed, scouring for some way to reclaim an identity and story that vanished with the jarring abruptness of an evacuated city. We're haunted by the personae—parent, student, athlete, extrovert, paramour—that were permanently compromised, if not lapped into oblivion. The demons in afterlives are not uncontrollable dimensions of our selves, that is, but rather unreachable ones—the people we once were and the lives they led. The insuperable conflict at the heart of many afterlives is between the competing impulses to resurrect that person and turn our back on them forever.

DESPITE SUFFERING A traumatic brain injury in September 2014, by the following January, Sophie was determined to cautiously return to her plans of attending college. That semester, she took two classes at Camosun College, a community college near her home in Victoria—the trial period she'd signed up for without telling anyone—and they were an emphatic success. She traveled to the smaller of the school's two campuses and found the peaceful, sparsely populated walkways and greens to be the ideal setting for her, soothing her tendencies toward overstimulation and distraction. The less hustle and bustle there was around her, the easier time she had getting to her classes, focusing on her assignments, and keeping hold of her squirrely attention. She did, on a few occasions, step out of classrooms because she felt overwhelmed or sensed a surge of fear, anger, or panic welling up inside her. But she held it together during the more jagged, turbulent stretches and kept up with her work.

The anxiety that had metastasized during the first months after the accident was still there, but Sophie found that she could train it on her academic tasks. She learned to channel her anxiousness into homework, papers, and exams, using its razor edge to keep her zeroed in on her academics. The sublimation worked: In both introductory courses she took, in psychology and chemistry, Sophie earned an A-plus. "They went spectacularly well," Sophie said. "And that gave a lot of confidence to my doctors, but also my family, in that my resolution to start up at the University of Victoria that summer was going to go well, too."

After her success at Camosun, Sophie enrolled in two summer courses at the University of Victoria. Throughout 2015 she'd continued making strides in her physical recovery, improving her coordination, balance, and control over the left side of her body, which had been partially paralyzed during the car accident. On the first day of classes, in May, she felt physically able enough to ride her bicycle from her house to the lush, lively campus in the northeast corner of Victoria. After everything she'd been through—the coma and the personality changes that followed, the sensory overload and self-doubt that could make her feel so helpless—it was a quiet moment of glowing triumph. Cycling along the road, her backpack slung over her shoulders as she pedaled past the cherry blossom trees ornamenting the city with their snowy-pink blooms, she flashed back to the first month after the accident, when she questioned whether she'd be able to accomplish any of the things she wanted in life. Here she was, on her way to the University of Victoria, long before anyone thought she'd be. Recognizing how far she'd come, she started tearing up. "It was just sort of everything—I was officially starting my journey," Sophie said. "I had done my trial period through Camosun, and it had clearly been successful, so I was riding a high." Though it was a stirring personal vindication, the euphoria wouldn't last.

At the University of Victoria, Sophie would be taking the second part of the psychology course she'd started at the community college, followed by a class on academic writing later that summer. During one of her first days in the psychology class—held in a lecture hall with long beige tables that circled the stage like horseshoes—the professor was discussing how frontal lobe damage affects behavior. Quietly registering the coincidence, Sophie listened as the professor explained how altered executive functioning in these individuals' brains changes their sense of humor. To illustrate her point, she offered a joke that, she said, only people with frontal lobe damage would find funny—something about nonwaterproof watches being submerged underwater. The lecture hall remained dead quiet following the joke; after a beat, Sophie erupted in peals of loud, uncontrollable laughter. Shattering the silence, her convulsive laughs drew classmates' craned necks and lasered glances. The spell persisted for long enough that she eventually slunk out of the room to try to collect herself.

At first Sophie had found the joke's peculiar construction hilarious. Individuals with frontal lobe damage occasionally report a phenomenon sometimes called Witzelsucht—German for "joking addiction"—in which they find non sequiturs, puns, and other one-liners hysterically funny while losing an appreciation for other varieties of humor. What really sent her over the top, though, was the uncomfortable surrealism of the situation. "It was the awkwardness of however many hundreds of students were there, and this one student was just killing herself laughing at a joke that was not supposed to be funny," Sophie said. The moment contained an absurd situational irony that served as a tart crystallization of her entire experience leading up to her enrollment at the university.

Since Sophie's accident the previous summer, nobody around her expected her to return to school anytime soon. Now here she was, sitting in a college classroom, and it was the professor who presumed she was not there. She was continuing to spurn everyone's expectations, and at the same time everyone's expectations seemed to continue spurning her. Observing her classmates' hard, appraising expressions as she slid out of her seat and left the room, Sophie felt exposed in an oddly circuitous way: By assuming she did not exist, the professor had paradoxically revealed her and her neurological differences to the rest of the class. If she'd begun to convince herself that her TBI symptoms would not, in fact, play much of a role in her college experience, the episode was a jolting illustration to the contrary.

During her second summer course, on academic writing, Sophie's relationship with her coursework intensified. When composing essays, she rewrote individual sentences over and over before she could move on from them. Editing her writing assignments, she reread paragraphs up to forty times, examining grammar, punctuation, and word choice with a fastidiousness that eventually degraded into empty repetition. A sense of rapacious perfectionism was setting in, one that verged on obsessive-compulsive disorder. The distressing traits that materialized during the class would follow her through much of her college career. Though this seemed like the start of another baffling development in Sophie's mercurial disposition, it was actually closely associated with traumatic brain injuries. TBIs have been found to affect specific neural circuits that are associated with OCD, including those in the frontal subcortical region of the brain. But Sophie couldn't recall the physicians at Victoria General Hospital ever discussing any of those possibilities with her. With no medical context to illuminate her neuroses, she lacked the insight to recognize the worrying habits that were rapidly evolving into a more pathological behavior.

For the writing course's final exam, Sophie was scheduled to meet her professor at her office to complete her test there. When the professor opened the office door to greet her, however, Sophie's chest suddenly tightened, and she felt as though she couldn't breathe. Dizzy, gasping for air, and overcome with fear, she broke into tears. When her teacher asked her if she was having a panic attack, at first Sophie didn't know how to reply. Considering it for a moment, though, she realized it was the only way to explain her visceral, immobilizing terror. "I felt like I was losing my mind," she said.

Though the courses Sophie took at the University of Victoria were more challenging both emotionally and intellectually, she still managed to receive A's. But the following fall, when she matriculated into the University of Victoria as a full-time student, Sophie would grapple with another ordeal: the way her drive to succeed concealed an even more powerful compulsion—to nullify her injury's effects. If the twelve months immediately after the accident could be characterized as a largely successful physical recovery, the ones that followed were more ambiguous. Her narrative through college would come to possess a Möbius strip–like quality, in which apparently novel paths would twist in such a way as to reveal themselves to be continuations of older dimensions of her experience. Any hopes of linear orientation during these years were impossible, because her successes and her failures were never quite what they seemed, and often led back to each other.

Sophie began the fall 2015 semester majoring in general science. She signed up for three courses that all included a multihour lab component every week. It was a big leap in difficulty level and time commitment, and the dramatic increase in workload blindsided her. Within just a few days of classes, she was spiraling—her mind careering out of control, her body sputtering. Her anxiety soared, and her thoughts, trapped on a hamster wheel, kept her awake at night. She reviewed the same assignments, the same tasks, the same details over and over, her brain cycling through a progressively decaying loop. She experienced such wallops of dread that her limbs were often numb and her lips an icy, waxen blue. She moved through the campus greens and her own house with the stiffened, halting posture of someone shuffling around in a straitjacket. "She was so cognitively exhausted," Jane said. "She didn't have facial expressions, she barely talked. We knew she felt really unwell. She was pale and gaunt looking." Her pallid complexion and brittle, faraway gazes gave her the look of a high-strung zombie, someone both on edge and bloodless, feeding on her own fear.

Jane was so worried about her daughter that she began seriously considering pulling her out of school and deferring her for another year. When Sophie found out, it became even more fodder for her voracious anxiety. She resisted sleep and, on the rare occasions when it did come, was seized by the irrational fear that her mom could sneak away and defer her enrollment while she lay unconscious in bed. By the end of September, Jane, Jamie, and even Sophie's brother, Alex, were seriously concerned about her mental health. It didn't take a seasoned physician to recognize that her psyche was raw and frayed, a bone popped loose from the sheath of flesh that was supposed to be sheltering it. No one could say with any measure of certainty how long she'd be able to last in her exhausted, addled state, how much further she could stagger forth before collapsing from the utter depletion of her thrashed and battered nerves.

One evening, with her family gathered for dinner, Sophie attempted to convey the depths of her psychological unease. Sitting at the dining room table with Jane, Jamie, and Alex, she explained how the emotional distress caused by her anxiety often became so acute that she felt as though someone else were experiencing it. It was a jarring shift in perception, she noted, that felt like she was observing herself from the third person. She also shared with them a disturbing theory she'd been harboring. Periodically, she would find herself gripped by a conviction that she was still in a coma, "somewhere in the bottom of a hospital basement," living out her days in an unconscious state cleverly mimicking waking reality.

When she finished speaking, her family paused to process everything she'd told them. Their eyes were heavy and searching, moving slowly across each other and the room. Her parents realized that Sophie was describing episodes of depersonalization—also called derealization—a serious psychiatric symptom in which a person becomes detached from their own reality and begins to doubt whether the world around them is real. (Individuals with traumatic brain injuries are at heightened risk for the phenomenon.) Jane and Jamie pleaded with her to consider seeing a psychiatrist, a measure she'd resisted for months. That evening, Alex offered his perspective, too. "Sophie," he said softly, his gentle, sincere voice releasing some of the tension in the room, "this time, Mom and Dad are giving you some really good advice."

In the days that followed, Sophie and her parents arrived at a shaky détente. Jane and Jamie would not withdraw Sophie from her classes. In return, she would start seeing someone to help her address her anxiety, insomnia, and palpable mental deterioration. During her first appointment a month later, the psychiatrist suggested that Sophie try a low-dose SSRI, a type of antidepressant frequently prescribed to people with traumatic brain injuries to remediate some of the condition's long-term symptoms. The medication, mercifully, took rapid effect. Within a week, Sophie was sleeping for several hours each night, and her anxiety was ratcheted down, slightly, from its vertiginous heights.

But Sophie's struggles as a first-year college student went beyond the sum of her considerable symptoms. After all the research she'd conducted into her TBI the year before, she'd become tangled in her own trawling net, caught in an intractable obsession with academic success. The notion that her intelligence had been blunted by the traumatic brain injury was too much to bear, and she'd dedicated herself to rebutting it through the evidence provided by her grades. According to Sophie's logic, succeeding in her college classes would serve as proof that either her cognitive faculties had not been negatively affected by the brain injury or she'd managed the astonishing feat of reversing its effects through her persevering efforts. But by framing her coursework in this way, Sophie was putting a great deal of weight on her academic performance. Her recovery, well-being, and sense of self-worth all hinged on how she managed in her classes. "I was just so worried that I was no longer capable," she said. "My trust in myself and my abilities was gone, and I was looking for something to prove that I was worthwhile . . . something to hold on to, some tether of perceived truth. And that was my GPA."

As the semester progressed, the medication curbed Sophie's stress and sleeplessness just enough to keep her functional. Her anxiety about her injury's potential impact on her intelligence drove her OCD-like perfectionism over her work, which fed right back into her anxiety. It was a vicious cycle, but also, in a perverse way, a virtuous one: The pressure she felt to perform in her classes provided bottomless motivation and drove a maniacal work ethic. "I owe my GPA to whatever anxiety I had," Sophie said.

Sophie succeeded during her first year to a jaw-dropping degree. By the end of her second full semester, she'd received all A's and A-pluses. If this was the tether of truth she was after—an exhibit objectively demonstrating her intellectual capacities—then she was clearly seizing it. Her success, however, came at a steep price she hadn't prepared for. She spent her weekends either in bed or staggering through her house, recuperating from the lengths she'd pushed herself to during the week. She was pouring so much of herself into her schoolwork, meanwhile, that scarcely any remained for other aspects of her life. The recovery-by-proxy logic she subscribed to—whereby academic success equaled health and normalcy—was being decisively refuted. "I could excel in my classes, and yet things on a more personal level were just as shitty as they had been," Sophie said. "I was having angry outbursts, I was crying at weird moments, I was laughing inappropriately, I was socially unaware, I couldn't walk at night. Just because I was quote-unquote doing it didn't mean that I was having a good time, or back to normal, or healthy in any way. And that was really hard."

Even at Sophie's extravagant levels of achievement, academic success was not reversing the ways her traumatic brain injury had transformed the rest of her life. Because of how her studies were exhausting her finite resources, they were actually damaging those other aspects of her identity. Recognizing this set off a painful disillusionment. Her hopes had reflected a flawed logic, a false assumption that one realm of her life might somehow stand in for them all—that by making things right there, she would be making them right everywhere else, too.

On a corkboard above her bedroom desk, Sophie had pinned a quote she found online: "Sometimes I feel like giving up, but then I remember I have a lot of motherfuckers to prove wrong." According to Jane, the quote was "so consistent with Sophie" and her desire to defy the doctors, researchers, and everyone else who, she felt, doubted her. The scientific studies she'd suffered over had the force of fate—perhaps today's counterpart to the prophecies of antiquity— and by defying them she was changing that fate, reclaiming it as something that could still be determined, and determined by her. But slowly, Sophie began to wonder how much more of herself she could sacrifice in the name of defiance, especially when it was not yielding the gratification she'd expected. She started to see that her "reality was very, very different from before the injury, and no amount of external validation could affirm that I was a good person," Sophie said. "It's not a logical feeling, unfortunately." She was gradually realizing that the person she was trying so desperately to return to—her mind, her faculties, her stamina, and her poise—was not hiding underneath the ever-shifting composition of her symptoms. That Matryoshka doll, she would have to accept, was simply no longer there.

MY DEMONS ARE not constant companions; they stride in and out of my thoughts with the haughty elegance of a neighborhood cat, moving across the road, through the grass, and between white fence posts, throwing me several daggered glances before disappearing back into the enveloping scenery. There's a basketball court near my apartment, and I have no choice but to pass it on my way to pick up the mail. Before developing CFS, I loved playing basketball; what running was for JR, basketball was for me. I found that the game rewarded my strengths—ingenuity, aggression, a decent vertical leap—while forgiving my weaknesses, and stepping onto an asphalt court was the closest I'd come to that temporary transcendence athletes sometimes describe feeling. Walking by the court near my apartment now, I stare up at the carbon steel rim and white rope with wariness. I brush shoulders with my younger self: Though his brows are pinched in a scowl, he's clearly absorbed on some deep instinctual level, a mustang ripping into full career. He embodies focus, ferocity, fervor—the antitheses of the ambivalence I feel so often now. There's a simplicity and certitude in his relationship with his body, a harmony and clarity of purpose, that I miss so badly I do not dare feel the ache for long.

We are accustomed to invoking demons as avatars for wickedness or shame, fugitives from our reasoning, ordered selves that inspire loathing and anguish. Perhaps just as often, though, our demons are the echoes and remnants of our most consummate selves, the people we gloried in waking up as every morning. In these instances, the pain issues not from the sudden intrusion of a rogue vestige of ourselves that we never wanted to see again, but from fleeting glimpses of someone we never wanted to part with in the first place. These demons are the arresting flickers of the people we were in less complicated times, in ebullient eras that chance wrenched away from us. They serve as proof that sometimes life twists in such a way that the greatest source of our happiness becomes the most eloquent author of our haunting.

JR STAYED AT St. Luke's Medical Center, just outside Manila on the island of Luzon in the Philippines, for a month. The plan had originally been for him to spend three months at the facility, undergoing the intensive physical rehabilitation required for amputees adapting to their dramatically altered bodies. But by the middle of October, he'd had enough of hospitals. He wanted to go home to Guam, where he felt he'd be able to better focus on his recovery in surroundings that were comforting and familiar.

After flying back to the island with his mother, Amalia, JR moved into the lonesome slog of long-term rehabilitation. His body had deteriorated significantly during the month-and-a-half-long coma: While his organs sputtered to function on their own, much of his muscle mass had wasted away. JR started by focusing on restoring his upper-body strength. He spent hours in his room each day, doing push-ups and dumbbell exercises while maintaining a regimen of stretches that combated the stiffness from sitting hunched in a wheelchair all day. But his workouts were more than just dispassionate physical acts intended to aid in his recovery. They were also JR's way of trying to salvage something he'd cherished more than anything in the years before the accident: the surge of exhilaration that flowed out of pushing his body and running up against its outer limits.

For JR, losing his legs imposed a staggering physical and psychological adjustment. He was forced to change not only the mechanics of his daily life but also the way he thought about his appearance and identity. The coldly specific facts of his loss—he was now a bilateral above-knee amputee—moved across everything else about him like the shadow of a jumbo jet. The procedure had left JR with the single most challenging form of limb loss. While his right leg had been separated at the knee, his left had been removed several inches higher, and above-knee amputations are far more difficult to recover from. "Not only did I lose my legs, I ended up with the worst combination of amputations for walking," he said. "Losing two legs above the knee is hard."

As Guam's rainy season pushed into December and evening storms left the roads and jungles slick and shimmering, JR spent most days inside his parents' one-floor concrete house in the village of Dededo. He'd begun to see how his traumatic injury was more complex and insidious than the mere sum of his physical changes, with psychological dimensions nobody prepared him for. The car accident had triggered two transformations: There was his personal experience of losing his legs and becoming—at least for now—largely dependent on a wheelchair to move through the world. But there was a second metamorphosis, too, one that he could only as-certain by inferring: People now saw a different person when they looked at him. "In the wheelchair, I just saw the world differently, and saw how people reacted to you," JR said. "You're a legless man in a wheelchair, people look at you differently, they react differ-ently."

These two perspectives—JR's and those of strangers and passersby—formed a sharp, insistent dichotomy. Never aligned, they instead pulled and tugged at each other, creating a perpetual ten-sion that left JR's sense of himself fractured and indeterminate. Al-ready struggling to gain traction in a new, arduous reality with precious few guidelines, trying to reconcile the man he thought he was with the person people were mirroring back to him made everything harder.

Like Valerie when she returned to Stuyvesant for her senior year, when JR resumed life on Guam, he discovered just how overpower-ing the physical presence of a wheelchair could be. The struggle to overcome the prejudices of an ableist gaze is hardly a rare one. Strangers often conjure hazy portraits of people with visible dis-abilities that are little more than caricatures, flimsy sketches that fail to recognize the depth and multiplicity of their lives. Such tired conceptions put disproportionate weight on the physical loss and the wheelchairs and prosthetic limbs that become its outsize sym-bols. Nondisabled people with little or no exposure to amputations, paralysis, and other physical disabilities are captivated by these ob-jects and the marginal corner of humanity they evoke in their minds. As one wheelchair user with a spinal cord injury told me, people staring at her in the grocery store see her as "a difference. A curios-ity. I represent a kind of borderland of human experience. It's pretty rare that someone is staring at me because they see me as who I am. As Laurie."

JR resolved not to be the "legless man in a wheelchair" pass-ersby saw. Avoiding that identity, he felt, demanded one measure above all else: acquiring prosthetic legs. Ever since they returned from St. Luke's, JR's parents had been encouraging him to look into prosthetics and how they could help him recover much of the mobility and functionality he'd lost. "That's what our focus was on—getting him to walk again," Amalia said. Prosthetics promised to give him back some, even most, of the independence, initiative, and vigor he'd been so suddenly stripped of. Perhaps of equal importance, it would bring greater alignment between his perception of himself and the one behind people's expressions as he wheeled past them on the island. Whatever it was people were seeing when they glanced in his direction, it was a painful misrepresentation of the active, willful person he'd been for his entire life. He didn't want the man those gazes telegraphed to form a collective weight that dragged down his sense of himself. With the help of prosthetics, he would be able to walk again and hopefully change all that.

But securing prosthetics is never a simple matter of driving to a clinic and getting fitted, and the challenge was even greater on Guam. The island didn't have any facilities that manufactured them; they weren't available anywhere on the island. Residents who needed prosthetics had to fly to a mainland, often either Asia or America; go through the multiweek process of getting fitted; and finally have the legs manufactured to their specific measurements. That fall, JR—who did not have health insurance when he got into the car accident—learned that he qualified for Guam's Medically Indigent Program (MIP), which covered medical expenses for low-income individuals. MIP contracted with a prosthetics clinic based in Hawaii, and in February 2012 JR and his parents made the eight-hour flight to get him fitted for a pair. It was the first major advancement on the path toward reclaiming as much of his pre-accident existence as he could. "People had shown me life with prosthetics, and what was possible," JR said, referring to both his parents and the research he'd done online. It was "the next logical step."

When JR returned to Guam with the pair a month later, though, his expectations were immediately cut down. "Attempting to stand up for the first time," JR remembered, "I knew right then and there that I wouldn't be able to walk with them the way they had set them up." The Hawaii-based clinic built the vast majority of its prosthetics for below-knee amputees—only around a quarter of major lower-extremity amputations occur above the knee—and the legs' mechanics made it extremely challenging for those with above-knee separations to maintain balance and ambulate smoothly. After several frustrating days wobbling around the house, crashing to the floor, and withstanding severe pain, JR happened upon a work-around. Over the course of his extensive research, he learned that one of the best ways for bilateral above-knee amputees like himself to regain their balance is by practicing walking on foreshortened prosthetics—something people in the amputee community called "stubbies."

JR's younger brother, Michael, went about modifying the pros-thetics himself. He took the legs apart and kept only the upper sec-tion with the sockets, which he fitted onto wood-and-rubber feet he'd built himself. With a lower center of gravity and less pressure on his hips and core to maintain his balance, JR immediately found them easier to walk on. Within days of converting his prosthetics into stubbies, he was far more active, playing with the family's four dogs in the backyard and joining his parents on grocery store runs. He even started wearing his stubbies to the office where he worked as a development coordinator, a position he'd resumed a few hours a week shortly after returning to Guam in October. Though pros-thetics can be physically taxing, JR was wearing his modified ver-sion up to sixteen hours a day. "I'm a very independent person, so I didn't like someone having to care for me," JR said. He remembered thinking, "I'm going to learn how to use these, get used to wearing them all the time, so that when I do get my full-length prosthetics I'm completely independent again."

Though he exhibited a matter-of-fact approach to his new cir-cumstances, underneath JR was struggling to let go of the stinging memories of who he once was. He thought constantly about the young man headed to a running session the previous July, "the strong-willed, entrepreneurial guy at age thirty-one," he said. "A guy who ran seventeen-minute 5Ks, who was training for a half-marathon." One of the last memories he had of that person was of him climbing a ladder to replace a malfunctioning ceiling fan. When the last screw shook loose from the steel threads and the fan dropped from the ceiling, JR caught it without missing a beat, his feet still firmly planted on the ladder steps. That's the person who lingered at the edges of his thoughts each day: someone limber, agile, and dexterous, capable of handling himself on the jungle trails and beaches he raced through daily or on an aluminum ladder in his office workplace.

Even if some aspects of JR's identity remained unresolved in the years leading up to the accident—particularly his sexuality—his days held a sense of euphoric anticipation. Whether through his running routines and competitions or his entrepreneurship, an expectant thrill glazed itself over even the most mundane stretches and kept him keyed into what made him feel most alive. After the crash, though, those enthusiasms seemed likely gone forever. Apart from his physical rehabilitation and the five or ten hours a week he worked in the office, much of his time was spent watching *Law & Order* and *CSI* episodes with his parents and coming to grips with how severely his life had changed. For months, he found it to be a barren and punishing existence, a "loss of everything" for which there seemed little remedy or recourse.

As with the basketball court outside my apartment, for JR the roads, sidewalks, and jungles of Guam all evoked painful reminiscences of the vigorously active life he once led. Passing the villages he used to run along—now from the seat of his parents' car—set off recollections that smarted in the same places that used to radiate enthusiasm. "Anytime you're out driving, running errands on the main roads, most of it was places I used to run," JR said. "Those were definitely triggers." The triggers juxtaposed his past life with his present one, producing a cognitive dissonance that confounded his sense of identity. Those two men—the "strong-willed, entrepreneurial guy at age thirty-one" and the struggling amputee he was now—were chasms apart, with daily lives that did not resemble each other's in any way. Reconciling those two figures seemed impossible, like trying to force two languages into one voice. All JR could do was push the momentary incursions out of his mind and try to move on with his day.

In the fall of 2012, a little over a year after the accident, a pastor from the Southern Baptist church JR and his parents attended put the family in touch with a friend who ran a prosthetics clinic in Oklahoma. The man—whose clinic specialized in prosthetics for lower-extremity amputees like JR—had heard about his story and wanted to offer him a new pair of legs at no charge. A few weeks later, JR, Anthony, and Amalia flew out to Tulsa for the fitting. While the second pair had a hydraulic system that powered more responsive, natural-feeling knees, JR found that he still needed the support of a cane to walk. Though a step up from the stubbies, the prosthetics still weren't coming close to providing JR with the mobility he was desperate to regain.

Long before he'd even heard about Tulsa, JR had pinned his highest hopes for reclaiming independence on a specific model of prosthetics known as C-Legs. Arguably the most sophisticated prosthetic legs in the world, the C-Legs were manufactured by a German company called Ottobock, and a single pair cost around seventy thousand dollars. After discovering them while researching prosthetics on the internet, JR grew enthralled by their possibilities. YouTube videos showed bilateral above-knee amputees wearing C-Legs and walking in smooth, steady strides, ascending stairs, navigating uneven terrain. The legs used a powerful microprocessor to execute dozens of calculations every second that determined the level of resistance to apply to the prosthetic knees. If their marketing videos were to be believed, the C-Legs' cutting-edge technology allowed above-knee amputees to walk with a level of control and fluidity that was unparalleled within the prosthetics field. As he moved from one pair to another during his first year and a half following the accident—the ill-fitting legs from Hawaii, the stubbies, the hydraulic model from Oklahoma City—JR remained privately fixated on the state-of-the-art C-Legs. Like Sophie's academics, they took on deep, almost totemic significance in his mind. In them, JR divined an avenue for reclaiming what catastrophe had compromised. They were, whether he knew it or not, a vehicle for wish fulfillment operating below logical thinking. He reasoned that if he ever got them, "I could go back to normal—normal life."

Throughout 2012, JR sought different ways to get the expensive C-Legs covered. Early in the year, he'd applied and was approved for Medicare. But because of the way the system delayed its benefits for new recipients, he wouldn't be eligible to get prosthetics covered until the middle of 2013. With the help of his boss, he appealed to the Division of Vocational Rehabilitation, a Guam agency that covers services that help disabled citizens return to work. The agency agreed to pay for roughly half the cost of the legs; JR would need to look elsewhere for the rest. He eventually circled back to the Medically Indigent Program, which agreed to cover the balance. It took months of research, phone calls, and bureaucratic maneuvering, but by year's end he finally had the funds to cover the C-Legs. The dream he'd clung to for well over a year was finally being fulfilled, the shot at a "normal life" no longer an abstract aspiration but a concrete reality embodied in the sophisticated prosthetics whose slick marketing promised a new level of mobility.

In January 2013, JR and his parents flew to a prosthetics clinic in Orlando, Florida, to get him fitted for the C-Legs. After spending a month there working with the company's prosthetists to have the pair manufactured to JR's physical specifications, they returned to Guam. Back on the island, he started testing out the new legs: walking around his parents' house and yard, trying to ambulate on rugged terrain, going up and down stairs. As he spent more time in the prosthetics, the hope and anticipation that had been building for upwards of a year started draining out of him. The technology was impressive, there was no question. But JR found that the prosthetics were still falling short—painfully, heartbreakingly short—of everything he'd imagined. "It was just a gradual process of realizing, as amazing as these are, I'll never be able to run like I used to," he said. "I'll never be able to be as mobile as I was before." The C-Legs suffered from many of the same limitations as all prosthetics, particularly on slanted or bumpy ground, and JR hadn't adequately prepared himself for those stark constraints. He felt emptied out. In the weeks that followed, he drifted into despondence that would evolve into a monthslong depression.

JR had invested a disproportionate amount of hope in the C-Legs, and when they underperformed he faced an equally disproportionate blow of defeat. "I had these high expectations for the legs," he said. "Unrealistically high." Because he'd projected so much onto them, their limitations forced him to do more than adjust his expectations for the prosthetics; he needed to recalibrate his prospects for everything that was possible in his life. It was an irrational investment I recognized all too quickly, having allowed my own fantasies of recovery to seep into and saturate any number of dubious CFS treatments. They all served as temporary vessels for the stubborn dream of slipping back into one's old body, of being returned to a story that had ended abruptly in the middle of a sentence. And when those vessels shattered—as they invariably did—they also damaged whatever I'd surreptitiously tucked inside them. It was a peculiar truth demonstrated by afterlives: Hope itself could be deceptive, even treacherous, luring you into a position that managed to lift your spirits and leave them perilously vulnerable at the same time.

In the weeks after acquiring the C-Legs, JR came to terms with the fact that he would have to move past his dream of reclaiming his pre-accident existence. He might inch his way toward progress on one front or another, but nothing out there had the power to restore his pre-accident body or its exquisitely fine-tuned movements. He'd ultimately need to earn his gains through his own perseverance and the narrow gradients of improvement it achieved. "I realized there's no going back to normal, there's no going back to pre-accident," he remembered. How he would ever be able to fully, wholeheartedly accept that, he honestly didn't know.

CHAPTER FOUR

Seeking

IN ONE OF THE NOTEBOOKS HE CARRIED WITH HIM, NIETZSCHE wrote, "We have art lest we perish from the truth." For those leading afterlives, the unadorned facts of what's happened to them can be brutish to bear on their own terms. Contextualizing that hardship through our intellects and imaginations is a critical salve, an act of transforming our perception that can guide and color how we experience our lives. We can knead our experiences into a larger arc, providing the cohesion that helps us form new narrative identities. Or we can look deeper into our afterlives until we ferret out a way of construing them that rouses our spirits or points them toward salvation. In her essay collection *The White Album,* Joan Didion delivered a pronouncement that was a natural descendant to Nietzsche's line, an admission of how desperately we rely on the subjective fictions we construct: "We tell ourselves stories in order to live." Those stories—whether they take the form of redemption narratives, personal parables, or the pearlescent beliefs we kneel before each day like shrines offering eternal grace—can elevate our lives and serve as the vessels of private deliverance.

In some cases, even just a subtle reframing, an infusion of dignifying poetry, makes a magnificent difference in how we feel about our lives. When the poet Anne Sexton reached out to a Catholic priest, in a desperate bid to bridle her mental illness and fortify herself through faith, he said something that—for a time, at least—breathed bracing life into her: "God is in your typewriter." We need to see the glory, the valor, the spiritual glamour in the imperfect lives we embark on after tragedy and trauma—even if it is we who are projecting those qualities. If we can do that, we can draw profound meaning from suffering that might otherwise only batter us into benumbed submission. It can become Nietzsche's "tension of the soul," pushing us to adapt, refine, transcend, and transform. If happiness encourages stasis—"joy accompanies, joy does not move"—then the circumstances people find themselves in following catastrophe encourage its diametrical opposite, a disequilibrium they will cover great lengths to rebalance. The search for faith, self-knowledge, or intellectual illumination is often at the heart of that vital, fraught, and all-consuming journey.

BY HIS SECOND year at Limon Correctional Facility, Sean was growing disillusioned with the cyclical violence and self-defeating thinking that characterized gang life. He wanted to start living with a firmer sense of intentionality, longed to feel that his actions and lifestyle were in greater harmony with his developing moral compass. Though Sean was raised in the Methodist Church, during his time in prison he would turn to the religion of Islam to help him achieve these goals. The more he was exposed to it—reading its texts, listening to its adherents, praying to its God—the more strongly he felt that it was an inestimable path for pursuing the righteousness, atonement, and forgiveness that were becoming the definitive yearnings of his young life. A spiritual hunger was growing in him, and what he needed, more than anything, was a source of boundless nourishment.

When he was first incarcerated, in 1989, Sean knew only a little about Islam. He knew that his father, Kenneth, who was serving a long prison sentence over a thousand miles away in Marquette,

Michigan, had converted to the religion. When Sean was a boy, Kenneth sent him letters from the various penitentiaries he was being held in. The rectangular white envelopes always had the name of the facility postmarked in the upper left corner, and the letters inside were filled with illustrations—stars, crescent moons, bold stylized lettering. In them, his dad often discussed Islam's messages and principles, its pillars and articles of faith. Sean didn't expend too much thought on the letters' contents back then, but he did cherish the fact that they'd been sent by his father, a man so many family members insisted he bore a striking resemblance to. "I would save the letters, even though I didn't really understand what he was saying in them," he said. He stacked every last one in the top drawer of a tall wooden dresser that sat against the wall of his bedroom. "I was happy to have the letters," he recalled. "I've always wanted to know this man."

Sean was first reexposed to his father's religion two years before being transferred to Limon, while he was awaiting trial in the Denver County Jail. A man in his early twenties with long, rangy arms and a sinewy build was walking back from the shower, his feet still wet and his sandals smacking against the concrete floor, when he stepped in front of the iron bars of Sean's cell. "I'm Anthony, Adam's older brother," he told him. Adam Anderson was one of Sean's close friends before he'd been incarcerated, and he recognized Anthony from their neighborhood. "They call me Rydhwan now," Anthony told him, "and I'm a Muslim. I'm going to send some stuff down for you." Over the next few weeks, Rydhwan sent Sean packs of his preferred brand of cigarettes, along with a steady stream of foldout pamphlets on Islam.

Starved for ways to occupy the time and rescue his idle mind from the predatory guilt that prowled through it, Sean began glancing through the pamphlets. He learned about the five pillars of Islam: faith, prayer, charity, fasting, and pilgrimage. He was introduced to Islam's founder and central prophet, Muhammad. And, as the weeks passed, he started contemplating the religion in a more personal light. He tried to make sense of what Islam said about

Jesus Christ, the God-like figure to whom Sean had long directed all his prayers, while also pondering how the path of righteousness it espoused might be applied to his own life.

By the time Sean encountered Islam at the county jail, the religion had been a potent force in American prisons since at least the late 1940s, when Malcolm X converted to the religion while serving part of a ten-year sentence at the Norfolk Prison Colony in Massachusetts. In the decades following his conversion, Islam would continue to attract incarcerated Black men looking for moral and spiritual guidance from an institution that was not tainted by legacies of white supremacy and racial oppression.

Perhaps not incidentally, the rise of the religion inside U.S. prisons coincided with the rapid and largely unchecked expansion of America's carceral state. From 1973 to 2009—a span of less than four decades—the state and federal prison populations rose from around 200,000 people to 1.5 million (jails currently lock up another 700,000 people). Black Americans bore the brunt of this proliferation of the prison industrial complex: They're incarcerated at six times the rate of whites, and young Black men account for 34 percent of the entire male prison population. Islam's popularity in America's prisons—particularly among the people of color disproportionately housed there—continues to this day: 80 percent of all religious conversions that take place inside U.S. prisons are to the Muslim faith.

Weeks turned to months in the redbrick facility as Sean waited for his trial to begin. Lying on his stiff cot, his thoughts occasionally drifted to those loose-leaf letters his father had sent him years ago. As a boy, Islam seemed hopelessly obscure, miles beyond the purview of his Methodist childhood filled with church pews and youth choirs in Denver and Aurora. Now that Sean himself was in prison, though, Islam no longer felt so remote.

The recollections offered a salient, sorrowful type of symmetry. Sean's father had found the religion while he was in prison, and now here his son was, learning about Muhammad, the Hadiths, and the language of Arabic while awaiting a trial that would result in a life sentence. The imprisonments of Kenneth and Sean fell right in the middle of America's incarceration explosion; they were a family defined, in many ways, by the evolution of the nation's criminal justice system. For his part, Sean didn't read too deeply into the sullen parallels between him and his father. He focused instead on what was uplifting—how embracing Sunni Islam might bring him closer to a man he hadn't seen since he was eight years old.

By early 1990, Kenneth had gotten word that his son was incarcerated. About six months into Sean's stint in the Denver County Jail, he sent him another letter. When Sean opened it, he found a photograph inside: a picture of his father with a kufi resting atop his head and a prayer rug slung over his shoulder, holding up a copy of the Koran. Sean kept the photograph in his pocket and pulled it out for anyone he thought might want to see. He felt proud, he said, "proud of my dad for the first time. Because I've always known him as just an addict."

Following his sentencing in the fall, Sean was transferred from the county jail to the Denver Reception and Diagnostic Center, a classification prison. Rydhwan was sent to the DRDC around the same time, and the two continued to bond over their shared backgrounds and growing enthusiasm for the texts and tenets of Islam. At the time, the facility didn't offer any Islamic prayer services, and so Rydhwan—a bundle of skittering nerves and careering energy—started lobbying the prison administration to accommodate Muslims who wanted to practice the traditional Friday afternoon congregational service known as Jummah. For months, he pestered correctional officers up and down the prison's chain of command, and his indefatigable efforts eventually wore the bureaucracy out. Every Friday at twelve-thirty P.M., Rydhwan, Sean, and a third young man named Donny were permitted to travel to the prison chapel with their Korans and prayer rugs to take part in Jummah.

Several months into these prayer services, Sean felt strongly enough about Islam and its teachings to take his Kalima Shahada—the ceremony where a person declares his faith and officially converts to Islam. That afternoon, all three men were escorted into the small chapel that the DRDC shared with a neighboring facility. After clearing some plastic chairs out of the way, they sat in a circle on the chapel floor behind the wooden pews, their legs folded over ornately patterned prayer rugs. The space around them was covered in Bibles, crosses, and crucifixes, but they did their best to put the Christian symbols out of their minds. Sitting in between the other men, his back perpendicular to the floor, Rydhwan started the service by delivering a short sermon and then leading the two others in a silent prayer. After that, he moved into the Kalima Shahada. With his face turned toward Sean's, he asked him to name the five pillars of Islam and explain what each meant to him. He then instructed Sean to raise his right index finger and recite the Shahada, or statement of faith, in Arabic. After Sean repeated the lines in English, the ceremony was complete. "Congratulations, you are a Muslim," Rydhwan told him. "Now it is as if your slate is clean."

Donny took his Kalima Shahada that afternoon, too, and once they were finished all three men wiped tears from their eyes. "Rydhwan was doing a ten-year sentence, I had just been sentenced to life, and my friend Donny had just been sentenced to a hundred and four years," Sean recalled. "We were at a time in our young lives where we were just seeking some type of guidance, or some kind of meaning, or even a reason to live." They'd managed to come together and take this one consequential step forward under the relentless blight of prison life, and the sense of pride that conferred was so rare and piercing that it flooded them with emotion. That afternoon represented so many of the things that were in grievously short supply in the concrete cellblock behind the facility's sweeping gray walls and looping razor wire: an identity that they themselves had consciously chosen, a sense of agency and active participation in the trajectory of their own lives, a purpose that was inviolable and could not be wrested away from them.

After he was transferred to Limon Correctional Facility, in 1992, Sean would stray from his fledgling faith. But following the episode in the prison gym—when he felt obligated to take part in an act of gang-related retribution—his walloping sense of remorse made it clear he needed to cut his ties to the Bloods for good. Standing in front of his fellow gang members at Limon's basketball courts, he told them he wanted to walk away from the Bloods and devote his time to becoming a Muslim. There were four or five young Black men opposite him, appraising his words that afternoon, and two of them made it immediately clear they didn't like what he had to say. He would, they intimated, have to brawl his way out. "We can go in the bathroom right now and take care of this," one of them offered. "If that's what it takes," Sean replied, "let's go." He agreed to fight both men at the same time. But Sean was six foot two and weighed 260 pounds, and he moved with the swiftness and force of a college linebacker. Catching glimmers of Sean's invigorated sense of purpose entering the fight, his would-be opponents quietly backed out. Sean was free to part ways with the gang he'd been affiliated with for much of his young life.

No longer under pressure to make appearances with the Bloods, Sean started spending more time in his cell reading. He gleaned the surahs of the Koran, parsed the words and deeds of Muhammad that were recorded in the Hadiths. He was starting to develop a foundation for his faith that was firmer and deeper than the one he'd cultivated at DRDC. "Everything about Islam made sense to me," Sean said, "as it pertained to the journey of my life, and how, if I would have made more righteous decisions, I wouldn't be in the place that I was in." According to the Islamic texts Sean was poring over, the righteousness of one's choices determined one's destiny. Sean felt a powerful desire to make sure that, going forward, everything he did came from a place of unclouded, uncompromised righteousness.

Sean's daily life was transformed. He got up at five in the morning—when it was still dark and the sun had yet to start trickling through his cell's postcard-wide plexiglass window—unrolled his prayer rug onto the concrete cell floor, and knelt for the first of five prayer sessions each day. During these sessions, he often thought about a saying of Muhammad's that Rydhwan invoked at DRDC: If you had a river in front of your house, and you bathed in it five times a day, would you ever be dirty? The prayers were the river in front of Sean's home, keeping him cleansed and protected from the temptations to stray that hung over every gang beef, drug-smuggling operation, and scheme of the month proliferating through his cellblock. Each time he bowed on his prayer rug, he was setting down breadcrumbs for that path, ensuring he would not lose sight of it amid the dizzying thicket of negative influences that carpeted the yards and dayrooms of Limon.

During each of the five prayer sessions he carried out every day, Sean quietly engaged in a more solemn personal ritual. First, he reminded himself of what he had done to receive a life sentence. Next, he spoke aloud the name of the person whose life he took. Finally, he cupped his hands together, each finger pressed against its counterpart and his thumbs tucked against his palms—"as if you were trying to hold water"—and asked forgiveness from Allah for the fatal error in judgment that was the culmination of his misguided adolescence. "Every day, after every prayer," Sean recalled, "I whispered that to God." The process would end with him repeating a mantra, over and over and over, hoping, perhaps, that some of his guilt might dissolve into its spiraling, incantatory rhythms. "Allah forgive me, Allah forgive me, Allah forgive me."

One of the aspects of Islam that interested Sean the most—obsessed him, even—was the concept of tawba. In Islam, tawba is the tenet of repentance to Allah. Unlike Catholicism and some other denominations of Christianity, in which followers must perform the sacrament of confession with a priest to receive divine forgiveness, tawba doesn't require intercession by a clerical figure. Repenting for one's sins and returning to a righteous path is a private affair conducted between the believer and God. In the Koran, the term is strongly associated with nasuh, which roughly translates to pure and sincere. Tawba nasuh is a sincere, fullhearted repentance before God, one whose purity is unalloyed by opaque intentions or transient passions. Subscribing to tawba nasuh requires Muslims to renounce any vestiges of sin or selfishness and embrace complete reform, aspiring toward moral perfection.

Sean was vivified by the concept of tawba nasuh, intoxicated with the idea that he could cleanse himself of past sin through un-wavering commitment to Islam and its principles. It was, in some ways, the answer he'd been searching for, a doctrine that crystal-lized his burgeoning desire to do everything in his power to rectify his crime.

Successfully performing tawba entails experiencing sincere re-morse for one's misdeeds, followed by a devotion to the divine du-ties that were overlooked leading up to the transgression, including daily prayer, charitable acts, and the improvement of all 360 degrees of one's existence. Through tawba, Sean could undertake the con-crete, practical work that yielded the sense of atonement that the diffuse vapor of regret never could. "I needed forgiveness in my life because I felt so bad about the crime that I committed," Sean said. Tawba became "the driving force" animating Sean's increasingly selfless acts. "I wanted to mean something in the eyes of the crea-tor," he said.

Later that year, a Black Muslim who'd given himself the name Hassan Latif was transferred to Limon Correctional Facility. Latif, who had sharp, lively dark brown eyes and wore a full beard that jutted out from beneath his chin like a crag, had learned about Islam and become devoted to its practice in the New York prison system of the 1980s and early '90s. In the Islamic communities at correc-tional facilities like Sing Sing and Attica, the religion was treated with fierce militancy: Prayers, readings, and discussions were not optional, and members of the community could be remorseless to-ward fellow Muslims who lagged in their commitment. Latif had used his time behind bars to examine who he'd become and rebuild that person from the ground up. He'd dedicated his days not just to daily prayers and Koranic readings but also to Islam's deeper, more elusive demands: interrogating one's core beliefs, asking philosoph-ical questions about the nature of God's relationship to humankind, and grappling with the implications of the afterlife. "Hassan was always very focused, and he had a purpose behind everything he did and said," Sean said. "And the purpose and the focus was always Islam."

Within weeks of Latif's arrival at Limon, the prison's Muslims voted to make him their imam, or spiritual leader. Wearing a beret-like kufi that, combined with his carefully kept beard, made him look like a political revolutionary, Latif began reshaping what had up to that point been a laid-back and desultory Islamic culture. Latif believed that if his fellow Muslims wanted the religion to change their lives and help pull them out from under years of lucklessness and institutional oppression, they needed to embrace structure, discipline, and cerebral rigor. Sean and the rest of the eager but inexperienced Muslims at Limon took to their charismatic new leader immediately. He and the other young men observed how Latif embodied so much of what they sought to achieve with Islam—speaking with force, acting with conviction, and possessing an imperturbable sense of his path forward.

Latif was forming a particularly strong bond with Sean, and several months after meeting the two applied to become cellmates. Once they shared the same cell, Latif exerted an even more profound influence over the twenty-year-old still learning how to root his life in religious faith. Latif's religious belief, it seemed to Sean, was crucially connected to the certainty and rectitude with which he carried himself, like a latticed trellis that gave a tangle of flowering vines the sturdy spine to blossom and grow. Observing Latif's decisiveness and confidence in his ability to carry out the changes he wanted to see in his life, Sean wondered whether his own feelings of hopelessness and condemnation were really as intractable as they seemed.

Sean and Latif often discussed Islam in their shared cell late into the night. With Sean seated cross-legged on his bed and Latif in a metal chair at the cell's steel desk, they analyzed predestination, interpreted Muhammad's aphorisms, and studied specific passages from the Koran. "He would ask me: 'What do you want to do? How are you going to grow? How are you going to elevate? And how are you going to allow Islam to help with that?'" Sean said. "'You can become a better young man. You can become a strong young man, and you can pursue your dreams.'" Latif, who was in his early thirties—more than a decade older than Sean—and had been incarcerated for far longer, also urged Sean to carefully examine his own life. He pressed him to grapple with why it swerved toward criminality the way it did, and whether the long chain of small and large decisions that led him to that fateful September day could have been broken by greater piety or a stronger grasp of moral righteousness.

Through the framework of repentance and Latif's bracing example, Sean was learning to harness what had long been a paralyzing sense of remorse. Carrying out Islam's injunction to improve all aspects of one's life, he worked out in the gym every day, began studying for his GED, and approached other men who'd also seen their futures razed by gang life. Though his guilt and self-loathing bogged him down like a thick, foggy mire, Sean was determined to make himself a positive figure in an environment that was too often enveloped in an atmosphere of noxious fatalism. His new religion demanded that of him, and Sean was increasingly motivated to live up to the strict expectations of tawba nasuh—to offer charity and aid to others and, in the process, continue his own moral and spiritual reformation. "I deserve to be here, I don't deserve a second chance at freedom, because I took someone's life," Sean remembered thinking. "At the same time, I'm not going to wallow in misery. I'm going to try to do my best to help people who are in here." By the fall of 1992—the end of his third year of incarceration—Sean was walking up to young Black men on the yard, asking them if they had any interests besides gang life, any skills they wanted to improve, or any plans for eventually getting released from prison.

For Sean, there was no recess or crevasse in his life that Islam could not irradiate in instructive light. Nevertheless, each morning was also a struggle to move past the familiar pain. Albert Camus wrote, "One always finds one's burden again," and Sean's continued to creak and sway in his cell like a prodigious rotting tree. Though his alignment with tawba and tutelage under Latif transformed his daily routine and instilled in him a sense of the value of his life, they struggled to budge his deep-seated convictions about the fate he'd sealed for himself. He would spend many more years convinced that he could not possibly be redeemed in this lifetime—that all the self-less good he carried out in prison was serving a final purpose and judgment that would be realized only after death. It was a deep but narrow comfort, a self-imposed narrative that imbued his actions with spiritual significance without promising that they would ever absolve his mortal guilt. "I wanted to do good where it could be re-corded for the afterlife, and not this life," Sean said. "Because I felt like I messed up so much in this life, that my only shot at a good life was the afterlife."

ISLAM IS HARDLY the only religion that offers adherents the spiritual wisdom and insight to cope with misfortune. One could argue that our major religions' doctrines and dogmas for working through our most profound trials are among the chief reasons belief systems like them have been around for nearly as long as misfortune itself. Few of them, though, are as intent as Christianity on serving as a prism for refracting hardship and suffering. The religion's narratives, tenets, animating figures, and most zealous followers have long intimated that our suffering has significance, and that significance—while mysterious and perhaps ineffable—may be approximate to truth, beauty, divinity, and redemption. (Recall the protagonist in *Kudos,* combing over her vague intuitions about how suffering "car-ried a kind of honor, if you survived it, and left you in a relationship to the truth that seemed closer.")

Christianity formed itself, after all, around the story of a man who surrendered himself to torture and crucifixion because he be-lieved it would redeem the whole of humankind and presage his own divine exaltation. For Christ, suffering was the path to every-thing his life was predestined for, and his narrative suggests that there is only a delicate membrane separating our agonizing hard-ships from the glory of our greater purpose. The art that Christian-ity has inspired—soaring ceiling frescoes, rapturously colored stained glass, and plaintive sculptures that find sublime folds in the

drapery of grief—attests to the religion's power to ignite imaginations in the face of life's wrenching heartbreaks. Few human projects have been more consistently, ardently focused on the aesthetics
and glorification of pain, affliction, and irremediable loss. From the
gold-suffused Byzantine mosaics to the inimitable masterpieces of
the Italian Renaissance, Christian art has long used Christ to en-
noble suffering and even sanctify it, painting a refulgent halo atop a
messiah whose torment changed the course of human history. For
the artists, priests, and hundreds of millions of inspired followers,
Christ's crucifixion—and the harrowing ordeals of the faith-seized
martyrs whose plights echoed his—stands as a testament to the way
our bitter desolations are but one face of a two-sided coin, heralding
rapture and salvation.

In the wake of life-altering catastrophe, many of America's 170
million Christians—around 65 percent of the country's adult
population—lean on their faith. They draw peace and comfort from
kneeling in the nave pews, contemplating the crosses in the church
and the crucifix suspended over the sanctuary. There's something
sustaining and even cathartic in the way Christianity portrays and
interprets suffering, and for centuries it has been vital to the religion's captivating power. But what exactly are people drawing from
the images, scenes, and narratives that make up Christianity's affecting iconography and never-ending Via Dolorosa?

Christianity invokes the word "passion" more than any other existing major religion. There is, most famously and canonically, the
Passion of Christ—Jesus's final days on earth, punctuated by his
trial, execution, burial, and resurrection. But the religion also cele-
brates the passion of its saints and martyrs, those devotees who
were willing to sacrifice themselves and withstand poverty, perse-
cution, and torture rather than renounce their sacred spiritual beliefs. The English word "passion" comes from the Latin noun
passio, which translates to "suffering" or "enduring," and the verb
patoir, meaning "to suffer, bear, or endure." Passion and suffering,
that is, share a common etymological root system; one might even
say that they're branches growing from the same tree. While the

two words diverged over the past few centuries, through the vessel of Christianity they've maintained a vivid, illuminating intimacy.

Christ and the martyrs who succeeded him were always suffering *for something*—their suffering was replete with meaning, because it was endured for the sake of their love and devotion to their savior, their faith, their God. Though the term "passion" still technically translated to "suffering" or "enduring" through much of the Middle Ages, in the context of Christianity's dramatic narratives it grew more nuanced and rarefied: To have passion was to suffer for your cause, to suffer for that which you love.

People enduring catastrophe find vitalizing solace in Christianity and its central figure because they embody this union of passion and suffering. The religion shows its followers that their adversities are not fruitless crucibles devoid of meaning—they are, rather, inextricably bound to their deepest purpose and the noblest aspects of their being, reminding them that they are always suffering *for*. The religion's elegiac tableaux continuously bring this relationship to the fore. The stations of the cross, the seven sorrows of the Virgin Mary, the mythologized rack and ruin of the saints and martyrs: All enact the idea that our suffering and our sense of passion and purpose can't be separated from one another. To have a passion at all—spiritual or otherwise—one need have suffered for it.

The narrative of Jesus Christ himself may be history's most powerful attestation that suffering possesses meaning and power we cannot always see. In his tortured last days—referred to simply as "the Passion"—Christ's agony and doubt are unified with his self-proclaimed destiny, and the result of that coalescence permanently reorganized human civilization and the world. Without his crucifixion, there would be no resurrection from the tomb, no redemption of humankind, no Christian faith at all. When Christians meditate on his narrative and the righteousness, atonement, and transformational power it invokes, they elevate their own adversities by affirming similar bonds. And when they gaze solemnly over the paintings, rituals, and holy pageantry glorifying Christ's trials, that ennobling reverence is quietly transferred to their own. It is a two-step vicariousness—the Christian lives through Christ, who then lives through him—whose deep catharsis can be its own quiet, mollifying salvation.

JASON'S FIRST YEAR at Somerset passed with the slowness and inexorability of a melting glacier, the thick blue ice of each day seemingly unconquerable until it ripped free and drifted into the surrounding ocean. There were precious few landmarks in prison's vast open water, a place where holidays only highlighted men's erasure from the outside world, birthdays signified even less, and the best way to cushion yourself against time's lassitude was to burrow into a routine until you lost sight of its passage. For a while, that's what the onetime addict and Florida native attempted to do. "I was going to Catholic mass, doing crossword puzzles, and working out constantly," Jason said. "That was the extent of my existence."

But after the incident in the sally port, which he passed through to reach the gym, Jason stopped working out for a while. Seeing that kind of human carnage up close—one of the combatants had a laceration over his cheek that you could reach two fingers into—left Jason distressed in a way few previous encounters with violence ever had. The jolting lightning strike of the attack, and the cascading helplessness he felt as it electrified into further bloodshed before him, embedded itself beneath his conscious thoughts. He had no way of knowing whether the brutality he'd witnessed might one day explode in his direction, leaving him wounded, disfigured, or worse. The perpetual state of high tension was leaving him ravaged by toxic stress.

As 2006 progressed, Jason leaned more and more on his Christian faith. He'd mostly taken the religion for granted during his childhood and adolescence, but now the words of Christ and his apostles—along with the assuaging ritual of mass—were the pillars keeping him together. Some of Christianity's subtler implications about human life's crucibles were also resonating with him more powerfully than ever before. "Christianity is full of these themes of purity through suffering," Jason said. "There are these stories of people wandering in the desert, people misunderstood, people being persecuted and suffering. I didn't think I was innocent or anything, but the trials and tribulations, and these things being tests by God—it's a nice spin to put on it." The New Testament, meanwhile, often spoke directly to the state of incarceration. "Christianity is filled with people in jail, filled with people under suffering and bondage," he said. "It made you focus on the eternal rather than the temporary suffering you were going through." He found an "element of freedom to it. This temporary suffering's okay, because Jesus was purified through his suffering, and the saints are purified through their suffering."

Somerset staff had supplied Jason with a copy of the Bible when he'd arrived there—a King James Version with a navy-blue jacket and white lettering—and he spent much of his free time reading scripture in his cell. He also started attending the prison's Bible study, held every Wednesday in a small classroom with glass walls that was attached to the prison chapel. A stout, scrappy-looking Italian deacon in his fifties headed the meetings, driving up from Pittsburgh to lead open-ended discussions centered on the life of Christ and the stories in the gospels. Each week after class, Jason walked up to the deacon and posed theological questions to him—probing Christ's parables, questioning the Old Testament God's capricious violence, examining the relationship between sin and salvation.

Jason's hunger to reclaim a Christian faith that had lapsed into indifference didn't stop at the Bible. He also began reading first-person accounts from some of the religion's most revered figures. Many of these hallowed disciples, he observed, recounted a supernatural experience that solidified their faith: Saul of Tarsus walking on the road to Damascus, stunned by a blinding light and Christ's pained lamentation. Saint Augustine pacing in his garden, hearing a cherubic child enjoining him to "take up and read, take up and read." Joan of Arc wandering a plot of earth in rural France, stumbling onto a dazzling vision of the archangel Michael delivering her divine purpose. Initially, Jason was moved by these mystical accounts of imperfect, even misguided people and their ascendance to inviolable belief. But when he continued reflecting on their lives, something else kept bubbling to the surface of his mind—how different they were from his. He couldn't square how he was expected to aspire toward the piety of saints and martyrs who were galvanized by a religious experience he'd never come close to having. "They're only who they are because they had this magical experience—they weren't this before," Jason said. "How am I supposed to have that degree of faith, to please God, Jesus? How am I supposed to achieve that when I haven't had the same shared experience?"

When he posed these questions to the deacon, the man never provided Jason with a satisfying answer. Instead, he grew visibly perturbed, countering impatiently that Jason needed to simply "have faith." The fact that these Christian luminaries—men and women he was supposed to see as inspiring examples of transformational belief—attained their faith through supernatural revelations the vast majority of Christians would never experience stuck itself in Jason's craw. Over time, it threw the entire concept of faith into question for him. If the religion's most exalted adherents went through these celestial experiences to crystallize their belief, why was everyone else expected to find the same degree of conviction without the same level of substantiation? Was it still faith when it was supported through divine proof? "That was the first crack," Jason said.

Leafing through the Bible, Jason applied an increasingly rigorous eye to its individual episodes and how they related to the work as a whole. He started to recognize inconsistencies—episodes when the commandments were temporarily thrown out the window, for example—and questioned some of the gospels' more overtly preternatural moments. As his skepticism grew, he asked himself more fundamental questions about his spirituality, including why he subscribed to Christianity in the first place. The answer was simple: It was because his parents did, his extended family did, and "when all the adults around you believe in God, you don't question that," he said.

By the fall, Jason still considered himself a Christian, but he'd grown far more ambivalent about the nature of faith and the moral rectitude of a wrathful, impetuous God. The following spring, he took a college correspondence course on Western civilization through Louisiana State University. The survey class covered ancient societies beginning in Mesopotamia and going through the Middle Ages. It placed a special focus on Christianity, showing the growth and evolution of the religion in a sociopolitical light Jason had never seen before. The course's textbook detailed how it wasn't an omnipotent God but a Roman emperor who determined what made the final cut of the New Testament. Jason was in disbelief. "These gospels were selected to retain and enforce the power of the emperor," he recalled thinking. "Regardless of spirituality, the final product was constructed for a political purpose." The religion's supposedly holy, word-of-God texts were actually the work of shrewd editing, carefully curated to help rulers control their subjects. The course seemed to be validating Jason's increasing skepticism, and he felt like he was experiencing a reverse revelation, the scandalous inverse of what those elevated saints and apostles encountered to solidify their belief. The lessons were exposing the seams behind what he'd long regarded as unassailable theology. Instead of being derived from divine authority, the Bible was the result of canny machinations that sought to manipulate the masses and guide them toward a life of meekness and subservience. "I had taken a clinical view of it," Jason said, "and it was disturbing."

After Jason finished the correspondence course, he asked his mother to send him an Oxford annotated edition of the Bible. He was determined to keep following the lines of inquiry the college material had opened for him until they led him somewhere conclusive and final. He needed to know, once and for all, whether or not he believed in God, in life after death, and in everything else the religion—which had come to mean so much to him—unequivocally espoused. With each passing week, the stakes ratcheted higher. "Once the seed had been planted in my head, that there is a very serious possibility that you have been wrong your entire life, and everybody else that believes this is wrong also, I had to find out," he said. "I thought it was the most important question of being a human, and I had to answer it for myself."

The Oxford Bible delivered the final blow to Jason's belief. Religious scholars provided detailed context before each book, and it reinforced everything he'd learned in the Louisiana State course. For him, the text's divine authority was finally undone, its halo of infallibility dismantled for good. Once it lost its patina as the word of God, many of the stories and events Jason had passively subscribed to now strained credulity. In some cases, they appeared outright fantastical. In a last-ditch effort to salvage his moribund faith, Jason scoured the Bible and any other Christian texts he could find for concrete evidence of God's existence. But he turned up nothing; the dissolution of his belief was complete. After months of searching and doubt, the final confirmation led him to a chilling conclusion: There's no God, which means there's no afterlife, which means that when you die, "it's just lights out," he said.

Jason's loss of faith struck him like an affliction. Christianity was perhaps the last safe harbor he had; without it, he was left even more distressed by his shameful past, bleak present, and opaque future. He stopped attending mass and Bible study, turned away from his religious texts, and quit asking theological questions. The disillusionment was so excruciating that it seemed to trigger a somatic response, sending him spiraling through successive bouts of physical illness. He suffered headaches, vomiting, even an ulcer that needed to be treated at the prison infirmary. "There was a good four months where I just shut down," Jason said. The idea of mortality—which took on a sharper edge after all the violence he'd witnessed at Somerset—had for him been robbed of its glittering implications, the promise of eternity wrenched away. What remained was stark and frightening. "It doesn't matter what the fuck you do," Jason said. "There's no goddamn redemption, there's no punishment. It's just lights out like when you go to sleep . . . lights out like before you were born."

In the midst of his harrowing disaffection, Jason wandered into

Somerset's library. A dim, pungent space, it was filled with waist-high stacks and lined with barred windows. Scanning a section on philosophy, he ran his eyes over an introductory text on existentialism. Taking it back to his cell, he opened the book and began reading about a philosophy he had only the vaguest conceptions of. He was desperate, prepared to grasp onto anything that might fill the portentous void inside himself. As he read, he became more and more intrigued by the text's organizing idea: the individual's quest for meaning and purpose in a cold, disorienting world. Here, he felt, was a perspective that fearlessly probed the essence of our existence after it had been shucked of religion's comforting sheath.

In the weeks that followed, Jason returned to the library and rented out works by Kierkegaard, Kafka, and Camus. He found that these European philosophers were speaking to him in a tone and register that felt forceful and even intimate, as though they were cornering him in silent confrontation. He was astonished to find, further, that works like *The Plague*, *The Stranger*, and *The Trial* resonated so closely with his specific circumstances. Those novels ushered readers into spare, alienating worlds shorn of detail but pregnant with suppressed emotion. To Jason, their austere atmospheres bore an uncanny resemblance to his own incarcerated life. "In most existential literature and some of the fiction that they wrote, it's always a simplified version of reality," Jason said. "Prison is like that, though, because so much of the world is stripped away." What remained was "this super, super reduced existence, down to the bare bones of what it is to be human."

He'd found a foothold in something, gained purchase in a hazy frontier whose trenchant metaphysical insights seemed to reflect and speak to his intellectual growth. Though he wasn't sure where it was leading him, he knew he needed it. When he renounced his belief in God, it desolated the final remnants of the person who turned himself in to police in November 2004. These philosophers were showing him a way out of the blasted ruins of those toppled certainties. As winter fell on the Laurel Highlands and Jason's third year at Somerset came to a close, he spent hours each day sitting with his legs crossed on his cell's bottom bunk, chewing over dense concepts like being, freedom, and the absurd. He read and reflected with a solemn guilelessness that could be called innocence, as though he were the first person to ever encounter these ideas and arguments. Over time, his fraught literary pilgrimage shifted something inside of him. Jason resolved that he would never blindly subscribe to anything again. From now on, he thought, his beliefs must be rooted in his perception and not his proximity.

During one of his regular trips to the library, Jason spotted *The Gay Science,* Nietzsche's 1882 collection of essays, poems, and polemics. He would come to find that reading Nietzsche was like running into the prophet just after the prophecy had been fulfilled. The philosopher's views on Christianity, his fearless deconstruction of its laws and tenets, vindicated Jason's searing estrangement from the Catholic faith. He finally understood that he was not the first person to carefully examine his religion and be forced down the anguishing path to nonbelief. "These are old ideas, and old pains," he thought. "Other people have felt this and gone through it." Nietzsche provided more than just the comfort of a fellow atheist, however. He would also be the thinker most responsible for revealing to Jason the blueprint for living in a godless world.

As he read *The Gay Science,* Jason eventually encountered Nietzsche's formulation of the eternal recurrence for the first time. In it, the philosopher sketches a supernatural scenario with weighty existential implications: "What if some day or night a demon were to steal after you into your loneliest loneliness and say to you: 'This life as you now live it and have lived it, you will have to live once more and innumerable times more.'" How would you respond? "Would you not throw yourself down and gnash your teeth and curse the demon who spoke thus? Or have you once experienced a tremendous moment when you would have answered him: 'You are a god and never have I heard anything more divine.'"

For Jason, the demon's proposal struck a plangent chord—or, to borrow from Kafka, was like "an axe for the frozen sea within us." It framed the way he'd been leading his life up to that point in the baldest terms possible. "Are you happy with these choices that you're making?" he asked himself. "Is this something you'd be okay with for eternity?" He knew the answer; perhaps he'd always known the answer. This was the first time in his life, though, that he'd been prompted to forthrightly ask the question.

Jason saw Nietzsche's eternal recurrence cutting two ways. Yes, the demon made it incontrovertibly clear to him that he would not want his life replayed for him on endless repeat, as it had been largely an ignominious one, defined by selfishness and apathy. But it also revealed to him something nothing else in his thirty years on earth had been able to: the notion of absolute, unfettered agency. "I did this," he thought. "There's no other forces pushing me into this. I can't blame Satan for making me a sinner." For him, the implications of Nietzsche's demon at the level of his own accountability were nothing short of monumental. "You're left with supreme responsibility," he said. "Way more responsibility than the court could ever have put on you, than your family sobbing over what's happened could put on you."

Incarceration had dispossessed Jason of his previous life and the persona that stood at its helm, peeling away an identity built on getting fucked up and flippantly dismissing everything else. Now his imprisonment was sending him on a private inquisition, one whose questions and answers might eventually lay the groundwork for a different sort of character. "I didn't ever want to go back to that person that came in," he remembered. "That person was largely dead. But I was in some weird limbo state between not being that person and being this person I didn't understand."

WHILE INCARCERATION PUSHED Sean toward religion and led Jason away from it, they were both searching for ways to interpret their afterlives and find the courage to look toward their futures. They were telling themselves stories not just in order to live, but in order to replace the identities they no longer wanted to define them.

Periods of ceaseless searching—and the stretches of contemplative solitude they inspire—often lead individuals to the first glimpses of a more permanent way of seeing themselves. In the years after catastrophe, many people seek out ways to reframe the diminishment they've experienced, to compensate for what's been lost by reimagining the story of their lives. This might begin with the perception that they've grown stronger from their adversities; over time, though, the process evolves into a more intimate and subjective project: making meaning. One person might center herself around the conviction that her traumatic injury paved the way for a more compassionate character to emerge; another may come to see his racking bereavement as the seed that bloomed the passionate activist he would one day become.

This meaning-making process is often realized through the construction of what psychologists call narrative identities—the stories we craft and subscribe to about the trajectory of our lives. Dan P. McAdams, a psychologist at Northwestern University and perhaps the foremost scholar on narrative identity, has defined the phenomenon as "the internalized and evolving story of the self that a person constructs to make sense and meaning out of his or her life." This story, he continues, "is a selective reconstruction of the autobiographical past and a narrative anticipation of the imagined future that serves to explain, for the self and others, how the person came to be and where his or her life may be going."

By developing narrative identities, we are synthesizing our lives' loose collections of partly remembered facts, anecdotes, successes, and failures into something cohesive and replete with thematic meaning. Rarely acknowledged aloud, narrative identity is a gauzy film, draped over a consciousness whose moods, mien, and grasp of events are often colored by it. At once omnipresent and exquisitely subtle, it operates beneath the level of language but is frequently revealed by it. When someone mutters, with rueful sarcasm, that a stroke of bad luck or an unintended blunder is "the story of my life," they're inadvertently gesturing toward the way they've constructed their narrative identity. A friend whose stories all seem to adopt the

same self-aggrandizing framework and climax—they face an un-
foreseen predicament, then courageously resolve it—is reflecting
theirs. "Over developmental time," McAdams writes, "selves create
stories, which in turn create selves."

Narrative identities range from arcs that illustrate how a person
rose above a hardscrabble background or formidable life challenge
to achieve great things (known as the agency or mastery narrative)
to how they overcame their mistakes and wayward choices to
achieve stability and self-betterment (the redemption narrative) or
were victimized by pernicious forces outside their control, resulting
in their failure, degradation, or downfall (the contamination narrative). Psychology researchers use these categories and several others to classify how we conceptualize the story of our lives—the
decades-long process we undertake to flesh out who we believe ourselves to be. While their work has found that people typically begin
developing narrative identities in late adolescence or early adulthood, catastrophic life events can rupture those identities and leave
us bereft of the underlying chronicles we were crafting. As a result,
many people leading afterlives are forced to rebuild narrative identities that no longer match the external circumstances of their lives.
Like astronomers gazing up at a conspicuously altered night sky,
they must devise a novel constellation—one that salvages some
points from the old clusters while also incorporating a blazing new-
born star.

Humans have an instinct, an adaptive response likely forged long
ago, to extract some kind of deeper value or importance from their
most challenging experiences. "We love finding meaning," Sophie
told me during one of our conversations. "We're just trying to create
meaning. We're trying to create a narrative that we can understand
and that sits right. And that might not be the truth—and that's okay.
That's just how it is." When catastrophes cleave our lives apart, in
order to restore purpose and cohesion we need to stitch our stories
back together with a new through line. I've found that many people
leading afterlives have a potent, galvanizing relationship with their

narrative identities, drawing on them to imbue a sense of redemptive purpose to what are otherwise senseless tragedies and traumas.

"Exploratory narrative processing"—a mouthful of a category that describes how a person thoughtfully examines their identity and subsequently expands self-understanding—may take root in minds that were not fertile soil for it prior to catastrophe. In the aftermath of a paralyzing spinal cord injury, subscribing to themes of agency and self-mastery can be a rousing schema, shifting the focus from loss to transformation and renewal. And individuals living under incarceration often embrace a redemption narrative that weaves together the person who committed the crime with the individual being punished for it and the one who'll one day be released. The framework of redemption lends a wonderful cohesion to their lives, giving them permission to change who they were without banishing that person forever.

Indiscriminate loss and abasement are not plot points that endear themselves to us—not in our art and our fiction, and not in the vicissitudes of our own lives. No matter how coldly logical or secular we believe ourselves to be, how thoroughly we've surrendered to the haphazard forces of the universe, we persist in asking "Why?" The question is as existentially vital as Hamlet's "To be, or not to be"—the need to understand, in our own carefully constructed way, "the slings and arrows of outrageous fortune." In many cases, the answer to our appeals is embodied in our narrative identities.

When animated by catastrophic life events, they can become more specific versions of Nietzsche's aphorism: What doesn't kill me redeems me, illuminates me, drives me to seize control over my impossibly precious fate. While the philosopher's valiant but specious maxim has always been itself a kind of narrative identity—at least for me personally—these are equally compelling, and less convoluted, alternatives.

Conceiving of a narrative identity in the wake of catastrophe is, however, only the first step in a longer metamorphosis. People leading afterlives must "tell themselves stories in order to live," but they must also go about the private, demanding labors of making those stories true. They must live the narrative they choose until it becomes indistinguishable from their everyday reality.

AFTER A LONELY, punishing gap year focused on regaining her physical sensation and strength, in the summer of 2010, Valerie—the Stuyvesant grad in a van accident two years earlier—prepared to return to school. By late August, she would officially be a first-year student at Harvard College, the only wheelchair user in a class of 1,734 students. (Though approximately 1 percent of the U.S. population uses a wheelchair, she represented just 0.06 percent of that group.) Valerie obtained permission from the school's disabilities services office to move onto campus two days before her peers—allowing her the vital accessibility support she needed—and she and her parents spent several days packing the family's taupe-colored Toyota Camry full of clothes, books, snacks, and medical equipment. A family friend offered to join the trek to Massachusetts in his minivan, providing the trunk space required to house Valerie's unwieldy standing frame and an old wooden coffee table her parents insisted on off-loading to her.

On a muggy, overcast morning in August's waning summer days, Valerie wheeled herself over the ramp leading out to her family's driveway, past the small rectangular garden where her parents planted tomatoes and arugula, onto the warming Brooklyn asphalt, and into the packed sedan to set out for her first year at Harvard. It was a four-and-a-half-hour drive from the Piros' home in Bay Ridge, Brooklyn, to Cambridge, where Harvard's campus stood, and heavy, thwacking sheets of summer rain battered the windshields as they rode along the Long Island Sound. They carved through the quiet rustic towns that peppered central Connecticut, turning east along the Massachusetts Turnpike before arriving at the elegantly filigreed wrought iron gate that signaled the main entrance to the fabled campus.

Valerie would be living on the second floor of an accessible first-year dormitory named Thayer, a five-story redbrick building constructed in the Georgian style ubiquitous on Harvard Yard. (Thayer was one of only two first-year dorms with elevators.) Once Valerie and her parents finished unpacking everything and setting up her room, her parents drove to a nearby hotel. Two days later, the rest of her class's student body descended on the campus, droves of teenagers and their families fanning out into the dormitories and surrounding grounds. From her single-person dorm room, Valerie listened tentatively as peers and their families bustled into Thayer. She overheard the rapid footfalls, the spurts of laughter, the voices shot through with the unmistakable collision of anxiety and exuberance. It bore all the tender, tottering characteristics of those lustrous threshold days that marked the first words of the first sentence of the first page of a new chapter of life. All afternoon, Valerie could feel the weight of the day zipping around her. She wondered, nervously, whether she should put herself out there, make herself a part of what felt like a consequential, formative moment.

Valerie felt a lot of pressure to make a good first impression. Though she'd moved in days earlier, she didn't want to squander those fraught, fleeting hours whose chance encounters and cursory conversations held an outsize importance that would reverberate through the rest of the semester. Her senior year at Stuyvesant had taught her how much of a distraction her wheelchair could be for nondisabled adolescents, and she wanted to make sure her warm, wry personality was not prematurely supplanted by it. When she tried introducing herself to a neighbor who lived next door, though, she felt ignored. She struggled to synchronize herself to the social rhythms thrumming around her, and observed silently as the other first-years in Thayer formed what she perceived to be bonds that would only take deeper root in the weeks to come. "Part of my brain just immediately felt like 'Everyone's already making friends,'" Valerie said. She asked herself how she could have possibly become excluded so quickly. The sense of glaring social isolation, of being both immersed in a vibrant milieu and secluded from it, immediately evoked memories of her senior year. "I think high school made me hyperaware, to the point of mild paranoia, that it could happen again."

By the late afternoon, Valerie's wary enthusiasm about a rejuvenated social life at Harvard had clattered to the ground. In its place was a sense of lumbering dread that the loneliness of her last two years had already resurfaced, infiltrating the manicured greens and painted spires of her new college campus. Sitting in her room with her parents later that day, she pleaded with them to take her home. "This is going to be high school all over again," she lamented. "I want to go back to Bay Ridge." But they gently refused, telling Valerie not to worry so much about the first day. Things were sure to get better, they promised. She didn't entirely believe them, but she didn't force the issue, either. Much of her adolescence up to that point—study sessions on the train, writing marathons in her room, SAT practice exams at the hospital—had been a vehicle for reaching this rarefied echelon. Retreating now would be a failure to live up to, perhaps even a renunciation of, the girl whose work ethic earned her admission into the best college in the country. She was meant to be here, and there was simply no turning back.

During her first week on the Harvard campus, Valerie left the door to her dorm room open all day, so other first-years could wander in whenever they pleased. Eventually, she started establishing herself within Thayer's fledgling ecosystem, developing acquaintances that nodded toward more lasting friendships. Move-in day notwithstanding, Valerie's Harvard classmates proved to be warmer than Stuyvesant's teenage cliques. And when classes started a week later, she shifted naturally into the familiar, exacting grooves that had long characterized her academic life. She began the process of sublimating her time, energy, and cognitive space to learning each class's material, plowing forward with the unfussy, self-effacing tenacity that prized intellectual work for its own sake.

In early September, Valerie participated in something called shopping week, a Harvard tradition where students sit in on different courses before finalizing their schedule for the semester. On her way to the mailroom, she spotted a flyer for a survey course on medieval history. Having been a longtime fan of the Monty Python movies—and intrigued by an era in human history she felt was always being mythologized or lampooned but almost never captured with historical accuracy—she decided to give it a try. An ebullient professor named Michael McCormick taught the class. "He had ridiculously high expectations for everyone's work," Valerie remembered. "I found that so refreshing, because when I was in high school, after my injury, some teachers were asking, 'Oh, do we need to lighten the course load? Can she handle the course load?'"

When Valerie's teachers at Stuyvesant lowered their expectations for her, the shift had left her demoralized. "I'm just like every other student in the class," she remembered thinking, "except I might have a slightly more masochistic work ethic." This graying, hawk-nosed medieval history professor, who lectured with the velocity of a bullet train and vibrated enthusiasm with his roving eyes and sharp, emphatic gestures, treated her like any other undergraduate. "I wanted to put in the effort that I knew I was capable of," she said. In McCormick's class, she remembered, "I felt like I was a real student."

Though Valerie eagerly took to her first semester's classes, she also learned that academic life at Harvard would be starkly different from her years at Stuyvesant. She no longer had the freedom to surrender all her free time to coursework when she felt classes required it, as she so often did before her injury. At least three days a week, she rode the functional electrical stimulation bike she'd set up in her room. The process of applying electrodes to her legs, attaching her wheelchair to the bike, and cycling for the prescribed time took three full hours. She spent another hour every night in her standing frame, a large metal apparatus that holds wheelchair users in a standing position to help them retain bone density and improve range of motion. In total, Valerie committed over sixteen hours a week to the ongoing rehabilitation that kept up her health and staved off complications that could land her in the hospital. In line with her continuing efforts to maintain a neutral, self-possessed outlook on her injury, Valerie equated her obligations to Harvard's student athletes'. "They have to get up early, they have to go to practice," she said. "The only difference is they get teammates."

The following semester, Valerie took a second class with McCormick, a challenging research seminar focused on the period immediately following the fall of the Roman Empire. The medieval course was geared toward upperclassmen, and Valerie was one of only two first-years enrolled. Though daunted by the more experienced students, she was also thrilled by the "adrenaline rush" of being in an advanced seminar. Learning more and more about medieval history and the patience, rigor, and industriousness required by scholars to excavate and illuminate it, her ardor for the subject blossomed. She became friendlier with McCormick, and over the spring semester, she began seeking him out after class and during his office hours. Sensing her uncommon fervency for medieval history, McCormick started recommending books to Valerie—hardbound texts with thick, rounded spines and affectless titles that might help her better understand the era's sprawling panoply of hell visions, barbarian law codes, and religious inquisitions.

That spring, Valerie became increasingly captivated by medieval history and its idiosyncratic intellectual demands. Above all else, it seemed, being a medieval scholar required a willingness to plow into dense thickets of text and bushwhack through obscure manuscripts, exhaustive footnotes, and dead languages for extremely minute, fine-grain discoveries. But it also demanded an enterprising imagination, one willing to fathom not just the grandiosities and caricatures of the so-called Dark Ages but also the nuanced dynamics of class, religion, and politics that undergirded the period. The field's boundless esotericism, she grew to understand, was not an indulged quirk but its raison d'être, the riverhead for so much of the zeal and fervency that flowed through medieval history departments. Valerie delighted in immersing herself in the layered textures of societies and civilizations that rose and fell many centuries ago. The Middle Ages felt to her both familiar and exotic, fantastical in their tableaux and the figures that landscaped them but recognizable in the central forces roiling underneath—patriarchies and power struggles, corruption and immiseration, the demands of faith and the snarling moral contradictions of the churches and clergymen that imposed them.

Whenever McCormick recommended specific books to Valerie, she'd head to Widener, the campus's main library, wheeling herself along the smooth asphalt pathways of Harvard Yard. Because Widener Library's white-columned, Romanesque front entrance is not ADA accessible, Valerie always wheeled into the building through the more mundane back doors. After riding two elevators to the upper stacks, she quietly traversed the aisles, procured the suggested texts, and took another elevator down to the circulation desk to check out the pile of door-stopping books teetering on her lap. She loved the feeling of independence that researching gave her, the internal validation that she was succeeding at something on a very high level and meeting the lofty expectations she continued to hold for herself. "This is really difficult and I'm doing it," Valerie recalled thinking. By the end of her first year, she "just fell in love with the process" of diving into different medieval eras. Holding her breath for as long as she could, she always tried to return to the surface with some glimmering, as-yet-undiscovered fragment of the deep past, a jigsaw piece that could be snapped into a much larger puzzle to provide a fuller, more layered portrait of human existence across time.

Valerie had spent much of her adolescence as an academic overachiever, committed to poring through textbooks, absorbing facts, laws, and concepts, and performing her knowledge on papers and exams. While her burgeoning interest in medieval history was clearly a continuation of that scholastic ambition, it also represented a purer, less goal-oriented pursuit of knowledge. As a high schooler, her work ethic was largely driven by a desire to live up to the lofty expectations so many students in Stuyvesant's competitive atmosphere internalized. Though Valerie was still motivated to earn high marks, her captivation with medieval studies was less attached to that culture of achievement, outcome, and results. Instead, it seemed to stem from a part of her that loved history as an end unto itself and drew a distinctive pleasure in submerging herself in it. The field was certainly reaffirming her talents as a student, but it was also providing something arguably even more vital, something she didn't know she was searching for: an anchoring force, a stabilizing sense of purpose. In a narrative stippled with uncertainties, her discovery of medieval history spoke emphatically to how the passion for knowledge that had spurred her academic success could also spawn its own fulfilling and novel identity.

Though exhilarated by the possibilities of scholarship, Valerie struggled in other ways during her first year at Harvard. There was not just her schoolwork and medical obligations to think about: She was a first-year college student, after all, and neglecting a social life could leave her wrestling with the same racking solitude that had plagued her senior year at Stuyvesant. But mustering the time and energy for all three was a stressful, depleting prospect, and stretching herself too thin carried serious health risks. Striking the right lifestyle balance felt all but impossible; one pursuit always needed to be sacrificed at the altar of another.

On at least three mornings a week, Valerie woke up at six A.M. so she could spend several hours on the FES cycle before setting off for the day. (When she had morning courses—which she tried assiduously to avoid—she needed to wake up at four-thirty.) By the time classes were finished, in the late afternoon, she was spent. But she would never lose sight of her therapy's critical, even dire importance. Her morning-spanning ritual—which cost her so much precious time—was the price of her survival. Valerie would not loosen the talon-tight grip she had on her studies, either. Academics had been the crux of her identity for as long as she could remember. For all the ways her spinal cord injury had cleaved her life apart, school was an irreplaceable through line that preserved cohesion. Socializing would always have to come behind that, too.

Valerie's first year at Harvard marked the beginning of what would become a lasting dynamic. To flourish in her academic career and continue regaining the sensation she'd lost to her spinal cord injury, steep sacrifices were required in other parts of her life. Recognizing this in her discreet, matter-of-fact way, she started to embrace the narrowed scope many of her nondisabled peers would have lamented.

Though Valerie cultivated friendships and valued them dearly, she rarely went to larger social gatherings and didn't attend a single party during her first year. "There was no time," she recalled. Weekends were opportunities to wade through as much reading as possible, lightening the forthcoming week's load. Dating happened in another universe—a parallel one that engulfed but did not include her. Just twenty years old, she was beginning to navigate the intricate ledger of trade-offs many of us are forced to confront much later into our adulthoods. Valerie needed to cash in more time, effort, and mental bandwidth than her nondisabled peers to make the gains she wanted as a college student and physically stable adult, and doing so meant letting go of certain recreational pursuits.

By the end of her first year at Harvard, Valerie caught the first glimmers of a powerful insight that would point a path forward for years to come: the discipline, commitment, and forbearance she needed to exemplify to manage her disability could also serve as the core principles for her nascent identity as an academic. If she could master those traits over time, she'd be able to progress, or at least hold her ground, on both fronts. Without being fully aware of it, Valerie began fostering a single persona—deepening her wherewithal and honing her most advantageous attributes—for the two preeminent theaters of her life.

PERIODS OF SEEKING in afterlives are not limited to external pursuits for faith, wisdom, or knowledge. In some cases, we plumb our own depths, seeking to interrogate our beliefs about ourselves and the underlying assumptions we've long used to solidify them. The un-

varnished truths we find there are the stuff of our formative deceptions, potsherds that reveal events and eras our self-fashioned
identities were intent on leaving buried forever.

In May of 2016, after a turbulent first year at the University of
Victoria, Sophie took a research position at a neuroscience lab at
McGill University in Montreal. She'd be spending the summer
working as an assistant to several PhD students, behavioral neuro-
scientists in training who were studying memory in the brains of
rats and mice. She sublet a small room in the city's LaSalle borough,
on the second story of an old brick apartment building with slanted
floors. Closing in on two years since her traumatic brain injury, Sophie had regained most of her physical abilities, to the point where
she could not only walk on her own but also hike, bike, and even put
in time at rock climbing gyms. She still struggled at times with her
proprioception at night, but her body's recuperation had largely
gone exceptionally well.

After spending a few days getting situated in Montreal and undergoing training in laboratory procedures and protocol, Sophie
moved into the work routine she would keep throughout the summer. She rode the metro for three stops to McGill, then walked the
half mile or so from the station to the Stewart Biology Building, an
imposing brutalist structure of austere concrete slabs laid over a
steel frame. Inside the neuroscience laboratory there, she prepared
microscope slides, analyzed and recorded data, and occasionally ran
experiments designed by her supervisors.

Although her responsibilities demanded the diligence and attention to detail required by anyone working in a research laboratory,
Sophie soon realized her workload was not nearly as onerous as her
first-year classes had been. For several months, she'd been contemplating the possibility of going off her SSRI, the antidepressant
medication she'd been prescribed nearly a year earlier, when her
anxiety was throttling her waking hours and her brain's dull turbu-
lence refused to let her fall asleep at night. She started wondering
whether her four months working as a research assistant might be
the ideal time to experiment with weaning herself off. If she at-

tempted to go off during the school year, it could trigger insomnia, key up her anxiousness, and leave her with the sharp edges that made her first months at college so nerve shredding. Here at McGill, the stakes were lower. She'd have wider margins to navigate any potential side effects or rebounding symptoms as her brain chemistry gradually shifted back to its pre-medication state. "I just wanted to see," she said. "Because there was a part of me that thought, 'I don't need this anymore. This isn't doing anything anymore.'"

Toward the end of May, Sophie stopped taking her medication. She'd resolved to pay close attention to the effects of deprescribing herself. Within a few days, she noticed herself getting up at five in the morning, unable to fall back asleep. She'd expected her insomnia to return—before she started taking medication, in the fall of 2015, she was barely sleeping at all—and she tried to take the afflictions of wakefulness in stride. When it was still mostly dark in her bedroom and morning light had just begun filtering through her window, she'd get out of bed, grab her journal, and walk to a small park near her apartment building. As dawn unfurled over the grass and trees, she perched herself on a wooden bench and scribbled down her thoughts in a large, leather-bound book. She penned insights, musings, and even diagrams that she felt might illuminate her traumatic brain injury, working to pinpoint how it had shaped her identity over the past two years. Her notes became smeared picture windows into her ongoing preoccupations, panes of fogged glass that revealed a mind grappling with its own mechanics and opacities. Sophie amassed pages and pages of self-documentation, a kaleidoscope of shifting insights into her efforts to decipher her own mercurial identity and the frameworks she used to make sense of it.

But it wasn't just the insomnia that staged a resurgence after Sophie discontinued her medication. Her anxiety ramped up, too, and she began compulsively picking at her skin—a condition called excoriation disorder that's most often seen in individuals with OCD. One minute, she'd be entering her dimly lit bathroom to pee; the next, her face would be pushed up just inches from the mirror, as she moved over each tiny pore with the engrossed precision of a surgeon. The derealization episodes she suffered from during her first year at the University of Victoria also returned. When conversing with anybody she'd met for the first time, she was often struck by the fear that they were figments of her imagination, hallucinations springing from a mind she no longer trusted. Stopping to talk to members of Montreal's homeless population—an example of her post-TBI extroversion—Sophie would find herself questioning the objective reality of their existence: Drifting through the streets and around metro stations and rarely acknowledged by other passersby, she had no proof outside of her own perception that they were actually there.

As if that weren't enough, Sophie's PTSD seemed to be expanding its repertoire, permeating her daily life in insidious new ways. Walking along the street, she'd see somebody in a position of physical vulnerability—a biker cycling alongside traffic or a pedestrian crossing an intersection—and abruptly imagine them suffering a gruesome head injury. Some haywire aspect of her brain was using the material around her to conjure morbid scenarios echoing her trauma. Like spores drifting through a vent, her body's memory of the car accident was leaking into her imagination. Though the microflashbacks, as she called them, were fleeting and easily distinguishable from reality, they remained discomfiting—a sinister reminder of how chance and violence could conspire to barrel into her or anybody else's fragile, oblivious bodies.

Most of these symptoms were not altogether unexpected. Sophie knew the anxiousness and insomnia that terrorized her first months at the University of Victoria would likely boomerang back into her daily life. And her PTSD had always been unpredictable, its intricate web of triggers and responses sensitive to even minor alterations in her environment. But as the extra serotonin floating freely in her brain was flushed out completely, she experienced an effect she hadn't expected: She became more searching and inquisitive. Her thoughts drifted, unbidden, toward weighty questions about the relationship between her traumatic brain injury and her sense of self. She pondered where the boundary lay between former and latter, whose perceptions of that boundary counted the most, and the agency she'd had in becoming the person she was now. "What makes me me? Is it free will or not?" she recalled asking herself. "It was a big rabbit hole."

In a journal entry from July 4, after she'd been off her medication for nearly six weeks, Sophie wrote, "I think that my car accident and subsequent injury led me to define myself as brain-injured. Along with the label came the constraints, the fear of the unknown, the possibility that I am less than who I was." In the same entry, she jotted several definitions of identity, including "a sense of coherence within the self, the world, and those around the self," and "confidence that fluidity of the personality does not mean the destruction of the person every time something changes." The entries spoke to somebody who yearned for the continuity of self that had been wrested from her, while contending with the lingering trauma of having her identity ruptured with such finality two years earlier.

Despite her tribulations, Sophie rarely went a day without traveling to the lab, taking pride in her reputation as a competent, dependable assistant. She also cultivated an active social life, venturing into different corners of Montreal on weekends with roommates and lab colleagues. A typical Saturday might include listening to live music, tracking down restaurants that specialized in the decadent poutine dish the city was famous for, or exploring the latest modern art exhibitions. There was something refreshing—emancipating, even—about being in an unfamiliar city three thousand miles from her home in Victoria. Because none of the acquaintances she'd made in Montreal knew Sophie prior to her brain injury, they weren't constantly comparing her to the baseline of a person who no longer existed. "They just met me there," she said, and the version of Sophie Papp they met that summer "was just normal for them."

During her first two months in Montreal, Sophie decided not to tell anybody she'd met about her brain injury. Her tacit hope was that if she came across as "normal" to others, it might serve as proof for herself that she'd made a thorough recovery. Over time, though, concealing such a defining aspect of her biography made her feel disingenuous, as though she'd secretly crafted a persuasive mask and was donning it every day. "As I made more friends and contacts, I felt like I was hiding something, like I was the elephant in the room," she said.

When Sophie finally started telling some of her new friends about her condition, they registered surprise but didn't seem to view her any differently for it. "They were like, 'Oh, wow, that's an interesting story,' but they didn't realize the impact that it was actively having on my psyche," she said. For her part, Sophie was gratified to hear how successful her concealment had been. Each person that responded to the disclosure of her traumatic brain injury with genuine unbelief was more evidence supporting the case that she was healthy and thriving, in no way notably different from any other twenty-one-year-old. "I was happy that they didn't know, and I thought I was an effective chameleon," she said.

Sophie's perspective on this type of external validation would shift dramatically years later, as she came to better understand her desire to be seen as normal and able-bodied as a manifestation of the ableism that had been embedded in her. Australian disability scholar Fiona Kumari Campbell has defined ableism as "a network of beliefs, processes and practices that produces a particular kind of self and body (the corporeal standard) that is projected as the perfect, species-typical and therefore essential and fully human. Disability, then, is cast as a diminished state of being human." Another definition might be the discrimination, devaluation, or even negation of disabled people, stemming from the underlying belief that able-bodied lives are inherently preferable and superior. It was this rarely stated but omnipresent "network of beliefs" that drove Sophie's decision to present herself in a certain way. Determining whether to conceal or divulge an invisible condition is a serious personal decision, one with weighty consequences for how the world sees you and how you see yourself. Covering up our illnesses and disabilities is a kind of "passing" that, unfortunately, can sometimes confer advantages in an ableist society that rewards conformity. Doing so, however, carries subtle unseen ramifications.

By concealing invisible disabilities from the people around them and the world at large, individuals can inadvertently reinforce and perpetuate the illusion that healthy, able-bodied people predominate in our society and disability is a rare, marginal phenomenon (despite sixty-one million American adults, or over one in four people, having one). This, in turn, strengthens the social force and capital of that ableist perspective and the ideology it generates, increasing the pressure on other people to conceal their invisible disabilities, too. The result is a vicious cycle that upholds a specious status quo, one where individuals with disabilities both visible and invisible—as well as the concept of disability itself—are never integrated into the dominant social and cultural imagination. Instead, they are kept in the conceptual silos that make the collective fantasy of immutable good health and unthreatened ability possible. Such invisible consequences mean the disclosure decision is a uniquely laden one, a choice often determined by whether or not a person has fully acknowledged the reality of disability in themselves.

Over the course of the summer, Sophie sat astride a peculiar dichotomy. In her LaSalle apartment, she was privately navigating a minefield of symptoms from her deprescription, navigating one explosion after another that only she could see. Outside of it, though, she was leading an exuberant social life shot through with the freedom of no longer having to lug around other people's memories of the girl she used to be. Somewhere between those two poles, meanwhile, was an intensifying compulsion to explore the heady predicaments her accident had brought to light.

In her journal, Sophie grappled over and over with the concept of identity, laboring to decipher what it really came down to once you accepted how much a person's personality and character were controlled by chance and circumstance. At the park, on the metro, and in her bed during sleepless nights, she scribbled down her thoughts, examining how others perceived her, how she perceived herself, and whether an authentic, "objective" selfhood even existed somewhere along that murky continuum. For her, people were defined less by a series of neat categories—each one laid squarely on top of the other—than by a heaving, churning chaos, like the ocean. "The tide is always moving, bringing new water, material, and it coincides with the moon," she wrote. "It's relatively stable short-term, even though there is always current, but over a lifetime it can change drastically to house different life-forms." Here, she felt, was the truth about identity: It was fluid, subject to change at any time, less the product of some imperishable internal self than the endless array of natural forces convulsing around it.

There had been an unfathomable aspect to Sophie's injury, an existential absurdity in how she'd been knocked unconscious and awoke, a week later, as a wholly different person. It sounded like an old fairy tale, perhaps a particularly vivid nightmare, but not biographical fact. She was finally reckoning with the powerful feelings such an extreme event evoked, the way it called into question universal axioms about coherent identities and continuous selves that everyone else seemed to unreservedly accept. The more she explored these concepts, the more she felt she was exposing their ephemeral nature and discontinuity, uncloaking the assuaging narratives others subscribed to and draped over more troubling truths. "Based on my model of personality, I am just a jumble of tendencies and perceptions, based on the input I'm given," she wrote.

Over the course of that summer, Sophie also started examining the habitual patterns of thinking that gained such baleful purchase during her first year of college—that her grades were the markers of her intelligence, letters and numbers possessing totemic importance, and that her intelligence was tantamount to her worth as a person. In Montreal, Sophie was attaining a measure of objective distance from that pathological thinking. Her view of what intelligence constituted was, in turn, evolving. In the wake of her accident, she viewed it as something static and fixed, a secret figure that was revealed through test scores, transcripts, and the perceptions of others. Like a price tag attached to a loop of white thread and tucked inside each person, intelligence was the equivalence of worth, and everyone could ultimately be boiled down to it. Sophie had become so enthralled by this definition of intelligence that she searched for its traces and clues everywhere, consumed with the prospect of reaching inside herself and unveiling her own numerical value.

But during that summer's restive nights and pensive strolls through Montreal's parks and ports, Sophie was beginning to see intelligence as something more fluid and subjective. Maybe the trait was not a single nesting doll that Sophie had to retrieve and preserve at all costs. Perhaps there was another variety of intelligence, one less purely quantitative, in her growing ability to navigate all the dolls. If she could relinquish her attachment to that single elusive Matryoshka—the brilliant, idealized Sophie her perfectionism had crystallized in her mind—maybe she'd open herself up to the novel truths and insights her extraordinary existence could yield. That type of wisdom and knowledge might be every bit as valid as her IQ and grade point average.

In August, Sophie's brother, Alex, flew across Canada to spend a few days with her. During a trip to pick up groceries one afternoon, Sophie experienced the most severe episode of derealization she'd ever had—one comparable in kind but far greater in degree than the intrusions she'd been negotiating that summer. After walking to the grocery store, Sophie and Alex split up so they could get through their shopping faster. Once Sophie had finished collecting everything on her list, she started looking for her brother. Circling the store, she scanned aisle after aisle, but she couldn't find him. After several minutes passed, she became unnerved; after several more, she was outright alarmed. Her panic escalated, and she began to question who it was she was actually looking for. Two years of anxiety, delirium, and cognitive dysfunction had eroded her faith in her perception of reality. Pushing her cart through the store, her dusty-blue eyes gripped in a hollow thousand-yard stare, she began doubting whether she had a sibling at all. "I resigned myself to the fact that I have made up my brother's existence in its entirety, and I have just been hallucinating him this entire time," Sophie said. She shuffled into a checkout line, paid for her groceries, and left the store by herself, "convinced that my brother was a made-up figment of my imagination."

The episode was a kind of reverse delusion. Instead of being convinced of the existence of something that wasn't real, Sophie's skepticism toward her own senses caused her to disbelieve in something—or someone—that was. The lack of faith in her perception meant that she was highly susceptible to frightening, hallucinatory experiences in which she became unmoored from her personal history, uprooted from the biographical narrative we all rely on to keep us anchored in reality. "Whatever fundamental trust that most people are born with, and they trust what they see and they trust what they hear, or their smell or emotions," Sophie said, "was destroyed for me in the accident."

By the time she was preparing to return home to Victoria, Sophie had experienced her share of disquieting trials in Montreal. But she'd also started pushing past some of the pernicious pathologies that had dominated her postinjury life. She'd spent four months forming relationships that didn't need to coexist alongside stubborn memories of "old Sophie," and she'd confronted the fraught nexuses between injury and identity and intelligence and self-worth. She was also gradually growing more comfortable with a definition of recovery that exchanged quixotic aspirations of an idealized normalcy for a model where permanent changes coexisted alongside personal growth. Buckled in on the plane, flying over wispy, sundering clouds and a mass of curving rivers, spidery ridgelines, and plots carved in a numberless panoply of geometric shapes that bespoke elegant cohesion while betraying endless instances of fracture, Sophie quietly basked in the warming afterglow of what had been a courageous and rewarding season.

Stories We Tell Ourselves

IN THE FIRST FEW YEARS AFTER I DEVELOPED CHRONIC FATIGUE SYN-
drome, I spent little time thinking about the reason *why* I'd gotten a
serious chronic illness. That is, why, in an existential or metaphysical sense, something like that might have happened to me. The
world didn't need reasons, of course. I knew that. Life consisted of
the cause and effect you could control and the cause and effect you
couldn't, and the first pool was a diminutive speck next to the colossal circumference of the second—a lagoon that emptied into an
ocean. My chronic illness was the random, microscopic collision of
a rogue pathogen, the cells comprising my immune system, and the
twenty thousand or so genes encoded in each of those cells.

There was a matter-of-fact neutrality to my condition. Illness, I
understood, was like the weather, affecting everything and signifying nothing. Mine had taken hold like a drought, and persisted utterly independent of my agency, choices, virtues, or vices. It wasn't
born out of my actions or behavior, and didn't speak to any aspects
of them. However logical this thinking was, though, it was not satisfying. Over time, I felt increasingly compelled to spurn that reasoning and understand my condition through the clarifying lens of
identity and character.

As this tension took stronger hold in my mind, a curious paradox emerged. Though my CFS did not grow out of my constitution or moral fiber, it nevertheless began illuminating something essential regarding my life's arc. I felt I had suffered another in a line of harsh twists of fate—never mind the fact that there was much in my biography that affirmed otherwise. I was gradually flipping the causality in my mind, until CFS no longer seemed to be a random collision at all, but part of a larger pattern that had already embedded itself in the first twenty-six years of my life. My illness was shape-shifting from a cause of my current circumstances to an effect of my long-standing narrative and its animating themes. I was enfolding it into the ever-advancing story I told myself about who I was and how my life was supposed to play out. It was subjective, to be sure, but it was also intimate, galvanizing, in some way imperative. Without this story, I felt, my existence would be stripped of its weight and meaning, reduced to a soap opera in which one convoluted dilemma after another confronted underdeveloped characters for no particular reason at all.

I couldn't accept the premise that CFS was just something that had happened to me, like a flooded basement, a fender-bender, or a turned ankle. Instead of swallowing the bitter pill of scientific materialism—the notion that my circumstances were no more significant than the arrangement of pool balls after the break—I imposed something more cogent and stirring onto them. Following the loss of my mother, and the way it devastated my father in slow, stealthy stages, CFS was another hardship that would both shape and motivate me. Observing peers who, I assumed, had experienced nothing approaching what I'd gone through only bolstered my belief that I needed to be stronger, more determined, able to reinvent my diminishments. I inserted myself into a story about scrabbling toward fulfillment under difficult circumstances and making the most of one's life in the face of loss. I was rebuilding my narrative identity, integrating my chronic illness into the larger drama I'd envisioned about myself. It was a flawed story from an unreliable narrator—incorporating Nietzsche's aphorism and Judeo-Christian views on the nobility of suffering while permitting a certain quantity of self-pity to seep in—but it was who I felt myself to be, the person I believed I amounted to when all things were considered.

In December 2005, seven years before I'd ever heard about CFS, I was home in Connecticut for the holidays. It was winter break at the small northeastern college where I was sputtering through my sophomore year, and I was in my family's unfinished basement after a night of hard drinking. As I tried in vain to fall asleep on our scratchy blue sofa, my silver flip phone started rattling. It was my best friend. When I called him back, he explained that he was having girl problems; he sounded distraught, edging on frantic. We discussed his predicament, pondering what might be done to soothe his teetering emotional state. With the wisdom only an adolescent could apply to such a delicate situation, I concluded that the solution to his heartache was a midnight joyride.

It was late by then, my house silent and the surrounding neighborhood dark and hushed. Having scarcely slept, I remained heavily intoxicated. Nevertheless, I stepped into my 1994 black Acura Integra—its license plate ending in "666"—pulled out of my driveway, and zipped into the night, the rattling snore of my engine and my headlights' cone-shaped beacons texturing the muted darkness.

I picked up my friend at his family's gray colonial a few miles away, and we sped off along the serpentine country roads that carved through the pastoral woods and lawns of our suburban town. My tortured logic that night was to pull him out of his fretting by enveloping ourselves in a sort of fraternal anarchy, a shared oblivion best achieved in the watery depths of the night. Our friendship was built on a sense of deep-seated loyalty, a natural sympathy earned over years of classes, house parties, basketball games, burn rides, teenage brawls, even legal troubles, and it allowed us to venture into dangerous spaces as consummate partners in crime. He trusted me, probably too much, recognizing a fearlessness in me that was likely less honorable than he intuited.

We darted through the moon-bathed back roads, vandalizing mailboxes, driving with the headlights off, screaming into the tree-silhouetted darkness. The object was to vanquish all our juvenile woes and surrender to a kind of devil-may-care madness. Insofar as two privileged white kids with their whole lives ahead of them could have any demons at all, we were conjuring them up and making them flesh.

After an hour or two of mischief, I felt an unaccountable urge to raise the stakes. We were hurtling down the main road that separated our houses, a flat, curveless stretch three miles long lined with neat rows of perfect colonial homes. I announced, apropos of nothing, that I was going to push the gas pedal all the way down, to the car's fabric floor. What was I thinking during that shameful moment? The only explanation I can imagine is that I was an adrenaline junkie with an invincibility complex, a teenager succumbing to a disordered brew of toxic impulses. Driven by the same fatal attraction that pulls people to climb free solo or ride one-ton bulls with skewering horns—and abetted by copious amounts of alcohol—I thirsted to push the outer limits of my hallucinated power.

I looked over at my friend to gauge his feelings. I can't recall exactly what his expression conveyed, but it said enough: He was on board. His propensity for trusting me had come to supersede much of the rational thought otherwise guiding a nineteen-year-old, one who'd come close to a perfect score on his SAT and was hailed as the kind of well-rounded achiever destined for success. But his wiser instincts were no match for the blinding fanaticism of teenage bonds. I pressed my right foot down against the rubber on the accelerator. Then I pressed it down farther. The engine let out an escalating howl and the coupe rocketed forward, blasting down the smooth asphalt into depthless tracts of darkness.

A maximum of several seconds passed. The brief string of instants—as we bulleted past a smeared blur of fences, tree lines, telephone poles, and dappled pools of light—felt even briefer. The vehicle's extreme speed seemed to curve time and collapse it into a single distended moment of sensory overload, like the crack of a bat against a ball or a sucker punch to the face. And, like anything that kinetic and crammed with energy, there was no keeping hold of it. One of my car's wheels smacked against a recessed storm drain and I lost control of the vehicle. I tried slamming the brakes, but it was too late; the car skidded down the road—its howl now a high screech—before slamming into a tree.

Amazingly, I didn't lose consciousness. Once the vehicle stopped, I tried to collect myself and scrabble together what had happened. I craned my neck to my right and saw that my friend, thankfully, was also conscious. Both our airbags had deployed. We pawed away the crinkled gray nylon smashed against our faces and took in deep, ravenous breaths. I swung the door open and stepped out of the car to assess the damage. It was extensive, grisly, total—the stuff of movie car chases that ended in lapping curtains of flame, or a scene from real life punctuated by the flashing of police lights, illuminated red flares, and yellow barricade tape.

The front of the vehicle had collapsed inward from the force of impact, and was now a concave jumble of warped, wavy metal. The Integra had struck the tree so hard that its trunk tilted backward, and its clod-covered roots hung suspended in the air like a claw. We could see a long trail of curving skid marks, scattered black ribbons undulating into the emptiness behind us. For several minutes we just stood over the mangled car silently, ossified. We were stage characters, awaiting the curtain's mercy. There was nothing left to say.

Someone living in one of the elegant houses nearby must have heard the collision and called 911, because the first car to pass us that night was a police officer's. He aimed his bright yellow spotlight on us, slowed his vehicle to a stop, and got out. After a brief, disapproving assessment, he directed me to slowly drive the half mile or so back to my house—my car was, unbelievably, capable of that—and he drove my friend home.

Back in my room, I examined myself in the mirror: I didn't have a scratch on me. The force of the airbag had torn some skin off my friend's nose, but aside from that he was unscathed, too. By then I'd been in trouble with the police many times, but that night I was let off the hook. Things almost certainly would have played out differently if I were a young man of color standing outside a totaled vehicle in a well-to-do residential neighborhood. Nineteen years old and even less mature, I did not grasp the good fortune cushioning what could have been a far more ruinous sequence of events. According to the police report, after skidding for over one hundred feet my car struck the tree at a diagonal angle rather than head-on. Had the center of my bumper collided directly with the trunk at the speed we were going, my friend and I almost certainly would have been either gravely injured or dead.

As it stood, however, I was released back into the wild no worse for the wear. The lack of consequences, legal or otherwise, only extended the impunity with which I led my reckless adolescence. It was a night that could have splintered at least two lives into irreversible befores and afters, in the same way that car crashes altered the trajectories of Valerie, Sophie, and JR. But instead, it left barely any legacy at all—despite the fact that I was, without a doubt, more responsible for my accident than those three individuals were for theirs. The totaled old coupe was shuttled to a junkyard, and that wanton night gradually faded from conversation, thought, and eventually memory, until there was hardly any trace of it at all.

Narrative identities are hardly beholden to objective fact. Rather, they're selective reconstructions of historical events that reflect our personal biases and unreliable memories. At once factually true and deliberately illusory, they play a powerful role in how we see ourselves and interpret our lives. They are allegorical fables with the power to steal or bestow agency, exalt experiences or condemn them, even trickle into the cryptic dye we sometimes call fate.

As far as I could tell, my narrative identity combined elements from two categories: the agency and contamination narratives. In cinematic terms, it was a character study spliced with the raw, serrated ordeals of a psychological thriller. I'd drawn a complicated hand, and the river card—the illness that would change my life forever—didn't do me any favors. But I'd managed to exert enough control over my circumstances that I did not let them lower my expectations for myself, did not permit my adversities to constrain the scope of my possible achievements. I was proud of that.

My narrative—one of agency over contamination—went something like this: After growing up in a single-parent household with a father who loved my sister and me but who was also aloof and alone, forever at a wraithlike remove, I had experienced several years of pleasant, highly privileged adulthood. Then CFS entered the picture, diablo ex machina, compromising my immune system and robbing that adulthood of much that made it whole. But I kept working, trying to salvage as much of my foregoing existence as I could, and sought treatments for my condition with furious persistence. When that model was no longer sustainable, I moved across the country, became a full-time writer, and looked for ways to replace everything I'd lost. Through it all, I'd exercised more courage, ingenuity, and fortitude than in all the years of my youth combined. In this way, CFS came to reinforce and even enhance the themes and subtexts that had, rightly or wrongly, colored how I saw myself since childhood, dispensing further evidence of character and worth. And it was deepening the contrast I observed between me and so many of my peers, whose lives never seemed to be subjected to the same lasting disturbances.

December 14, 2012, would always be a line of demarcation, a violent cleavage separating my biography into a before and an after. There was no getting around that. But I was also constructing a bridge between them, finessing a story in which I was moving deeper into the themes that had always been there, rather than abruptly shifting into a more disempowering tale. It was a narrative deception that preserved my deepest sense of identity, confirming everything about myself that I needed to be true.

Finding a way to sew the severed parts of our lives together can be critical to our survival and our sanity. Bereft of a narrative zip

line to whisk us through, we can get trapped in the crevasse between a past we can't let go of and a present we can't accept.

If we can't unify the before and after periods, incorporating our
catastrophes into the larger story we tell ourselves about our lives,
we risk getting "stuck at the point of fracture," restlessly circling it
forever.

At some point, after I'd moved from Hoboken to Lake Tahoe in the
hopes of getting on an experimental trial that might effectively treat
my CFS, I started revisiting the car crash from my adolescence. It
began as a rogue memory resurfacing seemingly of its own volition.
One of my "demons," perhaps. But over time, as I found myself revisiting the accident more and more frequently—in the middle of
work assignments, on soothing alpine hikes, and, appropriately, behind the wheel of my car—I started wondering if there wasn't something else going on. The recollections had a weight to them, a
gravitas that made them hard to dismiss. They felt more deliberate
than the random associations that normally trigger distant memories, and their emergence was ominous and incriminating: *Remember when you took your best friend on a kamikaze drive in the middle
of the night? Played Russian roulette by pressing your foot down on
the gas pedal and seeing where the chamber landed, just for the sheer
malevolent thrill?*

I did remember, but not with any particular vividness. The truth
was that for many years I'd stowed that memory away, stuffing it
into a steel lockbox far from my everyday lines of thinking. I'd never
fully reflected on—let alone processed—what had happened or my
responsibility for it. But now the memories and feelings were re-
appearing, drifting onto the shores of my mind like litter rolling in
with the tides.

My eventual recollection might have been the delayed effect of
guilt, a telltale heart thumping unbearable remorse through the
creaky floorboards. We unconsciously bury our most shameful

truths out of psychological convenience, and they can take a very long time to break through the boards we hammered over them. But something about this reminiscence reached beyond remorse and regret, to deeper correspondences that would take time to unpack and understand. If I was just processing my shit, trying to reconcile the reprehensible facts of what I'd done, then why was it all happening now, over a decade later? I felt sure there was something else underneath the shame spiral, something dredging these memories up for a more specific purpose.

By the time I turned thirty, my sense of my own narrative identity was growing even more entrenched. I leaned on the idea of my strength and agency in the face of tribulations more heavily than ever, clutching it with the intensity of faith. What I couldn't say, however, was where that night in December 2005 belonged in that valorizing vignette. Fittingly, while on a long drive in Northern California, the veiled connection finally snapped into place. The car accident was the most persuasive piece of evidence in my biography that contradicted the narrative identity I'd created for myself—the self-portrait that had hung for years undisturbed on the back wall of my mind. Here was a would-be tragedy—one that I'd been fully responsible for orchestrating—and I had the astonishing fortune of eluding it completely.

The cognitive dissonance was stark, rattling. I'd perceived myself as unlucky, misfortunate, bedeviled by crucibles born from illness and death that had all transpired outside my control. But here was a contravening exhibit, a crucial part of the record that was finally resurfacing. And instead of sharpening the picture, it was thrusting it into a place of ambiguity and doubt.

To borrow a term from the language of psychology, I was finally integrating the teenage car crash into the larger composite picture of my life. And while the reemerging memory was forcing me to reassess the person I'd long believed myself to be, its impact was also sending out more mysterious ripples. As I thought about the accident more and more, it became increasingly clear to me just how easily my friend and I could have died that night. The immense, sobering weight of what had happened—and what hadn't happened—was finally landing for me. I grew to feel *spared*. (Years later, speaking with Valerie, Sophie, and JR about their car accidents, that inimitable mixture of gratitude and guilt would only intensify.) But though I might have been spared injury, trauma, and even death on that particular night, I was not spared the serious illness that would befall me years later.

Beginning with that very fine, delicate thread, I started to think of the accident and my CFS as connected with each other—paired, even.

Even though I'm not an especially religious person, the car crash I'd emerged from literally without a scratch and the chronic illness that left me pockmarked with vulnerabilities began to possess an uncanny link. While I was shielded from any negative repercussions from the crash, I started seeing myself as marked—in one particular image I sometimes called to mind, literally, physically marked by God—for specific woe at some indeterminate point in the future.

My new occult logic deduced that my chronic illness was a form of delayed recompense. Having paid for my destructive abandon with credit that would eventually come due, I'd finally received my just deserts. The fact that the relationship between these two aspects of my biography was not remotely causal did not dissuade me from fervently subscribing to their correspondence. Life might have been one long chain of random events—the break of fifteen pool balls again and again—but when that randomness arranged itself in a way that yielded inexplicable connections, something else emerged: meaning.

When the accident and my illness fused themselves together in my mind, my attitude toward each was altered. On their own terms, the crash inspired guilt and shame, my CFS aggrievement tinged with rage. But when I considered them as a pair, a yin and yang that opposed and complemented each other, they obtained a kind of balance. Their unity seemed obvious, inevitable, like fragments of the same artifact at an archaeological dig. Fitted together, they elicited something more elegant and enigmatic than the strident ways I'd responded to each on their own. Here were the hands of the fates—their fingerprints all over both scenes—whose work evened out over the course of my life. It was enough to sew my thoughts shut and make me fall, quietly, into myself. So much of what we believe about ourselves—what I believed about myself—are painterly deceptions. Here was the truth.

In the psychiatry field, "magical thinking" is a term used to describe the belief that one's thoughts, fears, or wishes can influence the external world, or that certain actions and behaviors can affect events with which they have no logical relationship. Magical thinking is a hallmark symptom of people with obsessive-compulsive disorder: Individuals with OCD might believe they need to run through specific thoughts in a set order, repeat phrases aloud a predetermined number of times, or perform certain acts or gestures to keep themselves safe. The magical belief lies in seeing a causal relationship where there is no rational explanation for one.

But magical thinking is not exclusively the province of those with OCD or other pathologies. It also happens to be a mode of thought that serves as the fulcrum of many, perhaps even most, religious rituals and ceremonies. A rain dance hinges on the belief that causation exists between the gyrations of a person's body and the weather patterns forming in the sky. Ritual sacrifice is a grisly deployment of magical thinking: When Agamemnon sacrifices his daughter Iphigenia, it is according to the conviction that the bloodletting will stir becalmed ocean winds so that his ships might sail to Troy. Christian baptism is rooted in the belief that being submerged in consecrated water cleanses not only the skin of dirt and grime but also the soul of its original sin.

This magician's folly, as the British anthropologist Edward Burnett Tylor called it, permeates almost all organized religion. Indeed, it gives the rites and practices that are the bones and sinew of those institutions much of their captivating power. Houses of faith appeal to people, in part, because they serve as irreproachable sanctuaries for our magical thinking. Religions repeat acts that were originally performed as shared enactments of this nonrational thought, codify them over time into officially recognized rituals, and then declare that they are holy—fleeting spaces where the divine can seep into human tableaux like drafts through a cracked window.

Prayer is also an exercise in magical thinking, perhaps the preeminent one. Praying centers on the solemn hope that unvoiced thoughts organized in epistolary form will fulfill our deepest wishes, curing disease, forestalling war, or resolving suffering. And those who pray each night, as I do, know how easily those repeated clauses can slip further and further into the magician's folly, as we pause, scrap, and restart our appeals and petitions to ensure we deliver them with flawless care. Maybe one day, if we turn the phrases or enunciate the syllables in just the right way—perform the silent sacrament with enough sincere, somber belief—our prayers will break through the shadowy caves of our psyches and change our lives. As any diligent sorcerer knows, spells can take a lifetime to master.

The relationship I'd cultivated in my mind between my adolescent car accident and my adult illness was a special type of magical thinking. Though certainly not logical, the fantasized causation between one event and the other wasn't arbitrary, either, and it didn't rest on the fetishistic power of language or ritual. I was seduced by the conviction that my unpunished criminal act had both warranted and produced my ill health. This irrational belief had a distinct moral valence, a sense that a divine brand of retributive justice was being meted out post factum. This thinking sounds wildly irrational—and it definitely is—but by no means is it rare. It may be even more prevalent, in fact, than the other varieties of magical thinking. It's smuggled into adages like "You reap what you sow," "What goes around comes around," and "The chickens are coming home to roost." It's in the flawed Western interpretation of karma— the notion that we eventually get what we deserve, even if we can't always draw a straight line back from what we got to what we did to deserve it.

Fictional villains often face gruesome ends—they get what they deserve—even if there isn't any causal connection between their nefarious deeds and the specifics of their demise. In fairy tales, a single, easily dismissed erring in character or scruples can sow seeds that bloom lifelong imprecation. Horror movies wickedly revel in punishing sexually promiscuous teenagers by unleashing implacable killers onto them, wrathful gods delivering final judgment with white masks, finger-knives, and rumbling chainsaws.

Even our greatest novelists cannot resist the engrossing power of this morally charged storytelling device. In William Faulkner's *Absalom, Absalom!,* Thomas Sutpen builds an opulent mansion atop a sprawling estate in antebellum Mississippi, amassing wealth, notoriety, and a wife and several children to lord over. But as the secret sins from his past bubble forth into the labyrinthine narrative, he's forced to watch everything spoil away into sickness, rage, and murder. Sutpen built his garish American dream on lies, coercion, deception, and denial, using slaves, swindling Natives, and abandoning his progeny; in time, the soil rots beneath this mountain of moral corruption. He's punished for his greed and depravity, to be sure, but how and by whom? More than just direct cause and effect, his comeuppance is momentous, mythic, even spiritual. It represents our persistent conviction that our downfalls in the present are directly tied to the unreckoned wrongs of our past, and no amount of logical elucidation can persuade us otherwise.

These narratives don't just demonstrate their creators' magical thinking, though. They also betray a powerful desire for moral symmetry—an impulse to see transgressions paid or atoned for later in life. Though most of our major religions contain systems that reward or punish us based on the relative goodness with which we've lived our lives, those accountings are largely eschatological, final judgments dispensed only after death. We ache to see those circles closed in this life, and the moral symmetry we reach for as a result permeates the stories we tell. It should come as no surprise, then, that some of us look for that same hidden causation in our own lives. It can be stirring to see yourself as more than just a patient, a victim, or a statistic ground under blind fortune's revolving wheel. By dreaming up ways to hold ourselves accountable for our fates, we can restore agency, justness, and meaning—and we can also reframe identities that were not cohering our entire biographical picture.

One of the greatest examples of moral symmetry, of course, is the Judeo-Christian Genesis narrative: the primeval fall and ongoing redemption of humankind. Adam and Eve eat from the forbidden tree of knowledge and consummate the lust they learned from its fruit. When God finds out, he banishes them from paradise, forcing them to fend for themselves in a mortal existence from which they will inexorably perish. Christianity more broadly invokes moral symmetry through the interlocking concepts of sin, penitence, atonement, redemption, and salvation.

Perhaps it was these tenets, inculcated in me through one cultural vector or another over the course of my life, that inspired my sense of a mystical requital. Grasping my life story through this framework represented a major departure from the one-sided narrative identity I'd long subscribed to. But I felt drawn to the way that Christian doctrine mapped onto human biographies, its exquisite mixture of humility and grandeur. Despite its flawed and sometimes barbaric history, Christianity spoke movingly to the shades of folly and plight within my life. The religion seemed to understand how it could be appealing for somebody to think that each of his moral missteps was inextricably linked to a future misfortune, which itself joined up to a tortuous path that might one day be bathed in some glorious private light.

At one point in Flannery O'Connor's *Wise Blood,* street preacher Hazel Motes shouts to passersby, "In yourself right now is all the place you've got. If there was any Fall, look there, if there was any Redemption, look there, and if you expect any Judgment, look there, because they all three will have to be in your time and your body and where in your time and your body can they be?" The surface reading is that Motes is exposing the implausibility of Christian doctrine, evincing how those concepts could not possibly exist. But O'Connor seeds Motes's sermon with a deeper, more illuminating idea: that our fall, redemption, and judgment take place in our lifetimes, transpiring in "your time and your body." They are, that is, perpetually under way, our actions and our circumstances bearing ties to each other that enact these spiritual consequences.

It's true that superimposing these religious ideas onto my own life is another kind of narrative identity, and an arguably masochistic deployment of magical thinking. But the measure of a story, a narrative, or a myth isn't how logical, rational, or factually verifiable it is; it's how much of our lives it can unlock for us. And for a time, this particular story—about the mistakes I was responsible for, the misfortunes I wasn't, and how they might, when seen together, produce a clarifying coherence—unlocked inestimable insight into my own life. It carried out the remarkable feat of yielding an intimate, subjective "truth" about who I was and what I'd been through from a personal history spun, like everyone's, from a lifetime of persuasive illusions.

CHAPTER FIVE

Refinement

IN CONTEMPORARY PARLANCE, THE WORD "REFINEMENT" OFTEN carries a highbrow connotation. It conveys a decidedly genteel notion, the idea that those privileged enough to do so are pursuing self-betterment through sharpened diction, finer manners, and the air of elegance befitting heirs to high society. This sense of refinement conjures to mind—for me, anyway—chandeliered parlor rooms, prim Victorian courtships, and private academies where children learn to master the affect, comportment, and confidence to wordlessly express power. Its focus is on appearances: the ways we project our means and bona fides into a world of peers, rivals, and prospective partners who all extract a great deal from how we speak, dress, and even stand.

In my reporting, however, I observed a type of refinement that had nothing to do with social markers or the projection of class and privilege. Many individuals leading afterlives demonstrated a refinement that was a more solitary, internal endeavor, a process of elevating some qualities and paring back others in order to successfully adapt to their changed circumstances. Instead of cultivating external affectations, they were advancing their character in less visible ways, executing consequential decisions about which parts of their lives could be kept and which required revision or contraction. While some, including JR and Jason, honed their discipline and work ethic and redoubled their focus on their futures, others engaged in acts that looked more like sacrifice or renunciation. In either case, people recounted refining their lives and characters in ways that were deeper and more fraught than superficial modifications to appearance or mien.

Refinement in afterlives came across as an arduous but fulfilling act. People nurtured the aspects of themselves that were now critical to their survival while excising the luxuries too costly to afford under the stringency of their altered lives. Like so much else in their postcatastrophe worlds, refinement could be both dramatic and nuanced—sometimes at the same time.

BY 2009, JASON had served the first four years of his seven-and-a-half-to-fifteen-year sentence, including three at Somerset Correctional Institution. Once scrawny and pallid from heavy drug use, with close-cropped brown hair and a crescent of scruff that thickened under his chin, he'd shaved his head, grown a full goatee, and bulked up his arms and chest. Renouncing his Christian faith had set him spiritually adrift, but it had also led him toward another way of seeing the world. He spent hours reading about existentialism on the thin, squeaky mattress of his cell's steel-frame bunk beds, his legs crossed into a half lotus as he absorbed dense philosophical tracts. Writers like Nietzsche, Camus, and Kafka were showing him how to anchor himself in a finite mortal existence without religion, one that felt grounded in a rousing humanism. "The whole existential reading became about freedom, and that, ultimately, man is free to create himself," Jason said. "Our freedom is to give this void meaning."

A godless world might be bleak and frightening from certain angles, but Jason found that it could also be liberating. When an omnipotent deity no longer exerted influence or assumed responsibility, agency cascaded down to the street level of everyday people, like a mountain releasing a rockslide from its highest peaks. Jason felt emancipated by the notion that it was he and he alone who was making every decision, and that conviction electrified each choice with jolting significance. "That brought me just screaming out of this pit," he said.

But Jason's fresh perspective also forced an overdue personal reckoning. "I hadn't addressed my drug addiction, my violence, how bad I hurt everyone," he said. The way he saw things now, only personal accountability could control individual morality. A sinner's fall was not predetermined, nor would good works unlock heaven's gates. He was ultimately responsible for everything he did, and that insight pushed him to evaluate his past choices in a more searching light. He thought about his childhood, his adolescence, even his relationships with his parents, working to pinpoint why he'd developed into the criminal addict who'd robbed people at gunpoint. "By the time I'd gotten to adulthood, I was deeply, deeply ashamed of who I'd become," Jason remembered. "And I felt this great sense of loss of how much time I'd wasted being that person, and how much of my life I'd given away."

Thinking about the relationships he'd sabotaged and the years he'd squandered in frantic thrall to drugs pushed Jason to approach his future with a prudence nowhere to be found in his past. He had only so much time left, and he felt immense pressure to take advantage of everything that still lay ahead. The solace of eternity might have been gone, but in its place was what Camus called "divine availability": a full investment in the present moment that was not distracted by distant hopes of eternal paradise. "I realized I could make new choices, and I realized I could make a new life for myself," he said. "That was this glimmer of hope that I used to carry around with me."

By year five at Somerset, Jason mostly kept to himself, reading, working out, and planning how he would make the most of his freedom upon being released. He still lived inside the prison's implacable ecosystem, though, and no internal transformations were going to budge the dynamics that ran through it. One afternoon that spring, Jason was exercising in the prison's outdoor "weight pit"—a small pavilion outfitted with old weight lifting equipment and wrapped in chain-link fencing—when he noticed the area around him suddenly grow quiet. After everything he'd seen at Somerset, he instantly recognized what was going on. The cadence was off. It was a threat of violence, he had no doubt, that had ruptured it.

Glancing outside the weight pit, Jason tried to look for signs of an impending attack. His eyes were pulled toward a section of metal pull-up bars, no more than a few yards away. There, he saw a group of men rushing toward a younger prisoner. After they closed in around him, one of the assailants thrust his arm forward and stabbed him with a prison shank. The whole assault lasted no more than ten seconds, and appeared in some ways unremarkable—the swiftness, the premeditation, and the weapon of choice were all classic features of Somerset's culture of retaliatory punishment. But as the assailants fanned out across the yard, Jason noticed that the victim was still lying motionless on the ground. And he wasn't holding his stomach, as men often did after being attacked with a shank. He was gripping his neck with both hands, and blood was pouring out of it.

Several correctional officers sprinted toward the pull-up bars. When, panting for breath, they eventually reached the young man, the situation looked bad. A few other incarcerated men on the yard started yelling at the COs, demanding that they try to stanch the blood, which continued leaking out near the man's jugular in heavy pools that covered the cracked cement. But the officers only stood there, tense and frozen, following a prison protocol that required them to bar off the scene and wait for first responders to arrive. When they did, it was too late. "He just lay there and bled to death," Jason remembered. "That kid bled to death right there."

The young man's death scalded itself onto Jason's memory, and he would replay the event over and over in his mind in the weeks that followed. One minute, there was a kid no more than twenty-three years old; the next, an ugly void of blood and nothingness. "I just started processing, that, when that's me," he said, "when I'm the one leaking out all over the fucking cement under the pull-up bars, that's just it." If he was still holding out even a morsel of hope that some version of life after death did exist, that afternoon settled the matter with cold finality. The pressure to make the absolute most of his time on earth clanged inside him like a bell.

Though he rarely spoke to his ex-girlfriend or his daughter, Annabella, who was now seven years old, Jason remained close with his mom. It was perhaps the only relationship not tainted by his addiction or marred by the estrangement of incarceration, and he called her to check in weekly. Though she didn't approve of his atheism, she sent him books often, and that summer she mailed him a biography on Einstein after reading it herself. He'd never had much interest in math during his public school education; he got a D in the only algebra class he'd ever taken. But he found that Einstein's biography painted the subject in a refreshing, accessible light. Reading how the revolutionary mathematician proved his conjectures about the physics and mechanics of the world through equations and proofs made mathematics seem practical, powerful, even profound. By the time he'd finished the book, Jason was fascinated by math's rigor and concreteness, the way it explained matter, movement, and space through an objective, empirical lens. "It's like seeing New York City for the first time—I'd just never been exposed to it," he said. "And it completely reshaped me."

Philosophy may have delivered him from the paralyzing despair of losing his faith, but math, he felt, could serve as a durable bridge toward his future. When a relative passed away and left Jason a little bit of money, he started using it to pay for math correspondence classes through Louisiana State University (the same school where he'd learned about the early history of Christianity). For his first course, basic algebra, the college sent him a textbook and a lesson plan. The structure was straightforward and exacting: Jason read a chapter, learned its concepts, completed the problem set, and mailed his work to the professor. He repeated the same demanding sequence for each chapter, laboring through problems at the steel desk bolted to the wall of his cell. The textbook was his only resource—the course was almost entirely self-directed—and Jason found the class's difficulty humbling. "It made me feel very small, it made me realize I had been very arrogant," he said. Despite graduating from high school in a self-paced program housed inside a Florida strip mall, Jason had long considered himself a highly intelligent person. His reexposure to mathematics was revealing the dubiousness of that assessment.

It took nearly six months, but Jason eventually finished the introductory algebra course. Over the next three years, he took five more math correspondence classes, advancing all the way through trigonometry and calculus. During that time, he developed a meticulous homework ritual: For each problem set he was assigned, he puzzled through a messy rough draft, neatly rewrote all his work in a second copy in pencil, and then completed a third and final "formal" version in pen. "I was very slow and very deliberate in what my final product looked like, because I had never taken as much pride in what I was doing," he said. Math became a productive sanctuary, a place where Jason could be vaulted out of the immiseration of prison life and into a realm that rewarded mental effort and existed on a curve rather than a closed circle.

In *On the Nature of Things,* the Roman poet Lucretius defined "the sublime" as the art of exchanging easier for more difficult pleasures. After almost three decades of easy pleasures, Jason was finally performing that momentous exchange, discovering the exquisite gratification that came from grappling with a demanding, even onerous challenge and eventually mastering it. Through mathematics, he was developing a work ethic founded on bullheaded effort and rooted in personal accountability, one that helped him sustain his focus long enough to move toward goals that might take years to realize. He called it "working hard at hard things."

The correctional officers patrolling his block, however, remained unimpressed. On several occasions, vindictive guards used cell searches as an excuse to rip up problem sets Jason had spent hours toiling through. As his onetime cellmate put it, prison staff "are very threatened by seeing somebody take an interest in some kind of higher aspiration." Instead of showing support, "they understand it in terms of, 'How is this criminal going to use this stuff on the street to commit more crimes?'" But Jason was undeterred. His foray into existentialism had given him an unassailable conviction about how much responsibility and control he had over his own life, and guards intent on carrying out wanton attacks weren't going to jeopardize that. He was growing convinced that math would play a part in his postincarceration future in some as-yet-unknown but critical way. "It was a thing I was passionate about that took an intense amount of work," he said. "I had to keep trying, I had to keep learning. I had to go back and relearn, I had to go back and relearn again."

By the end of 2010, Jason had served six years in prison. He would soon be eligible for pre-release, a state program that released men and women with model records to halfway houses up to a year before they completed their minimum sentences. If all went well, Jason could be leaving Somerset inside of twelve months. That winter, for the first time in many years, he had an irrefutable sense of gaining positive momentum in his life. He was amassing college credits, sharpening his mathematical aptitude, and forging the unflappable determination he'd need ample supplies of once he assumed the often-stigmatized identity of a man returning from prison. His diligence and optimism would have been utterly alien to the twenty-five-year-old addict committing armed robberies under a thick narcotic haze that obscured the people left reeling in his wake. "I just became convinced that I could become this different person," Jason said.

Jason was scheduled to have his pre-release meeting with the prison review board the following summer. There, Somerset case managers would decide whether his personal history and prison record warranted an early transfer to a halfway house. As the weeks passed, Jason became increasingly invested in the prospect of getting out. So emotionally attached was he to being released that he started having nightmares of how it could be derailed. For months, falling asleep meant slipping into the same horrifying scenario. In the dream, he's just been released from prison. Later that same day, he violates his parole by using drugs. As night falls, he's behind the wheel of his car, frantically speeding down one road after another in an effort to evade police. Before long, he's surrounded by cop cars, their strobing haze of red-and-blue lights flooding the inky sky. Jason is so mortified by his actions—a crowning failure to a life pitted with them—that he pulls out a revolver and shoots himself. Waking up from the dream, his heart was always pounding and his forehead slicked with sweat, as though he were in the viselike grip of a panic attack.

In July 2011, Jason had his pre-release meeting. A staff member called him into a conference room on his block, where eight case managers and Somerset's deputy warden were quietly waiting. The first few minutes were little more than formalities; Jason sat silently, trying to read the expressions of the staff members and get a feel for the mood of the room. As more case managers began speaking, though, he quickly grasped where things were heading. Several of them voiced serious doubts about his ability to succeed outside prison walls. One woman told him she'd seen a long line of guys just like Jason—ex-addicts convinced they'd turned their lives around. Shortly after being released, she said, they all relapsed. Another was more direct, issuing a prediction: Inside of a month on the outside, he'd be back to shooting heroin.

The entire meeting felt like an ambush—a siege of humiliation from every corner of the room. Some of the pillorying didn't surprise him. He knew several of the caseworkers to be bitter, condescending people, jaded prison officials who genuinely hoped he didn't make something of himself with the math books he was always ferrying around. In other instances, though, he felt betrayed. Those he'd had good relationships with over the years revealed "a completely different side that day," he said. After the meeting, he waited another two months to learn of their decision. One day that September, one of the counselors assigned to his block called Jason into his office. "I just wanted to let you know that you got approved for pre-release," the counselor said. Despite the skepticism and vitriol of the July meeting, Somerset's staff had granted Jason's pre-release. Come the fall, he would be leaving the correctional institution for good.

On October 5, 2011, Jason's lawyer picked him up from Somerset and drove him to the halfway house outside Pittsburgh where he'd be serving the remainder of his sentence. It was a rainy, misty day, the mountains wreathed in coils of thick fog, and Jason sat in the passenger seat and quietly gazed out the window at the water rushing down the slopes. It ran through steep, narrow grooves in the slanting earth, gushing over winding beds of grizzled rock, skipping off sheer bluffs and turning into waterfalls that looked like clouds of whirling white smoke. During the hour-and-a-half ride, he remained almost completely silent. There were few words for the surge of hope and fear he felt, the fluttery sensation of wings whipping the air inside his chest. He cautiously allowed his mind to creep toward thoughts of what lay ahead, of the future he'd been concentrating on with such intense enthusiasm for the past few years. He could finally feel it looming before him, the goosebumps rising off his skin attesting to its wealth of possibilities and endless range of unknowns.

BY THE TIME he'd left prison, Jason had dramatically overhauled his identity. But the velocity and the clamor of twenty-first-century life make such changes surpassingly difficult. In environments blanketed by glowing screens, social media feeds, and the white noise of cultural static, it can be hard to find the space and stillness required to analyze ourselves. Examining our behaviors and thought patterns demands sustained, uninterrupted self-work, and the fullness of our everyday lives and the finite attention spans that rove through them sometimes appear engineered to thwart personal investigations. For many, such an undertaking is undesirable in any case: Those of us content with our lives are not compelled to confront or interrogate our habits, lifestyles, or underlying beliefs. Contentment doesn't incentivize change—it does everything in its power to forestall it. But those of us learning to survive in the ill-disposed, unaccommodating terrain of afterlives—marooned on a desert island we have little affinity for—must open ourselves up to it.

Following catastrophe, some people develop a monasticism they would never have anticipated for themselves beforehand. Incarceration is the most powerful, least ambiguous example of this: Because they're cut off from society and its never-ending supply of distractions, incarcerated people are forced to root themselves more firmly inside their own thoughts and consciousness. Many undertake spiritual or intellectual odysseys, renounce unhelpful habits or grooves of thought, and embark on precipitous paths to self-improvement with a fullhearted rigor that would not be possible under other circumstances. "You will see people in prison who have come in early in life, and have gotten started on reading, or studying, or theology, or philosophy, and have the time and the tenacity to really go deep," said Hans Hallundbaek, a minister with three decades of experience working with men inside New York prisons. "They are not distracted like the rest of us on the outside." These instances of transformative growth do not justify the overarching misery of incarceration, but for many they are an inextricable aspect of the experience.

Incarceration is not the only before-and-after experience to impose some degree of confinement. People who've been paralyzed, developed a chronic, debilitating illness, or had their brains altered by trauma find themselves living under new constraints and limitations. Though certainly less explicit, their freedom is also circumscribed, and they're forced to relinquish many of their previous diversions and pursuits. It is in this way that confinement begets refinement. When we can no longer spread ourselves horizontally, we must shift to a more vertical orientation, anchoring our focus within the self and cultivating an attention—which fifteenth-century French philosopher Nicolas Malebranche called the "prayer of the soul"—that is less cluttered and divided.

Many people leading afterlives speak to a more solid, voluminous sense of self. They express the quiet pride that arises out of being able to simply stand inside the void of one's consciousness, without anesthetizing buffers, for extended periods of time. The American poet Richard Wilbur wrote that "the strength of the genie comes of his being confined in a bottle." Wilbur was referring to how the restrictions imposed by meter and rhyme sharpened a poem's form, endowing it with a sense of concentrated power and swift, compact force. But the restrictions of form also funneled the poet's attention and intellect, crystallizing his creativity by trapping his focus inside the ballads, sonnets, and villanelles and their tightly structured stanzas.

The states of confinement found in some varieties of afterlives produce a similar consolidation and density of form, pressing individuals to apply their resources and wherewithal to the inflexible task of lives that can no longer be written in free verse. Absolute freedom can bring immeasurable joy, but it also requires little rigor or discipline. Those who enjoy it often find themselves spread thin, like a sliver of butter scraped across too much toast. Our forced concentration inside the genie's bottle can—in some cases—have the opposite effect, cultivating an internalized potency of feeling, ambition, and purpose.

SOMETIME IN EARLY 2012, JR was browsing the internet in his bedroom on Guam. Scrolling through forums for people who'd recently lost limbs and viewing YouTube videos of amputees maneuvering in prosthetics, he stopped at a clip of something he'd never seen before. It was a video of a bilateral amputee gliding through laps in a swimming pool. The video perked him up; he stared, rapt, as the man thrust his arms over and through the clear water in rapid, arcing circles, sailing from one end of the pool to the other. Besides the push-ups and dumbbell exercises JR performed in his room, the car accident had stripped him of the physical pursuits that once gave his days their secret, crackling frisson. He missed the anticipation that presaged a long run, the rush of adrenaline that surged through his body once his racing flats began striking the ground. Though he didn't expect swimming to fill that inexorable void, he was intrigued. It was, at the very least, worth trying. One late afternoon, JR asked his father if he would take him to the public swimming pool in Hagatna, a twenty-minute drive south of their home in the village of Dededo.

Within minutes of sliding into the water, JR realized the extremity of the task he'd dropped himself into. Without any legs to anchor his body under the water (he did not wear his prosthetics), he could swim only a few yards before his high center of gravity flipped him onto his back. Every few seconds, he'd be yanked out of his front crawl, his face turned up toward the dimming sky in an expression tight and clenched as a fist. For months, every trip to the pool ended the same way. "I quit, I'm done," JR groused to his father. "I'm never swimming again." But by the following afternoon, he was asking for another ride to the pool. Though he proudly carried a long-distance runner's DNA—a solitary intensity and flair for protracted punishment—it wasn't masochism that kept him returning to the pool every day. JR was determined to prove to himself that he could become proficient in a physical activity whose learning curve was steep. Beginning in brief sparks and flashes, like a thumb striking unsuccessfully against a lighter, swimming ignited something in him that had lain dormant for some time.

The following year, JR acquired the high-end, microprocessor-driven C-Legs. Though he was sorely disappointed by the legs' limitations—he'd fantasized that they would catapult him to an approximation of full functionality—they still expanded what he was capable of doing. Because the C-Legs' computer-controlled knees locked at several important angles, they gave him the physical responsiveness required to control car pedals and start driving again. His parents helped him pay for a gray Nissan Cube, and JR spent several weeks relearning to operate a vehicle as an amputee. It took time to ease into the controlled rhythms of shifting between the pedals, to learn to trust the way his prosthetic knees flexed and applied resistance to the carbon fiber feet, and to regain the confidence to safely negotiate Guam's notoriously foolhardy drivers. But by February, he was driving on his own.

Once he was comfortable taking the Nissan out by himself, JR threw himself into swimming with even greater élan. By the early spring, he was driving to the public pool every day, heading out at five-thirty in the morning to catch the hours when multiple lanes were sectioned off for long-course lap swimming. Swimming effectively is an exceedingly arduous task, at least initially, for a bilateral above-knee amputee. JR spent months mirroring techniques he'd watched online and picked up from the pool's solicitous lifeguards, refining strategies that helped him move in the water with a different body than he once had. Instead of generating power from his legs, he needed to control his body from his torso, using core and abdominal muscles to keep his frame parallel to the water. By anchoring his body through those muscles, he prevented himself from flipping onto his back. If he let his stumps drop too far into the water, meanwhile, it created drag that slowed him down and made his strokes choppy and inefficient. To keep his stumps horizontal near the surface of the water, JR learned to crane his neck forward, point his chin up, and train his gaze on a distant point ahead of him.

JR grew incrementally better with each passing week, strengthening his arms and shoulders and tightening his body control. Anthony, who still accompanied JR some days, remembered the lifeguards watching him from their chairs being "really awed at how he'd come around and learned to swim." His progress was not only a source of deep, abiding gratification but also a new avenue for the coveted runner's high the accident had left him bereft of. "Once I figured out the stroke and everything, it was the endorphins that kept me going back," JR said.

That same year, JR began researching the long-term psychological effects of limb loss. He learned that many amputees contextualize their experience through the stages of grief. Like the death of a loved one, a medical amputation leaves a grievous hollow, a sense of irreparable loss that may never be fully mollified. For JR, categories like denial, bargaining, and depression made the waves of heavy, alien feelings he'd been experiencing since the accident more comprehensible. Denial had attenuated the initial horror in the hospital in the Philippines, thinning out reality just enough to stave off the kind of tornado that might touch down if he took in everything at once. His outsize expectations for the C-Legs, meanwhile, had been a type of bargaining—if he could just get his hands on these state-of-the-art prosthetics, they would change everything—and when the bargain didn't pan out, depression was the flat, fathomless desert awaiting him on the other side. The stages' framing permitted him the time to process his loss and all the changes it wrought. "I had to mourn for my old life," he said.

During the first two years after the accident, JR was so focused on his physical rehabilitation that he stopped thinking about dating and relationships completely. Every day demanded so much physical effort and emotional fortitude that there was scarcely any time or energy left for contemplating sex or romance. He no longer thought about men the way he once did, and the entire psychic reorganization caused him to arrive at a new conclusion about his sexuality: He was no longer gay. Pondering the shift in the terms laid out by his family's Southern Baptist church, he started believing he'd been "cured."

By the following summer, though, that perspective was losing its purchase. It was 2014, and JR had spent three years adapting to the amputations in the aftermath of the accident. He was finally adjusting to his new body and the way it transformed his daily life, and that freed up some of the mental bandwidth that his grueling recovery had preempted for so long. "Once I had achieved the new normal, those thoughts started to come back," he said. And when those thoughts gained a foothold, all the ambiguity he'd craftily employed in the past seemed to fall away.

Now thirty-four years old, JR found himself struggling to call on the deceptive narratives he'd once constructed to keep the inconvenient parts of himself at arm's length. "The situation after the accident forced me to take a lot of hard looks at myself and see what was important," JR said. "You almost died, so you need to stop being afraid to be yourself." JR was finally looking down to the bottom of who he was, past the stories and rationalizations that long glossed over what was, given his religious background, a fraught sexual identity. He was gay—full stop, no qualifications—and he needed to see that, unflinchingly, and own it. Perhaps then he'd be able to look toward a future where he wasn't "cured" of his own fulfillment and happiness.

Later that summer, JR was sitting on his family's couch one evening, watching television. His parents had left the family's one-floor concrete home for a few hours that night to attend a church function. By then he'd come out to himself, but not to his parents, and the personal epiphany hadn't affected his day-to-day life in any meaningful way. "Nothing changed," he said. But as the television's soft glow rendered the living room in silhouette, JR nevertheless felt a sense of mellowing comfort. It occurred to him that he would be content living in Guam, under his parents' roof, for the rest of his life. His mom and dad watched over him, even cosseted him, and after everything he'd been through there was peacefulness in that. As he held that thought, though, his mind stopped cold in its tracks. "In that moment right there, I thought about that and it scared the shit out of me," he said. "Me staying there, and not doing anything with my life." In a sudden flash of clarity, the man he'd once been—an independent adult and aspiring entrepreneur with a dating life that was complicated but far from nonexistent—rose to the surface of his mind. If he was comfortable living under his parents' charge indefinitely, then he also needed to be comfortable letting that person fade away for good.

The whiplash of opposing realizations forced him back to that familiar cognitive dissonance, the jarring juxtaposition of his present and past selves. This time, though, he didn't feel the same sense of powerlessness. He saw that he had a choice, that there were ways to pull himself closer to the young man who stood in such damning contrast to the person he was gradually becoming. "At that moment I realized that I needed to leave Guam," he said. By the time he went to bed that night, he knew beyond doubt that he would move out of his parents' house, out of Dededo, off the Pacific island he'd called home for most of his adult life.

In the week that followed, JR thought about his future in very different terms. He began planning a permanent move to the States, where he would be forced to live independently and fashion a life for himself on his own. It would be a daunting, even staggering shift, but it would also help him regain control of a life trajectory that had skidded far afield. The move was going to be expensive, requiring him to pay for a long-term hotel until he found more permanent housing, at which point he'd be responsible for his rent, utilities, and all the other miscellaneous expenses he didn't worry about living at home in Dededo. He still worked part-time for the condominium complex, and he started stashing as much money from his paychecks as he could.

That fall, JR looked into job markets, apartment listings, and the cost of living in various parts of the country. His approach to his life was becoming more prudent and circumspect, his mindset keener and more focused than it had been in a long time. If he'd allowed an uncharacteristic complacency to settle over the homely trappings of his existence on Guam, he was now cutting through that ennui like a searchlight piercing the dozing murkiness of the night.

After some deliberation, JR decided that he would move to Orlando. There was a major prosthetics clinic there—where he'd been fitted for the C-Legs—and his parents were considering a permanent relocation to Florida in the future. Despite not yet solidifying what he would do for work or housing in the area, he targeted the end of the year for his departure. On the day after Christmas, Anthony and Amalia dropped JR off at Guam International Airport, and he boarded a plane for the seventeen-hour flight to Orlando. "It was very difficult to let him go, because we weren't sure how he was going to be able to handle it on his own," Anthony said. "There was a big unknown factor." When JR arrived, for the first time in his afterlife as an amputee, he would be completely reliant on himself.

ANOTHER SENSE OF refinement comes in the idea of distillation. The scientific process of distillation involves drawing out a composite substance's individual elements using steam or evaporation. Distilleries separate liquor from water to achieve higher alcohol content. Aromatic plants can be distilled to produce fragrant perfumes and essential oils. And, of course, oil refineries turn crude oil into the petroleum products we use to power cars, heat homes, and generate electricity: By channeling the oil through heated furnaces, they separate its constituent parts into different substances that become kerosene, heating oil, and gasoline. In each case, a heterogeneous mixture undergoes a chemical transformation that creates a purer substance.

People shifting into lives altered by catastrophe sometimes find themselves experiencing a corresponding distillation process. Due to changes to their bodies and circumstances and the limitations those changes impose, they must live between finer margins than they once did. Out of necessity or careful judgment, they opt to eliminate certain behaviors or pursuits, rarefying their existences down to a more simplified, even austere core. They may find themselves excising certain aspects of their social lives: alcohol or other substances they once used without consequence, late nights with friends that now leave them drained, or other leisurely pleasures their new parameters are no longer able to accommodate. One middle-aged father and husband I spoke to had been a hard-charging corporate banker with a nightly drinking habit that danced at the edge of alcoholism. Seemingly invincible, he put in seventy-hour workweeks, handled chores around the house, and took on child-rearing responsibilities—all while pounding liquor late into the night. But since suffering a stroke in 2019, he hadn't drunk a drop, as doing so could trigger another heavy blow to what had become a more fragile body. People leading certain types of afterlives simply don't have the slack rope to afford all the freedoms and excesses they once enjoyed; for better and worse, their rope has been rendered permanently taut.

This distillation process narrows the scope of one's existence, resulting in a diminishment of the panoramic life many of us prize for its vivacity and joie de vivre. But that tightened aperture also carries unexpected virtues. The sparer, less cluttered tableaux individuals cultivate within their afterlives can provide the ideal environment to ardently pursue a cause, craft, crusade, or discipline. The sacrifices spurred by refinement reduce the diversions and multiplicity that can sometimes jumble our lives, turning the forced narrowing into a deepening and sharpening of focus. These pruned conditions can pave the way for the states of devotion and reinvention that people spend years working toward. Without the process of refinement, such culminations would not be achievable.

IF VALERIE'S FIRST year at Harvard had been a delightful excursion into the intellectual frontiers of medieval history, her sophomore year was a fanatical pilgrimage. During her second semester she took one of the history department's most demanding courses, an intensive seminar focused on the early stages of medieval Europe. In that class she met a PhD student and teaching fellow named Shane Bobrycki, a walking encyclopedia of the Middle Ages who recognized a level of ambition in her that he'd rarely if ever seen before. Though most members of the seminar course were intense and precocious, Valerie "stood out in how far she was willing to go with research projects," he said. "She pursued these small, marginal advantages using the craziest technical problems, and delighted in the hurdles. The hurdles were clearly what was fun for her." Each hurdle, he recalled, involved learning an auxiliary discipline: translating Medieval Latin, deciphering old manuscripts, mastering medieval abbreviations.

Not everyone was enthusiastic about Valerie's academic zealotry. One of her closest friends at Harvard, an English major named Carina Livoti, observed with concern how much time she was pouring into medieval history. She remembered seeing Valerie in the dining hall of their residential house, "teaching herself Latin at two in the morning. It was fairly obvious that she was a bit of a workaholic." After Livoti got hired at the circulation desk of Widener Library—where Valerie spent long stretches burrowed away in the upper stacks—she tried keeping tabs on her friend. "There was growing concern among a few people that Val was just too wrapped up in the studying," Livoti said. One day, when Valerie and Livoti were hanging out in Valerie's dorm room, Livoti confronted her about her all-consuming focus on her classes. "I really think you're using your schoolwork as an emotional crutch," she told her. She urged Valerie to make an appointment with a counselor at the university health center.

By then, Valerie had grown adept at justifying the time she sank into her classes. She had long felt that her dedication to schoolwork was a vital, nourishing part of her identity, and she deftly deflected questions about why she avoided social events by reflexively citing the physical and academic obligations that sapped her resources. This time, though, her friend was more persistent. Livoti viewed Valerie's obsessive attitude toward academics as part of an effort to keep herself at a safe remove from uncomfortable social situations. "It seemed like, 'Okay, you go and study so that you don't have to deal with anything else,'" Livoti said. "That's just the one thing you deal with, and you're exceptional, and one of the smartest people I've ever met. But that's maybe not a path for not dealing with any of your other stuff."

To appease her friend, Valerie scheduled an appointment with a counselor at the Holyoke Center (now the Smith Campus Center), a brutalist high-rise that housed Harvard's university health facilities. After an hour-long session, Valerie was told she wasn't suffering from social anxiety, depression, or any other mental health disorder. Wheeling out of the Holyoke Center, she thought of the appointment as a bill of vindication, proof that her behavior was not a cause for concern, let alone a pathological condition. Years later, she would see where her friend was coming from. "Looking back, I definitely did use schoolwork as a way to avoid talking to people, or avoid social interactions," Valerie said. "'I can't do that thing, I've got work to do,' or, 'I'm working on my thesis, I can't do that.'"

Livoti recognized that beneath Valerie's immoderate work ethic was an undercurrent of unexamined motivations, psychological vagaries few people—including Valerie herself—took the time to fully parse. She funneled so much of herself into her coursework that little remained for anything else. Her passion for academics clearly drove one side of that equation, but what was harder to unravel was whether there were any underlying motives driving the other. It was an ongoing refinement as productive as it was fraught, with parts being separated out before a full accounting could be done of what was being lost.

Despite her friends' misgivings and their covert efforts to pull Valerie away from the medieval texts that landscaped her quiet, introverted days, her focus remained fixed. By the end of her sophomore year, she was starting to contemplate the possibility of applying to graduate programs in medieval history. Perhaps, she felt, the field could one day serve as the foundation for a career. She knew it was a rarefied dream, however, and harbored no illusions about the prospects of establishing a life for herself in scholarship. To give herself a legitimate chance of ascending one of the most exclusive keeps in academia's moat-wreathed castle, she'd need the strongest possible pedigree to get her through the drawbridge. Thus began yet another academic crucible, as Valerie turned her gimlet sights on what it would take to transform herself into a competitive graduate school candidate.

By the time Valerie started her junior year at Harvard in 2012, she'd become a clinical tactician at sharpening her curriculum vitae, employing a raft of intricate strategies that would strengthen her candidacy for medieval history programs. Having taught herself introductory Latin over the summer, she jumped directly into the intermediate-level course that fall and put herself in a better position to reach advanced proficiency by her senior year. She resolved to learn German, too, and enrolled in an intensive language course that met for an hour every weekday. (A substantial amount of medieval scholarship is written in German, and fluency in the language is often a prerequisite for competitive graduate programs.) In addition to learning two new languages, Valerie enrolled in the equivalent of five classes, one more than Harvard required students to take. Overextending herself was part of an overarching agenda to get into a top graduate school, but it also stemmed from her fierce dedication and the delirious work ethic that fed it. Under the Hobbies and Interests section of the notecard survey McCormick gave to all of his students on the first day of class, Valerie had once mordantly written "Torture and Pain." Now, it seemed, her masochistic impulses were on resplendent display.

Bobrycki, the teaching fellow, often invited Valerie to graduate student events, and over time she learned that medievalists hewed to a particular personality type. Embracing their "nerdy" quibbling over esoteric details and historical marginalia, they lived with one foot in a distant past rich with character and conflict: crusading knights and sprawling kingdoms, opulent emperors and avaricious kings, the glowering beauty of Gothic cathedrals and the mystics and martyrs stirred by them. A future in such a narrow and deep discipline, Valerie felt, might eventually yield not only a career but also a distinctive identity. Given the amount of specialized knowledge, technical skills, and intellectual acumen the field demanded, a medievalist was almost always a medievalist before she was anything else. The characteristics were exclusive and trenchant enough that they might one day even eclipse the parts of herself she'd been wantonly dragooned with—the wheelchair, the paralysis, the hours of daily rehabilitation for the smallest of gains.

Valerie's studying routine instilled sanctuary and ballast into her daily life. On most afternoons, she traveled to the fourth floor of Widener Library, wheeling to a column of carrels set against a wall lined with large vertical windows that looked out over crisscrossing walkways and the crowns of maples, yellowwoods, and oaks. Her favorite section of carrels sat directly across from an aisle full of tomes on medieval chivalry, stacks whose beige metal shelves few students ever passed. There, she put on her headphones—often playing the sweeping orchestrations from the Lord of the Rings films—and slipped into the immersive solitude in which she did her best work, poring over sources, translating long excerpts of Latin, and notating her minute discoveries in Excel spreadsheets. As the sun slowly withdrew behind the horizon, its fading rays drenched her sanctum in soft, yellow-gold light. Only when she became hungry or cold would she be stirred from her peaceful fugue. She could get so enveloped in the rhythmic flow of her work that she often missed dinner at her residence's dining hall, forcing her to make do with the peanut butter, jelly, and bread put out by Harvard's culinary staff during after hours.

The following summer, Valerie started working on her senior thesis. During her final year at Harvard, she would throw herself into the paper with a fervor that embodied everything fruitful and disconcerting about her academic career. For her subject, she chose the evolution of the medieval tournament across the eleventh, twelfth, and thirteenth centuries. While she took her time selecting a topic, once she returned to Harvard in the fall the project had become her great, galvanizing obsession, the magnum opus in which her three years of enthrallment to medieval history would culminate. "Any time that was available, I would be reading something for my thesis," she said. "It wasn't something I could detach myself from." Consolidating her mental resources and aiming them toward a single, formidable task, Valerie was pouring the totality of herself into her thesis and exemplifying the tireless patience and meticulousness of a professional scholar. Bobrycki invoked an analogy originally made by another historian to pinpoint Valerie's modus operandi. "The butterfly is beautiful, and flits from flower to flower, and everybody notices them," he said. "The caterpillar is a techni-cian. And every scholar, especially every medievalist, prefers the caterpillar, and the good ones want to be the caterpillar. And Val was a caterpillar—who sits on one leaf at a time, and slowly chews every bit of it."

Valerie lived on the first floor of Harvard's Currier House during her senior year, in a single-person dorm next to a common area. On Fridays and Saturdays, her fellow students threw parties in the common area that Valerie never attended. (She went to one party during her four years at Harvard, a *Star Wars*–themed gathering held on the same floor as her dorm.) The pulsing bass lines and din of voices during those nights made it so loud that Valerie found it impossible to sleep. In an encapsulation of how different her life was from that of her peers, she concluded that her best recourse was to treat her involuntary wakefulness as more firewood to pile onto the bright blaze of her scholarly ambitions. "If everybody's awake, and they're keeping me awake, I might as well just do some-thing productive during that time," she said. The late weekend nights became prime opportunities for her to plug away at laborious translation work, including Latin and Old French texts, fording through one sentence after another until long after midnight. Even-tually the clamor would drop away; only then would she transfer herself from her wheelchair to her bed, falling into deep, stony sleep.

Though Livoti continued running interference, there was little chance of displacing the scholarship that had risen to such an ex-alted place in Valerie's life. Her level of dedication was so intense that it had crowded out other aspects of her college experience, re-quiring sacrifices that weren't always made at a conscious level. The ways we choose to cope with life-altering events become only more complex over time. There's the familiar litany of maladaptive cop-ing mechanisms: alcohol, drugs, self-harm. But examine even the most reasonable, seemingly positive ones closely enough, and they're likely to yield ambiguities that speak to the difficult choices catastrophes force us to make. Even in our noblest efforts to distill our identities and refine the scope of our afterlives, our decisions reflect our blind spots and let in more than we can see. In Valerie's case, labeling her relationship to academics as either an animating passion or an "emotional crutch"—a fulfilling vocation that demanded and illuminated all her considerable talent, or a smoke screen to justify jettisoning the uncomfortable aspects of her life—was a false dichotomy. Academics was *both* a passion and a crutch, an adaptation that helped her realize her full potential while sequestering the rooms she resisted revisiting. "I may have gone overboard with academics," Valerie said. But "you need a goal, you need something to strive for until you're feeling stable enough in other parts of your life."

When Valerie submitted her senior thesis in March 2014, she'd toiled over it for nearly a year. The product of hundreds of hours of work, it was 150 pages long and included a bibliography that listed two hundred texts in six different languages. For her superlative efforts she won a bushel of awards, including the Hoopes Prize, a four-thousand-dollar award given to the top seventy or so theses in Harvard's senior class; the Colton Award for the best thesis in the history department; and a prize conferred for the best undergraduate thesis in medieval studies. Her work was also nominated for the prestigious Fay Prize, which recognizes the two or three most outstanding theses among Harvard's entire graduating class.

By the time she attended her graduation ceremony that May, in Currier House's sloping, ivy-wreathed courtyard, Valerie had developed a lasting fondness for her time at Harvard. She loved the way autumn cascaded gently through the campus, sharpening the morning air and transforming the trees' shamrock-green foliage into extravagant spectacles of orange, yellow, purple, and red, the serrated, symmetrical leaves a slightly different hue each day. She wistfully recalled the longer days, after the spring equinox, when she left the library in the late afternoon and wheeled herself through the campus. She loved traveling down one asphalt pathway after another, pushing the chair with enough force that it eventually rolled along on momentum alone, leaving her hands free for a precious few seconds.

Those soft-edged, exultant late afternoons reminded her of the rambling strolls she used to take before her injury. Heading home after classes in Lower Manhattan, she sometimes decided, on a whim, to follow Church Street or Broadway to wherever it might lead her. She wandered into Union Square or strolled through Columbus Circle, lingering over outdoor produce stands and drifting into bakeries and tea shops with an aimless serenity that allowed her to be carried along the various crosscutting currents around her, a leaf buoyed along the branching streams and channels of the city. Though her adolescent mind could not have understood it at the time, those freewheeling promenades were expressions of a glorious freedom that she would not have forever; anything that harked back to that feeling was worth holding on to.

Valerie's four years at Harvard helped her shift away from the stubborn dream of making a full recovery. In the years immediately following the accident, the idea of reclaiming her pre-injury body was the only narrative she could see, and therefore the only story she let herself subscribe to. But time softened those strident convictions. "You just get exhausted after a while," she said. "If you're focused on one thing, to the point where you put the rest of your life on pause, that is a really draining and exhausting thing to do." Assuming a more open-minded perspective on her life, Valerie saw everything she could accomplish and embody as both a wheelchair user and a disabled woman. She could become a scholar, a college professor, could nestle into a social niche that recognized her for the wound-up, wry, and disarmingly warm young woman she'd always been. Even her body image was changing—by her senior year, she'd swapped out her uniform of hoodies and sweatpants for blouses, T-shirts, and yoga pants.

Moving on from Harvard and into the rest of her twenties, Valerie grew more comfortable coexisting with uncertainty, better able to navigate the fluid, nebulous space that Romantic poet John Keats termed "negative capability." It was a stark alternative to the way she'd once fiercely clung to the apocryphal gospel of complete recovery—that complicated refuge for so many afterlives that consumes even as it sustains. She was finally letting go of the teenager she was before her injury and the body that girl inhabited, anchoring herself more firmly in an adult self that had seized on an absorbing passion. No longer married to the dream of walking again, she could now court a future brimming with a range of other worthy ambitions.

GINA ARRIVED IN Columbia, Missouri, in the summer of 2007 for her graduate program in geophysics. Almost immediately, she went about looking for opportunities to make the most of what she saw as her "blank slate"—her chance at starting over after everything that happened in Woods Hole and the trauma that engulfed her afterward. Once she settled into her apartment—a shabby but affordable one-bedroom in the Douglass Park neighborhood—she bought a used bicycle off Craigslist and set off for a solo cycling excursion. She packed some food and a few beers into her backpack, tied an old sleeping bag to a rack atop the rear wheel, and took a three-day trip along a smooth limestone trail that hugged the northern banks of the Missouri River. She rode through tiny midwestern towns, past old-fashioned country stores with dusty front porches and wooden rocking chairs that creaked in the hot wind like squeaking ghosts; slept along the wide, sinewy river; and read the historical plaques commemorating famous locations where Lewis and Clark stopped along their expedition. Gina could see only a few feet ahead of her bike, and the trail unraveled before her like unspooling ribbon, tumbling out of a middle distance that blurred into indecipherable abstraction. But she knew how to maximize what little vision she had, and the fact that there was so much around her she couldn't see became part of the adventure.

During her first semester in the geophysics master's program that fall, Gina taught two undergraduate geology labs. She showed students how to identify different rock strata, embarking on field trips to nearby caves and forests to observe geological structures and the dense tangle of natural forces that shaped them. After meticulously planning her first several lectures, she discovered that standing up in front of a class came naturally to her. It didn't hurt that she was the easygoing twenty-three-year-old teacher, the one who brought her fluffy, lumbering yellow Lab—her service dog, Mitchell—to class; played music as students worked quietly with their mineral samples and magnifying glasses; and opened the windows on warm, sunny days.

Gina's vision, meanwhile, continued its inalterable decline. Her case of S-cone syndrome had been a steadily graded downward slope since childhood, and she knew it wouldn't let up until there was no sight left to lose. By the time she started teaching at the University of Missouri, her vision had slipped below 20/2800. This meant that when she stood twenty feet away from something, she saw it as well as someone with 20/20 vision would see it from twenty-eight hundred feet (over half a mile). Though optometrists consider a figure that high skirting the outer limits of measurable sight, Gina still relied on the slivers of vision she had left to move through her everyday life. Wearing her thick-framed glasses, she could make out murky approximations of objects and people a few feet away, distinguish between light and dark, and read text that was sufficiently magnified. But a shimmering effect continued to disturb her visual field: Objects would start quivering without warning, as though a train had just blazed through her retinas. Her eyes were also losing the ability to cohere the images they independently captured into a single field, causing double vision. When she visited professors during their office hours, she often saw two heads speaking back to her. In the evenings, when she looked up at the night sky, she gazed at the milky glow of two moons.

From Gina's perspective, adaptation was a long, complex chess match, requiring patience and self-possession and rewarding strategy and forethought. There were always more openings and countermoves, an endless supply of additional measures to be taken that could strengthen one's position. Because she could no longer decipher the whiteboards and projection screens professors used in their courses, she started recording lectures on a small audiotape recorder. After class, she asked instructors for copies of any slides and PowerPoint presentations they used. Computers were becoming less legible, too—desktop icons little more than blurry swatches of color and words attenuated to inky fuzz—so she'd crank the zoom feature to the max to read academic texts and utilize oceanographic modeling programs.

Student papers, meanwhile, were often handwritten in dense, slanted scrawl that pushed her eyes to their limits and induced throbbing headaches. To make grading easier, she relied on a magnification device with a glass lens attached to an adjustable swing arm that she kept in her geology department office. The laborious repertoire of compensatory techniques could be exhausting. "There was just a lot of strain around it," Gina said. "The frustrating thing was that, even with all those tools, sometimes I still couldn't do the stuff. And it took me a lot longer to do everything." She nevertheless met every obstacle with a sense of harnessed poise and alacrity, a boxer who knew what to do when the brass bell rang and never hurt her chances by fretting before a round.

In the spring, Gina traveled to her first academic conference, at a ritzy hotel in downtown Portland, Oregon. There she delivered the first talk of her career, in a large conference room with a pull-down screen that covered most of the back wall. She distilled her nerve-racked presentation as "I don't really know what I'm doing, this is my project, please don't crucify me." Despite her surge of stage fright, her research attracted the attention of two male geologists who were leading an academic trip the following summer to the East Pacific Rise, a type of seafloor mountain range called a mid-ocean ridge, located off the coast of Mexico. Because Gina's work overlapped with the research they'd be doing there, they invited her to join the expedition.

That July, Gina and a cadre of students, geologists, and oceanographers set off on the navy-owned research vessel *Atlantis* from a dock in Manzanillo, Mexico, heading west several hundred miles to the jagged oceanic ridge. It was her first ocean voyage since the *Knorr*, which had taken place just a week after she'd been physically assaulted and raped by a fellow student at Woods Hole. She tried her best to not let the parallels evoke too many memories. "My love for the ocean is very old and very deep, and I wasn't going to let the trauma take that chance away from me," she said.

During the two-week expedition, Gina traveled down to the East Pacific Rise in *Alvin*, a world-renowned submersible shaped like the upper half of a rocket ship and engineered to withstand the crushing pressure that exists at extreme ocean depths. After *Alvin* was launched from *Atlantis*, the three-person crew descended three thousand feet underwater and passed into fathoms where sunlight never penetrates, otherworldly landscapes of craggy rock formations wrapped in freezing waters and permanent blackness. *Alvin* floated past mounds of bulging black magma oozing from beneath the splintering ridge; hydrothermal vents spewing dark, smokelike plumes; and bioluminescent creatures drifting blindly through their habitat's sprawling, light-starved oblivion. Though she couldn't see the mesmerizing underworld that surrounded her, Gina listened intently as other crew members described what they observed through the submersible's thick crystalline portholes. During *Alvin*'s return to the surface, she pumped mercury around the vehicle's exoskeleton so that it could ascend in the spiral-like trajectory required to avoid rapid decompression. Back on the ship, the crew dumped a bucket of ice water over her head, an *Atlantis* tradition for those returning from their first seafloor descents.

Over the twenty-four months since her assault, Gina's PTSD symptoms had gradually ebbed. She was no longer tormented by the nightmares that borrowed the physical grammar of the attack without ever quite reenacting it, and she found herself less and less sensitive to the words and stimuli that once invoked the assault and triggered swift meltdowns. Her rage, however, remained potent. "I distanced myself from the experience, but I connected fully with the emotion that I had around it," Gina said. Even as she eased into the challenging but steady rhythms of graduate school life, she continued nurturing an appetite for vengeance, one she saw as a propulsive force. She didn't know how much she would soon need it.

The following winter, in 2009, Gina moved into a new apartment on the east side of Columbia, near a charming park with a picturesque lake, public gardens, and paved running trails. She started getting up early in the morning to go on runs inside the park before strapping up Mitchell and heading south toward campus. With Mitchell leading the way, they carefully picked through the sidewalks and over the concrete pedestrian bridges she'd spent three semesters laying out in her head. On a Wednesday morning in early March, Gina woke up, grabbed her pack of cigarettes and lighter, and walked out to her apartment's small rectangular balcony for a smoke. She'd been looking forward to the day for some time: In the afternoon, she'd be taking one of her undergraduate labs on a field trip to Rock Bridge Memorial State Park, a geological preserve a few miles south of campus.

When Gina stepped onto her balcony and lit her cigarette, though, she recognized immediately that something was wrong with her vision. Everything around her was even less focused than usual, as though her corneas had been smeared with Vaseline. No matter which direction she looked, objects were cloudy and indistinct, coagulating into one hazy, abstract mass. A day earlier she could make out fuzzy renderings of faces, text, and almost anything that was directly in front of her. Now, though, "there was no useful visual information in there at all," she said.

Though Gina had been visually impaired for years, the eyes she was peering through that morning had undergone a sudden and severe decline. She was now almost completely blind, the last functioning cells in her retina having seemingly died off in the middle of the night (because Gina still perceived light, she was technically still not totally blind). Standing on the balcony, she frantically rubbed her eyes, closing and reopening them in an attempt to make out whatever she could in the apartment complex's dull, menacing blur. But nothing changed—every swatch of the world around her looked exactly the same. Her pulse quickened, and her breathing grew fast and shallow. A sense of anxiety fluttered up through her abdomen, fanning out into her chest like a ribbon of starlings. "I couldn't see anything," Gina said. "It was just gone. And I couldn't believe it was real."

Amid the blizzard of shock, Gina arrived at one clear decision: She would have to find a way to get to campus that morning. If she could reach the geology offices and find someone to cover the lab she was teaching that afternoon, she'd give herself the breathing room she needed to start mulling over a more long-term response to her situation. Throwing on a pair of tattered jeans and a black-and-white Misfits T-shirt, she headed to campus "praying that muscle memory and Mitchell the dog were going to get me where I needed to be."

A distance of just over a mile separated Gina's apartment and the University of Missouri campus—Mizzou, as everyone called it. That day, Gina traversed it far more slowly than usual, putting more trust in Mitchell than ever before. She faltered on the sidewalks, scraping her knees against a cement wall. On her way up one of Columbia's pedestrian bridges, she misjudged the stairs, crashing onto her hands and knees. It took her close to an hour, but Gina eventually made it to campus, far from unscathed but relatively safe. Once she reached the geology department, she went to see the professor whose class she was scheduled to lead on a field trip that day. (Though she conducted the labs, he was the course's professor.) Her plan was to explain to him what she was experiencing and together decide what to do about the field trip to Rock Bridge that afternoon. When she got to his door and tried to articulate the situation, though, she broke into tears. "Everybody knows I'm blind," she told him, her shoulders trembling as she scrabbled to push the words out between heaving sobs. "But I woke up this morning, and I'm really blind now."

The professor found someone to cover the lab, and he insisted that Gina head home and try to get some rest. With the looming crisis averted, she grabbed hold of Mitchell's harness and carefully made her way back to her apartment. There, she would attempt to make sense of the full magnitude of her new situation.

In the days after losing what remained of her vision, Gina weathered a sense of shock. "Suddenly it was gone," she said. "I thought I had been training myself and I was prepared for that moment, and I was not." While she'd known that blindness was a stark inevitability, it had always been at a comfortable remove, an abstract fact she could acknowledge without fully absorbing. The tatters of vision she'd still possessed were vital to her daily life, providing an invaluable sense of security and aiding her in innumerable ways. Now those shreds had been permanently removed, and in their place was a harrowing uncertainty and the oblivion that lurched and swayed over all loss.

As the week progressed, Gina labored to push away her sense of dispossession and shift her focus back to coursework. She spoke to her dad and sister, briefly, but she was determined as ever to negotiate her crucible without leaning too heavily on others. With her vision now completely gone, her ability to continue in her program was in grave jeopardy. As if that weren't enough, she was also experiencing other symptoms, including an odd blue light flickering across her field of vision and worsening migraines. But the vision loss was what most threatened her academic future. Given how total it was, she wondered whether she'd still be able to read academic papers, interpret data, or complete exams. Losing the rest of her vision was her second before-and-after event in just three years. A victim of rape not long before, Gina was now being forced to navigate the unforgiving world of academia as a blind person.

One large decision loomed: Would she try continuing with her studies or bow to her new circumstances and withdraw from her courses? In a meeting with her adviser that week—a woman in her forties who'd just started teaching at Mizzou—Gina laid out the harsh particulars of her situation. She also broached some of the adaptive technologies she could utilize to help her keep up with the course-work and finish her degree. Listening to Gina silently as she out-lined her predicament, the adviser grew uncomfortable. "I think you should strongly consider a medical leave of absence," she told her advisee. Gina could sense that the professor doubted her ability to successfully continue in the program. Her voice was shot through with skepticism, her words unfurling with a slow, cagey wariness. But Gina worried that taking a medical leave would kill all the mo-mentum she'd built toward her degree. Further, she feared—likely for good reason—that getting back into the program would be diffi-cult now that her impairment was even more severe. She refused to take a leave of absence, grabbing Mitchell's leather harness and ex-iting her adviser's office at peace with the knowledge that she'd have to face the challenge of adapting by herself.

Gina spent that first week letting the grief and distress take cen-ter stage. This loss had an aching finality to it, and it was going to make her academic dreams harder to attain than ever. But after that initial gloomy spell, she started trying to see her blindness from a novel point of view. She considered whether it was possible to con-ceptualize the loss as something more intricate and nuanced than just physical diminishment. Perhaps, she thought, the absence con-cealed a cryptic form of freedom. Maybe the last vestiges of her sight were holding her back, keeping her tethered to the dregs in her retinas when she could have been committing her considerable ingenuity to her other senses. Gradually, she began interpreting the dissolution of her remaining vision as the lifting of a weight that had been on her shoulders for years—the burden of having to straddle the irreconcilable worlds of blindness and sight. "I really saw it as a positive event in my life, as a release, as a liberation from a world that I couldn't make work into a mysterious and interesting realm that I could explore and be a pioneer in," she said.

Gina's sense of self did not depend on her vision. Because of that, she was able to process the loss relatively quickly and reframe it in a more vitalizing way. She might have mourned the further impair-ment of her functionality that came with her new stage of blindness, but she didn't mourn an entire person or identity. Instead, she was "excited about the transition and the possibilities and the opportunity to be radically free of typical perception," she said. "It gave me a license to transformation."

Gina started examining every possible resource at her disposal. From a practical standpoint, she had not been totally unprepared for this level of blindness. She relied on her memory to build maps in her head of her surroundings, including Columbia's streets and the campus's layout. She also extracted far more information from her hearing than most sighted people did, using voices, footfalls, engines, and other aural details to construct soundscapes that illuminated her surroundings. And when those maps and soundscapes evolved, she used her imagination to sketch the blanks. In those precarious early weeks, Gina relied on her "raw enthusiasm for life and learning" to keep her motivated and force her spirits aloft.

Gina needed to drastically alter the way she learned, and not during some theoretical planning phase, but in the turbulent thick of real time. One of the first measures she took that spring was teaching herself braille. She ordered learning materials through the Commission for the Blind and promptly went about poring over them. To grow more comfortable listening to class lectures she could no longer see at all, she rented audiobooks and courses on CD from the library. Before long, she was finishing several a week. By April, she started shifting her focus to computers, without question the steepest challenge she was facing. Geophysics relied heavily on advanced technology and the computer programs that powered it, and Gina could no longer so much as see a cursor. She needed to relearn how to operate a computer, only this time with all the codes, keys, backdoors, and sheer craftiness she could muster. She devoted several hours each night to experimenting with her computer's voice-command features and familiarizing herself with the deep array of keyboard shortcuts for opening programs, using drop-down menus, and accessing hard drives. Once a significant but limited aspect of her life, accessibility was becoming the defining feature of her academic career, the vestibule through which she had to pass to reach lessons, materials, technology, and even data. Accommodations were not handed out on a silver platter in an ableist society that often seemed loath to acknowledge disability; rather, they had to be mined, grasped, and excavated, hauled up from the margins to which they were sequestered.

Geological graphs presented another forbidding impediment. A computer could read out journal articles well enough, but a substantial part of her graduate work entailed producing and interpreting seismographs, wave graphs, and other visual representations of geological phenomena. Scouring the internet, she stumbled onto an obscure technology called data sonification, in which graphs, charts, and other visual data are converted into sounds that use features like frequency, pitch, and amplitude to communicate graphical material. Throughout the spring, she grew more and more comfortable with the process of absorbing data through the sonification process. There were also tactile displays, embossed printers, and sensational blackboards—all part of an extensive array of instruments she'd have to master if she wanted to continue her graduate career in geology. "Even though that energetic expenditure felt spontaneous to me and natural to me at the time, it was still a huge amount of energy and effort," she said. "I just worked my ass off all the time."

The opportunity to be a pioneer in her field—you could count on one hand the number of geologists with her degree of blindness in the country—provided much of the fuel for that energy expenditure, giving Gina a rousing new identity to work toward. "This is my statement now," she recalled thinking. "To be a monument to human possibility, in the face of some of the worst things that a person can experience."

As Columbia emerged from winter and its maples and dogwoods staged their vibrant resurrections, Gina carried out a prodigious spring-cleaning. She'd survived the semester, but she knew she'd need to be even more disciplined if she wanted to continue progressing as a geologist. Her life, she felt, would need to be stripped down to only those elements that were truly necessary and useful. In April, she purged her apartment of anything that was not serving a clear, consistent purpose. She gave away books she could no longer read, donated kitchenware she rarely used, and bartered off an antique organ that had been occupying a substantial amount of real estate in her apartment. The less cluttered her home was, the better she'd be able to memorize and navigate it. A simplified, even austere living space provided the ideal environment for her to start building a synesthetic coherence that might one day serve as a substitute for her lost vision.

Her pruning process only grew from there. Gina quit smoking, cut down on her drinking, and became a pescatarian. Unhealthy habits muddled her mental bandwidth and sapped her attention, and she felt she needed more of both to properly care for herself now. She sometimes joked that she'd become responsible for looking after somebody who could knock over a vase, press her finger to a knife, or stumble into traffic if her mind momentarily wandered or lapsed. "Suddenly I have to constantly pay attention to this person that is myself, and take care of her," she said.

When her sister visited that summer, she saw someone who'd overhauled her existence to a startling, almost unrecognizable degree. "She really just had this burst of energy to change her life," Andrea said. But she also took notice of how her twin had become rail thin, spoke in almost militant tones about her lifestyle changes, and appeared emotionally distant in a way that left Andrea uneasy. "She was really faraway," she said. "She became radical in a way that was hard for me to access." From her sister's perspective, the extreme discipline Gina was imposing on herself was also exposing her fragility, revealing a young woman who seemed to be holding on to her new commitments as if for dear life. Her intensity was propelling a metamorphosis, but it also seemed to be pushing her toward precipices she could not foresee. "The vulnerability is always there," Andrea said.

That summer, Gina got a tattoo of a chambered nautilus on her right wrist. When the aquatic creature—in a family of organisms called the cephalopods that includes octopus and squid—grows too large for the current chamber in its shell, it builds a new one. Though it never squeezes back into the old chambers, they remain a part of the cephalopod's structure, critical to the fantastical way it navigates the ocean's depths. "Identity is a dynamic, adaptive thing," Gina said. "Only when it becomes rigid and locked-in do you run into the problem of resisting change." It was her conviction that there was "a core something that has been here all along. But other than that, everything else is up for grabs."

CHAPTER SIX

Vulnerability

THERE'S A STORY IN GREEK MYTHOLOGY ABOUT THE GODDESS
Persephone called the abduction myth. One day Persephone
was strolling through a meadow, serenely gathering flowers, when
the ground broke open beneath her and Hades emerged from the
temporary fissure in the earth. Mounted on a gilded chariot led by
four rearing, sable-black horses, he captured Persephone and fer-
ried her back to his underworld kingdom. When her mother, Demeter, goddess of fertility and the harvest, discovered what had
happened, she fell into paralyzing grief. So immersed was she in her
melancholy that she stopped paying attention to her divine purview; soil soured, fields desiccated from drought, crops withered
away, and famine rippled across the human race.

To stanch the growing cataclysm, Zeus sent Hermes to the underworld to retrieve Persephone and return her to her mother. Once
the two were reunited on Olympus, however, Persephone revealed
that she had eaten a pomegranate seed during her captivity in the
land of the dead. Because of this, she was now bound to Hades's
kingdom forever. (Ancient laws, after all, could never be broken.)
Thenceforth, the gods agreed, Persephone would have to spend
one-third of every year in the underworld. She was, in effect, required to pay a recurring debt for that single seed, forced to surren-

der one-third of her life to a ghastly territory few could—or desired to—see.

It was a costly bargain that rescued her while also carving into stone a lifelong sentence of partial sequestration. Wherever Persephone ventured on the peaks of Olympus, whatever new myths she fashioned for herself, part of her would remain forever tethered to the pomegranate seed—pinioned to a specific moment in the past and the way it was bound up with absence, abeyance, and estrangement.

Like Persephone's fateful arrangement, afterlives foster an intricate relationship between the past and the future, one that might be called poetic if its symmetry of form were not also so cruel. Something that's already happened exerts its power over events to come in ways whose particularities may be beyond our grasp but whose expression—in one form or another—is all but certain. This is one way to understand the vulnerability sowed by catastrophic events: the way the limitations and psychic wounds they leave in their wake force people to surrender part of their lives to that event for years to come. By eating the pomegranate seed, Persephone unwittingly reconfigured the future geography of her existence. The traumas that constitute before-and-after experiences possess a similar power to affect the range and territory of our being and bind us to them. They become cyclical forces in our lives—as recurring as the winter season that flows out of Demeter's cataclysmic grief—and no amount of distance from the triggering event can emancipate us from them.

The vulnerability of afterlives manifests itself as a heightened exposure to not only concrete physical sequelae like injury and infirmity but also social issues like unemployment, marginalization, and poverty. Those leading these lives grapple with an increased susceptibility to future crises, trials that can be traced back—in one way or another—to the originative catastrophe. It's not just that these traumatic events have torn asunder and then permanently rearranged the landscape of our lives; it's that they have the power to do so again and again. They maintain their own arrangements, abiding by their own immutable laws, and the ongoing need to pay those recurring debts often renders permanent resolution impossible.

Life sails on, but for many individuals leading afterlives it does so on a slower, more delicate, and leak-prone ship.

BY 1997, SEAN was completing his eighth year of a life sentence. According to Colorado state law at the time, this required an offender to serve forty calendar years before he was even eligible to be seen by a parole board. Sean was still only twenty-five years old; the remainder of his sentence spanned his entire lifetime up to that point, plus another seven years (at minimum). At Limon Correctional Facility, behind the razor wire–topped chain-link fencing that walled the prison off from the surrounding prairie of southeastern Colorado, Sean continued his regimen of prayer, remembrance, and sacramental pleas for forgiveness.

That spring, Sean transferred out of a job that officials referred to as power-sewing, in which incarcerated men manufactured apparel that the prison profited from. Paying these men around seventy-five cents an hour, industrial jobs like those looked an awful lot like slave labor. (A 2015 piece in *The Atlantic* noted that prison industries "have ancestral roots in the black chattel slavery of the South.") Leaving Limon's manufacturing business, Sean took a position in the facility's library. "I got away from that fucking plantation," Sean said. "I just wanted to be around more stuff that would stimulate me mentally."

At the library, Sean worked forty hours a week staffing the circulation desk, restocking the aisles, and tidying up the space's wooden roundtables and plastic chairs. After a few months at the new position, he learned that his supervisor, a taciturn middle-aged man named Spencer, had hired an assistant. Her name was Alice and, Sean said, "She looked like Heather Locklear."

Alice was a white woman in her midthirties, a single mother

who lived in the town of Limon. She was tall, blond, and lithe, with a long, elegant stride. In her first few weeks at the prison, Sean showed her around the library, acclimating her to the day-to-day responsibilities they would both be carrying out as assistant clerks. The men who lived and worked at the correctional facility picked up on her presence right away. Accustomed to a stultifying sea of masculinity, they suddenly had an attractive woman striding through the halls, often in high heels, and the result was a comic frenzy.

Incarcerated men made excuses to walk past the library. When they got to the door, they peered through the window—their faces plastered with sheepish grins—to steal looks at Alice. One guard after another asked her out for drinks at the Rusty Spur Saloon, Limon's local hangout. Alice rebuffed the advances, paid little mind to the oglers, and generally appeared unfazed by the prurient farce swirling around her. She mostly tried to keep to herself, working alongside Sean and occasionally making friendly conversation as they stocked shelves, stamped books, and cleaned up after Limon's residents.

As Sean and Alice grew more comfortable with each other, "We discussed everything," Sean said. "Personal lives, ups and downs, old traumas." Alice had endured physical abuse at the hands of an ex-husband, and as a boy Sean had watched his mother cycle through her own turbulent, occasionally violent relationships. One day, when they were both sitting behind the library's circulation desk, Alice asked him what he'd been sentenced for. Sean paused, his large hooded eyes drifting to the floor. "I'm sentenced to life, for homicide," he replied. He told Alice his entire story, beginning with the wayward, tragic afternoon in September 1989. When he was finished, Alice's eyes had reddened and her face was streaked with tears. "I pray that one day you get out of here," she told him.

Sean and Alice continued spending hours together every day—wading into heavy subjects, making embarrassing confessions, and brushing up against each other in a way that carried an intense, unspoken charge. Eventually, they developed a romantic relationship.

Although they'd find ways to be alone and intimate together, for Sean the connection was about far more than physical attraction. "She didn't treat me like an offender," he said. "I felt very human to be accepted by someone who lived on the other side of prison." If close to a decade of incarceration had wrenched away much of the dignity, compassion, and emotional tenderness that nourish a person's humanity, his deepening bond with Alice was restoring some of those precious salves. He loved her. As painful and confounding as it was under their constricted circumstances, Sean sometimes tried to imagine what a more permanent relationship might look like. "I actually saw myself in a life with this woman," he said.

Sean was happier than he'd been in a long time, perhaps the happiest he'd ever been in his short, tumultuous life. His time alone with Alice allowed him to temporarily transcend the gravity of incarceration and the chronic pall that guilt cast over him. But after a few months, the physical intimacy Sean and Alice were sharing started weighing on his conscience. He was a devout Muslim—and had been so for several years now—committed to a religion that vehemently prohibited sex outside of wedlock. And after Hassan Latif had been transferred to another facility, he'd been named Limon's imam. What right did he have to guide and instruct the other men on the block when he was romantically involved with a woman who wasn't his wife? However much bliss and solace it brought him, Sean knew the relationship was also undermining his faith, a faith that had been a salvific force ever since he left the Bloods. "I felt like a hypocrite," he said. "I'm preaching all this stuff and teaching all this stuff, while at the same time having a relationship with this woman."

A year after starting the clandestine relationship, Sean asked Alice to marry him. She looked up at him, surprised, and for a moment they both stood silently, their eyes gently glancing off the other's. "I would love that," she replied. Because they never obtained a marriage license, Colorado state law never officially recognized the marriage. But they did sign an Islamic marriage certificate a friend of Sean's on the outside had prepared and mailed to them. Their union was recognized by Islam and consecrated by Allah, and for Sean that meant more than the imprimatur of any state or federal government. Their bond continued to blossom from there. Alice eventually converted to Islam, taking her Kalima Shahada in the library where she and Sean worked. Sean, meanwhile, started exchanging letters with Alice's children on the outside, offering them the advice and perspective that his faith had illuminated for him.

In January 1999, Limon Correctional Facility went into full lockdown for a month. Prisons typically impose full lockdowns as either a population-wide disciplinary measure or for security purposes, and men are kept in their cells for up to twenty-three hours a day. After several weeks behind the white steel door of his cell—barred from his work at the library and unable to see Alice—Sean used the prison phone to call a friend on the outside. He asked him if he could set up a three-way phone conversation with Alice. Prison regulations strictly forbade the incarcerated population from making three-way phone calls, and Sean knew going through with the call was a serious risk. But he loved Alice, and he missed her badly; he felt the risk was worth it. With Sean on the line, his friend dialed Alice's number. After several rings, she picked up. "Hey," Sean said. "I just want to say I love you."

"I love you, too," Alice replied. Then they hung up.

A week later, several correctional officers marched up to Sean's cell. Standing in front of his door in their light blue dress shirts and navy pants, they ordered him to face the wall and put his hands behind his back to be handcuffed. "We're taking you to administrative segregation," one of the officers told him. The guards escorted Sean to the wing of the prison where men are sent as punishment for disobeying officers and violating prison policy. There, he was led into a single bareboned cell, about six feet wide and slightly longer than a casket. Sean did not even have enough room to lie across the width of the cell. That night, a major came in and explained to him why he'd been sent there. Officials had suspected for some time that he and Alice were engaging in a romantic relationship. After listening to their three-way call, they had the concrete evidence they needed to prove it. Once they transferred Sean to administrative segregation, they turned over his cell and found letters and cards from Alice that further substantiated their suspicions. The major informed him that Limon's administration would be charging Sean with multiple infractions, including participating in a three-way phone call and carrying out an inappropriate relationship with a female staff member.

That same day, Alice was fired. Correctional officers filed into the library, handcuffed her, and escorted her through the halls of the prison, all the way to her car in the parking lot. Humiliated and afraid, she fixed her face to the concrete hallway floors and let out low, muffled sobs. When Sean heard about what Limon's guards had subjected Alice to—a "perp walk" that was as unnecessary as it was degrading—he immediately understood the purpose of the measure. It was an act of shaming and debasement, carried out to vividly illustrate to everyone at Limon what happens to employees who treat offenders as something more than criminals. "Back then, that's what they liked to do to people that crossed that line that they train them never to cross," Sean said. Like a public execution, it was a demonstration of state power performed to serve as a potent, frightening deterrent.

Two weeks later, Sean attended a hearing for his charges. It was held in the shift commander's office, a small, nondescript space near the facility's visiting room. Prison hearings at Limon functioned like mock trials, with different people filling the roles of judge, prosecutor, and defense attorney. For Sean's hearing, a female lieutenant served as the judge (also called a hearings officer); one of the prison's case managers assumed the role of prosecuting attorney; and Sean was eligible to use an inmate representative for his defense. If he was found guilty, he could face an extended period of time in administrative segregation, a state of solitary confinement that included twenty-three-hour lockdowns and minimal contact with other people. As Sean remembered it, "They were being vindictive, because they didn't like the fact that I was in an illicit relationship with this woman, whether it was because she was a white woman or because she was a department employee."

Sean opted not to use an inmate representative and instead represented himself. "How do you plead?" the lieutenant asked him. Sean's expression was tight and faraway, his large brown eyes falling just short of impenetrable. "Guilty," he said.

"Are you serious?" the lieutenant replied, her voice rising sharply. She pushed her finger down to pause the tape recorder. "Don't you want to explain any of this to us?"

"Guilty," Sean repeated, this time with even curter detachment. During hearings like this one, men accused of violating prison policy were expected to defend themselves, explaining their actions and providing details that contextualized their decisions more favorably. The lieutenant was not likely to look kindly on a defendant who didn't even attempt to plead his case, much less express remorse for his offense. Sean was sealing what was almost certain to be a cruel fate. But for him, depriving the officers of what they wanted to hear was worth whatever punishment they could throw at him. Limon's staff craved a juicy, salacious story, he felt, a slab of tabloid sensationalism to chew on during their tedious workdays, and he was refusing to give it to them. He didn't want his relationship with Alice vulgarized into some bawdy cautionary tale to be passed around and picked over to kill time and stoke the prison's culture of schadenfreude. He would plead guilty, and he would give them nothing.

"Okay, he wants to go to the hole," the hearings officer declared. "Let him go." The lieutenant sentenced Sean to up to five years of administrative segregation. His expression tense and stoic as officers led him out of the room, Sean silently faced down the barrel of over eighteen hundred days of solitary confinement. It was an unfathomably harsh punishment for one phone call and a short-lived romantic relationship, and an abuse of power far more severe than anything Jason faced during his seven years in the Pennsylvania Department of Corrections. And because Alice no longer worked at Limon, his ability to communicate with her and continue their relationship would be thrown into stark doubt.

In the hole, Sean was living on the margins of the margins, isolated and rendered invisible inside of a correctional facility that was itself isolating and largely invisible to the rest of the world. It was February, and his cell was cold and barren, four faceless concrete walls that boomeranged thoughts and forced the mind to crawl back into itself. When his beloved Denver Broncos captured their second consecutive NFL championship during the Super Bowl a week after his hearing, he had no television set to watch them. His material circumstances had always been subject to the callous whims of officials who saw him as little more than a numbered convict. Now, it seemed, they'd resolved to keep even the modest pleasures Limon allowed beyond his reach.

Toward the end of winter, gang violence broke out at Limon. Prison administration responded by cracking down on offending gang members, transferring one after another into the facility's administrative segregation unit. To free up more cells, officials decided to move Sean and a handful of other men to a different prison. That summer, they were transferred to a facility called Kit Carson Correctional Center. It was a brand-new private prison, owned and operated by Corrections Corporation of America, and it sat eighty miles east of Limon near the Kansas border.

Sean's time at Kit Carson would prove to be a ghoulish ordeal. When he and the other men from Limon arrived in a prison bus, Kit Carson had yet to finish training its staff. So ill-prepared were the facility's personnel, in fact, that officers didn't know the proper procedures for escorting prisoners into and out of their cells. As a result, the private prison's administration decided that the safest approach was to simply keep the men locked up for twenty-four hours a day until staff received adequate training. Days went by without Sean ever leaving his cell—not to eat, bathe, or even just stretch his crimped arms and legs. When the men ran out of toilet paper, correctional officers informed them that they hadn't received the training for replacing the rolls, either. They would just have to make do in their cells without them.

For one excruciating week, Sean and the other men who were transferred from Limon were robbed of the basic rights to clean and care for themselves. The psychic toll quickly became unbearable, the squalor and misery far exceeding Sean's previous experiences in solitary. Men were living immured in their own filth, barely able to move their stiffened bodies, and bereft of even the most fleeting human contact. As much out of incompetence as deliberate malice, Sean's living conditions during his first week at Kit Carson rose to a level of inhumanity that violated international standards for human rights. It was a set of circumstances that appeared better suited to another historical era entirely—one of rank dungeons and medieval torture chambers.

Pushed to the psychological brink, the incarcerated men eventually coordinated an effort to protest their abhorrent conditions. Sean and others on his block stuffed their bedding into the toilets to flood the tiers, slammed their plastic food trays out of the narrow rectangular openings they were served through, and pounded their feet against the doors in an effort to make as much noise as possible. The rioting eventually drew the attention of Kit Carson's warden, a towering figure who wore a long, thick mustache and whose ten-gallon hat and high-shafted leather boots gave him the look of an old-fashioned, swaggering cowboy. Advancing through the prison hallways surrounded by his security team, surveying a situation that was rapidly deteriorating, he stopped in front of one of the cells. "What are you looking at?" the inmate spat, his tone barbed with contempt. "I'm looking at a bunch of n—s fucking up the place they live in," the warden coolly replied. Sean's cell was just a few yards down the tier, and when he heard the vicious slur coming from the warden's mouth his stomach tightened into a stiff knot. The man behind the hellish nightmare they were living through was an inveterate racist, and he construed their efforts at improving their living conditions as proof of their inhumanity.

In Sean's second week at Kit Carson, officers finally started letting the population out of their cells for thirty minutes a day. It was a small reprieve, and he continued living under a state of solitary confinement that was not a temporary exception but a permanent rule. Administrative segregation allowed facilities to subject entire prison populations to the practice for years on end. In 2017, Colorado would outlaw the practice, prohibiting incarcerated men and women from being held under such conditions for any longer than fifteen consecutive days. In the late 1990s and early 2000s, though, Sean would spend nearly four years there. It was during this time that he developed the most severe trauma from his twenty-plus years of incarceration. "It was just that isolation, where there's not a whole lot of human interaction other than yelling outside of the door to other people," he recalled. "I went through some mental health issues at that time in my life."

For several months, Sean and Alice communicated through letters, with Alice using a pseudonym. Without all those hours together in the prison library, though, their relationship grew more distant, their affection feeling clumsy, forced. One day that spring, Sean received a letter from Alice telling him that she no longer wanted to continue their relationship. With neither of them at Limon, she felt, it just wasn't the same. This would be her final letter. Climbing out of the pit of each day at Kit Carson was already a monumental struggle. After reading Alice's letter, Sean plummeted further. He was already living in a state of sensory deprivation and extreme isolation, and now the woman he loved—who'd given his suffocating existence behind bars bursts of vaulting transcendence—no longer wanted him in her life. There was little left to live for, and for months Sean "just retreated inside," he said.

Sean's imprisonment imposed multiple layers of helplessness. He had no agency over his own circumstances, living as he did at the mercy of officers and administrators who saw him less as a human being than a six-digit number. He was herded through a system that grew out of American slavery, that incarcerated people of color at multiple times the rate of whites, and that subjected Black men to months or even years of solitary confinement like they were tossing them in county jail for the night. While the remorse he felt for his crime may have been unremitting, he was also able to use it to re-shape his identity, principles, and beliefs—even as the unpredict-able state of his incarceration spurned such attempts at adaptation. On any given day, Sean could be wrested from one set of conditions, attached to tight belly chains and leg-irons that rubbed his ankles raw, and thrust into another building, another cell, another barba-rous island on the nation's carceral archipelago. The reality for men like Sean was that the state's violent deprivation could sweep in at any moment—leaving them dispossessed of everything but their own incarcerated bodies.

Sean spent six months at Kit Carson before the Department of Corrections transferred him to Colorado State Penitentiary, a maximum-security facility run by the state. His time at the private prison would be a source of lasting trauma. He would never be able to forget the crushing isolation, the week of agonizing confinement, or the final letter from Alice. As the years progressed, he would also grow increasingly tormented by the power correctional officers held over every aspect of his life during those months. Their casual cruelty—the way they withheld from him the most basic human rights with bureaucratic indifference, an aloofness as monstrous as it was banal—would haunt him for the rest of his life.

THE TRAUMA THAT plagued Sean after Kit Carson did not make him stronger, and recognizing how those catastrophic experiences that don't kill us often leave us with a lifetime of vulnerability is one of the most forceful rebuttals to Nietzsche's aphorism. The maxim suggests invulnerability—at least in our most simplistic readings of it—and that has been a large part of its enduring appeal. He may have written it in 1888, but we have arguably become its truest au-thors, pulling it out of *Twilight of the Idols* and implanting it into our cultural DNA. As a society, our collective subscription to the attitude and ideology arising out of Nietzsche's aphorism has kept us from a more careful examination of what it means to be vulnerable.

Our enduring affection for the maxim reveals just how incompatible vulnerability is with so many of our American ideals. We prize attributes like power, achievement, and ascension. We continue to champion the characteristics of conquest: growth, expansion, accrual. For many, vulnerability represents the antithesis of those values. Instead of invoking power and bootstrapping individualism, it gestures toward our weaknesses, illuminating regions of the human condition we'd prefer not to think about: regression, depletion, failure, disempowerment. Rather than explore these uncomfortable spaces—which would, ironically, demonstrate the courage that the specious rhetoric of strength often lacks—our stories and art conceal them behind thrilling enactments of Nietzschean power-from-pain.

In an essay for *The New York Times,* Lena Wilson writes that many films about rape are not "particularly interested in the real aftermath of rape. Their characters may shed some tears, but there are no phone calls to loved ones, no visits to hospitals or therapists, no chronic depression or panic attacks. If anything, rape makes these women more resourceful, preternaturally capable of exacting justice without fear of retribution." What doesn't kill them, in other words, makes them stronger. My suspicion is that creators fear that revealing too much vulnerability threatens the narrative, complicating the principles of assertiveness and triumph embedded in our collective psychology. But what we fail to realize is that when we conceal vulnerability behind the language of power and ascendancy, we neglect how much compassion, self-knowledge, and solidarity spring from its taproot. We can feel empathy only for conditions that we've chosen to see and acknowledge in ourselves, and vulnerability means peering into the unexamined depths of our bodies, biographies, and selves. In this way, it is the subterranean passage to others—the routes that lead away from endless conquest and toward universal connection.

The Sufi poet Rumi wrote, "The wound is the place where the

Light enters you." The word "vulnerability" comes from the Latin term *vulnus,* or wound. Our vulnerabilities—those wounds that are never fully healed—can grow into receptacles for more than just pain, damage, and trauma. Rumi's "Light" is the transfiguring force that can be attained after tragedy splays us open, the personal enlightenment available to those who see a void as something that must be carefully filled. But the wounds represented by our vulnerabilities also bind us to others, cultivating deeper empathy than a life of more comfortable experiences could possibly achieve. The more we're forced to confront everything that is bruised and lacking in ourselves, the easier it is to feel moved by and connected to those qualities in the people around us.

Because of the compassion it makes possible, vulnerability is in some ways the antidote to dehumanization, the elemental human force that cracks open our neat, self-serving categories and silos. As the daughter of two Olympian gods, Persephone didn't need to waste a moment's thought on the innumerable souls writhing in the underworld. But after she was condemned to spend a third of each year living there herself, she witnessed those souls—indeed related to them—in a way that would have never been possible if not for the pomegranate seed. Her recurring tragedy and the vulnerability it created was a private revelation, exposing her to the vast outer reaches of human experience. Her plight, that is, was also her pathway to empathy.

In some cases, accessing our vulnerability requires an act of self-exposure—peeling away our carefully constructed personae to reveal dimensions of our identity that do not hew to Americans' reigning ideals. Such exposure allows us to share experiences and emotions we may have spent lifetimes burrowing away: trauma, loss, weakness, shame. Whether we're trying to connect through a painting, a poem, a podcast, or a one-on-one conversation, the more of ourselves we can expose—and therefore illuminate—the more vital and nourishing the bonds we can sew.

Vulnerability and exposure are the inheritances of afterlives, bequeathed to those leading them through their catastrophes and the

wounds they leave. The result, in many cases, is an expanded awareness of those struggling, marginalized, or otherwise cast aside in a
society that shuns people who fall outside its glossy reflections of
itself. Research has shown that individuals who've experienced severe adversities in their lives demonstrate higher levels of empathy
and compassion than those who haven't, and are more likely to take
action to allay the suffering of others. In these cases, vulnerability is
a type of knowledge, an understanding of ourselves and those
around us that, arguably, puts us "in a closer relationship to the
truth." It is the more honest alternative to our myths of strength and
invulnerability, a way of seeing the complicated depths of our own
identities and others' in all their irreparable wounds and brilliant,
inextinguishable light.

AFTER BEING RELEASED from Somerset prison, Jason was sent to a
halfway house in Arnold, Pennsylvania. Twenty miles north of Pittsburgh along the Allegheny River, Arnold was a major aluminum-
manufacturing hub in the twentieth century. By 2011, though, most
of its factories were closed. Along with the adjacent city of New
Kensington, the area's deindustrialization had hollowed out middle-
class jobs, creating the kind of blighted vacuum that the U.S. opioid
epidemic—which was burgeoning at the time—infiltrated and then
fed on. While New Kensington was slightly better off, for Jason,
large swaths of both cities were distinguished primarily by "heroin
and abandoned buildings."

The irony that the state of Pennsylvania was transferring Jason
to a facility in the middle of a city festering with opioids was not lost
on him. He'd undergone a dramatic transformation in prison, spending years shedding the shrewd, disreputable addict and replacing
him with a bookish, intensely focused thirty-two-year-old who
drew inspiration from Nietzsche and Camus and nurtured a geek's
awe for how mathematics anchored the world. But that entire metamorphosis took place in a state of incarceration, and now Jason was

a free man. For the first time in nearly eight years, he had the legal right to leave state premises, walk the streets, and make independent, unsupervised decisions. Powerful temptations skulked everywhere—especially in a city like Arnold. A cold-eyed counselor at Somerset bleakly declared that after Jason was released from prison, he would relapse within a month. Sand was now trickling through the hourglass of that prediction. Jason would be tested.

The halfway house was a two-floor redbrick building called Alle-Kiski Pavilion. Years earlier, it had served as a public elementary school. The walls between the classrooms had all been knocked down, leaving several huge rectangular rooms stacked with metal bunk beds. The tight, orderly living space resembled an old-fashioned orphanage, where dozens of individuals were forced to suppress their private traumas in order to achieve a state of peaceful, repressed uniformity. At night, Jason lay on his cheap, narrow mattress, gazing out the windows and contemplating his state of affairs. Apart from a check for $150 that the state of Pennsylvania issued offenders leaving prison, he had nothing: no job, no driver's license, no permanent address, and barely enough possessions to fill a small backpack. "Everything was extremely uncertain," he said.

The Department of Corrections had effectively erased any evidence of Jason's existence from society. And as fewer and fewer people traveled to Somerset to visit him over the years, he'd steadily faded from the minds of friends and family (save for his mom, whom he still spoke to over the phone at least once a week). Jason was not only marginalized by virtue of his joblessness and halfway house residence, but also bereft of the relationships and social markers that give people traction and solidity in the world. Returning from Somerset in his state-issued sweatpants and shabby white T-shirt, he resembled a ghost drifting out of purgatory, in search of the flesh, blood, and bone that might restore him to a more human form.

During Jason's first week at Alle-Kiski, staff permitted him to leave the facility to deposit his government-issued check and purchase living essentials. When he walked up to the building's large electronic exit door, a security guard pressed a button that popped it open. "All right, you can go," the guard offered. Instead of striding out, though, Jason froze. "Who's going with me?" he asked.

"No one's going with you," the guard replied behind a puzzled smirk. "Just go walk to the store." It was the first time in years that police or correctional officers weren't escorting Jason out of a building, and stepping outside on his own felt unsettling, even alarming. "It was extremely surreal, very uncomfortable, and I felt stupid for having those feelings," he said. Seven years after the culture shock he felt in the county jail when the iron bars rattled open and two hundred men trampled out of their cells, he was now experiencing its inverse. The world he was returning to was governed by everything he'd watched evaporate in that moment: freedom, space, volition. After so long living inside the deep, time-smoothed grooves of prison's cyclical routines—which didn't require conscious decision-making or even much thought—the life of a free person no longer came naturally to him.

At the grocery store, Jason walked the neatly stacked aisles with a mixture of anxiety and almost breathless excitement; he hadn't been deluged with so much personal choice in a long time. After depositing his check and buying shampoo, soap, and razors, he walked over to the deli and ordered a sandwich. Sitting down on a concrete bench outside the market, he attempted to recalibrate himself to the jarring lack of structure that defined life outside Somerset. As a balmy autumn wind blew against his face, he peered over the plaza's sparse parking lot—handmade signs sat in the windows of old storefronts; coin-operated kiddie rides collected dust beneath the overhang; passersby pushed shopping carts and pulled at the small hands of distracted children. "I didn't speak," Jason recalled. "I just sat there. And there was a whole toning down from being super amped-up."

After a few weeks, Jason got a job at a telemarketing firm in downtown Pittsburgh. He would be cold-calling companies, offering to help them secure contracts with the General Services Administration. During his first few months there, he became friendly with one of the firm's managers, a Ukrainian American woman named Tatyana with a sharp, irreverent wit and long brown hair that ran down her back in shiny tresses. Jason and Tatyana often found themselves conversing in the office's break room, discussing everything from the nuances of the firm's sales cycles to politics, religion, and their respective daughters (Annabella was now going on nine years old and living with his ex, and Tatyana had a six-year-old at home). In early December, as temperatures dropped below freezing, they went on their first date, to a Japanese steak house just outside Pittsburgh. Afterward, Tatyana dropped Jason off a block from the halfway house so he could stroll in pretending he'd just gotten off the bus (residents were permitted to leave the facility only for work or legal obligations). Their relationship continued progressing from there. By the time Jason was eligible to be released from Alle-Kiski that summer, they'd agreed that he would move in with her.

Tatyana lived a half hour east of Pittsburgh, in a one-floor mint-green house nestled inside a neighborhood with a small park, a firehouse, and a muddy yellow creek murmuring along the road. When Jason first moved in, he was thrilled. "She had a real bed, she had a real couch, and a real kitchen, and a real refrigerator," he said. The house wasn't all gray concrete facades and smooth steel doors; its decorations reflected personal style and individual choice. And he was relieved to finally be living somewhere that wasn't under the constant 24-7 surveillance that he was subjected to at Somerset and Alle-Kiski.

At first, the "tiny little house" in rural Pennsylvania was "wonderful." But as he spent more time there, Jason's perspective on his new living situation evolved. Cars whizzed by the road in front of the house all day long. The landlord's property was attached to theirs, and the neighbors' homes all felt a little too close. Tatyana's front door was nothing like the thick steel Jason was accustomed to, either. It appeared so creaky and fragile, in fact, that a strong gust of wind might rip it off the hinges. There were no firm, solid boundar-

ies separating one life from another in this nondescript neighborhood in southwestern Pennsylvania. Everything felt too exposed,
too permeable, a dense network of arteries with no walls between
them.

Jason had spent years inside the labyrinthine bowels of a concrete fortress, a place so hard to get into and out of that he and
his cellmate sometimes speculated—their voices inflected with
thoughtfulness—on what would happen if an army attempted a
siege. Tatyana's house, in contrast, felt frighteningly porous. He
couldn't shake the feeling that living inside of it was somehow un-
safe, critically exposing him to the ceaseless peril and lurking violence churning outside their door. At night, lying next to Tatyana, he
sometimes felt an urge to "lock the door to the bedroom and push
her vanity in front of it," he said.

Initially, Jason didn't know what to make of his fear and paranoia. But as he continued reflecting on it, a clearer sense of what he
was grappling with emerged. After fifteen months in a county jail
and five and a half years at Somerset Correctional Institution, this
was the thick, clotting residue of institutionalization. While he was
busy adapting to Somerset's strict rules and rigorous codes of conduct, his body and mind were adjusting to a life of unerring routine
and stringency. Even though he'd been removed from the mold, the
cast was still there, a deep impression intricately notched into his
brain. No matter how many small victories he'd amassed—a steady
job, a serious relationship, an absence of missteps—Somerset still
clung to his psyche, replicating itself over and over in his thoughts,
his dreams, even his nervous system. His existence felt bifurcated,
as though one part of him had successfully moved on from incarceration and the other was still being swallowed by it.

It would not be unreasonable to assume that Jason should have
felt *safer* in a home outside of prison, far away from a culture of
stabbings, beatings, and other bloody attacks. But studies on post-
traumatic stress disorder and post-incarceration syndrome show
that brains struggle to readjust once they're removed from traumatizing environments. Some people continue operating with the

draining hypervigilance demanded by more harrowing conditions, while others find the return to normalcy such an extreme transition that it introduces its own jolting shockwaves. For Jason, life on the outside felt insecure and unpredictable, threaded with unknowable forces and variables that Somerset had systematically eliminated. Pacing through the house and peering out the windows, his mind raced with possibilities, seized by an imagination accustomed to perceiving all of them as surreptitious threats waiting to erupt into violence.

In September 2012, after transferring the credits he'd accumulated at Louisiana State University, Jason started taking classes at a local community college. The effects of institutionalization notwithstanding, he'd spent the previous twelve months rebuilding the layers of his identity that incarceration had rent away. He was working, going to school, and adjusting to a homelife with Tatyana and her daughter, Adrianna. He'd come a long way since his release, fostering the kinds of relationships and personal advancements that pulled him out of the punishing margins so many formerly incarcerated people fell into. Through his progress, he was rebuilding the pride and self-regard he'd lost after his crimes, too, reinforcing the conviction that the foundation he'd laid at Somerset wasn't some childish fantasy. He began cautiously allowing himself to envision a stable, fulfilling future that built on his academic progress and growing intimacy with Tatyana. Then, without any warning, the nightmares came back.

They started as little more than visceral claps of terror awakening him in the middle of the night. "Out of a dead sleep, I feel like I'm having a heart attack," Jason recalled. Jerking up from the bed, his ears rang and his heart thumped. Just like at Somerset, his taut, edgy nerves felt like he'd had a panic attack. Over time, the night terrors evolved into the exaggerated narrative of a full dream: Jason finds himself back in prison, but can't recall the crime that landed him there. He sprints through his old tier, frantically searching for a case manager to inform him of his charges. The gray concrete walls are scoured clean and drenched in bright fluorescent light, but otherwise the prison is denuded of specificity. He runs up to a correctional officer, who tells him that the counselor assigned to his case won't be returning for another three years. As the wrenching horror of another long prison stint sinks in, shame and despair tighten around Jason's chest. As with the nightmares he suffered during his last months in prison, he cannot cope with failure at this magnitude. The dream ends with a gunshot.

In these dreams, Jason's deep-seated fears of recidivism mingled with the infuriation and hopelessness of life beneath an unfeeling bureaucracy, a scenario that echoed works by Kafka he'd read in prison. For nearly his entire adult life, he'd been either an addict or a prisoner, yoked to his desolating addiction or the carceral state. "But now I was building up this life that I was scared to lose," Jason said. "Everyone that believed in me, I feel like I have let them down." When he woke up, usually in the early morning, he'd need to swallow the jagged pill of his own fantasized suicide and prepare for the day. "I was just in prison, three minutes ago, and I made a completely lucid decision to put a gun to my head and kill myself," he said. "And I heard it, I heard it happen. And I felt it. And now I'm here, and I have to pretend like none of that happened."

The dreams leaked out of the night, leaving a patina of corrosive dread bleeding through Jason's waking hours. Still, he was determined to continue moving forward in his life. That fall, he and Tatyana got married, holding a small ceremony at a city park centered around Pittsburgh's white-domed Allegheny Observatory. But even Jason's wedding was not without an ominous underbelly. Just weeks before the event, Tatyana's parents received an unmarked package in their mailbox. Inside, they found a copy of Jason's Pennsylvania court docket, including his criminal charges, conviction, and sentence. Jason and Tatyana had yet to tell her parents about his past, and the sudden, cryptic nature of the disclosure was shocking—not least because of the seemingly vindictive timing. Though Tatyana's parents responded with a level of composure and empathy that heartened them both, the unexplained package would have more insidious consequences.

For months, Jason and Tatyana speculated on the culprit behind the malevolent exposé. He considered people he knew in Pennsylvania and Florida, scrutinizing their motives and whether they were cunning enough to think of something so careful and calculating. Over time, his relentless probing yielded a frightening realization: Whoever sent the package to Tatyana's parents could also send a package—or place a call, or dash off an email—to his employer. "I spent years terrified that someone was going to call my job and get me fired," he said. The package was a concrete fulfillment of all the fears Jason harbored about how his past could suffuse his present, jeopardizing everything he'd accomplished. In its aftermath, all his anxieties and doubts seemed bolder and more threatening, the specter of his criminal record possessing more verisimilitude than ever. He badly yearned to make his postincarceration successes permanent, but the package cast a pall of fragility that made that impossible. He would have to live with that fragility, accepting the gnawing feelings of insecurity that made all his positive momentum feel provisional.

During his first few years out of prison, Jason learned just how deeply incarceration had been etched into his identity. It was a real-life scarlet letter, one nearly as oppressive as Hester Prynne's—not because it was emblazoned on his chest for all to see, but because it could be concealed, and therefore exposed at any time. Whether with colleagues, friends, or potential employers, there was a dizzying array of scenarios in which his ex-convict status could be unveiled without warning to destabilizing effect. He knew how little power he had to control any of them, and the helplessness that inspired was not a feeling he'd prepared for.

No matter how Jason changed or reconstructed his identity, the fact of his incarceration would always be there, a black obelisk bisecting his horizon line. For many people, his criminal record was decisive evidence "that I morphed into a violent criminal, and that's what I will always be under the surface," he said. "The worst possible part of my life, when I was at my lowest and didn't think I was going to survive—I now have to live with that forever," Jason said.

GINA TOOK AN extra year to finish her master's degree in geology, defending her thesis and completing her coursework in the spring of 2010. By the time she graduated, her passions had shifted: She'd become just as interested in bringing geology and other scientific fields to students of all backgrounds and capabilities as she was in studying specific geologic phenomena. Her experience losing her vision and being forced to stumble alone through research and coursework not designed to accommodate her was revelatory, demonstrating just how ill-equipped science education was in teaching students with disabilities. She now wanted to pursue a career in higher education that focused on increasing accessibility in college classrooms and laboratories. It would be her way of trying to ensure that other students didn't face the same obstacles, doubt, and institutional inertia that she had been forced to suffer through.

Through online research and conversations with other disability advocates in academia, Gina had caught glimpses of inclusion technology being developed at different universities across the country. But she'd also experienced firsthand just how little of that technology was making it into classrooms and course designs, leading to a more frustrating reality on the ground. Maybe she could be the person who helped carry out the revolutionary act of closing that gap.

After receiving her master's degree, Gina was admitted to the University of Missouri's doctoral program in science education. She'd be starting the following fall. In truth, a righteous enthusiasm to expand accessibility in the sciences wasn't the only reason Gina had switched academic tracks. She'd also gotten married, somewhat spontaneously, to a longtime friend and fellow scientist named Savas. He'd proposed in December, and they held a small ceremony on Christmas Eve along Charleston's Ashley River, among the regal gardens of a historic property her dad helped manage. (The place was empty for the holidays, and they snuck in using his keys.) Savas was still working toward his PhD in seismology at the University of Missouri, and starting a marriage, she felt, meant staying in Columbia. Pursuing a doctorate in geology would have required her to apply to programs all over the country. By accepting a spot in UM's science education program, she'd be able to start a life with her husband and stay in the college town that had come to feel like a second home.

Gina and Savas—who grew up in Turkey and moved to the United States to pursue a scientific career—rented a duplex less than a mile north of campus, one half of an old wood-framed house with a covered front porch and a spacious backyard. Gina brought her beloved Mitchell, now eight years old, and two impish cats named Pixie and Misfit. Once her doctoral program began in September, she settled into what she thought of as her "efficacious" rhythm: waking up around sunrise to go for a long run in the tree-studded park near the house, then heading south to campus for classes in the late morning and afternoon. She often spent the rest of the day at a corner table in her favorite bakery—the air redolent with leavening bread and the sticky scent of sugar-creased parchment paper—where she'd put on headphones and listen to journal articles through her screen reader, complete writing assignments using her laptop's braille display, and work on her research. Though she'd stopped teaching geology labs after losing the rest of her vision, that fall she secured a job for a university program focused on improving teaching practices in the STEM disciplines. The paycheck provided a much-needed infusion of income to help offset her tuition and living expenses.

For three years, Gina's life had a sense of both security and forward momentum. Precarity was no longer a constant adversary, and a career in academia seemed more attainable than ever. Her ramshackle duplex on Windsor Street was warm and easygoing, with a growing troupe of pets and a mellow, companionable husband creating the kind of cozy atmosphere that had long appeared out of reach. Along the concrete pathways and ionic limestone columns of Mizzou, meanwhile, Gina's confidence as a teacher and researcher was growing. She began allowing herself to entertain the possibility of actually becoming the trailblazing figure in inclusion and accessibility she'd been envisioning ever since her grueling years as a blind geology student. But Gina's fortunes were always fickle, and the mellifluous hum of a stable life would prove to be less a prelude than a peaceful interregnum. It seemed that type of neat, propitious narrative just wasn't meant for her.

In the fall of 2013, the intermittent migraines Gina had been experiencing since losing the rest of her vision started getting worse. The pain between her temples could be so sharp that it would leave her completely laid up—supine on the couch for hours on end, unable to read, study, or even hold up her end of a conversation. One day that November, she'd been struggling with a particularly fierce migraine that took hold in a van on her way back from an academic conference. After walloping her for several hours, it finally receded and was replaced by the warm wash of postdrome euphoria (a phenomenon commonly described by sufferers after a migraine has fully subsided). Gina was unwinding at her house, letting the waves of serotonin tumble over her, when she began noticing that the blue light—which initially emerged after her 2009 vision loss—had become more active and turbulent. Brighter and faster, it flashed through the muddled blur of her visual field like strobe lights strafing across a pitch-dark room. She also noticed a burning sensation near the back of her head, a kind of intense, concentrated heat that was fundamentally different from her recurring migraines.

Two weeks after the puzzling symptoms surfaced, Gina was taking a nap on a couch in the corner of her husband's campus office. Between the throbbing migraines, the burning feeling, and the distracting bright lights, she often grew overwhelmed during the day and tried sleeping the turmoil off. When she woke up that afternoon, though, something had changed. The luminescence, which she'd previously perceived as a "big flashing light field," was drastically altered: When she closed her eyes, it assumed the blurry, glowing shape of her hands and arms. "Oh my God," she mouthed, her voice slowed to a hypnotized half speed. Shooting up in her seat, she waved both her arms in front of her like windshield wipers, shocked at what she was seeing with eyes that had seemingly lost all useful vision years earlier. "I'm seeing with my eyes closed," she told her husband, her voice rising with disbelief as she peeled words from her mouth that bespoke a reality she knew could not be possible.

After several minutes, Gina realized that she was visualizing other parts of her body, too. Her legs, her torso, her feet—they all appeared to her as incandescent shapes quivering with movement. The "continual flickering, electric blue light" she'd experienced for years had been a distinctive but not shocking variety of blindness. Many people who've lost their sight report still being able to perceive light, and some experience blindness less as darkness than as an endless spectacle of brilliant, pirouetting beams and flickers. BBC journalist Damon Rose once described his blindness as "bright, colorful, ever-changing, often terribly distracting, light." Gina's perception of light, however, seemed to have consolidated into something else entirely.

As she waved her arms and tilted her head like a slack-jawed mime, Savas looked on from his desk with a practiced lack of judgment. Over the years, he'd learned that being closed-minded got you nowhere with someone whose empirical reality always seemed to be evolving, a kaleidoscope whose fragments of shimmering glass kept turning in search of new symmetries. Sometimes all you could do was dutifully assume the role of unbiased witness. "That's crazy," he said when Gina related what she was experiencing. "We'll just have to wait and see if it continues." Flooded with shock and awe, Gina left Savas's office to finish up some work for the day. She had an irrepressible sense, however, that whatever it was she'd seen in the cramped, disheveled office where her husband read seismographs and graded undergraduate exams, it wasn't going away.

Over the next few days, Gina's visualizations expanded. When her eyes were closed, she could see a fuzzy but luminous first-person rendering of herself, a kind of wavy blob of light with the crudeness of an amateur cartoon. If she opened them, she perceived objects she came into physical contact with—coffee cups, countertops, sidewalks, blades of grass. "My whole body, and objects and surfaces, and the world around me began to crystallize into this visualization," she said. She hadn't regained her sight, however, and she wasn't capturing light the way sighted people do. Gina speculated, rather, that years of honing her synesthetic perception had culminated in the ability to maximize all the sensory information from her surroundings.

All the time Gina put into reconnoitering in the borderlands of perception—in soundscapes and felt sense and the reconstructive power of the imagination—appeared to have catalyzed in a single thrilling adaptation. The result was a sensory cohesion that gave bleary, resplendent form to the world around her. She described it as a "technicolor wonderland," where the "sounds, the embodied and extended felt sense, my memory, knowledge, and imagination, all fed into a very colorful, dynamic visual world of glowing light." Though it was at times thrilling, she also found the adjustment to this brave new world at the borders of vision stressful and overwhelming. "It was confusing, it was disorienting," Gina said. "I really had to sort of stretch and reconfigure my understanding of reality and my relationship to it, and how this whole perceptual shift speaks to whatever that relationship is. Because I wasn't seeing pigs on the wing. I was seeing myself and buildings and sidewalks and trash cans."

Gina had a friend in the college's psychology department who put her in touch with a Mizzou neurologist named Joel Shenker. Around three weeks after waking up in Savas's office, Gina started meeting with Shenker in his clinic at the University Hospital. After administering some exams to make sure Gina wasn't suffering from a brain tumor or any other serious neurological condition, Shenker began carrying out impromptu experiments in his office. He wanted to determine whether what she was experiencing should be categorized as hallucinations, mental imagery, or a form of sensory perception that actually corresponded with the physical world around her. Over the course of several appointments, Shenker put everyday objects like screws, buttons, coins, and batteries in front of her and asked her to identify and describe them. He would sometimes re-arrange the objects and ask her to try pinpointing them again. He tested her with her eyes open, then told her to close them and re-tested her. He even pressed tuning forks against her hands to see if she could visualize the vibrations they emitted. (She could.)

After spending enough time observing Gina's abilities and listening to her recount the vibrant visualizations that sparked to life when she grasped a coffee mug or stepped in front of a tree, Shenker grew excited about the case's research implications. "It was immediately obvious that what she was having was not a hallucination," he said. He suspected that what he was observing "was a unique set of perceptual experiences." By the end of the year, he'd brought a young resident named Matthew Roberts into the fold, and together the researchers began collecting data and performing more structured experiments. They hoped to publish their findings in a research paper that would systematically lay out Gina's uncanny abilities, introducing a variety of perception that had rarely if ever been documented before.

Shenker and Roberts's research on Gina was published in 2016, in the peer-reviewed medical journal *Brain and Cognition*. In their paper, they postulated that Gina, whom they referred to as patient NS, had developed a synesthetic perception that they termed "non-optic vision." "We think that patient NS represents the most developed case yet reported of high-level veridical synesthesia-like visual perception," they wrote. They went on to speculate that Gina's other senses were lighting up the region of her brain responsible for visual processing, resulting in the perceptual experiences that constituted her remarkable non-optic vision. "If there's another human being on the planet who's ever had these, I can't find any evidence of it in the literature," Shenker said.

For her part, Gina was handling the experience in the same way that she'd navigated so many other challenges before it: by plunging in headfirst, applying her bottomless curiosity to the formidable task of grasping her fluid, ever-changing reality. She read about a Hungarian psychologist named Zoltan Torey who went completely blind in his twenties after battery acid splashed onto his face in a power plant accident. Torey spent years cultivating his ability to visualize the world around him, refining his focus and deepening his powers of concentration. Eventually, he reached a level of mastery where he could produce meticulously detailed "blueprints" that replicated the scenes and spaces he could no longer see. Gina read Oliver Sacks's "The Mind's Eye," the famous essay in which the neurologist recounts several case studies of individuals robbed of their vision who leveraged memory, imagination, and synesthesia to recapture lustrous fragments, painterly impressions, and intricate simulacra of a visual world otherwise lost to them. Though Shenker believed Gina's perception exceeded even those unusual cases, they nevertheless gave her a sense of solidarity across time. Knowing that she was not a straggling, forlorn pioneer, stranded by herself on some wind-whipped island hugging the unmapped edges of human experience, was a source of profound consolation. Being the only person to see the world how she saw it, she felt, would have left her with a deep, bruising sadness.

Though Shenker and Roberts's investigations provided Gina's experiences with a measure of objective validation, not everyone at the University of Missouri was equally persuaded. As word spread around campus that a blind doctoral student was claiming to be experiencing unusual visualizations, "there was a subset of people that thought I was delusional," Gina said. "This girl is crazy," she remembered them suggesting, "and she thinks she can see again." Gina struggled to feel her way through the unpredictable social gamut, and the near-total blindness she now lived with did not make the experience any easier: She struggled to gauge where the harshest judgments were coming from, deepening her sense of vulnerability and exposure. Her days on campus, which she once cherished, were tense and disorienting. When the semester finally ended in December, she felt unburdened.

On New Year's Eve, Gina boarded a plane for Chile, accompanying around two dozen geology professors and graduate students making the trip to study the country's sprawling mountain ranges and arid, alien high plateaus. Centering herself within the natural world following crucibles and trauma had become a leitmotif in Gina's life, and in the first days of 2014, she did her best to take in the breathtaking landscapes around her. Like an artist piecing together a mosaic, she used everything at her disposal—including colleagues' descriptions, her non-optic vision, and the rest of her senses—to perceive the country's coarse, cragged beauty. There were the Andes' snow-topped spires and striated peaks, splintering deserts and salt flats swarming with herds of giant flamingos, and bleached coastline embroidered with spindly succulents and shrouded in sheets of fog. For twelve days, she tried to clasp her fingers around a chunk of that gorgeous, mystifying flank of the world, and draw some peace from it.

But when Gina returned for the spring semester later that month, the pall of skepticism surrounding her synesthetic perception had only grown thicker. Gossip seemed to linger around her, its trails now longer and harder to subdue. Some of her colleagues believed she was experiencing a manic episode, and they perceived the emergence of her unprecedented vision—along with her intensifying enthusiasm and boundless energy—as evidence. Disturbed at how the university milieu could turn on her so quickly, she traveled the campus halls and stone paths in a state of self-protective silence. Savas had left in December for a postdoc at the University of Southampton, in the United Kingdom, and Gina was on her own to navigate the chilly atmosphere. Even her supervisor at the graduate office where she worked, whom Gina thought she was close to, began expressing doubts about her mental health. Her supervisor heard everything, Gina recalled, "all the stuff around, 'Can she really see again? Is she delusional?' And on and on." Concerned about both her employee's mental health and her own reputation on campus, the woman urged her, on several occasions, to take a medical leave of absence. Just as she'd done after losing the rest of her sight in 2009, though, Gina refused.

Nearing the end of her fourth year in the science education program, Gina was only two semesters away from attaining her lifelong dream of a PhD. For her, there was just no logic in jeopardizing her degree because a few students and colleagues were drawing unfounded conclusions about her. Her plan was to forge ahead, defend her dissertation, and get her doctorate. But after her supervisor tried a final time to persuade her to go on medical leave, she sent Gina an email informing her that she would be terminating her position. Suddenly, Gina had no clear way of funding the remainder of her PhD.

The situation only unraveled further from there. That winter, Gina's supervisor had introduced her to a colleague, a woman named Olivia (not her real name) who worked at the university. As the semester progressed, Gina found Olivia becoming increasingly involved in her life—inviting her to lunch, placing calls to see how she was doing, even popping up at her home with bags of groceries. At first, Olivia's intentions appeared kind and guileless. Gina was a young blind woman living on her own, with several pets, in a large duplex apartment; perhaps she'd benefit from a supportive maternal figure checking in on her once in a while. Over time, though, Olivia's agenda grew harder to parse. By the middle of spring, she was urging Gina to explore counseling and psychotherapy, perhaps even consider going on psychiatric medication. She seemed to suspect that Gina's non-optic vision was a pathological delusion, and that she could be careering toward a larger, more serious mental breakdown. Without telling Gina, Olivia started sending concerned emails to her sister, father, and husband—she'd found their contact information online—outlining a situation she felt was rapidly deteriorating under what she saw as a state of unchecked mania.

One particular afternoon that May, Olivia persuaded Gina to visit a counseling facility nearby. Driving her there herself, she remained vague on the specifics of where they were going. "They've really helped my son," she offered, referring to a stepson who'd suffered psychiatric issues in the past. When the two parked and walked through the building's automatic double doors, Gina grew wary. Inside was a vast lobby with a dense, cacophonous soundscape. Everything Gina was picking up on—voices, footfalls, shapes, light—spoke to a large, complex facility. A woman sitting at the front desk asked her to sign herself in. After that, a nurse clipped a pulse oximeter onto her finger and wrapped a blood pressure cuff around her whippet-thin arm. Taking everything in, Gina finally realized where she'd been taken. They weren't in a counseling center, not really; instead, they were sitting in the lobby of the University of Missouri Psychiatric Center. She'd been misled, even deceived, and now she was on the verge of being admitted into a psychiatric unit. Internal alarm bells clattered in her head, and a wash of anxiety flushed through her body. As the nurse finished gathering vitals and Olivia sat quietly a few feet away, Gina could feel herself lurching toward full-blown panic.

Despite Gina's palpable discomfort, Olivia convinced her to stay. They were already there, she pleaded. And if Gina was as healthy as she claimed to be, there was nothing to worry about. Nurses led her into the bowels of the facility, and over the next several hours UMPC staff put her through an extensive battery of tests and examinations that she found physically invasive and emotionally distressing. Her blindness had made her more susceptible to Olivia's deceit, and now the hospital rigmarole and all the doctors, nurses, and medical equipment she could not see were worsening her helplessness and discomfort. "The place was horrible," she said, "and they just treat you like an animal."

Sometime in the late afternoon, a psychiatrist entered the small conference room where Gina had been told to wait in a flimsy plastic chair. In a voice that was affectless and remote, he informed her that a team of clinicians had concluded that she was experiencing hypomania. When she said she didn't think she was mentally ill, he laughed. "Well, all mentally ill people say that." After running through a list of her symptoms, the doctor presented her with two choices. The first option was to admit herself for inpatient treatment, allowing psychiatrists who believed she was exhibiting bipolar mania to observe her for days or weeks and prescribe her psychotropic medication. The second was to discharge herself and leave. For Gina, it was barely a decision at all: She thanked the man and left. Walking home in her T-shirt and tattered blue jeans—her body wound tight with anger and her mind cycling around the deception that led her to such a frightening precipice—Gina tried to anchor herself by remembering everything she'd been through. It was always her instincts, she knew, that best guided her.

Her ordeal, however, was far from over. When Olivia discovered that Gina had been diagnosed with hypomania and left the facility anyway, she staged an even more aggressive intervention, sending an email to Gina's dad, Steve, and twin sister, Andrea, stating that Gina was not capable of feeding, clothing, or caring for herself and that she may be suicidal. According to Gina, Olivia embellished facts and exaggerated certain aspects of her homelife in an effort to depict her as somebody on the edge of sanity, posing an imminent danger to herself. "In this email she used very specific language for a reason," Gina said. Gina believed that Olivia hoped to convince her family to carry out an involuntary commitment—also known as a psychiatric hold—that would send Gina to an inpatient psychiatric facility without her consent.

When Andrea read the email, she became immediately alarmed. "In my mind, I had this nightmarish vision of Gina at her worst experiences and struggles, in real danger," Andrea recalled. "There was a shift in Gina's behavior, and there was a shift in what I was hearing from the people around her." Though she'd never met Olivia, her note came across as an urgent dispatch from a life collapsing under chaos and neglect. Rather than seek an involuntary commitment for her sister, though, Andrea urged her father to drive to Missouri to check up on Gina. Later that month, Gina heard a knock on her door. It was Steve. "He'd driven halfway across the country," Gina said, after Andrea insisted he needed to "rescue her."

After spending a few days with her, Gina's dad felt more comfortable about her situation. She may have been weathering a rough stretch, but she was also more stable and functional than Olivia had suggested in her foreboding missive. Getting back into his Dodge pickup, he drove home to South Carolina. Months later, when Gina finally cooled off, she was able to better grasp Olivia's perspective.

"She saw a person whose husband had gone for the postdoc," she said, and was "going through what's, from the outside, a totally incomprehensible transition." She eventually understood how Olivia could have surmised that it "must be a mental breakdown."

Gina had managed to convince her family that the confounding changes she was going through did not amount to a psychotic break, or a loss in her fundamental capacity to care for herself. But she also felt humiliated and even betrayed: Steve and Andrea hadn't trusted her, and they felt compelled to follow up on a stranger's intrusive speculations. As summer began, though, she would need to face up to an even more agonizing truth. For months, she'd searched frantically for a position to replace the one she'd lost, applying to everything from administrative work on campus to research posts in university labs. Without the money from one of those positions, Gina was slowly coming to realize, in the fall she would not be continuing with her PhD.

In some ways, Gina felt as though she was being ostracized from the larger campus milieu and shut out of her program. Andrea remembered getting the sense that "there were personal politics and mean motives involved" in her sister's struggle to solidify her place on campus and finish her PhD. It seemed highly likely that there was more to her situation than just a lack of job openings on campus. Everything about Gina—her blindness, her outspoken determination to effect change, and her sui generis non-optic sight—made her a consummate outsider, a woman who would never be able to conform, even if she wanted to. By standing out as much as she did, she exposed herself to a collegiate culture that rewarded conformity and staying inside the lines. Her honesty about her sensory experiences and her refusal to pathologize them represented a costly defiance.

Savas was transferring from his postdoc in England to another in Zurich, Switzerland, and would not be returning to the United States. Though he urged Gina to join him in Europe, she didn't want to forfeit her academic track—as imperiled and uncertain as it now was—in the States. "I wasn't up for it," she said. "I could have just gone overseas and been the wife, but I didn't want to go to Switzerland. When it really came down to it, I didn't love him enough to throw my life away and move." She opted to remain alone in Columbia, her future now murkier than ever, again struggling to make the most basic ends meet. She found some work through the Commission for the Blind—menial jobs that were hard to travel to and for which she was laughably overqualified—and she discovered a state-sponsored pension for blind Missourians. But the lofty academic aspirations she'd harbored with such untempered exuberance had been, for now at least, dashed. She was achieving little more than subsistence survival, scraping by on pension checks and low-paying temp gigs and bereft of the overarching purpose that had given so much meaning to her life. It was a juncture she found "devastating," one where her identity had in some sense been stripped back down to her disability, the person all her perseverance and intellectual vigor had led her to become spoiling away to a papery husk in a matter of weeks. Even her sexual trauma had never dealt her such a torturous blow. There was no denying that her blindness had always been an inextricable aspect of her biography, its challenges a persistent feature of her adult life. But over the course of that spring and summer, that relationship seemed to have inverted itself: Her biography now felt like little more than an unalterable expression of her blindness. Would nothing else ever take as deep a hold?

Dual Citizenship

IN THE EARLY MORNING HOURS OF A MONDAY IN FEBRUARY 2020, I
awoke to a dense, immovable pain. While I'd slept, an excruciating
ache had settled over my entire body. The throbbing radiated from
the soles of my feet to the nape of my neck, and I struggled to make
it to the bathroom cabinet where I kept the ibuprofen. I fared no
better in the morning light, shuffling, like a hunched wraith, to the
extra bedroom I'd converted into an office to open my computer and
cancel my scheduled calls for the day.

The following morning was much the same, and as the week
progressed it became clear that I was in the throes of the season's flu
virus. My symptoms were a noxious but familiar horde: inflamed
sinuses that barred any airflow and kept me congested and struggling to take full breaths; shivers that rumbled through my coiled
body; scabrous coughing fits that culminated in long, disturbing
wheezing. My body hurt, all over. Watching the week slip away from
my rumpled perch of disheveled pillows and twisted bedsheets, a
laptop queued to Netflix glowing in the shuttered half-light, I felt
the sense of industriousness and professional exigency I'd spent
years cultivating suddenly under attack. But the flu was a known
quantity, its course vexing but predictable. Enfeebling though it felt
at the time, it would do its worst and then be over.

On Thursday, I felt well enough to return to a mostly full day of work. By the following morning, though, my body faltered, stumbling back into infirmity. I felt dizzy and disoriented, laboring to fix my eyes on my laptop as the text in emails and documents blurred and frayed. I struggled to concentrate, too, my mind fluttering as though it were a compass whose magnetic needle couldn't stop swinging. And while the aching pain all over my body had abated, it was replaced with a feeling of acute weakness that sapped what limited mental and physical vigor I had. To an even greater extent than normal, I felt shucked and barren.

By midmorning I'd given up on working entirely. I hurried across my apartment complex, got into my car, and headed to the nearest pharmacy. There, I snatched a bottle of grape-colored cold syrup and a box of tangerine-flavored immune support tablets. Even driving required the marshaling of maximum effort, as I strained to shift lanes safely and execute smooth turns amid the illness's stifling malaise. By the early afternoon, I was growing legitimately concerned. Had the flu somehow destabilized my body's defenses, exacerbating my chronic fatigue syndrome?

Since I first fell ill with the Epstein-Barr virus that evolved into CFS seven years earlier, I'd grown thoroughly accustomed to my chronic illness's repertoire of intractable symptoms—how they muddled my memory recall, shrank my stamina to a fraction of its youthful peaks, rendered my sleep unrefreshing and my days washed-out. These were not flare-ups, waxing symptoms, or a fleeting exacerbation of my condition; they were my everyday reality. Though my own experience with CFS had been stable and—in the wider scheme of this illness—relatively mild, I knew how much worse some sufferers had it. When the author Laura Hillenbrand, who has CFS, told *The New York Times,* "Fatigue is what we experience, but it is what a match is to an atomic bomb," her analogy spoke for the experience of perhaps close to a million Americans. Though the burden of my symptoms remained significant, I often wondered what, exactly, was separating me from CFS's worst victims, and how sturdy and dependable that invisible border actually was.

A week had passed since I'd first fallen ill with the flu, and my condition had only declined. Worse, my symptoms were becoming less and less recognizably flu related. The regression evoked some of my worst fears, as I thought about the more disabled people with CFS I'd seen over the years. "What a match is to an atomic bomb." I was scared.

It was the first time since the onset of my condition in late 2012 that I'd experienced this palpable sense of dread surrounding my illness. That Friday—Valentine's Day—I struggled to string together more than a couple hours' worth of work. I was too weary, the effort to corral my torpid thinking into sustained focus too much. My capacities all seemed to be diminishing, and I felt like a country whose borders were shrinking on all sides by the day. I had my intuitions about what was happening, but I dared not give them too much credence. I told myself, over and over, that this spell of infirmity would end soon.

It had been an unusually warm, dry February, even by Northern California standards, and as the day's temperature rose to the mid-sixties, I kept the blinds shut and contemplated a single inescapable question: How long would this downturn last? If the past week was establishing a new precedent, ushering in another chapter in my existence—and coexistence—with this condition, then the life I'd painstakingly constructed since first developing CFS was in terrific jeopardy. Continents away from acceptance, all I could think to do was remain relatively calm. I had to remember to breathe, keep myself centered, and do my best to remain confident that whatever I was experiencing was most likely the transitory effects of a flawed immune system thrown into further disarray.

This particular Valentine's Day signified more for me than couture chocolate and teddy bears. It was the eve of the weekend I was planning on proposing to my longtime girlfriend. We'd made plans, earlier in the year, to drive up to Redwood National Park, which sat several hours north of us near the Oregon border. There, we'd spend a few days hiking through the sprawling redwood groves that hugged the Pacific Ocean and scanning for the majestic Roosevelt elk that roamed beneath the dense, towering canopies.

I'd spent weeks planning the proposal with meticulous care: We would watch the sunset on a secluded beach next to a quaint white-brick lighthouse, as a violinist emerged on the rocky banks to serenade my girlfriend while I made a brief speech and knelt on one knee. Now, though, I was ruminating in our ground-floor apartment, the romance and anticipation replaced with aggrievement and shock. "I'm not sure my body can handle making the trip right now," I told her in a strained voice. As we exchanged gifts and dangled toys in front of Lucas, an azure-eyed snowshoe cat we'd recently adopted, the balmy night was glazed with the mutual recognition that my frailties were once again tainting our plans. I'd contended with this truth enough times before, but watching as my illness not only diminished my own life but also affected my significant other's never failed to reopen the old gash. These little frustrations and heartbreaks were always repeating themselves, my vulnerability an open wound that was seldom as sealed as it looked.

The next morning, I decided to go through with our trip to Redwood. I was far from recuperated, but there was just too much riding on the long weekend for me to surrender it. The dissonance was not lost on me: What was once a carefully orchestrated romantic getaway would now be doubling as a precarious gamble on my health. When a person's CFS symptoms worsen, most specialists recommend that patients allow themselves a commensurate amount of time to rest and regain strength. Pushing through, most think, risks making things worse. Given those widespread prescriptions, I wondered whether resigning myself to a weekend of convalescence would have been the more prudent decision. I could have let go of the beach, the lighthouse, the serenade, and started brainstorming another plan for my proposal from the safety of my bed. My condition was foisting a familiar ultimatum onto me: Maintain your grip on your life and risk exacerbating your condition, or relinquish that grip to cut your losses and forestall further deterioration.

Heading north up Route 101, we drove through curving mountain passes and flitted by lakeside resort towns peppered with spiky succulents and ramshackle boats marooned on patchy square yards. As we grew closer to the park, the surrounding landscape gradually transformed into the sprawling evergreen forests and gauzy wreaths of mist signaling entrance into the Pacific Northwest. Spruce, Douglas fir, and western hemlock stood alongside the mammoth coastal redwoods, forming an immense, largely unbroken wilderness that carpeted thousands of miles of coastline in lush tangles of Pacific rainforest.

Though I remained dizzy, weak, and swaddled in malaise throughout the weekend—symptoms that had become familiar over the years but were now more jarring and intense—the trip went as well as I might have hoped. On Sunday night, we sat on a sunbleached log on a narrow spit of beach overlooking the lighthouse keeper's one-room cottage. Getting down on one knee over the shifting heaps of salt water–smoothed gray stone and fractured scallop shells, I pulled open the small velvet box I'd kept hidden for weeks and asked my girlfriend to marry me.

Though it was a beautiful evening, full of bright eyes and bursts of elation, my mind couldn't help drifting toward the dichotomy I'd found myself in. Amid this weighty life event, I was straddling two starkly different realities. As dusk fell over the tumbling Pacific waters and the muted beaches that dipped toward them, we walked to a small restaurant pitched over a mossy cliff overlooking the white-capped surf. Peering out of the dining room's floor-to-ceiling windows toward a silvery horizon, I wondered whether this was a dichotomy I was destined to be pinioned to forever—and if, under the current strain of worsening symptoms, it would be able to hold. For years I had quietly exercised my dual citizenship in what Susan Sontag called the kingdom of the well and the kingdom of the sick. But that weekend, I felt the delicate balance teetering. If those borders were suddenly shut down, what power did I have to stop it?

The long weekend I'd crafted with dioramic care now firmly behind me, I cautiously moved into the following week. Each day my symptoms showed no signs of improvement, the stakes were ratcheted higher. Every project or task I toiled over in futility was full of dreadful portent, a notch on the wall signifying another defeat. I just didn't know whether my functionality would return to its previous baseline, and the uncertainty was tormenting me. By pushing myself and maximizing my abilities and functionality—such as they were—I'd long been able to retain something approximating a full life. But the arrangements had changed, without pretense or warning, and now that precarious pact was collapsing.

My mood was grave, serrated, my mind slipping into its own tense and isolating atmosphere. I observed my attention span grow smothered and frantic, darting through constellations of possibilities but incapable of considering them thoughtfully. Because of a mixture of my worsening symptoms and their emotional toll, I was scarcely speaking to friends, family, or even the woman who had just become my fiancée. The alarming scenarios reverberating across the corridors of my mind, it seemed, had sewed my mouth shut.

One afternoon, as I was taking a walk along an asphalt bike path that snaked past duck ponds, backyard patios, and squat orange trees, I was struck with a flash of insight. The previous two weeks had very closely mirrored the experience of falling ill seven years earlier with the virus, mononucleosis, that triggered my development of CFS. There was the acute onset of an aggressive viral infection, the wobbly convalescence, and then the mysterious excrescence of new symptoms that left me distraught and unwell. Only this time, of course, I already had CFS, and so what this virus was leaving in its wake was a sudden escalation of everything I'd spent years adapting to at lower degrees. My experience possessed the air of resurgent trauma, the terrifying sense that your most agonizing trial was repeating itself, resurfacing for another sadistic go at you.

While I didn't consider this experience traumatic in the strict sense of the word, the current development was revealing the recurring, cyclical nature of my life-altering event. I had spent seven years adapting to my condition—changing careers, moving across the country, discovering new passions to replace the ones I'd lost— and yet here was proof that those adaptations were not nearly as secure as I had thought. My sense of stability was an illusion: I could not truly indemnify myself against new crises stemming from that day in December years ago. This, as I came to understand it, was the true face of my vulnerability. No amount of progress, adjustments, concessions, or even time would be enough to grant me a full separation from that day. Part of me would always be tied to the pomegranate seed, forever subject to the replication, in one form or another, of my illness's onset. In some genuine, irrefutable way, my body had never really exited from that moment.

During the worst stretches of my illness, long afternoons when the muscle pain twinged my arms, hands, and wrists or bleary mornings when my mind felt like an echoing void, I longed for time to slow. Just give me a day or two to hunker down and recuperate, I would think. But life did not slow down; instead, it surged from the spigot. My fiancée and I now had the prodigious task of planning a wedding ahead of us, with numberless venues and vendors and wedding party details all awaiting our time and solicitude. My sister, who lived across the country in Connecticut, near where we grew up, was thirty-odd weeks pregnant, with a baby boy due any day. We spoke daily, as she recounted her sleepless nights and nerve-racking false contractions, the hormonal cyclone of emotions wheeling through her.

Though I permitted myself to be only dimly aware of it, the second half of February also held a pair of painful milestones. The anniversaries of my parents' deaths were three days apart, on Wednesday the nineteenth and Saturday the twenty-second. It would be the twenty-eighth anniversary for my mother, and for my father, the first. I looked with melancholic apprehension toward the fast-approaching week, the dates lodged like twin IEDs tucked a few feet away from each other under February's frozen dirt.

But it wasn't the grief, sadness, or memories those anniversaries might dredge up to the surface of my mind that troubled me. What concerned me most was how my illness and all the additional bandwidth it now demanded might sap all my attention, leaving no room for me to take a deep breath and remember my parents. I feared that I would be deprived of the serenity necessary to conjure the mirror-shard memories of who they were and in what specific ways they acted out their love for me. My thoughts were hijacked, and I worried I lacked the breathing room necessary to feel anything besides the fear and desperation CFS itself evoked in me.

So instead of preparing to mourn my parents, I shifted into pre-emptive bitterness that even grieving was a luxury I would not be afforded. Still, my sister and I spoke about them both, briefly, during the week, and I eventually found the time and space to let myself slip into several clear, untarnished recollections—my dad diving into the collapsing waves of the Atlantic Ocean in his cream-colored swim trunks, coming up for air with the sunbeam grin of an untroubled boy, and my mom giving my sister and me a bath in our porcelain enamel tub, scooping up the warm water in an oversize plastic cup and letting it cascade like a gushing fountain over our slick, matted heads.

By the time the anniversaries were behind me, two weeks had passed since I'd first fallen ill. I remained nowhere close to a full recovery. Between the worsening fatigue and concentration problems and the question of what the sudden decline portended for my future, days took on a phantasmagoric quality. I'd catch myself zoning out as I gazed through the slatted blinds of my dining room windows to a cerulean sky painted over sun-speckled pine trees and Spanish tile roofs. Some days I would be lying on my bed in a run-down daze by noon. I slept long enough at night—an attempt at recovering my strength—that the textures and images of visceral, gothic dreams trickled into my mornings, leaving my grip on reality noticeably loosened. One afternoon after another of debilitation, doubt, and escalating paranoia were taking a toll on my psyche, and my thoughts had developed the sharp, jumpy edges of an exhausted fugitive.

Though I would eventually climb back to my pre-February levels of health and energy, the month served as a brutal reminder that there was little insulating me from deeper infirmity. I was left, finally, with two options: Either live with the premonition of decline, waiting anxiously for the next shoe to drop, or hope, quixotically, that there was some kind of divine, invisible thread keeping me on bearable ground.

CHAPTER SEVEN

Devotion

AFTER SERVING FOUR YEARS IN SOLITARY CONFINEMENT—THREE
months in Limon's administrative segregation unit, six months
at Kit Carson's private prison, and over three years at Colorado State
Penitentiary—Sean was transferred to Arkansas Valley Correctional
Facility. There, ninety miles southeast of Colorado Springs in the
state's sparsely populated high plains, he rejoined the general population. Arkansas Valley housed a thousand inmates of various security levels. By the spring of 2002, when he was transferred there,
Sean was a few months shy of thirty years old. He had by that point
spent nearly half his time on earth in Colorado's state prisons, moving from one sprawling complex to another at the behest of the officers, lieutenants, captains, and wardens who governed his life.
The texture of existence inside the matte concrete walls had become deeply interwoven with the fabric he recognized to be his
own life: the sharp chemical smell of state-issued soap and laundry
detergent and the pungent aroma that saturated the prison gyms;
the specific way certain gang members moved through the yard,
hunched over conspiratorially with guarded expressions and eyes
sharp as bayonets; the pregnant silence just before dawn, when
Sean knelt in his cell's relinquishing dark to pray as the men on his
block slowly rustled awake. Every morning, he put on his hunter-

green pants and V-neck shirt, laced up his size-eleven-and-a-half black boots, and psychologically prepared himself for another day of wading through a world that could be both torpid and violent, familiar and alienating, capable of slowing down time and devouring it at once.

Twelve years after the Kalima Shahada ceremony that symbolized Sean's official conversion to Islam, the religion remained his foundation. The imam at Arkansas Valley, a bald, bearded man in his midforties, was impressed with Sean's grasp of Islam's core texts and facility for Arabic, and asked him to become a vizier, or Islamic teacher, for the several dozen Muslims there. As he settled into his new surroundings, Sean instructed new Muslims in the Hadiths, which recorded the words and deeds of Muhammad; led in-depth discussions of passages in the Koran; and even taught Arabic to those with the patience and diligence to learn.

Sean hadn't spoken to Alice in over three years. Though their marriage was recognized by Islamic law, it was never legally certified. As heartbreaking as the dissolution of their relationship had been for Sean, its nature and limitations meant that it had vanished from his life all but without a trace. After the brutal, yearslong punishment for his relationship with her, Sean was determined to be a blameless figure at Arkansas Valley. He took a position working for the Colorado Department of Motor Vehicles, a so-called industry job that paid better than most. His eight-hour shifts taking calls for the DMV made him close to a dollar an hour—still exploitative, to be sure, but a boon compared to the twenty or thirty cents an hour men earned serving meals in the kitchen, mopping the tiers, or laundering uniforms. Sean also collaborated with several others on his block to undertake a major initiative: lobbying the facility's administration to create an "incentive unit" for the prison's most exemplary residents.

Sean and the other men argued that it wasn't right for decent, hardworking individuals who never got in trouble and steered clear of the prison's array of illicit operations to suffer because of the transgressions of a single bad actor. There should be an opportunity for the most upstanding members of Arkansas Valley's population to avoid the blanket punishments that swept through the entire facility following a violent assault in the weight room or the bloody fallout from a gambling debt.

"I was tired of hearing people next door to me have their heads bouncing off the concrete while screaming for someone to stop beating them," Sean said. When presenting the idea to correctional staff, he would ask them, "Even though I'm not involved in anything like that, why do I have to endure even listening to it? How can I prosper from being in an environment like that?"

It took several years, but Sean and the rest of his cohort eventually persuaded the administration to establish the incentive unit they envisioned. (The staff likely felt the existence of such a unit would motivate everyone in the facility to walk the line.) In the incentive unit, incarcerated men could move freely from one cellblock to another, order food from the same menu as correctional officers, and even use videogame consoles set up in each pod's common area. One afternoon in 2007, Sean was in the incentive unit's dayroom talking with a close friend everyone called Papa T. Papa T explained to Sean that he'd just finished a powerful book, one that was transforming his whole perspective. By the time he'd reached the last page, he knew he'd never think about his future in the same way again. When Papa T asked Sean if he wanted to borrow the book, he nodded emphatically.

Almost two decades had passed since the crime Sean haphazardly committed as a teenager. The most forceful emotion in his life, however, remained his guilt—the stubborn conviction that he deserved to suffer forever for what he'd done. The book Papa T gave him that afternoon was *The Secret,* a self-help work published the previous year espousing the idea that changing one's thoughts and beliefs can alter future experiences. In the days that followed, Sean sat cross-legged on the narrow mattress in his cell and pored through the book. When he finished reading it, just days after Papa T lent it to him, he felt an unmistakable shift inside himself. "That book was the first time that I ever read that you shouldn't make yourself suffer for the rest of your life for mistakes," Sean said. "Because if you do, then you're bringing more mistakes to you. You're bringing more negativity to you. If you want life to be better, if you want to be an improvement upon the world that you live in, then you're going to have to forgive yourself."

What the book had to say regarding Sean's specific circumstances was galvanizing in its utter lack of ambiguity: Start living your life as though you're going to get out of prison. "They are going to come to me one day and tell me that I am going home," he said. "And so I have to prepare for that right now." Over the next few weeks, Sean did start preparing for that, giving away any possessions he felt were tied to his incarceration or would not be needed once he was freed. He gave one friend a favorite plastic knife he'd used for years to cut the commissary's holiday sausage, and gifted one of his beloved prayer rugs to another. He walked up to one of the Muslims on his block and offered him the very first Koran he'd ever owned, a green hardbound copy with gold lettering given to him by Rydhwan, the man who introduced him to Islam seventeen years earlier. When the Muslim asked him why he was giving it away, Sean told him, simply, "Because I'm going home."

"What are you talking about? You have a life sentence," the man replied.

"Well, yeah, I do now, but I believe I'm going home, and I'm going to start preparing to go home now."

For the first time since he turned himself in at seventeen years old, Sean began seriously considering how he might go about working toward his release. He would not technically be up for parole until he'd served forty calendar years, which meant his earliest ostensible chance to be freed wouldn't come until the year 2029. But that summer, Colorado governor Bill Ritter announced the creation of the state's first Juvenile Clemency Board. In a press release, the governor explained that the board would "bring an added level of expertise to the review process and help ensure that the interests of justice are served in cases where juveniles are tried and sentenced as adults."

Cagey political phrasing notwithstanding, the board's establish-ment was an auspicious development for Sean. A clemency board focused exclusively on juveniles meant that more eyes would be on cases like his, where a teenager had been tried as an adult, trans-formed himself during his time in prison into a model individual, and was searching for the second chance his draconian sentence all but precluded. Sean knew it was the rare chance he'd been looking for, a path that made the early release he was preparing for actually possible. He'd started a clemency application years earlier, but he'd possessed little faith that it would ever amount to anything. But after reading *The Secret* and then hearing about Governor Ritter's announcement, the hand of the universe seemed to be extending its palm toward him.

For the clemency application, Sean compiled letters of reference from a cousin, a man he'd become close friends with during his time in prison, and his older brother, TL. When Sean first turned himself in, in 1989, TL had just had a baby girl named Ashley and was getting ready to leave Aurora for basic training in San Antonio. Now he had three daughters, served as a technical sergeant in the air force, and lived with his family on a base in Southern California. "I want you to put it on your official air force letterhead," Sean told his brother, "explaining to the clemency board why you believe your little brother should come home."

Sean also composed a letter to Governor Ritter, detailing how he'd been "part of the problem" in the 1980s, but had spent the years since "striving to be part of many solutions in this world." Even if he wasn't granted clemency, he told the governor, "I am still going to be doing positive things right here where I live, sir." Finally, Sean de-cided to write a letter to the victim's family, taking responsibility for his actions that September afternoon. Sitting at his desk, in front of a gray daisy-wheel electric typewriter his brother had sent him, he groped for words to express the illimitable guilt and sorrow he'd felt every single day since the fatal shooting. "If I am ever in your pres-ence, I would probably just fall to the ground and beg for your for-giveness until you allowed me to get back up," he wrote. He finally submitted his application to the Arkansas Valley assistant warden in the summer of 2009. From there, it was sent to Colorado's Juvenile Clemency Board.

Months went by, and Sean heard nothing. By January 2011, it had been well over a year, and he rarely gave much thought to the application. He always knew clemency was a long shot—everyone in prison knew that—and he'd done his best to keep any unrealistic hopes at a safe distance, grounding himself in the routine that made life under incarceration bearable.

One afternoon, Sean was sitting in his cell, crocheting. It was a pastime he'd taken up in prison after recalling the calming influence it had on his mother when he was growing up. Casting yarn onto her crochet hook, she'd had an expression of serene absorption that he never forgot. Sean was on his bed crocheting a teddy bear—other men at Arkansas Valley often bought his crochet bears to send to family on the outside—when a friend named Dietrick motioned him to come out. Men in the incentive unit could move freely outside their cells, and Dietrick had just returned from the visiting room when he waved Sean over. "Hey, listen," Dietrick told him breathlessly, his baggy green prison uniform hanging loosely from his skinny frame. "My aunt told me that we were in the paper, and we got our sentences commuted."

Sean locked eyes with Dietrick. His large, bearded face, only a minute ago engrossed in hypnotic focus, softened with disbelief. For several seconds Sean remained silent, laboring to grasp the implications of the words his friend had not so much uttered as expelled. He could feel whorls of anxiousness and excitement eddying in his chest and stomach, spiraling like dough in a mixer at the prospect that something so glorious might actually be true. For the sake of his own protection, though, he headed off Dietrick's words. He needed to maintain a strong sense of skepticism, and he implored his friend to do the same. "Just calm down, and let's look for proof," Sean said.

But instead of searching for some evidence that might corroborate Dietrick's words, Sean strode back into his cell and returned to making teddy bears. He needed to soothe his startled nerves, and he didn't want to abandon the perennial rhythms of his life before he had any confirmation he was truly free from them. Dietrick was rash and excitable, like the incentive unit's version of Tigger from Winnie the Pooh, and Sean remained wary of investing too much hope in someone with less-than-perfect credibility. Sitting back down on his cot, the rusted old springs squeaking loudly as they sank beneath him, he picked up the crochet hook and hoped its pacifying cadence would hush a mind and body suddenly keyed up to the ecstatic possibility of freedom.

About an hour later, Sean was called to one of the sergeant's offices. When he arrived at the door, the sergeant was sitting at his bulky desktop computer, looking up at him. "Hey Sean, I want you to read what's on this screen," he said. As Sean walked over, he could see that it was displaying some kind of letter. It was an official press release, issued from the office of Governor Bill Ritter. "What's it say?" The sergeant asked him. Sean bent his bulky six-foot-two frame and quietly scanned the press statement. Then, with muted intensity, he read it several more times. Finally, he uttered the words aloud. "It says, 'Sean Taylor, who in 1990 was sentenced to life for first-degree murder. Eligible for parole in 2029, he is granted parole, for the maximum allowable term of five years, effective July 1, 2011.'" It was the proof he'd been looking for, evidence that he'd received a commutation from the governor. Still, he struggled to bring himself to believe it. "Does this mean that I get out in July?" he asked the sergeant. "Yeah, Sean." As he stood up from the computer, two decades' worth of powerful emotions, frozen like thick, glassy ice sheets, began melting away and coursing through his body. Standing in front of the sergeant and two other men, he broke down in tears, sobbing for joy at the prospect of being a free man for the first time in more than twenty years.

Sean, Dietrick, and two other men tried as juveniles were the first Coloradans to receive commutations under the Juvenile Clemency Board established by the governor four years earlier. That Friday was—in its own humble, unnoticed way—a historic one for the state. For Sean, it was one of the happiest days of his life. In the five months between when he learned his sentence was commuted and when he was released to a halfway house, Sean worked to inspire as many other incarcerated men as he could. During Friday prayer sessions, the imam often asked him to speak to the rest of the prison's Muslims. Standing in front of the other men, he insisted that they, too, could alter seemingly immutable fates and find their way back to lives that had long slipped clear of their grasps.

On May 18, 2011, Sean was released to the Independence House, a yellow-brick halfway house in the Sunnyside neighborhood of north Denver. Waiting for the transport van to pick him up from Arkansas Valley and take him to DRDC for processing, he realized he "wasn't wearing shackles and handcuffs," he said. "I wasn't wearing the belly chain. I wasn't wearing any of those things. I was just walking around in the holding cell, and the holding cell wasn't even closed." Although Sean was elated to be a returning citizen and a free man, his first few weeks at the halfway house were a challenging adjustment.

On the cusp of his forties, Sean fumbled through basic competencies he'd never learned in prison: reading a bus schedule, operating a computer, navigating the internet. Fortunately, it wasn't all a humbling slog up the learning curve of modern life; buried in those first few taxing weeks were also the seeds of his life's next chapter. Once the Independence House permitted Sean to receive visitors, a man showed up whom he hadn't seen in well over a decade: Hassan Latif. The imam from Limon Correctional Facility—who'd inspired Sean to think deeply about the tenets of Islam and use them to reflect on the pathways behind and before him—had been closely following his case. By the time Sean was transferred to the halfway house in May, Latif was eagerly anticipating his release.

When Sean first laid eyes on his old mentor, standing in the halfway house's office, a bright, unguarded smile formed across his face. As the two men embraced, Sean wiped tears from his eyes. Latif brought him a watch, a wallet, some clothes, and an iPod, and they caught up on everything that had happened in the years since they last saw each other. After that, the two stayed in close contact. Latif eventually told Sean about a project he was working on: founding a reentry organization focused on helping men and women recently released from prison face the staggering challenge of rebuilding their lives on the outside. "As soon as we've got the word that we've got funding," Hassan told him, "I want you to be a case manager."

In 2012, Sean reconnected with another person from his past—a woman named Tiffany whom he'd known since his childhood days in and around Denver. The two had grown up together, playing football on the scruffy lawns in front of their apartment buildings, racing go-karts they'd jury-rigged from plywood and lawn mower motors, and rendezvousing in the dark, empty basement laundry rooms to practice kissing. Even as the years separating them piled up, Tiffany had never forgotten about Sean. During his incarceration, she'd whispered to herself every September 6, "Happy Birthday, Sean." During Sean's first year outside of prison, Tiffany helped him develop the skills and proficiencies required to gain a foothold in a society whose technology had advanced dramatically in the twenty-two years he'd been locked up. "Her guidance helped me transition back to life in general," he remembered. On September 7, a day after Sean's fortieth birthday, the two were married.

That same year, Latif received a grant to start the reentry organization he'd told Sean about. Its name succinctly reflected its mission: the Second Chance Center. Latif wanted the center to be a wide, robust safety net for people returning from long stints in prison, a place where they could go to secure housing, find employment, and even work with counselors to address the negative thought patterns that proliferated behind bars. The organization wanted returning citizens to have the opportunities they needed to assimilate back into society and piece together lives that looked different from the ones that landed them in prison. As soon as he was awarded the funding to start the Second Chance Center, Latif followed through on his word and made Sean one of the first hires.

The program's early days were hectic and exhausting. Latif had received only enough money to bring on a few employees, and the organization was largely run by just three men—Sean, Latif, and an older man named Adam Abdullah. The trio had collectively served over seven decades in state and federal prisons, and part of what made the Second Chance Center so revolutionary at the time was its founding conviction that those who'd experienced incarceration themselves were in the best position to help returning citizens land on their feet. "We're here because these men and women who are coming to us are our friends," Sean said. "We met them in prison. We ate ramen noodles with them, walked the track with them, lifted weights with them." Men like Sean, Latif, and Abdullah understood that successful reentry wasn't only about finding a steady job and a place to live (although those were critical steps): People needed to repair and fortify self-esteem that was being constantly whittled down by a society that persecuted and marginalized them.

Following the organization's inception, many in the community corrections field regarded the Second Chance Center and its team with doubt. Officials from halfway houses, probation offices, and parole agencies in the Denver area discouraged returning citizens from connecting with the group. In some cases, they went as far as explicitly prohibiting them from seeking assistance there—an injunction that vulnerable men and women living under strict probationary supervision were in no position to question. Sean, Latif, and Abdullah would have to work their way up from the presumption of failure, fighting for every client they got.

Though he was hired as a case manager, Sean spent dozens of hours each week interfacing with contacts throughout the community. He needed not only to gain the trust of community corrections officers and other professionals in the field, but also to convince employers and landlords to offer jobs and leases to his organization's clients. Because the Second Chance Center was guaranteeing employment for the returning citizens it worked with, Sean was forced into a position where he was simultaneously building the plane and piloting it: meeting with formerly incarcerated people and opening cases on their behalf, and then driving around Denver persuading local employers and landlords to hire and house them. It took a year or two, but the gambit paid off: Over time, businesses started gaining trust in the competence and dependability of returning citizens, and apartment complexes and housing facilities grew more comfortable offering them leases. By late 2013, the Colorado Department of Corrections even started referring people to the organization. Latif and Sean were successfully reshuffling decks that had been perennially stacked against individuals like them.

Though "overworked and overwhelmed" in the organization's early days, Sean also felt that his efforts harmonized powerfully with his own moral and religious principles. He found what he was doing at the Second Chance Center to be "exactly in line with the pillars of Islam, and the spirit of Islam," Sean said. Although the organization is not faith based, he framed the work he did every day as "helping people in the name of God." He'd spent years in prison taking pains to be a righteous influence on the men around him, both because it advanced the cause of his own Islamic repentance and because it offered the possibility of lifting those men's lives out of gang culture's blinkered psychology and lethal violence.

At Second Chance Center, Sean continued pursuing the same abiding sense of purpose. The catastrophic mistake that yoked him to a life sentence had also, over time, begotten a devotion to changing people's lives for the better. A single stark, irreducible fact rooted itself in the back of his mind: That horrific error in judgment and the ardent commitment to helping others improve their circumstances that he'd developed in the decades since were inextricable from one another. The fluctuating equilibrium between those two forces was, in some way, the clearest expression of his identity. "It was those strong emotions that drove me to be who I am right now," he said. "The feeling of extreme guilt, of not really ever being able to feel relief for what I've done. So instead of trying to get relief, which will never happen, I'm just trying to redeem. And believing that, from that day forward, I just need to do good things. I need to do good things to make up for that life."

In the decade since his release, Sean often found himself ruminating on all the time he'd lost: the memories, milestones, and shared experiences he was deprived of having with the people he loved. But he never let those brooding spells last for long. Whenever he lapsed into bitterness or melancholy, he was swiftly reminded of the other seventeen-year-old whose life—and death—his own would always be bound to. "I start thinking like that, and then I'm like, 'Man, imagine what Dean's family feels,'" he said. "They don't get a chance to watch him grow, what he could have been, what he could have accomplished, the relationship between him and his mother, his sister, his brothers. That's the weight." In forging a three-decade path devoted to seeking the divine forgiveness that might lift that weight—and never quite finding it—Sean had left a measureless trail of small, selfless acts that has been arguably even more salvific.

THE PAINFUL ODYSSEYS we embark on after tragedy—in search of meaning, answers, or some form of recompense—do not usually yield precisely what we seek. They do, however, still offer something of value: a more nuanced, sophisticated understanding of what befell us. At the outset of afterlives, many grasp their catastrophes through the lenses of diminishment and bereavement. We question why it was our lives that needed to be ravaged, staggering through self-pity and refuting the permanence of our displaced fates. But through the slow, often unconscious process of adaptation, in which we strengthen parts of our character and refine certain aspects of our lifestyle, we grow more thoughtful and discerning. We may eventually arrive at a humble but dignified truth: For all the pain and desolation our catastrophe has caused us, there is some measure of good that has come from it, too. For many people, that good—the radiant thread of redemption stitched into a darker, more saturnine tapestry—is in the cause, craft, or discipline they've discovered and become devoted to.

Reaching a state of devotion often requires individuals to pass through the periods of seeking, refinement, and even vulnerability discussed in the preceding chapters. A simplified, refined existence—shorn of excess and distraction, consolidated through its unflinching focus—provides the ideal environment for dedication to take deep, imperishable root. And vulnerability can push us to seek out a cause or pursuit that functions like a circle of protection. When we pour ourselves into our passions, we are less susceptible to the vagaries of our illnesses, disabilities, and traumas. Those who are consumed by something are also fortified within it. Many of us scour for some nugget of meaning or cryptic purpose behind our traumas, as though groping around for a secret note hidden in the back of a picture frame. Amid our ceaseless searching, we eventually find ourselves immersed in something that honors our journeys without necessarily vanishing the pain that prompted them—be it a fight over gun control, a crusade to counter addiction, or a newfound love for painting. These pursuits may be consolation prizes in the place of desperate prayers to reverse the past, but our devotion to them can become a worthy substitute for the answer we've been seeking.

In many afterlives, devotion becomes the engine, the apparatus from which we create meaning from our before-and-after experiences. Nowhere is this on more stirring display than among parents who've lost children. In the aftermath of the Sandy Hook Elementary School shooting, in which his seven-year-old son was murdered, Mark Barden cofounded Sandy Hook Promise, a nonprofit organization dedicated to preventing future gun violence inside schools. "For me it's not like a car accident that I went through and how horrible that was," he said. "This was a redefining experience that has completely changed me, rewired me as a person, and it was a catalyst moment for everything being different afterward. It started a process in motion and it's never going to let up." For Barden, the catastrophe on December 14, 2012, was the "big bang" that birthed a new universe, one where he's dedicated his life to ending gun violence in schools.

Diannee Carden's son, Michael, had been a leading voice in the harm reduction movement for intravenous drug users before he died of a heroin overdose in 2012. Following his death, Diannee plunged into the world of harm reduction, syringe exchanges, and public health—her son's world. "I've probably become consumed with wanting to help people who use drugs continue to stay alive until they do something else—at the expense of my family and my bank account," she said. "I'm not who I used to be. I won't ever be that person again."

For parents like these, devotion is tantamount to salvation. It has helped them scrabble a sense of purpose from unfathomable pain, has given them a way not only to conceive of a novel narrative identity for themselves but also to live out that identity every day by acting in a way that reflects and memorializes the person they lost. Devotion following catastrophe is a source of protection, resilience, even regeneration, a clandestine promise, doubtful but rousing, that the object of our prodigious investments will reciprocate our efforts by making us whole.

AFTER GRADUATING FROM Harvard in 2014, Valerie spent a year overseas, studying for her master's in medieval history at the University of Cambridge. There, she explored a topic she had not encountered as an undergraduate: disability in the Middle Ages. Working in her dorm and a favorite café near the college, Valerie dug up perspectives that challenged traditional conceptions of how the medieval period treated physical impairment. Some Catholic women in early medieval Europe were so devoted to Christ, she read, that they prayed for disfigurement to become less attractive candidates for arranged marriages. Writing in the fifth century, Saint Augustine opined how "the love we bear for the blessed martyrs makes us desire to see in the kingdom of heaven the marks of the wounds which they received for Christ's name." These wounds, he continued, "will not be a deformity, but a badge of honour, and the beauty of their virtue—a beauty which is in the body, but not of the body—will shine forth in it."

Here, Valerie felt, were deeper, more probing ways of contemplating disability. One might even argue that they served as counterpoints—if not outright confrontations—of today's ableist perspectives. These accounts saw scars, disfigurements, and limb loss as emblems of rarefaction, distinguishing the physically disabled from the nondisabled masses and sanctifying their passion through the symbolic power of the wounds themselves. The views may have been steeped in a Catholic theology that fetishized suffering—even self-mortification—but at least these medieval figures saw threads connecting injury and disability to so much more than just degradation and loss. "It certainly makes you think about it a bit more," Valerie said.

Valerie decided to write her master's dissertation on perceptions of disability in the early Middle Ages. Casting a wide net in her research, she soon ventured beyond medieval texts and into contemporary works exploring disability rights and theory. She learned more about ableism and how it pervaded nearly every corner of modern society. While its physical manifestations could be seen in sidewalks, storefronts, and architectural design, the more internalized beliefs and assumptions it perpetuated braided themselves through film, television, fiction, and the onslaught of homogenous cultural imagery. Immersing herself in these texts, Valerie was nudged toward a sharp, clarifying insight. She realized that, although she'd never had the language to identify it, she'd been subjected to the institutional and psychological forces of ableism ever since her accident in 2008. There were the restaurants she couldn't dine in, the academic buildings she had to wheel around the back to enter. Even some of her favorite books and television shows betrayed ableist assumptions; for example, wheelchair-using characters were either healed or ushered out of the story, the implication being that not only miraculous recovery but also death was preferable to a life of paralysis. Like so many of society's problems, ableism was sprawling but difficult to call out, an underlying belief to which large swaths of Americans reflexively subscribed while defensively wielding their plausible deniability.

The lens of ableism also helped Valerie to illuminate a recurring experience that had discomfited her for years. Ever since her accident, she'd noticed herself being watched in grocery stores, subways, and city streets. It felt almost as if these public spaces had become a stage, one where she was forced to deliver the performance of her wheelchair-using life. Eyes flitted about her like bustling flies, glancing off only when she'd moved out of view. This phenomenon created a stifling sensation that was comparable to the double consciousness experienced by people of color in oppressive, racialized societies: Valerie was forced to fathom, if not altogether internalize, the imaginary person onlookers conceived of when they surveyed her (an experience much like JR's in the months following his accident). "I know that when people who don't know me very well or don't know me at all see me, they think that the trauma has completely shaped my identity because the first thing they see is me in the wheelchair," she said.

For strangers in these fleeting moments, Valerie was defined completely by her paralysis. Rather than representing a single finite part of her identity, to passersby her wheelchair represented the entirety of it. During these unsettling episodes Valerie felt as though she was both standing out and disappearing: Nondisabled people stared at her but could never see the specific, three-dimensional person beneath the injury. Being seen, in a strange but undeniable paradox, equaled being erased.

Valerie moved back to Brooklyn in 2015, and the following year she returned to Harvard as a graduate student in its higher education program. A second master's degree hadn't been her original plan, though. While at Cambridge she remained intently focused on a career in medieval history, and she applied to several PhD programs throughout the United States. For the first time in her life, though, she failed to achieve an academic goal she set her sights on: That spring, she'd received rejection letters from them all. Valerie remembered the letters as a "gut punch," she said. "I couldn't believe it. I was just staring at my laptop in disbelief, like, 'How did this happen?'"

Valerie was only a month into her yearlong master's program

when she started feeling a void, and by October 2016 she was pulled back into the Harvard medievalists' inimitable orbit: attending talks, participating in workshops, and going to meetings held in a small library inside elegant Robinson Hall. She remained captivated by the field's overarching framework: the way every era's patchwork of tensions and motivations suspended themselves before her like tantalizing mysteries, polyphonic stories whose secrets could always be chiseled away at but never fully solved.

Valerie decided that she would give her dream of getting into a PhD program in medieval history one more shot. "If I don't get in this time," she thought, "I'm never applying again." In her statement of purpose—revised for her second round of applications—she described wandering into a medieval history survey course during her first year at Harvard, "expecting to learn about heroic knights and burned heretics. What I learned instead was far more interesting— political and social networks that involved individuals of every status, questions of legal procedure and access to the law, and rich evidence from written, archaeological, and scientific sources to illustrate the past." While researching her master's dissertation, she "found that, as is still true today, there were contradictory perceptions of disability in early medieval Europe." She wanted to continue studying marginalized groups in the Middle Ages—individuals who, she felt, might have been disenfranchised and pushed far from the levers of power, but whose relationship to the larger society was far more revealing and consequential than powerlessness alone could convey.

As winter's morning temperatures dropped near single digits and a layer of hard, pearly snow glazed over Harvard's frozen greens and pitched Georgian roofs, Valerie became less and less interested in her current coursework. But by February, the first replies from PhD programs began trickling into her inbox. Though she'd been shut out two years earlier, Valerie now found herself accepted into nearly every school to which she applied—Princeton, Columbia, Brown, Rutgers. "I was feeling relief, and I was really excited," Valerie said. "It was like getting another chance." When she called her mom to tell her, her mother burst into laughter at the absurdity of the about-face.

Valerie decided to accept the offer from Princeton, at the time the top-ranked history program in the country. When she visited the suburban campus during recruitment weekend that March, before making her decision official, she met with the department's director of graduate studies. He informed her that, should she accept, she'd be the first wheelchair user in the program's history. "Oh, okay," was all Valerie could muster in reply. Though rendered nearly speechless—there were no pithy, winsome responses to disclosures like that—she wasn't necessarily surprised, either. During her four years as a Harvard undergraduate, she'd met exactly two other students in wheelchairs. Princeton's history building, a white stone, citadel-like structure built in the lofty Beaux-Arts style, was technically not ADA compliant—there was no way for wheelchair users like Valerie to reach the upper floors. If she accepted, the director told her, the department would immediately begin installation of a stair lift in the building.

When Valerie started classes at Princeton the following fall, she did so in the lonely, momentous fashion of a pioneer. Thousands of students had passed through the university's graduate school of history in the decades preceding her admission, and not a single one of them used a wheelchair to do it. If her position as a doctoral candidate at a top university was unprecedented, it was largely because the process of adapting to a spinal cord injury is hard, long, and exasperating. Before arriving at Princeton, she'd spent a decade rehabbing her body: relearning how to write with her right hand, transferring in and out of wheelchairs, managing her fickle bladder, and maneuvering her body through a network of core muscles she'd spent hundreds of hours regaining sensation in. Rarely does that amount of effort leave room for scaling a second punishing peak.

Because of the physical limitations, the everyday demands, and perhaps most of all the cultural barriers spinal cord injuries impose, only around 35 percent of Americans with paralysis are employed. By accepting admission into Princeton's PhD program in medieval history, Valerie would be receiving a living income from one of the world's most prestigious universities. What made her different? Valerie didn't spend much time pondering the range of possible answers (though work ethic, intellectual aptitude, and familial support might have been fair places to start). Whenever her thoughts drifted toward the reality of her status as the first wheelchair user in the program's history, she automatically defaulted to a terse, unsentimental point of view. "I better not screw this up," she'd remind herself wryly. In her mind, the unparalleled circumstances she'd arrived at were not some glorious showcase for her own surpassing merits, but rather a pressure cooker she needed to approach with imperturbable focus and diligence. She saw herself crossing a tightrope above an audience that had never seen a person who looked like her make it to the other side. Lacking the comforting assurances conferred by predecessors, Valerie instead felt the added weight of all her possible successors—at Princeton, anyway—whose opportunities, she felt, would widen or narrow in accordance with her own performance.

Life at Princeton did not begin with the same frictionless enthusiasm as nearly all of Valerie's previous academic endeavors. During her first few weeks navigating the campus's Gothic labyrinth of sweeping towers, vaulted ceilings, and ivy-draped stone, pressure, expectations, and apprehension about committing six more years of her life to academia all snowballed in her mind. She struggled to eat and sleep. She had a difficult time concentrating on the assignments that were piling up before her like unpaid bills. And she suffered panic attacks each day at sundown when she thought about how little she'd accomplished since the sun had risen. Running through her battery of anxieties was an acute case of impostor syndrome: She was convinced that the peers in her cohort were all smarter, more capable scholars who weren't hindered by the rehabilitation commitments that eliminated multiple hours of her potential output every day. "I thought, I've been out of this for so long, I don't know if I can turn in the work they want me to turn in," Valerie said.

As the semester progressed, though, Valerie's anxiety waned.

She learned that many of the colleagues she felt intimidated by shouldered similar stress. Her time deficits were real—and would likely remain so for her entire career—but she was far from an impostor. All the strategies she'd honed and refined over the years—becoming a nimble reader, a deft translator, a surgical manager of time—had arguably made her a uniquely capable scholar. She was now an established student in academia's highest echelons, her abilities beyond question.

After completing two years of coursework, Valerie moved to the dissertation phase of her PhD. By 2020, she was writing it, and her life as a scholar had become the fulcrum of her identity. At Princeton, "I'm treated like a colleague, like an equal," she said. Some of her most fulfilling moments have come when that identity fully eclipses the one that was born on that frigid January afternoon in New Hampshire in 2008. "I've had mentors who often forget that I use a wheelchair," she said, "in a good way."

It's impossible to know whether Valerie would have discovered medieval history if she had never suffered a spinal cord injury during her junior year of high school. But it's also not particularly difficult to see how the injury might have paved the way for the scholarship. The accident narrowed the scope of her life, cleaving away her blissful rambles through the city, her track practices and meets, and much of the socializing that had once landscaped her adolescence.

Though she'd never lead the kind of active, well-proportioned lifestyle she'd imagined during her teenage years, what she could do was devote herself to a specific discipline in a way that would not have been possible under most other circumstances. The ardor she cultivated for medieval history was a force that propelled her through some of the most difficult years after her injury. It was a level of commitment many peers—and sometimes even Valerie herself—could not make sense of in real time. But she felt a powerful attachment to it, for reasons that were in some cases unambiguous and in others more abstruse. "I needed medieval history to remind myself how capable I am of doing things," she said. "I don't regret having any of those drives and motivations, because I needed those at the time." Over the years, those drives and motivations came to shape her identity in a way that's only possible when we bring a desperate, needful passion and an exposed self to the altar of a particular endeavor: Our seeking and vulnerability lead to our devotion, and that becomes the sturdy, galloping horse we ride out of one story and into more distant, far-flung frontiers.

A LIFE OF dedication following a tragic event is even woven into the mythologies of major religions. In Christianity, Mary Magdalene was one of Jesus Christ's most devout followers, traveling with him all over the crumbling Judean Desert and along the riverbanks and briny lakes where he preached to growing crowds of fishermen and their families. The Gospels attest that Christ delivered "seven devils" out of Mary—which could refer to a physical malady or psychological affliction he somehow ameliorated—and for years she financially supported his ministry. She was there for his crucifixion and his entombment, and was allegedly the first person to see him resurrected—shouting "Rabboni," the Hebrew word for teacher, when she realized who it was standing before her.

Jesus gave Mary Magdalene the inestimable gifts of moral passion and spiritual ardor, and when he departed from this world for good she was never the same. She is purported to have taken up a quiet, solitary existence filled with prayer and contemplation, her heart still swollen with sorrow and awe for the fearless figure who'd performed beneficent miracles and prophesied his own betrayal and death. Renaissance painters often portrayed Magdalene seated in mournful contemplation before a wispy candle flame, a flickering symbol of her spiritual enlightenment and inextinguishable love for Christ. Hers became its own afterlife, one that can only be understood as a long and unquenchable act of devotion.

The nineteenth-century Hindu mystic Ramakrishna likewise drew deep passion out of irremediable loss. Ramakrishna was born into a poor family in eastern India in 1836, and when he was seven his father died and his family slipped deeper into poverty. As a teenager, Ramakrishna moved from the small village where he grew up to Calcutta, where his brother had founded a Hindu temple. But just a few years later, when Ramakrishna was only twenty years old, his brother also passed away. Desperate and crestfallen, Ramakrishna prayed to the Hindu goddess Kali Ma, begging for some kind of divine vision or confirmation of his spiritual path.

Alone in the world and swallowed by grief, the young priest was on the brink of killing himself when he finally got his vision—what he would later recall as an "infinite shoreless sea of light." From that point onward, Ramakrishna transformed himself into a determined, devout yogi, practicing various Hindu mystical traditions with fearsome discipline. He would develop followers throughout the world, acolytes who subscribed to his principles that all religions were routes to the same spiritual endpoint and the Divine Mother is the supreme manifestation of holiness. His religious devotion seemed to have been born, in part, out of the desolate place his grief and loss had left him in.

Many of our most beloved artists have also exemplified this interlacing of catastrophe and ardor. Vincent van Gogh suffered from severe mental illness (what we would likely diagnose today as bipolar disorder), endured numerous psychological breakdowns, lopped off half his ear with a razor, and in 1889 committed himself to an asylum in Saint-Rémy-de-Provence for a year. Out of this, we say, grew nearly a thousand paintings of vibrant landscapes, windblown wheat fields, suns, moons, aching starlight, and bright, quicksilver clouds that hold, like moisture, the diaphanous pleasure of watching them. Van Gogh is hardly alone. From John Milton to Frida Kahlo to Sylvia Plath, artists have used their misfortune as both grist and motivating force, providing the material and the compulsion to produce transcendent works of art.

"Look at the data," Paul Bloom wrote. "Bad things are bad." But when we end the investigation there, we fail to see the way those bad things can simultaneously make life harder and more charged with passion, heavier with the dark matter of grief but vitalized by private visions of starry skies and everlasting flames and shoreless seas of light. The Lebanese American poet Kahlil Gibran wrote, "The deeper that sorrow carves into your being, the more joy you can contain." The catastrophes that carve themselves deep inside of us also leave us with increased depth, augmenting the volume of feeling we're able to hold. And how can we measure devotion but by how much the vessels that we become for our art, faith, saviors, and crusades have the capacity to contain?

AFTER GINA LOST the funding for her PhD at the University of Missouri, there was nothing left tying her to Columbia. Her husband, Savas, would not return to America for at least another year. She'd agreed to accept an EdS, or education specialist degree, and was no longer enrolled at the college. Though she could have begun another doctorate elsewhere—because the EdS was a terminal degree, she could not transfer its credits—that would have required painstaking effort and initiative: reaching out to academics in her field, applying to programs all over the country, and doing everything on the fly, so soon after her wings had been clipped. "At that point I was so heartbroken over the old PhD, I wasn't ready to run off and start a new one," she said.

Instead, Gina eventually decided that the one place she could go to gather herself and plan the next chapter of her life was the city she'd left seven years earlier. In October 2014, the fall after her final semester at the University of Missouri, she attended a geological conference in Vancouver and reconnected with some old colleagues from the College of Charleston, her undergraduate alma mater. A few of them mentioned a science grant they'd recently received. Should she decide to return to the area, they promised, they would keep a position open for her. Maybe, they offered, she could pick up some geology labs at the college, too. "That's when the seed got planted to come home," Gina said.

In late November, as snow started dappling the bare branches of trees and frost bloomed into tiny crystals over downtown storefronts at night, Steve arrived in Columbia in a rented Suburban to help his daughter move back to South Carolina. She packed up her jeans and black tees, her ripped boxes of vinyl records, her rare rock collection. She lured her cats, Pixie and Misfit, into their carriers. And she contemplated her bittersweet departure from a city that had served as both a bastion for her cherished academic aspirations and the place where she helplessly observed many of them dwindle away. While her dad steered through the rugged, hilly interior of West Virginia, Gina listened as the rain pelting the windshield in rapid fusillades slowly turned to the soft swishing of wet, heavy snow. They stopped in Durham to spend a night with Gina's twin sister, Andrea, before heading down the coast, to the South Carolina Lowcountry where she'd been homeschooled two decades earlier—to the old cobblestone roads, dollhouse Victorians, and spidery live oaks that had long been Gina's home. There, she would pick up the pieces that had been shattered in Missouri and try to repair her battered scholarly hopes.

While she searched for a place she could afford in Charleston, Gina spent a month living with her dad in a log cabin along the leisurely paced, tea-colored waters of the Edisto River. The lackadaisical atmosphere of rural South Carolina didn't suit her, though, and she pined to return to the kind of intellectual environment where her hungry mind could be roused from a slumber it hadn't asked for. Toward the end of January, Gina found an affordable room for rent in downtown Charleston, on the ground floor of a duplex she'd be sharing with two older men. Though her roommates mostly kept to themselves, they were aimless bachelors and the apartment was a grubby hovel, with dirty plates littering the kitchen, cockroaches skittering across the linoleum floors, and the scattered pockmarks of illicit drug use. Gina didn't have Mitchell anymore, either. He'd turned ten years old during her last year in Missouri—the age when most guide dogs are retired—and she'd sent him to live with her dad. She was on her own to navigate a disheveled apartment where nothing ever seemed to be in the right place, and the perpetual disarray made her homelife exasperating. By the start of the spring semester, when she began work on the science grant, Gina—who would turn thirty the following fall—had returned to the pitiless configuration that had grafted itself over most of her twenties. She was laboring through academia in narrow, uncertain pursuit of her professional ambitions while living under the precarious financial straits that made sustained forward momentum seem impossible.

For Gina, however, the superficial markers of circumstance were always just one layer of her story. She acknowledged them but also saw through to all the possible transformations buried underneath, as though she were peering into the striations of a quarry and discerning everything she might excavate from it. To Gina, returning to Charleston was the next step along a painful but profound rebirth that began the afternoon she woke up with what neurologists would later call her non-optic vision. It had been over a year since that startling shift, and she'd learned, the hard way, to treat the subject with the discretion required to buffer herself against a stigmatizing world. But she continued perceiving luminous visualizations of both herself and her surrounding environment, further proof that it had not been the fleeting delusion of a manic episode or psychotic break. That astonishing leap in her perception had also had a powerful effect on her broader sense of self.

By the time she'd settled back in Charleston, the sexual trauma from nearly a decade earlier no longer held the same primacy in her thoughts and emotions. The more Gina examined it, in fact, the more she seemed to feel that it no longer bore the characteristics of trauma at all. Gone was the rage that dangled a struck match over the flammable memory of that night. The psychic transformation reminded Gina of a rare phenomenon geologists sometimes observed in metamorphic rocks. These rocks withstand staggering supertemperatures, crushing pressures, and other extreme environmental forces that get recorded in their composition. They become palimpsests for everything that happens to them over millions of years, layered testaments to the intensity and permanence of the past. Every once in a while, though, an event comes along that's so potent and seismic that it overprints one or more of the incidents that preceded it. The non-optic vision, Gina felt, was one of those epochal occurrences. It transformed her perception and rearranged her psyche so drastically that it effectively overwrote the sexual trauma, nullifying the psychological scars that had long persisted in the deeper layers of her composition. She'd endured two before-and-after experiences in the span of just three years—being raped and suddenly losing the remainder of her functional vision—and in a singular, serendipitous way, the ripple effects of the latter actually came to ameliorate the former.

The upheaval from the previous year inspired Gina to make other changes, too. Unhappy with a marriage that was stretched across continents, and unwilling to sacrifice her career prospects by moving to Europe, she filed for divorce in February 2015. No longer yoked to a stagnating relationship, Gina started committing more of her time and energy to the intellectual pursuits that filled her "mind-palace." Though her academic interests ranged widely, her unstinting devotion to a life of the mind ran cleanly through them. Ever since she had devoured the myths of Camelot and the adventures of teenage detectives in her tree house in Summerville, it had been her one abiding polestar. Years of trauma had only further crystallized that bond.

When Gina wasn't in the geology offices working on the grant, she was auditing university courses. In the wake of her synesthetic breakthrough, she found herself increasingly drawn to new subject matter—disciplines like religion, philosophy, and psychology that she'd never had much interest in before. In 2015 and 2016, she audited courses in Buddhism, existentialism, classical mythology, and theories of consciousness. She was using the prism of academia to grapple with both her past and her future, trying to find a schema that might frame her perplexing adaptation while casting about for what the next stage of her star-crossed career was going to be.

When she discovered Carl Jung and transpersonal psychology, during a course on dream analysis, Gina knew it was the framework she'd been searching for. Unlike the institutional versions of psychology she was herded through after her assault and, later, at the University of Missouri's psychiatric center, transpersonal psychology didn't contextualize human experience in terms of illness and pathology. Instead, it incorporated spirituality to interpret torturous life events through a lens that embraced neutrality and personal insight. Rather than drawing from an ever-expanding litany of disorders and diseases to diagnose, medicate, and assign the lifelong labels Gina felt society stigmatized, transpersonal psychology perceived our internal troubles as spiritual crises, alternative mental states, and mystical experiences. A mental breakdown or a period of tumultuous tribulation was not evidence of a permanent underlying pathology, the field stipulated, but rather a temporary crucible that often broke through to consciousness-expanding growth.

Some experts and laypeople feel that transpersonal psychology and its unscientific theories whitewash the bleakness of traumas and illnesses that don't possess an iota of redemptive power, neglecting the pernicious biological shifts underpinning them. For Gina, though, the field was a stirring actualization of her longstanding impulse to construe catastrophe and misfortune as bridges to opportunity, keyholes of self-knowledge, and passageways to universal wisdom. Her narrative identity was one of recurring metamorphosis—less the caterpillar threshing away its silky chrysalis once and for all than the quaking aspen altering its form with each changing season, its bright lime-gumdrop leaves conflagrating into yellow-orange blazes before fluttering to the forest floor and starting the cycle anew. Transpersonal psychology illumined the sense of mystery and inexpressible nuance underneath the changes a person experiences over a lifetime better than anything she'd ever come across. "There were a lot of perspectives and questions and nascent beliefs that had emerged for me since 2014 that I was recognizing in the work," she said. "I saw for myself a potential academic home, where I thought I was never going to find it again."

Funding for the science grant dried up in 2016, and Gina again found herself scrambling to make ends meet. She picked up work tutoring College of Charleston undergrads, guiding students through everything from geology and physics to philosophy and anthropology, her polymathic aptitude brilliantly displayed in what was otherwise a humble, unideal position. When that didn't cover the bills, she'd take shifts at the modeling gig she'd held as an undergraduate, sitting nude on a large metal platform in the paint-spattered studios where the college's drawing and painting classes were held.

Though her professional life may have been sputtering, the field of transpersonal psychology threw a clarifying light on where her academic peregrinations would lead her next. When a mentor who taught at the College of Charleston introduced her to the California Institute of Integral Studies—a San Francisco–based university that offered a PhD program in transpersonal psychology that could be completed largely online—she knew she had to apply. In the spring of 2017, she submitted her application, which included a statement of personal and spiritual growth that she found herself spending weeks suffering over. "Closer to chaos is where transformation occurs and accepting adversity is critical for the natural texture of our experience," she wrote. "On another level, our diversity, and any adversity arising in interrelation, challenges us into extraordinary adaptability and growth we would not otherwise discover in ourselves."

Andrea had moved to Athens, Greece, in 2016, and the summer after Gina submitted her application to the California Institute, the twins scrounged up the funds for her to book a flight there. During her three-week stay at her sister's fifth-floor apartment in the Pangrati neighborhood, Gina used synesthesia, soundscapes, and the accounts of Andrea's sighted friends to take in the city's evocative splendor. She strolled through the white stone pathways at the National Garden, passing hulking fragments of fluted columns and towering sculptures of angels, poets, and statesmen. She and Andrea rode a cherry-red tram to the Apollo Coast, where they swam along beaches bookended by chunks of hot white marble tumbling into the translucent blue Aegean Sea. And she lingered over the archaeological site of Aristotle's Lyceum, fathoming the philosopher and his Peripatetic school amid the earth-awakening smell of fresh rain. She remembered thinking, "It's been a long time, but I bet the way that the earth smells when it rains in Athens is the same as it was when Aristotle was here."

Andrea had only recently moved to Pangrati, and the twins spent several days doing the difficult, troubleshooting work of mapping out the area in their minds. (Though Andrea's vision was better than Gina's, her visual impairment remained severe.) Each morning, Andrea strapped her seeing-eye dog, a black Lab named Mercy, to a harness and let her lead the twins along the narrow stone sidewalks snaking through Athens. They walked past overflowing cafés and ornate burbling fountains, over treacherous crosswalks, and up the towering staircase that led to the city's central Syntagma Square. One day, after they'd ascended to the very top, panting for breath, Mercy led them to a craggy hillside overlooking the entire city. Before them lay a teeming expanse of bushy canopies, terra-cotta roofs, and crumbling antiquities hugging glittering turquoise water. Though Gina couldn't see Athens that way, she took in her own vibrant panorama: a rich, rustling soundscape, the feeling of sharp alpine breeze gusting over her face, and the city's blurry rendering in an undulating, incandescent spectacle of lights.

Much like the wayfaring of Gina's past, though, her trip to Greece could not safeguard her from the adversities of life back home. In early July, the California Institute of Integral Studies informed her that she'd been formally accepted into its PhD program in transpersonal psychology. She was ecstatic: After reading the email on her sister's couch, she leaped to her feet, hugged Andrea, and ran around the apartment in a fit of childlike ebullience. Gina's successes, alas, were rarely that straightforward. As was so often the case, complications ensued that threatened her forward progress.

Just a few days later, she received a second email. This one was from the University of Missouri, explaining that she owed around a thousand dollars in student fees dating all the way back to 2007. Until it was paid in full, the school wouldn't release her transcript to the California Institute. Because a transcript was required to be officially admitted into the program, Gina's enrollment was no longer guaranteed. The next chapter of her academic career was already imperiled, two months before it was even scheduled to begin.

As the summer wore on and Gina returned to the United States, the stakes kept ratcheting higher and higher. Given her long-standing financial precarity, she didn't have the money to pay back the student fees. Instead, she'd have to assuage her alma mater through other, more creative strategies. By late August, she'd booked a flight to San Francisco for the program's weeklong orientation. Her transcript, however, was still under lock and key in an admissions office in Columbia, Missouri. Gina spoke on the phone with the University of Missouri nearly every day, playing "harass the bureaucrats" and trying to locate a sympathetic figure somewhere along the administrative hierarchy. Finally, a week before she was scheduled to fly across the country, the onetime president of the College of Charleston—an old friend of Gina's—stepped in and agreed to pay off the student fees. Even by her extreme standards, Gina had been working between the absolute narrowest of margins. But she managed to preserve her spot in the PhD program and keep her academic dreams alive.

Gina spent the next two years working toward her PhD at the California Institute. She covered her living expenses through modeling shifts, tutoring gigs, and around nine hundred dollars a month in disability payments from the federal government. But even those multiple income streams were not nearly enough to lift her out of the peripatetic shuffle of moving from one squalid living situation to another. Desperate for a secure place to call her own but unable to afford even the more modest studio apartments in Charleston's safer neighborhoods—most were upward of eleven hundred dollars a month—she eventually conceived the idea of building a tiny home. By gradually raising money on GoFundMe, Gina was able to construct the 450-square-foot home piece by piece. The foundation came first, from the Tumbleweed Tiny House Company, followed by the framing, the siding, the windows, and the roof. Despite not yet having electricity, water, or plumbing, in the fall of 2019 she officially moved in.

The miniature light gray house sat on a small lot at the end of a cul-de-sac in the central part of the city. Gina entered through a narrow wooden porch, no more than eight feet across, where a silver wind chime dangled over glass candles and the spiky leaves of an aloe vera plant. Inside was a single large room with two compact lofts on either side; a green shelf lined with cardboard boxes full of her vinyl records sat against the wall, opposite a record player and unconnected PVC pipes. Without any connections to water or sewer lines, the bathroom served as storage for Gina's pots, pans, clothes, and toiletries. In a class paper she described her Thoreau-like existence in the tiny home: "Climbing down the metal ladder from the bed loft, into the large, open living space. Opening seven casement windows, the practiced counterclockwise turning, lighting the tall candle in the soft dawn light." Each morning, she would "welcome the new day with the blackbird, a few robins, my beloved chimney swifts."

Though friends offered to put her up in a spare bedroom or let her sleep on a couch until the home was completed, she always demurred. "I had many offers—just come stay with me, drop in and take a shower anytime," she said. "I'd rather be independent. And it's the same piece of me that stole food when I was broke in college, instead of relying on somebody for it." In the meantime, she used the college's geology department bathrooms to shower each morning, cooked over an iron camp stove on her porch, washed the dishes on top of a rusting SUV adjacent to her lot, and lit candles so she didn't have to live in full darkness at night.

By the time she'd moved into her unfinished tiny home that fall, Gina was thirty-four years old. The scrawny girl with hickory-brown eyes who'd once survived on restaurant leftovers and groceries slipped under her baggy sleeves had been replaced by an athletic, sinewy woman who'd spent years developing the strength and agility necessary to defend herself in any situation. She was muscular in the efficient, imperfectly apportioned fashion of a gymnast—rounded shoulders cresting to a firm neck, short, powerful arms, and calves sculpted from the miles and miles she walked each day. Her skin had the deep tan of someone who spent most of her time traveling beneath the sultry southern sun, and several nautical tattoos scattered over her body immortalized the treasured insights from a hard but rewarding life. As dedicated as she was to a life of the mind, there was also a rugged physicality to Gina's existence. Her body was coarsened and lived-in, her bufferless circumstances pushing her against life's elemental forces in a way that garnered immense respect and even reverence from friends and acquaintances.

Her PhD in transpersonal psychology would be Gina's fourth college degree. Whether it was the mesmerizing nightscapes of the ocean floor, the ingenuity and initiative that went into increasing accessibility in the sciences, or the self-affirming work of identifying archetypal experiences in human psychology, Gina had long devoted herself to the bright wonder and quiet toil of academic pursuits. Though she hoped to teach at the university level after finishing her program, she would never stop being a student enthralled by science and psychology and philosophy and religion, forever hunting for a fresh lens through which to examine her uncanny world. Her passion for expanding her knowledge had proven itself inviolable, capable of surviving rape, hunger, poverty, blindness, and the insidious inertia of institutional discrimination. Her intellectual zeal had for years been her sheltering sanctum, a stronghold that shielded her from starker confrontations with the pitiless forces that shaped so much of her life.

Yet it remained unclear where her narrative was headed. It did not seem to be moving along a linear arc so much as a tight, expanding spiral, its concentric circles curving around one another in a motion that seemed suspended halfway between repetition and growth. It was difficult to tell whether she was pulling closer to her academic aspirations or falling deeper within the clutches of the circumstances that kept them chronically out of reach. Perhaps she remained the same distance from them both as she'd always been, engaged in a struggle that would persist, unceasingly, for years to come.

For Gina, such questions were—at least on some level—secondary to the more overarching significance of her existence. The multiple before-and-after experiences that forced her to continue developing new layers—ringed around the old ones like the perfectly spiraling chambers of the deep-seafaring nautilus—had contributed to a beloved identity. All the adversities she'd been through had added depth to her relationship with her own life. She knew what she'd overcome as a blind academic battling everything from poverty to prejudice, and her ability to process the full scope of her story and draw spiritual sustenance from it was a crucial part of her sense of self. Her life had been hard, at times unforgiving, and she had found so much to love in it anyhow. She told me, unprompted, that if Nietzsche's demon were to confront her in the middle of the night, vowing that she would have to live her life innumerable times over, "it would be totally worth it, one hundred percent worth every single ounce of suffering that I've been through to also have those numinous experiences that I've had.

"Why would I ever want a regular experience?" she asked. "This is extraordinary." If there was a cure for blindness, she said, she was absolutely certain that she wouldn't take it.

CHAPTER EIGHT

Reinvention

OVER THE COURSE OF WRITING THIS BOOK, I'VE TRIED TO MAKE sense of how tragedy and identity interact in so many of our lives. The subject obsessed the ancient Greeks, who wrote, performed, and attended tragic plays in which protagonists were transformed by devastating turns of events that splintered lives, sealed fates, and inspired the catharsis of "terror and pity" in audiences. The protagonists of Greek tragedies—Oedipus, Antigone, Orestes, Electra—face pain, loss, estrangement, deracination, and horror. Nevertheless, for thousands of years readers and audiences have returned to the plays that dramatize their catastrophes, finding something exquisite and exalted in the way these men and women's arcs are twisted into baroque, arabesque forms. In these stories, the catastrophes we endure and the noblest aspects of our character are intimately twined, and the interplay between the two over a lifetime is both stirring and fiercely enigmatic.

Sophocles begins *Oedipus Rex* with the titular king delivering a speech rife with dramatic irony, urging the citizens of Thebes to root out the man who killed their previous king—a man that, by play's end, Oedipus discovers is himself. He pays dearly for the discovery of his true provenance, as his family is wrested apart and, blinded and traumatized, he is forced into a disgraced exile.

Though Sophocles was using the play to caution against those who would try to escape their preordained fates, he was also conveying a subtler but equally powerful thesis: that tragedy unfolded identity, and without the former we could never access the truest expression of the latter. In his Oedipal saga, this relationship is writ large: Oedipus's tragedy *is* his identity, his wrenching catastrophe the full realization of who he is and has always been. They are inextricable, one and the same, and Sophocles's literalization of this relationship tells us all we need to know about how he felt these events shaped our stories and our selves. In his telling, our tragedies define us, discover us, and overwrite whoever it was we fleetingly assumed ourselves to be. While I don't take the extreme view that our catastrophes completely create or reveal us—or that we require them to realize our fullest foreordained selves—I do believe they become indistinguishable from our identities, the two creating an amalgam that looks, in retrospect, like an inevitability.

While some living afterlives find meaning in steady devotion to a cause or pursuit, others undergo even more dramatic shifts in their efforts to reclaim a sundered existence. In their quests to adapt, evolve, or forge themselves anew, people sometimes move on from everything that once constituted their lives. They change their faiths, philosophies, and careers, move to the other side of the world, or overhaul how they conceptualize their life's purpose. Sophocles and his fellow tragedians might read this as one of the ways catastrophes unfurl deeper layers of identity—revealing truths about ourselves only the most searing crucibles could evoke—but such a one-sided interpretation does not account for the active roles we play in reimagining our lives and then reinventing them. In *Far from the Tree,* Andrew Solomon writes, "It takes an act of will to grow from loss: the disruption provides the opportunity for growth, not the growth itself." Catastrophes do not trigger transformation; they only establish the conditions that increase the likelihood that we will pursue them. Only through our willful, persevering actions can we gradually remake our identities.

And so there is a third ingredient in the struggle between tragedy and identity: our own free will, that metaphysically fraught blend of agency, autonomy, and self-assertion that manifests through the choices we make and the efforts we put into changing our lives. Like continental plates colliding and forming magnificent mountain ranges, our tragedies and our free will assert themselves against one another, shifting, pushing, buckling, and lifting the other until a new equilibrium is achieved. The result is the spectacle of transformation we see on the outside, the upheaval and re-formation born of conflict, friction, and subterranean drama that alters landscapes forever. Catastrophes may facilitate the birth of new identities in the tumult of afterlives, but they are not the only parent.

People who have led multiple lives seize our imaginations: the repentant sinner who labors through years of humble atonement to reach someone approximating a saint; the timid prairie girl who takes a Greyhound to Hollywood and transforms into a glittering starlet; the rich banker who flees the soul-crushing corporate world to live in blissful serenity along the curving lagoons of a secluded island paradise. Individuals who have swept through multiple selves appear both mystifying and alluring, glinting with romance but also tinged by the melancholy of having lost someone forever. Rarely do we reinvent ourselves just for the sake of doing so—it is almost always a desperate measure. Reinvention is an act of intense ambivalence, a drastic instrument of adaptation carried out from a place of pitiless necessity. But it also possesses an unmistakable frisson, a thrilling testimony to our unseen multitudes and the valiant mutability of the human spirit.

The reinventions that succeed catastrophe do not play into popular culture's quixotic clichés of metamorphosis. They are not vibrant wings beating away memories of the sluggish caterpillar, or a vermilion bird resurrected by the same flames that consumed it. These are quieter, less glorious reinventions, ones that include a level of sacrifice, renunciation, and loss that our favorite stories and myths prefer to steer clear of. But they are equally brave expressions of agency and imagination that enable us to spurn Nietzsche's aphorism in favor of something more fulfilling and radical.

JASON ENROLLED AT the Community College of Allegheny County in the fall of 2012. His plan was to get his associate's degree, transfer to a four-year college, and then work toward his BA in mathematics. When he allowed himself to dream, what he dreamed of most often was becoming an aerospace engineer. Growing up in Cocoa, Florida, locals idolized the men and women who worked at the Kennedy Space Center just a few miles off the coast in Cape Canaveral, regarding them with the breathless reverence more often reserved for athletes or musicians. If a lofty career like that was too far out of reach, though, he still reasoned that a math degree would open doors to other engineering fields.

As part of his credit requirements, Jason needed to take three computer programming courses. It was not something he was looking forward to. What little he knew of coding and programming suggested an icy realm of arrogant, aloof men laboring in darkened rooms, observing the Luddites around them with thinly veiled contempt. Jason wasn't that kind of person at all. He was affable and outgoing, even charismatic, a natural storyteller who recounted his experiences with a sense of pacing and an eye for detail. He set up elaborate jokes using narratives that came full circle. When he dug into heavy subject matter, which he often did, it was with a sense of humor and an infectious enthusiasm, exuding the kind of honesty and openness that pulled people into conversations as if by gravitational force.

That semester, Jason reluctantly signed up for an introductory programming course. After a few weeks, many of his preconceptions about the field started to fade away, and he was astonished to discover that the language of coding was coming naturally to him. Each project felt like an intricate puzzle, one that required him to determine the jigsaw pieces he needed to build before snapping them into place. He felt himself drawn to the way programming's rules were flexible and open-ended, less balancing equations than pounding out proofs. Even more appealing was the rush of satisfaction that came with finishing a piece of code, an affirmation that his fledgling expertise had made something concrete and practical that other people could use. Sensing his potential, Tatyana encouraged his interest. "You're really quantitative, you're really logical, but you also have this creative side, too," she told him. "The intersection of that Venn diagram is a programmer."

Jason took several more programming classes that spring, and his fascination with the field only intensified. He started neglecting his other courses so he could spend more time delving into coding tasks and programming languages outside his assigned coursework. The following year, he used a cross-registration program at his community college to take a course at Carnegie Mellon University. "It was so wild," he said. "Two years ago, I was in a prison. And now I'm sitting in this illustrious school."

Jason started spending his evenings researching the history and development of the field, tumbling down internet rabbit holes as he read up on the industry's brainy pioneers and leading lights. His wife's insight had hit on something deeper than she even realized: Programming was a dynamic evocation of the subjects that constituted his intellectual pilgrimage at Somerset. There was math, of course, which could be found in coding's quantitative side. But Jason also saw programming as a "philosophical endeavor," requiring coders to ask fundamental questions about knowledge and information while adhering to the logical structures underpinning how programs were developed. He even found a strong correlation between software and fiction: Both challenged authors to balance competing demands of creativity and rigor with elegance and brevity in an invisible space governed by a loose set of rules. "I started realizing that this might be it," Jason said. "I think I found a thing that I really love, and I think this might be where I should have been all along."

Later that year, Jason applied for an entry-level programming position at a small company based outside Pittsburgh. Because most background checks go back at least seven years, he knew that his record would come up on just about anything the firm ran. His best strategy, he decided, was to identify the presence of the elephant before it lumbered into the room. During the in-person interview held in the company's offices, he explained his personal history and the actions that led to his incarceration. After recounting his descent into heroin addiction and the crimes he committed to sustain it, he watched in real time as his prospective employer tensed up, his bearings stiffening and his face pinched in an expression that did not bother concealing its disapproval. But Jason also detailed all the math and programming he'd learned in the intervening years, sculpting his narrative into one that hairpinned toward redemption. The owner appreciated Jason's up-front approach to his checkered past, and he decided to give him a shot. It would be the first of many restive conversations in professional settings. The fact that he'd gotten the job at all, though, was likely a testament to the programming industry's willingness to take on outsiders. He knew that in any number of other related fields—including, more than likely, aerospace engineering—his disclosure would have hastily ended his candidacy.

Jason found programming to be "very much a meritocracy." Coders weren't Silicon Valley hotshots with fancy pedigrees and trophy degrees; they were hackers, hippies, stoners, and loners who wrote code as well as or better than anyone else. Coding was a world where misfits and rogues with blemished histories got a chance to be judged less on personal biography than on their dexterity with JavaScript, Python, and Ruby on Rails. In the years following his first programming job, Jason moved to several different companies, each subsequent position a level above its predecessor. His work ethic was dogged and propulsive, and seventy-hour workweeks were not uncommon. He never lost his beginner's infatuation with learning new code, either, and kept pursuing outside projects in whatever free time he could muster between work hours. At night, he watched lectures by esteemed professors on YouTube's *MIT OpenCourseWare* program. Sentiments that held colleagues back—

complacency, lassitude, indecision—no longer existed for him. Nietzsche's demon was still whispering to him, its proposition reverberating through the years and reminding him how desperately he'd wanted to transform himself and forge a life he'd be content to live "innumerable times again."

The pressing urgency to shape his own circumstances that Jason discovered in prison had never left him. It was a bright, blazing star formed out of the wreathing dust of an aimless past, always reminding him of the "supreme responsibility" he had to live a life he would choose to live again. He'd wrested away a core truth from the existentialism he read at Somerset, and he still clasped his fingers around it like a sacred talisman: In a world without God, there's no will but your own, and the time you have to exercise it is immeasurably precious. Because he'd snapped that insight into such a personal place—making it a plot point along his own narrative identity—it remained an essential, regenerative part of him years later. He'd used the philosophers' rousing metaphysical logic to tell himself a story about the person he could become, and then he persevered through the humble odyssey of coaxing that story into existence.

In 2018, Jason was hired as a senior programmer for a company that developed code for smart TV devices. It was not only a career breakthrough—one born of six years spent zealously absorbing the field's language—but an opportunity to give his family the financial security they had struggled for ever since he'd moved in with Tatyana in 2012. Jason was like a father to Tatyana's daughter, Adrianna, and his biological daughter, Annabella, often stayed with them for weeks at a time. His success would have a significant impact on all of them. But as gratified as he was by the professional advancement, his achievement did little to quell the fear of having his biography exposed. Recurring nightmares still throttled his sleep every few nights, propelled by the insuppressible feeling that the life he'd attained was ephemeral—a charade whose jubilant pageantry could be torn away at any moment to reveal the criminal pariah underneath. It was another exhausting postincarceration paradox, one suggesting that he could reinvent himself completely and still never change at all.

That May, Jason was scheduled to spend a week doing some work in New York City. One of his company's executives, a bluff, raspy-voiced programmer named Manny, invited him to stay at his condo in a brownstone just two blocks from the East River. When Jason got there, he looked out the windows and was floored by sweeping views of the waterfront and the stone arches anchoring the Brooklyn Bridge. One night, after his host left to meet some friends, Jason was wandering the apartment, admiring the abstract paintings lining the halls, when he saw an old news clipping framed in a plaque. The newspaper article described how the executive had been in a gang on the city's Lower East Side as a teenager. Involved in an armed robbery, he was sent to New York's Rikers Island, at the time one of the most notoriously violent prisons in the nation. The piece explained how a mentor figure, looking to steer the teenager away from gang culture, introduced Manny to computers and coding. He quickly became engrossed, and the field completely altered the trajectory of his life.

Standing in front of the wall in gray pants, sneakers, and a plaid button-down shirt, Jason scanned the article several times over. His face was squinched in disbelief. Perhaps he'd misread or misunderstood some key detail in the story. Was it possible that this highly successful, even renowned programmer had spent time in prison, just as Jason had—and for what was essentially the same crime? "It's all I could think about," he said.

Later that week, the two went out to dinner in Manhattan's Financial District, at a restaurant overlooking the East River. After Jason cautiously broached the article he'd read a few days earlier, Manny was disarmingly candid, openly recounting his troubled adolescence and the intervention that gave him something positive to strive toward. Strolling down Water Street, passing mismatching brick storefronts and gleaming skyscrapers on their way back to

Manny's apartment, Jason felt a powerful urge to reciprocate Manny's disclosure and share his own past. "If there's ever going to be a good time, it's after he just volunteered almost identical information," Jason thought. As they settled in the apartment and situated themselves around Manny's dining room table, Jason took a long, slow breath. "I need to talk to you about something," Jason began, sotto voce but also firm, steady. Sitting opposite Manny, who was leaning over the kitchen island standing between them, he proceeded to share his own story: how he got hooked on OxyContin, switched to heroin, and eventually carried out a string of armed robberies to support his voracious addiction.

Jason remembered his decision as "this gigantic fucking gamble." His company never ran a background check when they hired him, and none of his colleagues or supervisors knew about his past. One way or another, the admission would have major ramifications. Once Jason finished speaking, they both stood quietly in the dining room's soft evening chiaroscuro. Manny's expression was thoughtful and hard, but not shocked. After a short but palpable silence—in which the air felt thick with both vulnerability and hope—Manny replied in his gravelly voice. "Everything you've done over the past six years is a testament to your worth," he said. "You came home with nothing, and nobody gave this to you." He promised to support Jason and his career however he could. At ease with one another in a way unique to those who have shared a common plight, they delved deeper into their respective experiences in prison. Manny, whose personal narrative mirrored Jason's but was a few chapters further along, offered him two pieces of advice. "You need to start talking about it," he said, "and you need to find a way to give back."

In the days following his conversation with Manny, Jason was exultant. Receiving that kind of support and affirmation from one of his company's executives uncorked an intoxicating wash of relief. He'd finally achieved the sense of stability and permanence he'd been yearning for, fruitlessly, since his first job after prison. There was something else, too. After sharing his crimes in such unvarnished detail, he felt his relationship to his narrative shift in a subtle but not undetectable way. Excavating his personal history not only allowed him to shrug off the stifling burden of secrecy, it also reminded him what was in the past and what was in the present, crystallizing everything he'd gone through and all the ways he'd changed. No longer suffocating beneath its predecessor, the present was finally permitted to let out a long, full exhale.

Over the next few months, Jason followed Manny's recommendations. He began working with a criminal justice think tank based at Pittsburgh's Duquesne University, working to develop restorative justice programs in the community. He started volunteering at a nonprofit organization focused on men and women reentering society after long stints in incarceration, helping them prepare for job interviews in the technology sector. And he permitted himself to talk about his prison experiences more often. The measures helped assuage his nightmares, which became less and less frequent. "The more I've been giving back, whatever is in my subconscious that's driving this fear, and driving this demon up there, is going away," he said.

A few years after Jason was released from Somerset, a friend of his forwarded him an open call for submissions from a law journal. The publication was asking formerly and currently incarcerated people to share their stories, reflections, and emotions surrounding their time in prison. "I was incarcerated for a little over seven years," Jason began. "I had been a heroin addict, and committed a series of robberies during what I believed were my last days." Later in the essay, he asked, "Have I been corrected? I am finishing college, majoring in mathematics. I am raising two intelligent, beautiful daughters. I am getting married to a type of woman I didn't know existed. I sit at this desk and listen to the rain on the windows, and the gusts in the trees. There was a rabbit in our yard, and I brought our girls to the window and we watched it eat our grass." But his serene, family-centered narrative is counterbalanced in the final paragraph, when he reflects on how he "cannot forget the emptiness" he felt in prison, "the gaping maw of a hole that was my deepest identity." In that gaping maw—where a person, a life, and a firm if flawed sense of self once stood—Jason carried out the quiet, arduous act of creation, and re-creation, that made everything afterward possible.

HIKING IN THE Sierra Nevada range near where I live, I've seen trees growing under astonishingly severe conditions: pines that take root on the jagged lips of sheer bluffs; firs hugging compact fists of parched soil along tracts of sweeping granite; junipers wrapping their sinewy trunks around crags of rock protruding, like the prow of a marooned ship, into sheer alpine air. These trees are twisted, curved, kneaded, and coiled by the elements, lashed by winds and tugged by gravity and sunken by smothering blizzards of heavy mountain snow. They've become malformed monuments, their bark, branches, and crowns warped into grotesque, implausible shapes that are both celebrations and subversions of their classical form. They are specimens in extremis, survivors bearing the transformations demanded by their harrowing lots.

Looking at these trees, I've often wondered whether their onerous circumstances do not in fact provide the ideal conditions to demonstrate their species' most beloved qualities. Resilience, malleability, resourcefulness, and dynamic force of will are all are on resplendent display in these battered, buffeted, and bent flora. Even the crooked trunks and spidery branches suggest a certain uncanny beauty—the kind that unravels something so completely that we are reminded of everything bracing and fantastical about its form. Their contorted aesthetics give us the chance to see trees as if for the first time. But when we imagine these woody plants, conjure to mind what we think of as the tree's platonic ideal, how often do we picture these lonely pioneers and weather-walloped survivors? Rarely, I think. Instead, we're more likely to invoke the towering sequoias or the majestic redwoods, those stout sentries holding court in their sheltering groves. They grow into marvels of size, stature, and girth, taking advantage of their idyllic conditions to achieve their full genetic potential. But is that something we should revere, let alone be inspired by? Isn't there more to admire and draw strength from in those embattled trees—their roots clinging to hostile, bitter land—that have been bent backward by fate yet still reach toward the sun and the sky?

It's fair to assume that Nietzsche would have chosen the trees smitten by nature, the specimens that have suffered, scrabbled, and survived. For him the amount you endured was tantamount to your worth as a person, and your adversities lifted you to a nobler plane of human beings. While there's a limited measure of truth, however deceptive, in the aphorism "What doesn't kill me makes me stronger," it might be more accurate to say, simply, that what doesn't kill us makes us. Catastrophes change us in such a dizzying myriad of conflicting ways that Nietzsche's adage manages to be both accurate and profoundly misleading. Like a tree clutching the sloping face of a snow-covered peak, it's possible to be both stronger and more vulnerable, to stand as a testament to wherewithal and still live on the precipice of fragility.

AFTER SPENDING NEARLY twenty-four hours traveling across the world, JR arrived in Orlando on December 27, 2014. In the days that followed, he would reach another monumental decision: It was time, he felt, to come out to his parents. His mother and father had been there for him through his entire ordeal—by his bedside when he woke for the first time, feeding and bathing him when he was too weak and incapacitated to care for himself, traveling with him all over the United States to get fitted for prosthetics. Indeed, they were prepared to look after him for as long as was necessary. He needed them to know who he was, even if that identity was something their Protestant denomination told them was morally wrong. He would be turning thirty-five on January 17, just a few weeks away. He resolved that he would wait until his birthday, and then call his mom and dad to share a part of himself that he'd kept hidden from them his entire life.

JR's introduction to life back on the mainland was choppy and haphazard, far from affirming his life-changing decision. While trying to get settled and find more permanent housing in Orlando, he moved into an extended-stay hotel in a suburb called Altamonte Springs a few miles north of the city. Though he began aggressively applying to jobs in the area, few employers were responding to his applications. Further, he'd hoped that a move to the continental United States would at least offer respite from Guam's sweltering tropical climate—which can be especially punishing for amputees whose stumps are sealed into prosthetic sockets all day—but found that January temperatures in Central Florida were already climbing into the upper seventies. By the time April rolled around, locals warned, the heat index would commence a precipitate ascent. Between his cramped hotel living quarters, unpromising job prospects, and climate miscalculation, JR's brazen leap of faith had landed him in a rocky place.

But moving across the world on your own was meant to be erratic and flawed, prone to error. A few hapless weeks were just that, nothing more, and JR didn't let the string of setbacks cast a pall over his decision to leave Guam. They certainly weren't going to dissuade him from taking the one step he'd been set on since his very first days in the States. On his thirty-fifth birthday, JR called his mom and dad from his hotel room on the outskirts of Orlando. "You know me," he told his mom, his voice quivering with emotions that had been pent up for years. "You've known me since I was a little kid, a little boy, and I just wanted to let you know that I'm gay." After JR finished speaking, there was an extended pause. "No, no, you can't be," his mom stammered, her voice at once firm and incredulous.

"No, Mom," he replied. "This is what I know, and I can't deny it any longer."

The conversation didn't proceed much further from there. JR's mom gave the phone to her husband, who came on, briefly, to emphasize that they both still loved and supported their son. Then the call ended. Amalia had been stunned, blindsided, the revelation that her son was gay sending her into a stubborn denial that couldn't navigate further discussion. Following the phone call, she and JR, who'd grown closer in the years after the accident, didn't speak for over a month.

Part of the reason his mother had such a hard time accepting that he was gay, JR believed, was because of her preexisting ideas about the kind of man a firstborn son should be. It was a conception deeply rooted in a traditional Filipino culture that—like so many other cultures' mores and expectations—did not accommodate a pluralistic view of manhood. Instead, it reinforced a sharply defined portrait of a straight, successful professional, husband, and father who eventually matures into the patriarch of his own family. For JR, that image was another elusive persona to make permanent peace with. The competitive runner, the coffee-roasting entrepreneur, the firstborn Filipino son—they were all doppelgängers from lives that had passed or were never to be. They served no purpose now.

Despite his mother's speechlessness, in the days following the call JR felt an overwhelming sense of relief. His parents finally knew him for who he was, and it was "a great weight off my shoulders," he said. Coming out to them represented a vital advance along the path to transforming himself into the person he felt he needed to become. Because so much of his past identity had been irrecoverably lost, he now assumed an acute sense of responsibility for everything that remained—including the parts of himself he'd once obfuscated. Every once in a while, he'd remind himself of the undecorated facts of his accident: He'd lost both his legs, suffered a traumatic brain injury, and repeatedly flatlined in the hospital, nearly dying. Now was no longer the time to neglect or suppress anything about himself. Much of the sum total of who he'd been was wrenched away in the wake of the crash; he felt an imperative to never willingly surrender any more. "The accident had put this sense of urgency that I need to go do things before I get too old to do things, or before it's too late," JR said. "Because life is short."

It took only a month for JR to realize that he wouldn't be putting down roots in Orlando. Though he'd sent out dozens of applications, by early February he'd received only one job offer, an administrative assistant position that paid $12 an hour. The humidity left him sweating after even brief walks—JR expended much more energy ambulating in his prosthetics than nondisabled people use walking—and tourist traffic regularly bottlenecked Interstate 4, making travel around the metropolitan area an exasperating ordeal for long stretches of each day. He needed to move on—but to where? He couldn't afford to live on his own, not yet; he'd need a roommate, at least for a while. He started running through everyone he knew in the continental United States. He had college friends in San Diego, but most of them were married, some with kids. He remembered that an old friend and ex-coworker from Guam had moved to Seattle a few years earlier. Maybe she would be open to a new roommate? He still had her number in his phone, and he called her up to see if he could stay at her place until he figured out his next steps. She was heartened to hear from him, she said, and of course he could stay with her. Within days, JR was packing up his possessions and preparing for his second major move in three months.

Orlando had been something of a misfire, but JR gained more traction in Seattle. He secured a job scoring aptitude tests for Pearson Education, working full-time in their headquarters in Kent. On weekends, he explored the surrounding Pacific Northwest environs with his roommate—strolling through Pike Place, having lunch at the Space Needle, visiting the quaintly charming German village of Leavenworth. But after a few months, he started getting the feeling that this wouldn't be his final stop, either. The succession of overcast, drizzly days was affecting his mood; he missed the sunshine. By the springtime, he was revisiting a dream that he'd tucked deep down inside himself for years: returning to Southern California, where he'd gone to college. "The first time I moved back to Guam," JR said, "after a few years I started to regret leaving California. I should have never left."

In addition to pondering his third move in less than a year, JR was also mulling over another ambition that had been suspended indefinitely: returning to school for his MBA. Business school had been part of his larger life blueprint before the accident, something he'd had in the back of his mind as he put together plans to launch a coffee roaster. That spring, as he contemplated a future still hazy and undefined, he applied to MBA programs in Southern California. By July, he was preparing to haul up his life yet again, this time to Orange County. In late August, he would be starting school at California's public university in Fullerton.

Since JR first left Guam on the day after Christmas, the shape of his journey had been scattershot. While partly a function of his laid-back planning, it also reflected his imperfect circumstances. Sure, he'd had only the fuzziest outline for what he wanted his life in the States to look like, but he also had no family in the lower forty-eight and scarce financial resources to draw from. He was a double amputee with limited savings essentially couch surfing around the country. One had to give it to him—it was ballsy. He'd privileged instincts and intuition over comfort and security, setting himself up for a lifestyle subject to constant flux. But those seven months were hardly fruitless, and while he never established himself the way he'd hoped in Orlando and Seattle, he said, "I think it was a good period for me. A lot of growth."

JR arranged to stay with another friend in Southern California. The woman, whom he'd known since his days in San Diego, flew up to Seattle to meet him, and from there the two drove down the Pacific coast together, riding alongside the tawny cliffs and curling breakers that gave raw, dynamic texture to California's famous Route 1. His friend lived in Calabasas, an upscale Los Angeles suburb perched in the picturesque foothills of the Santa Monica Mountains, and JR lived with her for several months while starting school.

That fall, JR began dating a man named Bart, who worked as a dean in the fine arts department of a local college. The two men bonded over the respective adversities life had foisted onto them: JR's accident and the staggering crucible that emerged in its aftermath, Bart's divorce and the challenge of staying close with two adolescent daughters amid a sundered family structure. By connecting through their hardships and the subsequent vulnerabilities they'd been left with, their relationship quickly accelerated. Within two months, Bart was regularly uttering a refrain he deployed with a comic verve that only partially veiled its naked candor: "I'm all in."

JR's blossoming relationship with Bart helped cushion the blow when he realized how difficult his traumatic brain injury was going to make his graduate coursework at Cal State Fullerton. He struggled with the level of memory retention required for some of the classes, and eventually withdrew from the program in the spring of 2016. He remained determined, however, to become an entrepreneur—a dream that he was just beginning to realize when his car struck a telephone pole five years earlier. He knew he didn't need a business school diploma or graduate-level math proficiency to start his own business. Attributes like vision, persistence, and resourcefulness ultimately mattered just as much, perhaps more, and he felt he'd demonstrated those to an estimable degree in the preceding years. He would continue pursuing a calling he was certain was still available to him.

JR and Bart got engaged in late 2017. The following year, they moved into a one-story home in Newport Beach, just a few blocks from the Pacific Coast Highway and the ocean. It was there where JR—finally grounded in a place he'd long harbored hopes of returning to—found ways to reincarnate more of the vibrant life he'd once led on Guam. Part of the reason he'd wanted to return to Southern California was because of how many adaptive sports were available in the region, and after settling in Newport Beach, JR started experimenting with activities like archery, hand cycling, and rowing (he continued swimming regularly, too).

When one of Bart's colleagues invited him and JR to go sailing off Dana Point, a scenic surf town thirty miles south of their home, JR found the experience breathtaking. Pacific trade winds gusted over the boat and pulled the sails into taut, fluttering arcs, as dolphins hurtled through the careening waters in a dazzling synchronized spectacle. It was an invigorating communion with the ocean's sublime balance of potency and succor—its thrilling power and arresting harmony—and he would not soon forget it. "It was just so peaceful being out there," JR said. "I was amazed and awed by it." JR would sail many times after that, and he eventually founded a nonprofit, California Dream Sailing, dedicated to building an accessible catamaran for wheelchair users and other disabled populations on the West Coast.

Ever since his accident, JR had been searching for opportunities to fill the void left by running, often in ways he didn't even consciously realize. "What happens when you can't do the one thing you love?" he asked. The unfathomable answer to that question defined a significant portion of JR's afterlife. Mythologist Joseph Campbell asserted that people are not so much in search of an abstract, disembodied "meaning" in their lives as they're seeking "an experience of being alive . . . the rapture of being alive." Running, for JR, bestowed "the rapture of being alive," and when he lost that pursuit he was dispossessed of nothing less than his access to that rapture.

Catastrophes frequently deprive us of those experiences to which we are most ferociously attached—acts as universal as walking, running, seeing, or watching our children grow—and without them we are forced to cling more fervently to the facets of our identity still available to us. Following my diagnosis with CFS, I could no longer lead the exuberantly active lifestyle I once did, and had to hastily forfeit mornings at the gym, afternoons on the basketball court, and my slipshod running regimen. In response to these comparatively minor losses, I immersed myself in literature and a writing craft I'd long taken for granted, which had each played spirited but supporting roles in the before period of my life. After her accident, Valerie's social circles were partially diminished and her athletic career cut short; she responded by ramping up her commitment to academics and cultivating a passionate attachment to medieval studies that would evolve into an anchoring force. When we lose the headliners that strut across the stage of our lives—those natural performers who've commanded our time and attention for as long as we can remember—we must keep the production going with what members of the cast we have left. Understudies get bumped up to top billing, minor roles are expanded, and the narrative acquires an element of pathos and loss that it never had before. The show goes on, recast and reinvented with many of the same parts and players on hand before it lost its stars. But the story—and the meaning performers and audience alike will glean from it—has been profoundly altered.

In the summer of 2019, JR and Bart got married. The ceremony was held in the same Presbyterian chapel where they attended weekly mass, inside a Spanish revival church with red-tile roofs, swooping rounded archways, and a quaint, lofty bell tower topped with a wrought iron cross. The couple sent no formal invitations, but on their wedding day the polished-wood pews quickly filled. Friends, family, old classmates, fellow churchgoers, and amputees JR met in the preceding years got word and huddled, elbow to elbow, for the nuptials. (Whether because they lived a thirteen-hour plane ride away or because of their ambivalence about the relationship, JR's parents did not attend.) After they were pronounced married, the couple shared drinks with their guests on the church's stucco patio. A jazz band, featuring the head pastor on saxophone, played rhapsodic harmonies into the dry, balmy night.

JR's reinvention along the piers, marinas, and seaside cliffs of Southern California straddled a revealing paradox. He moved six thousand miles from home, came out to his family, discovered swimming and sailing, and settled into a married life that would not have been possible on Guam. But many of those transformations could be traced back to the bones and tissue of his life before the car accident. Whether it was his sexuality, entrepreneurship, or fondness for challenging his body and stretching its outer limits, everything about JR's life that blossomed in Southern California had an earlier permutation on Guam. His reinvention was not into an utterly unrecognizable person, fabricated out of whole cloth. It might be better understood as a series of reincarnations he'd fought hard to usher into existence, analogues to the person and life he'd left after walking through afterlives' one-way looking glass.

The result, for JR, was a dramatically rearranged biography that supported a surprisingly similar underlying identity. "There's things that were down there that I never knew or acknowledged or realized," JR said. The car accident that night a decade ago in Hagatna "forced me to look at all those things and use them." In his case, tragedy did, eventually, reveal identity, precipitating a transformation into a version of himself who had—deep down—always been there.

THERE'S A WORD that comes up over and over in conversations with people who've endured catastrophic life events: perspective. Direct quotes I've heard include "I've gained a completely new perspective," "I have a much different perspective than I once did," and "My perspective into other people and their lives is much different than it used to be." But what, exactly, do such impassioned declarations actually mean? The human condition exists along a vast spectrum, and those who've endured catastrophe watch their placement along that spectrum shift—in some cases drastically so. As they settle into their new position and adjust to their unfamiliar surroundings, they acquire a different point of view than they previously had. Their "perspective" along the continuum of human existence has been altered, and their new position brings them into closer proximity to what had long been remote and inaccessible lives.

Like two flashlights whose beams combine to illuminate everything in between them, lives split into a before and an after can recognize and identify with a broader swath of humanity. This coalescence deepens individuals' "capacity to view things in their true relations or relative importance," to invoke one definition of perspective. Having witnessed the inexorable randomness of fate, those leading afterlives come to understand that their situation could be not just better but also far worse. The lives of the least fortunate, meanwhile—which they might have once regarded as sympathetic abstractions—become full and three-dimensional, integrated into how they gauge and conceptualize their own circumstances.

Struggling with chronic illness has illuminated for me not only the million-plus Americans who live with CFS but also those people living with multiple sclerosis, lupus, Sjogren's, and a host of other autoimmune conditions that fly beneath the radar of our culture and medical establishment but nevertheless affect quality of life for millions. My vexing array of symptoms—ones I cannot escape for so much as a single day—have demonstrated for me the fortitude, willpower, and self-possession required by individuals living with serious health conditions. These groups are no longer hypothetical to me. My own life experience shines a light on theirs, offering a broader, more inclusive view of humanity and its hidden frailties.

My blow of misfortune has also had the paradoxical effect of illustrating, even emphasizing, the degree to which my existence had long been bolstered by good fortune. Once my illness had shifted my position along the human spectrum, I suddenly saw more clearly where the accident of birth had originally positioned me. It was like being a random point on a coordinate plane with no x- and y-axis and suddenly having them unveiled to you. The myopia I once saw the world through conferred a kind of ignorant bliss, an innocence tantamount to obliviousness. The perspective of my life-altering adversity, on the other hand, has brought me just a little bit closer to the immutable hardships that define the lives of so many people around the world. It is the unnerving wisdom of experience, one that reveals how unequal and disparate the human condition is, how random and unearned the circumstances that press down on people's fates.

Aeschylus wrote that we "suffer into truth." If the merging of before and after perspectives is not quite suffering into truth, it is suffering into several of its correlatives: insight, empathy, awareness, depth of understanding. Gaining perspective means being able to counterbalance the knowledge of everything we've lost by awakening to the unacknowledged windfalls we've always had. In this way, it is often a prerequisite for reinvention, a necessary reexamination of our biographies that rescues our gratitude and inspires us to embrace lives that are neither perfect nor doomed.

IN THE SUMMER before her second year at the University of Victoria, Sophie had enjoyed an insightful, liberating four months on the other side of the country. In Montreal, she'd confronted some of the most daunting questions her traumatic brain injury had left, gradually coming to accept the fluidity of her identity and growing more comfortable in her own skin. But year two as a full-time college student, alas, began much like year one. When classes started in September 2016, her anxiety began climbing almost immediately, inching upward like mercury expanding in a glass tube during the summer's most sweltering months. The rigid associations between her grades, her intelligence, and her self-worth came howling back, and she resumed fixating on every sentence she wrote, every multiple-choice question she answered, every simple assignment as part of her headlong pursuit of academic perfection.

As Sophie's second year progressed, it was clear her compulsive work ethic and extreme investment in her schoolwork were extracting a hefty price. In addition to her suffocating anxiety and insomnia, there was also the physical and cognitive exhaustion she suffered before and after each semester's major exams. Those were grim, haggard hours, spent shuffling around like a shadow, too vacant for even perfunctory conversation and too depleted to consistently feed herself. Her mom, with whom she still lived, often prepared her meals and helped her with other tasks. "We were cooking for her, waking her up, sometimes getting her clothes out of the closet, making her breakfast, making her lunch, dropping her to the university, picking her up," Jane recalled. "What she doesn't know is that I'm supporting her all the way, and I needed to keep that connection with her."

Like neglected crops, nonacademic aspects of Sophie's life shriv-

eled away during the school year as she expended her deepest reserves on homework, papers, and exams. Her steely focus and
avowed determination to blaze through her bachelor's and immediately move forward with a PhD earned her the nickname Little
Professor among her peers. It was a sobriquet that might have ac-
curately spoken to the strident, severe persona she projected around
campus, but one that also failed to capture just how thorny and convoluted her relationship with her schoolwork actually was. To get
the grades she pined for, she offered up her body, her mind, even her
sanity.

By the summer of 2017, Sophie was finally asking herself a question she'd avoided for two long, grueling years. Were the steep sacrifices of her mental health and physical well-being worth whatever
sense of validation an impeccable transcript conferred? Her hell-
bent insistence on academic excellence, which had inoculated her
from the years of listlessness that could have easily followed a traumatic brain injury, had turned into a poison dose. She was actively
deciding, over and over, to keep swallowing it.

The following winter, Sophie began a relationship with a deaf
male student at the University of Victoria. The two had met through
the Society for Students with a Disability, where she worked as a
community liaison and later a chairperson. They dated for a year,
and she found the experience "world altering." Seeing the gauntlet
of obstacles he faced on campus every single day—from straining to
follow lectures he couldn't hear to communicating with professors
through a limited number of available interpreters—opened her
eyes to the innumerable ways access, privilege, and physical capability paved so much of each individual's academic path. When Sophie was later exposed to the larger Deaf community in Victoria,
through him, she witnessed his social barriers on an even larger,
more devastating scale. Deaf Victorians faced pervasive levels of
poverty and illiteracy and profound social marginalization, and
even suffered disproportionately high incarceration rates. The
group's single physiological difference, she observed, seemed to ripple outward into a slew of socioeconomic disadvantages. But it was

clear these afflictions didn't stem from the biological fact of deafness; rather, they arose from the way society operated as though that difference was not there (in other words, ableism). The structures and institutions surrounding the Deaf community habitually overlooked its existence, and the people in that community suffered dearly for it.

When Sophie saw the systemic effects of ableism firsthand, it shattered her long-standing conceptions about intelligence and worth. She'd finally stumbled onto a vantage point that exposed just how flawed her thinking had been. Allegedly objective measurements like grades and test scores were subject to a litany of confounding factors, including a person's physical capacities, socioeconomic position, and the inherent prejudices of the institutions that shaped and administered such measurements. "Even the idea of doing well in a class is such a privileged idea," she said. "Why," she asked, "am I holding myself to such standards, when I can logically see how that's not the whole story?"

The men and women Sophie met in Victoria's Deaf community—including Native populations and people of color who strode atop some of intersectionality's densest junctures—galvanized her growing sense of empathetic solidarity with disabled and disadvantaged groups. As she observed her deaf boyfriend collide with cyclists whose bike bells he couldn't hear and navigate tense encounters with police officers he couldn't communicate with, Sophie was gradually pulled out of the excruciating introspection she'd long enshrouded herself in. Her gaze was shifting outward, lifted from the repetitive paralysis of proving her self-worth toward an intensifying affinity for the people negotiating a world seemingly engineered to keep theirs debased and demoralized.

After Sophie saw the glaring flaws in her perspective, her relationship with her studies began to evolve. By her fourth year at the University of Victoria, in 2018, her yearslong thralldom to schoolwork was dissipating, a spell that had finally been broken. Though imminent tests and deadlines still aroused Sophie's anxiety, she also found herself growing emotionally detached from her classes. The result was a bizarre dissonance in which her firmly entrenched re-lationship with her coursework coexisted with an increasing sense of indifference. "Clearly this is activating my nervous system," she recalled observing, "but I don't feel like school is hitting my needs or my values." Her disillusionment with academia went beyond skepticism toward grades and performance; she also started ques-tioning her long-established ambitions to become a scientific re-searcher. "When I reflect or imagine wanting to be a researcher, there's a part of me that's trying to fix myself, and there's a part of me that is absolutely terrified of the changes that my brain under-went," she said. "I'm trying to find solutions because I'm so deathly afraid of it."

But that thinking had changed over the years, too. Sophie was no longer steered by a dire wish to reverse everything that had hap-pened to her. Instead of dedicating her life to the hazy prospects of discovering treatments for Alzheimer's or Parkinson's—conditions she was several times more likely to develop than the general population—she wanted to effectuate a greater difference in the present. "What can I do now?" she asked. "How can I make a life that's meaningful for both me and other people?"

Widening the aperture of her perception, Sophie became in-creasingly involved in communities she felt passionate about. As a chairperson for the University of Victoria's Society for Students with a Disability, she planned workshops and discussions, orga-nized conferences, and worked to shape college policy surrounding disability. She volunteered at Victoria General Hospital—the same facility where she'd spent a month recovering from the car accident—where she spoke to teenagers about the long-term effects of trau-matic injuries. And she attended weekly meetings held by the Victoria Brain Injury Society, meeting with other TBI sufferers with backgrounds and experiences that sometimes mirrored her narra-tive and other times diverged from it. When her scientific aspira-tions were juxtaposed with activities that bettered lives in the present, the research dreams that once held such primacy no longer felt nearly as consequential.

By the winter of her fourth year at the University of Victoria, the facts of Sophie's biographical narrative had changed only slightly. The thoughts, feelings, and preoccupations that once landscaped its interior spaces, however, had been replaced to a startling degree. Her journal entries attest to a twenty-four-year-old woman ardently focused on the humanitarian and environmental crises enveloping the world. "When people look back in history, at what point will they say the end is considered to be?" she wrote in one entry. "Will it be the first acid rainstorm blanketing a city in the States? Will it be the moment the last tree in the Amazon is cut? Will it be when another shooter chooses to murder people praying in a synagogue? Will it be the nth bomb dropped in Syria? Is it to be considered when the last tree frog goes extinct?" By prying herself away from the fixations arising from her brain injury, Sophie returned her attention to the global exigencies that inspired such fiery passion in her during her adolescence. This borderless compassion was an aspect of her identity that had existed long before her TBI, and by finding her way back to it she was reclaiming some of the territory her injury had long usurped.

Interestingly, the TBI itself may have affected the way she approached issues like poverty, war, and climate change. In addition to making her more impulsive and sharpening her communication style, Sophie's disinhibition also pushed open the invisible pathways between her and other people. The result was a level of warmth and empathy that is inaccessible to most of us. Examples of unusual beneficence were scattered through her daily life: She pulled up to the bus stop near her home in Victoria to offer rides to total strangers, befriended and bought food for members of Victoria's homeless population, and regularly supported disabled friends at college by walking with them to classes and talking them through emotional crises.

By the winter of 2019, Sophie had become so tuned in to the suffering and catastrophe wreathed around the planet that it was plunging her into bouts of desolating sorrow. Her emotional engine had been supercharged ever since the accident: She slipped more easily into the fits of rage and sobbing meltdowns, paroxysms of laughter and glittering spurts of exuberance that represented rare states for most people. Now, as her attention slowly returned to the issues and causes that engrossed her adolescence, it was her compassion that was pushed to woozy new heights.

Some days, as sunset fell on Victoria and she contemplated the unhoused refugees in Syria or the children starving in Yemen, Sophie would feel a sharp sense of melancholy knife through her thoughts, slicing deeper and deeper until it pierced her troubled heart. Tossing and turning in bed, unable to expel the heartrending images or stark news stories from her mind, she'd wake up her partner, drive to the ocean, and wade up to her waist in the frigid, quickening water. "It's winter, it's dark, there's no one else around," she said. "And I can just put my head underwater, and hear the ocean, and scream." In those protracted, desperate nights, Sophie wept into the churning blackness of the sea, hoping its stabbing coldness might expunge a throbbing sadness for people she'd never met but nevertheless felt immensely for.

During the following semester Sophie took just a single class. She spent the winter wrestling with a depression whose torturous provenance—burnout from school, uncertainty about her future, plangent sorrow for the world—reflected the dense tangle of struggles she'd endured over the preceding five years. Semester after semester of pushing herself to the precipice of physical and cognitive collapse had taken a cumulative toll, and the ambivalence she now felt toward everything she'd been doggedly working toward made it hard to stay motivated with her schoolwork. She decided that it was in her best interest to take an additional year to graduate.

In June 2020, Sophie completed enough credits to earn her bachelor of science in biopsychology. That summer, she started a job working as an assistant to a project manager in Victoria. A few months later, she would accept a part-time position at the Society for Students with a Disability at the university, where she'd volunteered as an undergraduate. She was still only twenty-six years old, a raw bundle of unsettled biography and experience who likely had several more permutations to come.

While her life hadn't changed in the sweeping, extravagant fashions of some of the other people in this book, her perspective had, and those changes became the crux of her reinvention. After all her experiences distrusting her perception and relentlessly plumbing the slippery depths of her identity, Sophie had arrived at a singular, unorthodox point of view, one that ranged over the full scope of the human condition and suggested a different sort of self. "I have had people ask me, 'So who is Sophie?'" she said. "And I legitimately cannot answer that. I don't know.

"I have rejected the notion of having an identity, and I take so much meaning from the things around me," she continued. "The birds coming out, the mushrooms growing, the rain coming back, the smoke rolling in." She was, she said, "just a witness, a witness to everything wonderful and awful going on." It was a reconfiguration of how she saw the world, a view that promised to honor everything she'd been through without relinquishing the person she was before she stepped into the blue Volkswagen Golf on that fate-twisting September morning.

Sophie's story transposes the patterns that appear in most of the other afterlives in this book. Instead of spending years slogging through the laborious internal work of reinventing her identity, in at least one narrow sense her transformation was complete as soon as she awakened at Victoria General Hospital in the fall of 2014. Rather than following a trajectory in which an individual pursues the dramatic changes that help them build a more fulfilling afterlife, Sophie needed to reconcile herself to the ones that had already taken permanent hold before she even started hers. Looked at from one angle, her narrative emphatically demonstrates the way catastrophe shapes identity: Her traumatic injury literally transformed her emotions and personality, altering the way she felt, behaved, communicated, and interacted with the wider world.

But that was only the beginning of her story. For years, she was at the tense, roiling center of the push and pull between catastrophe and identity, and her sense of self today is defined as much by her insights and decisions during that blistering odyssey as it is by any of the changes that emerged in the immediate aftermath of her brain injury. Despite what the broader contours of her story might suggest, she was never going to be fixed in place by her catastrophic experience, trapped in the translucent amber of a single biographical event. No afterlives are, and her narrative also conversely illustrates the folly in seeing our greatest adversities as the sole sculptors of the people we become. Sophie's TBI was only the beginning of all the changes she would undergo over the next seven years, and her compassionate, ego-renouncing perspective—a view earned through her psychological travails—is perhaps her truer reinvention.

Afterlives testify to many things. One is that the catastrophic events we live through can sow a lifetime of obstacles that play an outsize role in determining our future. But those obstacles and the vulnerabilities that produce them will always be just one side of a larger equation, the first line of a longer mathematical proof. Everything that we do after catastrophe—in the midst of our losses and impediments—is what matters most: our feats of adaptation, crises of faith, and hard-won ground where we carry the backbreaking weight of making our identities over again. Sophie's story appears, at first, to demonstrate that "what doesn't kill us makes us." But interpreting her adulthood in that way would miss much of the point. For her and for so many people leading afterlives, what doesn't kill us makes us make ourselves.

~

Impossible Things

IN *ECCE HOMO*, NIETZSCHE WROTE, "MY FORMULA FOR GREATNESS in a human being is amor fati: that one wants nothing to be different, not forward, not backward, not in all eternity. Not merely bear what is necessary, still less conceal it . . . but love it." The Latin phrase Nietzsche invokes translates to "love of one's fate." Though his reference is the most well-known today, the concept of amor fati has been around since at least the first century, when Greeks practicing the philosophy of Stoicism argued that we should embrace everything that happens to us because each incident is inextricably linked to the totality of our lives. You cannot reject one specific aspect of your narrative, the philosophy asserted, because if you tried to pull it out everything else would unravel with it. There is a dense web of cause and effect that holds everything together, and parsing it is fruitless and even self-destructive.

Nietzsche and his predecessors saw amor fati as a form of unconditional acceptance, an attitude that trades the futility of hypotheticals—the what-ifs and if-onlys—for gratitude and amazement before the irrevocable trajectory of one's fate. And the love within amor fati is also an analytical one, probing our misfortunes for the seeds that would later bloom into what we cherish most about our identities. There is simply no extricating the good from the bad, because they are perpetually creating one another. If we appreciate anything about our existence, the philosophy suggests, we must appreciate everything.

Perhaps it was inevitable that Nietzsche's own adage about life after catastrophe, rather than the concept he inherited from the Greek Stoics, would gain more purchase in the modern world. The notion that what doesn't kill us makes us stronger is more immediately gratifying than the dense tangle of implications that amor fati asks us to glean. While the former acts like a spell, transforming all our hardship into the personal enhancement we may feel our adversities entitle us to, the latter charges us with a far more difficult task: examining our lives exactly as they are, and then accepting them without romance or valorization. Nietzsche's maxim does all the work for us, superimposing exaltation onto our most agonizing trials; amor fati, on the other hand, demands that we stumble through our lives' labyrinth of cause and effect and endeavor to memorize the layout.

I didn't hear of the concept of amor fati until my late twenties, a case in point for the cultural supremacy of Nietzsche's maxim. It was only after that revealing constellation therapy session in 2018, when I was thirty-two, that I began doubting the philosopher's claim. As my adversities were pulled away from their long-standing prism and laid out like courtroom exhibits before me, I realized, perhaps for the first time in my life, that I didn't know how they'd influenced my identity and character. Though it was a disillusionment in the truest sense of the word, it would also be the first step on my path to grasping the validity of amor fati. In attempting to trace the aforementioned labyrinths in six afterlives, this book also pushed me to examine the cause and effect in my own winding biography. Over time I came to understand that the aspects of my life that I most loved could not be so easily disentangled from those that caused me the deepest pain.

I set out to write this book with a straightforward, almost artlessly simple question. How valid was Nietzsche's claim that what doesn't kill us makes us stronger? And if it was only partly valid—or not at all valid—then what did the broader picture of those lives transformed by catastrophe look like? I needed to unearth the layers of truth beneath our fears and our fantasies about trauma and tragedy, and I could do so only by mining the stories of others who've endured their own. Whatever I uncovered in their lives, I hoped, would yield illuminating insights into my own.

By the time I'd finished the dozens of interviews I had with Sophie, JR, Jason, Valerie, Sean, and Gina—which came to feel like one long conversation shared over two years—they'd each affected and even uplifted me in ways that I couldn't possibly have foreseen. I was moved by their collective embodiment of so many of the characterstics we revere in our culture but rarely see on full, unconcealed display in the people around us. Quantities like theirs of courage, flexibility, imagination, and equanimity do not spring up spontaneously; they are summoned by commensurate measures of pain, fear, bewilderment, and doubt. Beneath those qualities, I also observed a gentler, more graceful feat: These men and women retained a positive attachment to their lives, an affection for their selves even after catastrophe dramatically disarranged them. In *Far from the Tree*, Andrew Solomon writes that under the most unexpected and arduous of circumstances, "Cleaving to our own lives, with all their challenges and limitations and particularities, is vital." These subjects demonstrated that essential instinct, refusing to become estranged from themselves. They all saw one or several aspects of their identities that they still cherished, and they cleaved to them ferociously. Each person began with the irreducible task of survival but eventually found their way toward wisdom, growth, empathy, and transformation.

It would not be an overstatement to say that these subjects have inspired me—but not, I believe, in the fraught, exploitative sense of "inspiration porn." The full range and depth of their lives, rather than a single tragedy or triumph, has moved me to perceive and respond to my own circumstances differently. These are people whose relationships, careers, circumstances, and general well-being evolved over the course of my reporting, and not even a book-length project could hope to capture the entirety of their protean layers. Their complexities overlapped with one another in surprising, instructive ways. Sean and Sophie both felt a galvanizing need to lift up the lives of those around them, improving their material conditions and brightening their spirits with dignity, possibility, and hope. Gina and Valerie each found a regenerative sanctuary in their respective intellectual arenas, disciplines that provided them with a means of coexisting alongside their disabilities without surmounting or "overcoming" them. And Jason and JR plunged into the nerve-rattling free fall of wholly reimagining their lives, from where they lived and who they loved to the personal philosophy underpinning how they rose to each day. Though afterlives encompass a heterogeneous swath of society's invisible kingdoms—from disability and chronic illness to incarceration and trauma—our means of adaptation and deliverance are often the same. The faces of salvation are timeless and undiscriminating.

THE SIX SUBJECTS provided no shortage of insights into afterlives and the realities of how we lead them, and a handful have proven especially meaningful to me. I was surprised to find how many individuals held fast—for a time—to a sense of irrational conviction that was often sharpened by defiance. In the years immediately following their catastrophes, they insisted that their lives would eventually return to "normal." Frustrated and sometimes scornful of the lowered expectations held by those around them, they flung themselves toward one vessel of hope after another.

Their mindsets reminded me of my own bargaining and rationalizations, the way I preserved for years a stubborn confidence that I would eventually make a full recovery. Though my own irrational belief did not prevail indefinitely, the people I spoke to showed me that—in the context of an afterlife—it was hardly a frivolous impulse. Believing in futures and possibilities that appear dubious, far-fetched, or even outright impossible can change the mood and tenor of one's life, granting it a levity and expansiveness that is, in some ways, its own reward. In *Through the Looking-Glass*, Alice tells the White Queen, "One can't believe impossible things."

"I daresay you haven't had much practice," the Queen replies. "Why, sometimes I've believed as many as six impossible things before breakfast."

It's hard to say with certainty what Lewis Carroll was winking at here, but I'd like to think that the queen is an unlikely vehicle for the author's notion that releasing ourselves from reason and rationalism—at least once in a while—can be a wondrous emancipation. We may tell ourselves stories in order to live, but sometimes we must also free ourselves from the stories we've heard too many times, the ones that confine and sequester us. Seeing how individuals leading afterlives believed in their own "impossible things" validated that instinct in myself, reminding me that—as long as we're not too attached to our chimeras—we can be cast aloft by our generous imaginations and audacious beliefs.

I also found myself recognizing a particular pattern that's hard to describe but indispensable to understanding many afterlives: the exchange of one's lightness of being for increased weight and depth. Lifestyles that were once vibrant and intoxicating often become, in the months and years after life-altering events, slower, quieter, and more reflective. Individuals like Jason and Sean, whose identities thrived off of velocity and thrill, were forced to sink into themselves in a way they'd never needed to before. In the absence of daily exhilaration, they began to examine their priorities, ideals, and assumptions with a sophistication and nuance previously unavailable to them.

It was an evolution I related to, and one that became increasingly recognizable as I moved deeper through my reporting. People's catastrophes weighed them down, even curbed their vivacity, but they also gradually deepened their convictions, resolve, and emotional discipline. Those leading afterlives woke up in the morning with heavier crosses to bear, but that act of bearing changed them in ways few could have imagined. I read somewhere that the ego emerges only after the id is rejected for the first time, and I think, on some level, a similar relationship holds here. After the sources from which people long drew their joy were ruptured, they felt an urgency to seize on something else—a sense of overarching purpose and meaning. The lightness and gusto of their "before" lives might have been gone, but through dedication and focus they cultivated a sense of gravity and responsibility that served as an abiding substitute.

Another abstract truth I observed in the subjects came to feel to me like a saving grace. The law of conservation of mass, first discovered by French chemist Antoine Lavoisier in 1789, states that mass and energy can neither be created nor destroyed. Atoms can be rearranged, reconstituted, and transferred through the universe to create new forms, but they cannot be permanently lost. Based in large part on the many afterlives I learned about for this book, I would assert a comparable law at work in our own hearts and minds. Tragedy, trauma, and their resulting diminishments breach and even shatter the objects of our passion, whether that be running through the jungle, jaunting around the city, or plugging into catharsis on a basketball court. Those catastrophes cannot, however, eradicate the passion itself underlying those pursuits. Like salt in the oceans, nitrogen in the atmosphere, or the atoms themselves ricocheting in and around us, that is inextinguishable.

The physical trauma suffered by Valerie and JR, for example, put an end to some of the pursuits they most loved. Though it might have taken years, they ultimately discovered new vessels for their displaced passions. It was a law I'd long felt manifested in my own life, as the sports I could no longer play and the weights I could no longer lift without triggering debilitating malaise were replaced with a soothing affection for the natural world and its magnificent array of wild inhabitants. Seeing this conservation phenomenon in other lives bolstered its veracity. Catastrophes can demolish the forms atoms take, but they can never destroy the atoms themselves— the sum total of our ardor for the world. It is the essential, affirming work of afterlives to reclaim them.

In between my many conversations with these six people, I thought about them often. Were they struggling beneath the surface, as I often was? Were they still pulled into recollections of the before-and-after events that transformed their identities, forced to negotiate slinking reminiscences of the person chance cast into oblivion? I imagined them in joy and triumph—Valerie being recognized for her Harvard thesis, Sean learning that his life sentence had been commuted by the governor—and also in dejection and defeat, when their circumstances appeared to them irreconcilable with their selfhood and dreams. But I also tried to fathom those more quicksilver days when they felt both torn and whole, when their bodies or memories led them to the uncomfortable paradox that they'd changed and grown and accomplished so much, and yet had never truly divorced themselves from the very first moments of their afterlives.

IF WE ALLOW afterlives to work on us, they can burn clean our preconceived expectations for who we believe we should—or deserve to—be. What were once seemingly immutable attachments can come to be replaced with attitudes of grace and awe: grace in accepting a life we almost certainly never would have asked for, and awe that our biographies are unraveling with a mysterious and engrossing cause and effect we could not possibly have foreseen. In this way, the dramatic trajectories of afterlives are all but perfectly suited to the philosophy of amor fati.

Perhaps the Greek Stoics' philosophy is a more faithful, realistic mantra to live by than Nietzsche's indefatigable adage. It grants us a broader and more inclusive perspective into our lives, showing us how to reconcile ourselves to all the ways catastrophes change us beyond making us stronger. An unconditional love of one's fate can help people come to terms with the ambiguity and multiplicity of afterlives, the way the chapters in this book coexist, intertwine, and open pathways to one another. It's the before-and-after experience itself and the resulting diminishment, after all, that bring forth all the complex changes and adaptations that follow. A survivor of rape in 2006, Gina experienced a vision loss three years later that eventually led to the synesthetic breakthrough in 2014 that would, in turn, trigger a psychic reorganization that attenuated her sexual trauma: an exquisite expression of everything amor fati urges us to see. If the positive and negative are all but impossible to disentangle in most people's lives, they are even more dyed into each other's wool in afterlives. For those leading them, amor fati is a resonant, elevating appeal.

Although many people living after catastrophe grasp for devotion and reinvention, most will ultimately find themselves embodying the other chapters in this book just as fully. It is entirely possible to exemplify fortitude while sinking deeper into vulnerability, to intensify our devotion to what we love even as we negotiate the progressive erosion of other parts of our lives. Even those who have achieved reinvention—arguably the most extraordinary human act in the wake of catastrophe—secure no guarantee of quieting their demons or immunizing themselves from lifelong susceptibilities. The act of reinvention does not so much whisk people beyond those challenges as it sublimates the challenges to a new end, turning them into open questions to which one's evolving identity can serve as a long, passionate, unfinished answer. Those leading afterlives must accept the inherent tensions and contradictions of their fates and internal lives that cannot be neatly categorized. The catastrophes that don't kill us turn us into more fluid, layered texts, defying linear interpretation, straddling ambiguity and dissonance, and living with a loss that we silently wrestle with forever—perpetually shaping us, as we unceasingly toil to shape it.

It's easy to be "inspired" by those people who've endured calamity and continue to grapple with its lifelong effects. But the more important—and more humanizing—project is understanding the specific ways in which they endured, and how those choices, strategies, and adaptations made them into the person they are today. People searching to regain their equilibrium and revitalize their fondness for their lives following catastrophe require more than inner strength or sheer force of will. If afterlives throw light on anything about the human condition more broadly, it's that we demand more than just a survival instinct if we want to endure in any bearable way. In a line frequently misattributed to Nietzsche, Harvard psychologist Gordon Allport wrote, "To live is to suffer, to survive is to find meaning in the suffering." We need spiritual, intellectual, and moral sustenance, a kind of infrastructure of the spirit that can anchor us when so much else has been unceremoniously stripped away. Like nocturnal dreams or holy visions, this infrastructure takes a dazzling abundance of forms: Christianity, Islam, existentialism, mathematics, medieval history, bearing witness, or becoming a "monument to human possibility." I was astonished by how many people leading afterlives found *something* to pour themselves into that was not directly related to the reversal or amelioration of their life-altering events.

The seventeenth-century French philosopher Blaise Pascal once said, "In difficult times you should always carry something beautiful in your mind." We have a choice about where to point our lens—an active furnishing of the consciousness toward which we can all strive. Afterlives demonstrate for everyone the importance of conceiving meaning, divining purpose, and helming new stories—creative acts that, like great art, redeem and exalt—but they also exhort us to carry out something even simpler: to connect to the world in whatever forms we choose. At their sinister cores, our tragedies and traumas saw through the ropes connecting us to what we love, setting us adrift and unmoored in faceless waters oblivious to our suffering. It is our noblest task to tether ourselves back, lashing our ships to the jetties, piers, and unmapped islands that we discover. Only then will we find ourselves leading different lives with different identities and different beloveds, immersed in a new existence with only a passing resemblance to the old.

ACKNOWLEDGMENTS

THIS BOOK WOULD NOT HAVE BEEN POSSIBLE IF NOT FOR THE time, effort, and dedication of its six primary subjects: Sophie Papp, Valerie Piro, Gina Applebee, Sean Taylor, Jason Dixon, and JR Vigil. Each of these individuals committed themselves to a long-term project that required dozens of hours of interviews—often covering events and circumstances that were sensitive, painful to revisit, or even traumatizing—all while knowing next to nothing about what the final work was going to look like. Their patience, openness, generosity, self-reflection, vulnerability, intelligence, and candor were indispensable to my efforts to understand how human beings change in the aftermath of calamity. I owe them each a significant debt of gratitude.

My agent, Jennifer Herrera, was irreplaceable to the germination of this book, from its most incipient stages as a collection of desultory notes to the exacting and fastidious work of crafting a proposal. Her keen eye and quick, discerning mind pushed me to think about the book's themes, ideas, allusions, scope, and inclusion criteria with prudence, discipline, and rigor, and she encouraged me to forthrightly explore how my own personal experiences might snap into place alongside those individuals whose lives I was narrativizing. She served as an editor, guide, and friend—a kind of warm, enlightening chaperone through the labyrinthine intricacies of book publishing—long before the book had anything resembling a permanent, official home. There is little chance in overstating her importance to the inception, production, and successful completion of this work.

Emily Hartley, my editor, provided invaluable feedback, commentary, and guidance over many months of revisions. Equally important, to my mind, was her irrepressible enthusiasm—even as the project wended its way through the roughest, most nebulous stages—and a painstaking work ethic that helped me recognize and take deeper pride in my own. I am profoundly grateful for her willingness to take on, and commit so much time and effort to, a debut work that does not easily slip into category or genre. Her unstinting positivity gave me confidence, momentum, and validation when I needed it most. My thanks also goes out to the entire team at Ballantine for all the behind-the-scenes efforts, expertise, and acumen that helped this book come to fruition.

I began this project by casting a wide reporting net, and the means by which I found my subjects were highly varied. Nevertheless, I would like to extend my special gratitude to the nonprofit organization Blind New World, who introduced me to Gina Applebee, and the Second Chance Center, through which I was able to connect with Sean Taylor. I also owe thanks to Sandy Hook Promise, Disabled American Veterans Charitable Service Trust, Schizophrenia and Related Disorders Alliance of America, Grief Recovery After Substance Passing (GRASP), and Denise Cullen, who were all kind and generous enough to share a number of contacts with me. Thank you, too, to every person who was willing to share their lives and traumas with a journalist whom they had never spoken to before, much less met. You had nothing to gain—save for the faintest of connections and perhaps a glimmer of catharsis—and yet you took the time to open yourself up to me. I will always be appreciative of that.

A bright, dense constellation of books helped me find my way through the uncharted territory I was in while writing my own, and they include Judith Herman's *Trauma and Recovery*, Larissa Mac-Farquhar's *Strangers Drowning*, Eula Biss's *On Immunity*, the *Best American Essays* series, Jack Hart's *Storycraft*, Jon Franklin's *Writing for Story*, and especially the book-length works of Andrew Solomon. *Far from the Tree* and the *Noonday Demon* showed me what was possible in nonfiction bookwriting, that you could combine the honesty and depth of personal vulnerabilities with the curiosity and compassion of journalistic reporting, all in the service of broadening how readers conceptualize the sweep and breadth of the human condition. Few things have opened my eyes and perspective as widely, or soothed my heart as mysteriously.

Finally, I would like to thank my family, whose encouragement and excitement helped to sustain me, and my wife, Natalia, who has long been a flat, soft, sheltering sandbar in my own roiling, capricious sea.

NOTES

Introduction: Invisible Kingdoms

xix **"Suffering has always appeared to me"** Rachel Cusk, *Kudos* (New York: Farrar, Straus, and Giroux, 2018), 64.

xxiv **spinal cord injuries** B. B. Lee et al., "The Global Map for Traumatic Spinal Cord Injury and Epidemiology: Update 2011, Global Incidence Rate," *Spinal Cord* 52 (February 2013): 110–116, https://www.nature.com/articles/sc2012158.

xxv **the leading cause of death** "Leading Causes of Death Visualization Tool," Centers for Disease Control and Prevention, accessed June 15, 2021, https://www.cdc.gov/injury/wisqars/index.html.

xxv **the leading cause of spinal cord injuries** Yuying Chen et al., "Causes of Spinal Cord Injury," *Topics in Spinal Cord Injury Rehabilitation* 19, no. 1 (Winter 2013): 1–8, https://www.ncbi.nlm.nih.gov/pmc/articles/PMC3584795/.

xxv **Over a quarter of the U.S.** "Disability Impacts All of Us," Centers for Disease Control and Prevention, last modified September 16, 2020, https://www.cdc.gov/ncbddd/disabilityandhealth/infographic-disability-impacts-all.html.

xxvi **Around three hundred thousand Americans have suffered** "Spinal Cord Injury Facts and Figures at a Glance," National Spinal Cord Injury Statistical Center, 2018, https://www.nscisc.uab.edu/Public/Facts%20and%20Figures%20-%202018.pdf.

xxvi **over five million are living with** "CDC Research Finds Spinal Cord Injury Is a Leading Cause of Paralysis in the United States," Administration for Community Living, September 26, 2016, https://acl.gov/

news-and-events/announcements/cdc-research-finds-spinal-cord
-injury-leading-cause-paralysis-united.

xxvi **Another two million people** "Limb Loss Statistics," Amputee Coalition, October 7, 2015, https://www.amputee-coalition.org/resources/
limb-loss-statistics/.

xxvi **Data from the Federal Health** Paula Span, "A Child's Death Brings
'Trauma That Doesn't Go Away,'" *The New York Times,* September 29, 2017, https://www.nytimes.com/2017/09/29/health/children
-death-elderly-grief.html.

xxvi **Nearly 6 percent** "How Common Is PTSD in Adults?" U.S. Department of Veterans Affairs, October 17, 2019, https://www.ptsd.va.gov/
understand/common/common_adults.asp.

xxvi **One in four American women will** William George Axinn, Maura
Elaine Bardos, and Brady Thomas West, "General Population Estimates of the Association Between College Experience and the Odds
of Forced Intercourse," *Social Science Research* 70 (February 2018):
131–143, https://www.sciencedirect.com/science/article/abs/pii/
S0049089X16307128.

xxvi **fully 33 percent of those women** "Victims of Sexual Violence: Statistics," Rape, Abuse, & Incest National Network, accessed February
10, 2020, https://www.rainn.org/statistics/victims-sexual-violence.

xxvi **For American Indian and Alaskan** Garet Bleir and Anya Zoled-
ziowski, "Murdered and Missing Native American Women Challenge Police and Courts," The Center for Public Integrity, August 27,
2018, https://publicintegrity.org/politics/murdered-and-missing
-native-american-women-challenge-police-and-courts/.

xxvi **Over half of the transgender** "Understanding the Transgender
Community," Human Rights Campaign, accessed January 15, 2021,
https://www.hrc.org/resources/understanding-the-transgender
-community.

xxvi **The number of Black mothers** Span, "A Child's Death Brings
'Trauma That Doesn't Go Away.'"

xxvi **Black men are also** Thomas P. Bonczar and Allen J. Beck, "Lifetime
Likelihood of Going to State or Federal Prison," Bureau of Justice
Statistics Special Report, March 1997, https://www.bjs.gov/content/
pub/pdf/Llgsfp.pdf.

xxxii **Nietzsche's preface to** Friedrich Nietzsche, *Twilight of the Idols,*
trans. Richard Polt (Indianapolis: Hackett Publishing Com-
pany, 1997), 3, http://www.faculty.umb.edu/gary_zabel/Phil_100/
Nietzsche_files/Friedrich-Nietzsche-Twilight-of-the-Idols-or-How
-to-Philosophize-With-the-Hammer-Translated-by-Richard-Polt.pdf.

xxxiv **As Nietzsche put it** Friedrich Nietzsche, *The Will to Power,* trans.

Walter Kaufmann and R. J. Hollingdale (New York: Vintage, 1967), 366.

xxxiv **"Stuttering gave me my life"** Alan Rabinowitz, "We Are All Wildlife," interview by Krista Tippett, *On Being,* aired August 16, 2018, audio, https://onbeing.org/programs/alan-rabinowitz-a-voice-for-the-animals-aug2018/.

xxxv **"vigilant people are alert"** Meister Eckhart, *Selected Writings* (London: Penguin Books, 1994), 13.

xxxv **"The dragon sits by the side"** Flannery O'Connor, *Mystery and Manners* (New York: Farrar, Straus, and Giroux, 1969), 35.

Chapter One: Diminishment

11   **People who live with a chronic** "The Relationship Between Mental Health, Mental Illness and Chronic Physical Conditions," Canadian Mental Health Association, accessed March 15, 2020, https://ontario .cmha.ca/documents/the-relationship-between-mental-health -mental-illness-and-chronic-physical-conditions/.

11   **The prevalence of clinical depression** Sher-Wei Lim et al., "Anxiety and Depression in Patients with Traumatic Spinal Cord Injury: A Nationwide Population-Based Cohort Study," *PLOS ONE* 12, no. 1 (January 2017), https://dx.doi.org/10.1371%2Fjournal.pone.0169623.

11   **Because spinal cord injuries** Catherine Otis, André Marchand, and Frédérique Courtois, "Risk Factors for Posttraumatic Stress Disorder in Persons with Spinal Cord Injury," *Topics in Spinal Cord Injury Rehabilitation* 18, no. 3 (Summer 2012): 253–263, https://dx.doi .org/10.1310%2Fsci1803-253.

12   **Meanwhile, experiences like rape** Katherine M. Keyes et al., "The Burden of Loss: Unexpected Death of a Loved One and Psychiatric Disorders Across the Life Course in a National Study," *The American Journal of Psychiatry* 171, no. 8 (August 2014): 864–871, https://dx.doi .org/10.1176%2Fappi.ajp.2014.13081132.

12   **"Look at the data"** Bloom quoted in Ariel Levy, "A World Without Pain," *The New Yorker,* January 13, 2020, 24.

20   **A 2013 study carried out** "Prevalence of Paralysis in the United States," Christopher & Dana Reeve Foundation, accessed March 5, 2020, https://www.christopherreeve.org/living-with-paralysis/stats -about-paralysis.

20   **Among those living with** "Spinal Cord Injury Statistics," The Miami Project to Cure Paralysis, accessed April 27, 2021, https://www .themiamiproject.org/resources/statistics/.

22   **"physical injury to the body"** Karim Brohi and Martin Schreiber, "The New Survivors and a New Era for Trauma Research," *PLOS*

Medicine 14, no. 7 (July 2017), https://doi.org/10.1371/journal
.pmed.1002354.

22   **"physical violation or injury"** Judith Herman, *Trauma and Recovery: The Aftermath of Violence—From Domestic Abuse to Political Terror* (New York: Basic Books, 1992), 34.

22   **"Traumatic events produce"** Herman, *Trauma and Recovery*, 34.

22   **These changes, in turn** J. Douglas Bremner, "Traumatic Stress: Effects on the Brain," *Dialogues in Clinical Neuroscience* 8, no. 4 (December 2006): 445–461, https://dx.doi.org/10.31887%2FDCNS.2006 .8.4%2Fjbremner.

24   **"Once people realize you're blind"** Andrea Applebee, *Mercy Athena*. Narrated by Annie Wadman, Naomi Rhema Edwards, and Bryant Kirkland, abridged edition, Bandcamp, 2021. Bandcamp.com, https://andreaapplebee.bandcamp.com/album/mercy-athena.

34   **Less than 3 percent** "The Criminal Justice System: Statistics," RAINN, accessed June 18, 2021, https://www.rainn.org/statistics/ criminal-justice-system.

34   **Over 2 million Americans** Wendy Sawyer and Peter Wagner, "Mass Incarceration: The Whole Pie," Prison Policy Initiative, March 24, 2020, https://www.prisonpolicy.org/reports/pie2020.html.

34   **And even after years** Wendy Sawyer, "Visualizing the Racial Disparities in Mass Incarceration," Prison Policy Initiative, July 27, 2020, https://www.prisonpolicy.org/blog/2020/07/27/disparities/.

34   **Over one-fifth** Tara O'Neill Hayes and Margaret Barnhorst, "Incarceration and Poverty in the United States," American Action Forum, June 30, 2020, https://www.americanactionforum.org/research/ incarceration-and-poverty-in-the-united-states/.

42   **According to the Bureau** Jennifer Bronson and Marcus Berzofsky, "Indicators of Mental Health Problems Reported by Prisoners and Jail Inmates, 2011–2012," Bureau of Justice Statistics, June 22, 2017, https://www.bjs.gov/index.cfm?ty=pbdetail&iid=5946.

43   **The number of people in prisons** Tala Al-Rousan et al., "Inside the Nation's Largest Mental Health Institution: A Prevalence Study in a State Prison System," *BMC Public Health* 17, no. 342 (April 2017), https://dx.doi.org/10.1186%2Fs12889-017-4257-0.

43   **Some research indicates** Alicia Piper and David Berle, "The Association Between Trauma Experienced During Incarceration and PTSD Outcomes: A Systematic Review and Meta-analysis," *The Journal of Forensic Psychiatry and Psychology* 30, no. 5 (July 2019): 854–875.

43   **"Divided racial lines"** John Broman, "Upon Release from Prison, a New Kind of Nightmare," *The Fix*, November 14, 2019, https://www .thefix.com/post-incarceration-syndrome-ptsd.

52 **"even a desire to engage"** "Stances of Faith on LGBTQ Issues: Southern Baptist Convention," Human Rights Campaign, accessed May 15, 2021, https://www.hrc.org/resources/stances-of-faiths-on-lgbt-issues-southern-baptist-convention.

55 **The two major causes of amputation** "Limb Loss Statistics," Amputee Coalition, accessed April 10, 2020, https://www.amputee-coalition.org/resources/limb-loss-statistics/.

Chapter Two: Fortitude

68 **"courage over a long period"** "Fortitude," Cambridge Dictionary, accessed January 14, 2021, https://dictionary.cambridge.org/us/dictionary/english/fortitude.

68 **"mental and emotional strength"** "Fortitude," Dictionary.com, accessed January 14, 2021, https://www.dictionary.com/browse/fortitude.

79 **"Resilience presents a challenge"** Maria Konnikova, "How People Learn to Become Resilient," *The New Yorker*, February 11, 2016, https://www.newyorker.com/science/maria-konnikova/the-secret-formula-for-resilience.

79 **Psychologist Emmy Werner recruited** E. E. Werner, "High-Risk Children in Young Adulthood: A Longitudinal Study from Birth to 32 Years," *American Journal of Orthopsychiatry* 59, no. 1 (January 1989): 72–81.

80 **"is fleet, adaptive, pragmatic"** Parul Sehgal, "The Profound Emptiness of Resilience," *The New York Times Magazine*, December 1, 2015, https://www.nytimes.com/2015/12/06/magazine/the-profound-emptiness-of-resilience.html.

90 **"He who has a *why*"** Friedrich Nietzsche as quoted by Viktor Frankl, *Man's Search for Meaning* (Boston: Beacon Press, 1959), 76.

91 **"the sculptor, the hardness"** Friedrich Nietzsche, *Beyond Good and Evil* (New York: Macmillan Company, 1907), 171.

91 **"That tension of the soul"** Friedrich Nietzsche, *Beyond Good and Evil* (New York: Macmillan Company, 1907), 171.

96 **"go years without stepping"** Alex Burness, "Inside Centennial South, the Maximum Security Prison Colorado Could Soon Reopen," *The Colorado Independent*, August 8, 2019, https://www.coloradoindependent.com/2019/08/08/centennial-south-dean-williams/.

Chapter Three: Demons

109   **"When the integrity of the story"** Jordan Kisner, "Thin Places," in *Best American Essays 2016,* ed. Jonathan Franzen (Boston: Houghton Mifflin Harcourt, 2016), 132.

122   **TBIs have been found** M. L. Berthier et al., "Obsessive-Compulsive Disorder and Traumatic Brain Injury: Behavioral, Cognitive, and Neurological Findings," *Neuropsychiatry, Neuropsychology, and Behavioral Neurology* 14, no. 1 (January 2001): 23–31, https://pubmed.ncbi.nlm.nih.gov/11234906/.

131   **The Hawaii-based clinic** Bernadette Aulivola, Chantel N. Hile, and Allen D. Hamdan, "Major Lower Extremity Amputation: Outcome of a Modern Series," *The Archives of Surgery* 139, no. 4 (April 2004): 395–399, https://jamanetwork.com/journals/jamasurgery/fullarticle/396466.

Chapter Four: Seeking

137   **"We tell ourselves stories"** Joan Didion, *The White Album* (New York: Farrar, Straus, and Giroux, 1979), 11.

138   **"God is in your typewriter"** Anne Sexton, *The Complete Poems: Anne Sexton* (New York: First Mariner Books, 1999), xxiii.

140   **the religion had been a potent force** Allison Keyes, "Is It Time for a Reassessment of Malcolm X?," *Smithsonian Magazine,* February 23, 2018, https://www.smithsonianmag.com/smithsonian-institution/it-time-reassessment-malcolm-x-180968247/.

140   **From 1973 to 2009** Jeremy Travis, Bruce Western, and Steve Redburn, eds., *The Growth of Incarceration in the United States: Exploring Causes and Consequences* (Washington, D.C.: National Academies Press, 2014), 2, https://www.nap.edu/read/18613/chapter/2#2.

140   **Black Americans bore the brunt** Travis, Western, and Redburn, *The Growth of Incarceration in the United States,* 2.

140   **Islam's popularity in America's prisons** SpearIt, "Facts and Fictions About Islam in Prison: Assessing Prisoner Radicalization in Post-9/11 America," Institute for Social Policy and Understanding, January 2013, https://www.ispu.org/wp-content/uploads/2012/12/ISPU_Report_Prison.pdf.

147   **"One always finds"** Albert Camus, *The Myth of Sisyphus* (New York: Vintage International, 1955), 123.

149   **In the wake of life-altering** "In U.S., Decline of Christianity Continues at Rapid Pace," Pew Research Center, October 17, 2019, https://www.pewforum.org/2019/10/17/in-u-s-decline-of-christianity-continues-at-rapid-pace/.

159   **"the internalized and evolving"** a psychologist at Northwestern Dan P. McAdams, "Narrative Identity," in *Handbook of Identity Theory and Research,* eds. S. J. Schwartz, K. Luyckx, and V. L. Vignoles (Berlin: Springer Science + Business Media, 2011), 99.

160   **"Over developmental time"** Dan P. McAdams and Kate C. McLean, "Narrative Identity," *Current Directions in Psychological Science* 22, no. 3 (2013): 235, https://doi.org/10.1177%2F0963721413475622.

162   **Though approximately 1 percent** "Wheelchair Users," Physiopedia, accessed April 29, 2021, https://www.physio-pedia.com/Wheelchair_Users#cite_note-2.

174   **"a network of beliefs"** Fiona A. K. Campbell, "Inciting legal fictions: Legal Fictions: Disability's Date with Ontology and the Ableist Body of the Law," *Griffith Law Review* 10, no. 1 (2001), 42–62.

192   **"In yourself right now"** Flannery O'Connor, *Wise Blood* (New York: Farrar, Straus, and Giroux, 1949), 166.

Chapter Five: Refinement

199   **In *On the Nature of Things*** Lucretius, *On the Nature of Things* (London: H. G. Bohn, 1851).

204   **"the strength of the genie"** Richard Wilbur, "The Genie in the Bottle," in *Mid-Century American Poets,* ed. John Ciardi (Boston: Twayne Publishers, 1950), 2–8.

Chapter Six: Vulnerability

233   **"have ancestral roots"** Whitney Benns, "American Slavery, Reinvented," *The Atlantic,* September 21, 2015, https://www.theatlantic.com/business/archive/2015/09/prison-labor-in-america/406177/.

243   **"particularly interested"** Lena Wilson, "Catharsis Without the Healing," *The New York Times,* January 14 2021, https://www.nytimes.com/2021/01/14/movies/rape-revenge-films-flaws.html.

245   **Research has shown** Jill Suttie, "What Doesn't Kill You Makes You Kinder," *Greater Good,* January 25, 2016, https://greatergood.berkeley.edu/article/item/what_doesnt_kill_you_makes_you_kinder.

256   **"bright, colorful, ever-changing"** Damon Rose, "Do Blind People Really Experience Complete Darkness?" *BBC News,* February 25, 2015, https://www.bbc.com/news/blogs-ouch-31487662.

257   **"technicolor wonderland"** Gina Applebee, "Blind & In Technicolor," Blind New World, July 3, 2019, http://blindnewworld.org/blog/blind_and_in_technicolor/.

258   **"We think that patient NS"** Matthew H. Roberts and Joel I. Shen-

ker, "Non-optic Vision: Beyond Synesthesia?" *Brain and Cognition* 107 (August 2016): 24–29.

Chapter Seven: Devotion

292   **Because of the physical limitations** Lisa Ottomanelli and Lisa Lind, "Review of Critical Factors Related to Employment After Spinal Cord Injury: Implications for Research and Vocational Services," *Journal of Spinal Cord Medicine* 32, no. 5 (October 2009): 503–531.

297   **"The deeper that sorrow carves"** Kahlil Gibran, *The Prophet* (New York: Alfred A. Knopf, 1923), 29.

Chapter Eight: Reinvention

308   **Sophocles begins *Oedipus Rex*** Sophocles, *The Oedipus Cycle,* trans. Dudley Fitts and Robert Fitzgerald (New York: Houghton Mifflin Harcourt, 1977).

309   **"It takes an act of will** Andrew Solomon, *Far from the Tree* (New York: Scribner, 2012), 42.

325   **"an experience of being alive"** Joseph Campbell with Bill Moyers, *The Power of Myth* (New York: Random House, 1991), 4.

327   **"capacity to view things"** "Perspective," Merriam-Webster, accessed October 20, 2020, https://www.merriam-webster.com/dictionary/perspective.

Conclusion: Impossible Things

337   **"My formula for greatness"** Friedrich Nietzsche, *Basic Writings of Nietzsche,* trans. Walter Kaufmann (New York: Modern Library, 2000), 714.

339   **"Cleaving to our own lives"** Andrew Solomon, *Far from the Tree* (New York: Scribner, 2012), 41.

341   **"One can't believe"** Lewis Carroll, *Through the Looking-Glass: And What Alice Found There* (1872; repr. London: Macmillan and Co., Limited, 1899), 36.

345   **"To live is to suffer"** Gordon Allport, Preface, in *Man's Search for Meaning,* by Viktor Frankl (Boston: Beacon Press, 1963), 9.

Since graduating with his MA in English literature, MIKE MARIANI has worked as an English professor and freelance journalist, writing feature articles for *The New Yorker, The Atlantic, The Guardian, T: The New York Times Style Magazine, Newsweek, GQ, Vanity Fair, Mother Jones,* and *The Atavist* and essays for *The Believer, Slate, The Los Angeles Review of Books, Pacific Standard, The Nation,* and *Hazlitt*. Some of the topics Mariani has written about include long Covid and the history of medical gaslighting, criminal cases involving mental illness, the opioid crisis, and the neuroscience of inequality. Mariani and his wife live in Northern California.

Twitter: @mikesmariani

ABOUT THE TYPE

This book was set in Mercury Text, a family of typefaces designed by Hoefler & Co. The font is available in a series of grades that have different degrees of darkness but share the same character widths.

DISCARD